THE GOD WHO IS

THE GOD WHO IS

The Christian God in a Pluralistic World

Hans Schwarz

CASCADE *Books* • Eugene, Oregon

THE GOD WHO IS
The Christian God in a Pluralistic World

Copyright © 2011 Hans Schwarz. All rights reserved. Except for brief quotations in critical publications or reviews, no part of this book may be reproduced in any manner without prior written permission from the publisher. Write: Permissions, Wipf and Stock Publishers, 199 W. 8th Ave., Suite 3, Eugene, OR 97401.

Cascade Books
An Imprint of Wipf and Stock Publishers
199 W. 8th Ave., Suite 3
Eugene, OR 97401

www.wipfandstock.com

ISBN 13: 978-1-60899-434-2

Cataloging-in-Publication data:

Schwarz, Hans, 1939–.

    The god who is : the Christian God in a pluralistic world / Hans Schwarz.

    xii + 288 p. ; 23 cm. — Includes indexes.

    ISBN 13: 978-1-60899-434-2

    1. Religious pluralism—Christianity. 2. God. 3. Belief and doubt. I. Title.

BR118 .S368 2011

Manufactured in the U.S.A.

Contents

Preface vii
Introduction ix

PART I: Approaching the God Phenomenon

1 A Figment of the Human Mind? 3
2 Beyond Proof and Disproof 29

PART II: Discerning the God among the gods

3 The Enigma of Religion 65
4 Deciphering the Religious Landscape 107
5 Copernican versus Pre-Copernican Evaluations 143

PART III: The God Who Entrusts

6 The Lord of History 195
7 God's Ultimate Self-Disclosure 216
8 Theomorphous Humanity—Curse or Blessing? 239

Index of Names 273
Index of Subjects 278
Index of Scripture References 284

Preface

The vast majority of the more than six billion people who populate this earth believe in a God or some higher power beyond themselves. But what or who is it into which they put their trust? Is it something or someone they have simply imagined as the variety of religious beliefs might indicate, or is there something real behind humanity's religions? If we concede that this something is real, can that something be proven, or are we simply abiding by the principle that one must believe in something? If we leave the object of our faith to human arbitrariness, we might be politically correct, but at the same time we undermine our own faith, which calls us to total dedication. Yet how can I be dedicated to the right object if the person next to me is also totally dedicated, but to something or someone totally different? A discernment in what we believe is badly needed. Yet how can we discern which faith is right or more appropriate? Even if we have decided on a proper understanding of God, what would that entail for us or rather what kind of God would that be?

It is understandable that questions of this kind cannot be dealt with extensively or to everyone's satisfaction in just one publication. Nevertheless it is important to face these issues squarely and to deal with them honestly. I have had the privilege of teaching in the U.S., first at Trinity Theological Seminary in Columbus, Ohio, and for the past twenty-some years biannually at Lutheran Theological Southern Seminary in Columbia, South Carolina. My home is in Germany and I have taught at the University of Regensburg since 1981. In addition I have presented more than four hundred guest lectures mostly in Eastern Europe and Asia. I share this to say that I have discussed the following pages with many people, especially students in the U.S. and in Germany and with others around the world. Dealing with the issues both openly and honestly has helped clarify my thinking on the subject at hand.

I am thankful to my former graduate research assistant, Dr. Anna Madsen, and to Dr. Terry Dohm, also a former doctoral student of mine, for improving the style and the content of these pages, then to my longtime secretary Hildegard Ferme who typed the various drafts with unfailing speed and accuracy, helped compiling the indices, and who also detected many infelicities. My Old Testament colleague Ted Swanson of Lutheran Theological Southern Seminary who taught for many years at United Theological Seminary in Bangalore, India, and before that at the United Seminary in Kingston, Jamaica, also went through the manuscript with his usual care and suggested many improvements. Many thanks! My graduate research assistant Dr. Andrea König also deserves thanks for providing the necessary help with books and other supplies. Finally I am indebted to my wife Hildegard for putting up with a husband who all too often withdrew to his "catacombs" to put the finishing touches on yet another project.

Introduction

At a regional meeting of the American Academy of Religion I got into a discussion with a colleague whose expertise was not in theology or religion, but in one of the secular pursuits. He told me very bluntly that the belief in God should be eradicated altogether. His reasoning was that belief in God ensues in ideology, and ideology breeds violence. "Wherever you look," he claimed, "when there is an atrocity, it is motivated by religious causes. Therefore religion is the real culprit of people hating and murdering each other." Indeed, the veneration of something or someone higher than humanity has often led to an exclusive and arrogant attitude which to some extent still continues today. For instance more Christians have been martyred in the twentieth century alone than in all the centuries before. But most of these killings were not committed by adherents of other religions. The Communists, for instance, were strictly anti-religious insofar as a veneration of a higher being or beings was concerned. Nevertheless they left a trail of blood causing the death of approximately 70 million people among whom were many Christians and believers of other religions. The Communist attempt to eradicate religion, however, was without success.

People are intrinsically religious, always prone to venerate God or other higher beings. Though scientists have not yet discovered a gene that makes people religious, neuroscience has detected certain areas in the brain that are responsive to religious cues similar to other areas which are responsive to visual impressions. The question then needs to be addressed whether religion is really a human epiphenomenon, so to speak a reflection of the human mind or the human psyche, or whether that to which religion witnesses is something independent of humanity.

In other words: Do people believe in God because there is a genetic or psychological need to do so? Or is God, or the higher beings that are venerated in religion, an entity independent of humanity to which humanity responds through religious exercises? To approach this issue, we will first analyze the attacks on the God phenomenon through which it is has been declared a figment of the human mind. Then we ask ourselves whether there is any possibility to prove God's existence as an entity independent from ourselves.

Once we have wrestled with these preliminary issues, we can ask what kind of entity it is which we assume to be beyond ourselves. To that effect we will first tackle the issue of religion. What is religion and how is it related to the understanding of God? We should also not forget to ask whether we can ascertain a historical origin for humanity's religious consciousness. Moving beyond that, we will view the confusing religious landscape attempting in bold strokes to trace the different religions starting with pre-historic and tribal religions via polytheistic religions to monotheistic manifestations. We will concentrate in the latter field primarily on three embodiments that have been embraced by people from many different nations, tribes, and walks of life: Christianity, Islam, and Buddhism. The latter may sound odd being labeled a monotheistic religion. Nevertheless we want to consider it here because it too focuses only on one ultimate object, not naming it God, but Nirvana.

Having traversed the religious landscape, the decisive question is how we can differentiate these religions. Are they all equal? Are some better than the others? Or, are those questions already ruled out, since all religions are the manifestation of the same ultimacy? We will note that one cannot evaluate religions in a value-free vacuum, but can only approach them from one's own vantage point. While such a point is necessarily historically and geographically conditioned, for the believer it is the only standpoint he or she can occupy. For this person then it assumes the position of ultimacy. From our vantage point the decisive criterion for evaluating the religious landscape is Jesus the Christ. To establish this criterion, we can put down some significant markers. The God disclosed in the Judeo-Christian history is a God of history as shown especially in the Old Testament. It is a God who communicated God's self in an unsurpassable manner through Jesus the Christ. This self-manifestation is decisive because if God were different, salvation might be in jeopardy. Through its universality, entailing hope for everyone, this self-manifestation is not exclusive. The God whom we encounter in that history is also not a God of our likeness. To the contrary, God wants us to be in God's own likeness. To that effect God summons us to become ever more like the One who has guided humanity through the ages. This is, of course, but a brief introductory synopsis; it is now time to consider some details.

PART I

Approaching the God Phenomenon

The belief in God has a checkered history. In the first centuries the Christian faith and with it the Christian belief in God were outlawed in the Roman Empire. At times Christians were actively persecuted and at other times merely tacitly tolerated. During the expansion of Islam, from the seventh century onward, Christian believers in God again faced hardships or were even forcibly converted to Islam. The Spanish conquistadores of the sixteenth century then in turn used force in Latin America to make the Indios believe in the Christian God. These atrocities, though regrettable, were always carried out in the name of one religion against another religion or other religions. Only in the twentieth century did an anti-religious ideology evolve that wanted to wipe out every religion. Especially in Russia, the Communists tried every means to exterminate religion altogether, since they considered it to be superstition.

There were certainly political reasons that motivated this persecution. The Russian Orthodox Church was so closely connected with the Tsarist rule that abolishing the Tsar also meant to reduce the power of the Orthodox Church. But the Communist contempt for religion and anything resembling faith in God is a thought pattern that has its roots in the nineteenth century. That religion belonged to a bygone era was evident for the German philosopher Ludwig Feuerbach (1804–1872) and the revolutionary Karl Marx (1818–1883), and also to some extent for the founder of psychoanalysis Sigmund Freud (1856–1939) and many proponents of the Darwinian notion of human evolution.

Both Feuerbach and Marx were students of Georg Wilhelm Friedrich Hegel (1770–1831) and his philosophical system. For Hegel the notion of God was a most natural presupposition. Due to the rapid industrial progress, Feuerbach and Marx were more materialistically inclined. For Feuerbach, God was not the foundation and opposition of the material as Hegel had thought, but at the most an epiphenomen of the material. Being involved with the workers' movement, Marx noted the close association between the religious and the political establishment. Moreover, similar to Feuerbach, he was dissatisfied with the Hegelian system which saw a most natural logic in the antithesis of God and the world and their synthesis found in the incarnation. For Marx such a synthesis did not exist. God and the world were opposites.

Since Feuerbach had claimed that religion is a human product and "A god is man's striving for happiness, fulfilled in his imagination" the idea evolved in Marx that this God notion had to be eliminated.[1] The attempt was then made in Marxist Communism, the single most powerful political ideology of the twentieth century, to execute this idea. While religiosity took a heavy toll in Socialist countries, the God notion was not eliminated. In the West too skepticism has increased about anything religious. Especially "organized" religion has often been considered as a tool to keep people, especially children, under control. Religion is a means to pacify people and through religiously imposed rules to make them more docile. Yet such an understanding of religion as a political instrument already closes the door on the God phenomenon as a living reality which makes religion possible. Still religion in its various forms seems again on the upswing in Western countries.

---

1. Ludwig Feuerbach, *Lectures on the Essence of Religion*, trans. Ralph Manheim (New York: Harper & Row, 1967) 199 (Lecture 22).

ONE

A Figment of the Human Mind?

From the very beginning, the "New World," established by the Pilgrims and other persecuted religious minorities coming from the Old World of Europe, had a religious focus. The European immigrants settled in this "New World" and they tenaciously defended their newly won religious freedom. To safeguard this freedom the notion of inalienable human rights was introduced and monarchy as a form of government was rejected. In Europe, however, monarchies were too well established for this kind of freedom to gain much of a hearing. Attempts toward democratization were quickly squelched. The only exception was France where in 1789 a violent revolution swept away the old monarchy. But soon the French re-established a new monarchy of sorts.

Since in Europe religion was considered part of the government establishment, the questioning of religion became more and more an issue in intellectual circles and also among political radicals. Here the deistic critiques of John Locke (1632–1704) and David Hume (1711–1776) paved the way for the primacy of sense experience and reason while relegating religion and everything non-material to secondary status. The elevation of reason as a goddess in the wake of the French Revolution and with it the clear designation of religion as a private matter, had an impact beyond France. While Hegel could still wed revelation and reason, Immanuel Kant (1724–1804) showed that they belong to different dimensions; reason to the realm of phenomena, as that what we can see and touch, and revelation to that of the noumena, meaning that which underlies the world of phenomena and which is not accessible by reason. It was the criticism of Hegel's synthesis of reason and revelation that became the catalyst for Feuerbach's criticism of God and the Christian religion in general.

The Anthropocentric Turn: Ludwig Feuerbach

Feuerbach had been a student and follower of Hegel. But he could not accept his teacher's organic and developmental thinking when Hegel, for instance, postulated: "The development of Mind [i.e., the Spirit] lies in the fact that its going forth and separation constitutes its coming to itself."[1] For Feuerbach there was no thesis and antithesis, with a subsequent synthesis on a higher plane. Thesis and antithesis became identical for him. Hegel distinguished the absolute Spirit, i.e., God, from the subjective spirit in individuals, and the objective spirit of the human community which shows itself in the legal system and in morality. But Feuerbach collapsed all three into one spirit. "Consciousness of God is self-consciousness, knowledge of God is self-knowledge," wrote Feuerbach.[2] God and humanity are the same, because "the secret of theology is anthropology."[3] "Man's knowledge of God is man's knowledge of himself, of his own nature."[4] Humanity becomes the starting-point and the focus of human reflection. Feuerbach confessed very pointedly: "God was my first thought, reason my second, humanity my third and last thought."[5]

Theology, according to Feuerbach, must not (just) be seen as a derivative of, but must be dissolved into anthropology. The reason for this is that there is only one reality, the one given through our senses. There is no other reality, since "truth, reality, and the sensually given are identical."[6] Feuerbach objected here also to the idealistic notion of Hegel that reason would be the most truly real in humanity since hu-

---

1. Georg W. F. Hegel, *Lectures on the History of Philosophy*, trans. E. S. Haldane and Frances H. Simpson (Atlantic Highlands, NJ: Humanities, 1983) 1:23.

2. Ludwig Feuerbach, *The Essence of Christianity*, trans. George Eliot (Buffalo, NY: Prometheus, 1989) 12.

3. Ludwig Feuerbach, *Vorläufige Thesen zur Reform der Philosophie* (1842) in *Sämtliche Werke*, Wilhelm Bolin and Friedrich Jodl, eds. (Stuttgart-Bad Cannstatt: Fromann, 1959) 2:222 (Thesis 1).

4. Feuerbach, *Essence of Christianity*, 230 (ch. 23).

5. Feuerbach, "Grundsätze der Philosophie" in *Sämtliche Werke*, 2:388.

6. Feuerbach, *Grundsätze der Philosophie der Zukunft*, in *Sämtliche Werke*, 2:296 (32).

man reason is in touch with God as the world reason or the absolute Spirit. For Feuerbach the "sensually given is the essence of humanity."[7] This materialistic vision of Feuerbach focuses exclusively on humanity, because "man, especially the religious man, is to himself the measure of all things, of all reality."[8] This anthropocentric materialistic vision is now employed to analyze religion, because as Feuerbach asserted, his writings have "strictly speaking only one purpose, one intention and idea, one theme. This theme, of course, is religion or theology and everything connected with it."[9]

Since religion is a human phenomenon, Feuerbach sought to discover the origins of religion, primarily the God concept. He noticed that "the theist conceives God as an existing and personal being external to reason and in general apart from man."[10] The implications insist that neither God nor religion is primary, but humanity, since the concept of God is declared to be a projection of humanity. "The beginning, the middle and end of religion is MAN," Feuerbach summarized his assessment of religion at the conclusion of the first part of his book *The Essence of Christianity*.[11] God is perceived as a being outside and beyond humanity but "all the attributes of the divine nature are, therefore, attributes of the human nature."[12] Even the Trinity is brought into this anthropocentric focus. The Trinity is explained as the secret of the social life of the community, and the incarnation as the secret of God's love to humanity is seen as the secret of humanity's love to itself.[13]

However, Feuerbach sees that the problem with religion and the God concept is that it is not simply a projection of humanity's own being. Such a direct projection would pose no problems. But in religion God—in actuality an imaginary being—becomes a being that is differentiated and even contrasted with humanity. This God who is thought to exist in and of itself exists only in one's imagination, as an idea, but not

7. Feuerbach, "Wider den Dualismus von Leib und Seele, Fleisch und Geist," in *Sämtliche Werke*, 2:350.

8. Feuerbach, *Essence of Christianity*, 22.

9. Feuerbach, *Lectures on the Essence of Religion*, 5 (1st lecture).

10. Ludwig Feuerbach, *Principles of the Philosophy of the Future*, trans. with intro. Manfred H. Vogel (Indianapolis: Bobbs-Merrill, 1966) 8–9 (7).

11. Feuerbach, *Essence of Christianity*, 184 (ch. 18).

12. Ibid., 14.

13. Cf. ibid., 293 and 289 (appendix).

in reality and in truth.[14] Feuerbach now sees his task to deny this fantastic imaginative construct of theology and religion and "to affirm the true nature of man."[15] Religion and the God concept are dangerous, because they provide an illusory world that has nothing to do with humanity's actual world and humanity's actual essence. For Feuerbach, God needs to be discarded, and humanity emerges in God's place.

Feuerbach asserted: "The sentence, 'Humanity is God, the highest essence of humanity' is identical with the sentence, 'There is no God, no highest being as theology holds.'"[16] Still Feuerbach feels himself to be a follower of Hegel, because, "if in the consciousness which man has of God, first arises the self-consciousness of God, then the human consciousness is, *per se*, the divine consciousness."[17] While Hegel saw God reflected in humanity, this divine self-reflection is now identified with humanity. But this did not mean for Feuerbach that material humanity, able to be perceived by our senses, is finite like everything material. To the contrary, in nineteenth-century idealistic and optimistic fashion, Feuerbach declared that if religion is the consciousness of the infinite, then religion can be "nothing else than the consciousness which man has of his own, not finite and limited, but infinite nature."[18] Strictly speaking, human consciousness and consciousness of the infinite are inseparable, indicating the elevated status which Feuerbach accords to humanity. Feuerbach can even equate "the highest feeling" with the highest feeling of self."[19] Since humanity is so elevated, then the concept of God can emerge. "Thus God, as an object of feeling, or what is the same thing, the feeling of God, is nothing else than man's highest feeling of self." The affinity and yet the contrast to Friedrich Schleiermacher (1768–1834) is obvious, for Schleiermacher asserted that God is the feeling for the infinite. Schleiermacher, however, would have never dared to regard God as a human construct, since for him humanity did not yet possess such a high status as it did for Feuerbach.

---

14. Cf. Feuerbach, Preface to the 2nd ed. of *Essence of Christianity*, xviii.

15. Feuerbach, *Lectures on the Essence of Religion*, 23 (3rd lecture).

16. Feuerbach, "Das Wesen des Christentums in Beziehung auf den 'Einzigen und sein Eigentum'" (1845) in *Sämtliche Werke*, 7:297.

17. Feuerbach, *Essence of Christianity*, 230 (ch. 23).

18. Ibid., 2 (ch. 1).

19. Ibid., 284 (appendix) for this and the following quote.

This said, Feuerbach also realized that a human being is nevertheless finite and therefore he was opposed to the idea of a personal immortality. The reason for rejecting the notion of immortality is that, according to Feuerbach, any existence needs a material base. Therefore no disembodied existence is possible. Moreover, he claimed: "All proofs of immortality are insufficient, and even unassisted reason is not capable of apprehending it, still less of proving it."[20] But Feuerbach did not object to immortality altogether, since for him the species is still immortal. The human individual being "can become conscious of his limits, his finiteness, only because the perfection, the infinitude of his species, is perceived by him."[21] But according to Feuerbach such perception is a mistake. Every being is in itself infinite. From the infinity of the species Feuerbach conjectured the infinity of the Godhead, and thereby the human species became the foundation for the God concept. This notion of the infinity of the human species is typical of nineteenth-century optimism with its enchantment with advancement and progress. But it remains an unproven hypothesis.

Feuerbach did not only focus on the human species. In his later writings he expanded his anthropocentric base to include nature. He surmised: "If we now consider the attributes of the Godhead, we shall find that they are all rooted in nature."[22] Nature is related to humanity, since it is presupposed by humanity and without it, humanity would have no existence and no being. Conversely humanity also belongs to the essence of nature, because humanity is "the being in whom nature becomes personal, conscious, and rational."[23] We are reminded here of the Hegelian antithesis between the ultimate spirit and the human spirit. Somehow Feuerbach could not totally rid himself of his master's influence.

These convictions led Feuerbach to the conclusion that humanity and nature work together in producing religion. However, he precluded the argument that the reverse way to presuppose God is that God is the

---

20. Ibid., 135 (ch. 14).

21. Ibid., 7 (ch. 1).

22. Feuerbach, *Lectures on the Essence of Religion*, 104 (lecture 12). In *The Essence of Christianity* he expounds the anthropocentric base but later realizes that the actual real and true basis for reality is nature. Cf. Feuerbach, *Lectures on the Essence of Religion*, 20 (lecture 3) concerning *The Essence of Christianity*.

23. Feuerbach, *Lectures on the Essence of Religion*, 21 (lecture 3).

one from whom humanity and nature would have their origin. Feuerbach declared: "The God from whom nature is deduced . . . is itself a being originating from nature, deduced from it, and expressing the effects, properties and appearances of nature."[24] Infinity pertains not to God, but rather to nature. "The idea that Nature or the universe in general has a real beginning, and that consequently at some time there was no Nature, no universe, is a narrow idea. . . . It is an imagination without sense and foundation."[25] Nature is neither created nor brought forth by anyone or anything. "It is from itself and in itself, it has no beginning and no end; the beginning and end of the world are human concepts, concepts which humanity transfers from itself onto nature because humanity begins at a certain time and also ends."[26] Therefore not only humanity, but also nature is infinite, and a God is no longer needed.

Feuerbach's proposal is atheistic in the sense that it involves the "abandoning of a God who is different from humanity."[27] But this kind of atheism is not negative as Feuerbach asserted, since "we must replace the love of God by the love of man as the only true religion, the belief in God by the belief in man and his powers."[28] Feuerbach was convinced that Christianity and faith in God are passé. "In place of faith there is faithlessness, in place of the Bible there is reason, in place of religion and the church there is politics, in place of heaven there is earth, in place of prayer there is work, in place of hell there is the material want, and in place of the Christian there is humanity."[29]

Feuerbach certainly knew how to read the signs of the times, since the nineteenth century was the century of the large-scale desertion of the church by the working class, most prominently in Great Britain and Germany. Feuerbach also thought he realized what the problem was with God and religion. "Man deifies the being or thing upon which he

---

24. Feuerbach, "Über meine 'Gedanken über Tod und Unsterblichkeit'" (1847), in *Sämtliche Werke*, 1:204.

25. Ludwig Feuerbach, *Essence of Religion*, trans. Alexander Loos (London: Progressive, 1890) 28 (24).

26. Feuerbach, "Über meine 'Gedanken über Tod und Unsterblichkeit'," 1:204.

27. Feuerbach, "*Notwendigkeit einer Reform der Philosophie*" (1842) in *Sämtliche Werke*, 2:219.

28. Feuerbach, *Lectures on the Essence of Religion*, 285 (lecture 30).

29. Feuerbach, "Notwendigkeit einer Reform der Philosophie" (1842), in *Sämtliche Werke*, 2:218–9.

knows or believes his life to depend."³⁰ This conviction led to the fallacy that God is more efficacious than humanity and infinitely transcends human powers. Humanity in turn becomes limited, powerless, and has the feeling of dependence. This is the problem that Feuerbach endeavored to solve. Dependency on the transcendent God is wrong. While "the foundation of religion is a feeling of dependency; the first object of that feeling is nature."³¹ Since humanity is dependent on nature with every step it takes, nothing is transcendent or otherworldly in nature. Therefore humanity can tackle nature and focus on that which is the ultimate longing of humanity, the "pursuit of happiness."³² Here religion enters in because according to Feuerbach "a god is man's striving for happiness, fulfilled in his imagination."³³

Feuerbach did not want humanity to indulge in fantasy, i.e., in religion, since religion has it all wrong, "it does claim that the semblance of reality is reality."³⁴ "God does not exist in sense perception or in reason but only in faith, that is, imagination."³⁵ "For a god as such is an imagined, unreal, fantastic being, which however *is supposed to be* a real being."³⁶ God therefore is a superfluous hypothesis, and diverts our attention to a figment of the human mind, instead of focusing on the object matter, the material. God is supposed to satisfy our yearning for happiness, but because God is a mental illusion, such happiness can only occur in our imagination and not in reality. Therefore the whole idea of God and religion must be abolished to attain real happiness for humanity.

Although Feuerbach's wholesale accusation is too sweeping to be accurate, his diagnosis that humanity is yearning for happiness and love is certainly correct. But how can this be attained if we live in a finite world? Here the sentiment of the nineteenth century was much more optimistic than that of today. Even if we still believed in a universe without boundaries and without beginning or end in time, we people of modernity are painfully confronted with our own finitude and also with the finitude of the resources we employ to master our lives.

30. Feuerbach, *Lectures on the Essence of Religion*, 49 (lecture 7).
31. Ibid., 24 (lecture 4).
32. Feuerbach, *Theogonie*, in *Sämtliche Werke*, 9:79 ("Der Glückseligkeitswunsch").
33. Feuerbach, *Lectures on the Essence of Religion*, 199 (lecture 22).
34. Ibid., 183 (lecture 20).
35. Ibid., 180 (lecture 20)
36. Ibid., 183 (lecture 20).

The Radicalization of Feuerbach: Karl Marx

Feuerbach's ideas were too contagious to be soon forgotten. When Karl Marx came across Feuerbach's book *The Essence of Christianity* he "enthusiastically welcomed this new concept," since Feuerbach reestablished materialism as the prime concept.[37] As Feuerbach, Marx was influenced by Hegel and uneasy with his dialectic. While estrangement for Hegel is something positive in which self-consciousness objectifies itself and therefore posits a world over against itself, for Marx this is something totally negative, because "the objectification as such applies to an estranged relatedness of humanity which does not correspond to the human essence, to its self-consciousness."[38] For Marx estrangement is not a theoretical and abstract philosophical thought-pattern. It is something eminently real, though according to Marx, Hegel postulated "an estrangement of the *pure*, i.e., abstract philosophical thinking."[39] Marx, however, had no interest in philosophical abstractions but focused on the tangible, on economic matters.

Yet the charge against Hegel that he does not deal with reality, Marx also lodged against Feuerbach. In his *Theses on Feuerbach* which Engels published in 1845, Marx stated in thesis 11: "The philosophers have only *interpreted* the world, in various ways; the point is to *change* it."[40] Marx was not actually a philosopher, but a revolutionary who set out to change the world. Therefore he accused Feuerbach of not noticing "that the abstract individual whom he [Feuerbach] analyzes belongs to a particular form of society."[41] Feuerbach "conceives of men not in their given social connection, not under their existing conditions of life, which have made them what they are."[42] Since Feuerbach as a philosopher neglected the

---

37. According to Friedrich Engels, *Ludwig Feuerbach und der Ausgang der klassischen deutschen Philosophie*, in Karl Marx—Friedrich Engels, *Werke* (Berlin: Dietz, 1962) 21:272.

38. Marx, "Kritik der Hegelschen Dialektik und Philosophie überhaupt" (1844), in *Werke-Schriften-Briefe*, ed. Hans-Joachim Lieber and Peter Furth (Darmstadt: Wissenschaftliche Buchgesellschaft, 1971) 1:646.

39. Marx, "Kritik der Hegelschen Dialektik und Philosophie überhaupt," in *Werke-Schriften-Briefe*, 1:643.

40. Marx, *Theses on Feuerbach*, in *Karl Marx: The Essential Writings*, ed. Frederic L. Bender (New York: Harper, 1972) 155.

41. Ibid., 154 (thesis 7).

42. Marx, *German Ideology*, in *Karl Marx: The Essential Writings*, 157, for this and the following quote.

practical and societal aspect of humanity, he also neglected the historical aspect of human life and the concrete historical evolution of human history. Therefore, according to Marx, "he never arrives at the really existing active men, but stops at the abstraction 'man'." This goes hand in hand with the charge that Feuerbach neglected to ask why religion even came into being—in terms of social conditions—and how this religious self-estrangement could be overcome.

Marx had little interest in interpretation, but focused on inducing change. He surmised that humanity creates religion because humanity's world—and this means primarily the social world—is felt wanting. "But that the secular basis detaches itself from itself and establishes itself as an independent realm in the clouds can only be explained by the cleavages and self-contradictions within this secular basis."[43] Since humanity is dissatisfied with the kind of world in which we live, it creates this divine supra-world. Religion therefore becomes the fantasizing realization of the human being, because this "supra-world" society "is a wrong world." The origins of religion, according to Marx, are the warped conditions of this world, the actual estrangement of human existence from itself. Therefore religion serves as "the opiate of the people."[44] Karl Marx asserted that Feuerbach "does not see that the 'religious sentiment' is itself a social product, and that the abstract individual whom he analyzes belongs to a particular form of society."[45] This is a society which needs religion, which needs an opiate, because people are exploited. Yet Marx contends that "millions of proletarians feel by no means contented with their living conditions, if their 'existence' does not in the least correspond to their 'essence'."[46] Therefore they will "bring their 'existence' into harmony with their 'essence' in a practical way, by means of a revolution."

One cannot just talk like Feuerbach about religious self-alienation and the dichotomization of the world into a religious world and a secular one. This opposition has to be resolved and "after the earthly family is discovered to be the secret of the holy family, the former must then itself be destroyed in theory and in practice."[47] Humanity will not attain

---

43. Marx, *Theses on Feuerbach*, 153 (thesis 4).
44. Marx, *Zur Kritik der Hegelschen Rechtsphilosophie*, in Karl Marx-Friedrich Engels, *Werke*, 1:378.
45. Marx, *Theses on Feuerbach*, 154 (thesis 7).
46. Marx, *German Ideology*, 156, for this and the following quote.
47. Marx, *Theses on Feuerbach*, 154 (thesis 4).

its true essence as long as it perceives its essence above and beyond itself in a heavenly realm. Marx detected the main culprit for this dilemma in Christianity. "The social principles of Christianity preach cowardice, self-contempt, abasement, submission, dejection."[48] Since the proletariat needs courage, self-esteem, pride, and a sense of independence to attain its goal, it must do away with religion. "The criticism of religion ends with the teaching that *man is the highest essence for man*, hence with the *categoric imperative to overthrow all relations* in which man is a debased, enslaved, abandoned, despicable essence."[49]

Since the religious world is but a reflex of the real world, Marx demanded that we abandon the search "for a superman in the fantastic reality of heaven" where we find nothing but a reflection of ourselves.[50] Marx therefore claimed that "the abolition of religion as the *illusory* happiness of the people is required for their *real* happiness."[51] As soon as religion as the general theory of this world is abolished—a theory which according to Marx provides the justification for the exploitation of the working class and the consolation for a better future—we will abandon the fantastic heavenly reality and face our reality on earth. His conclusion therefore was: "We do not change the secular questions into theological ones. We change the theological questions into secular ones."[52] Indeed, this was the agenda of Marx and the Marxist Communist Revolution, not only to see religion wither away, but to make it wither away through closing churches, monasteries, and theological faculties and, worse yet, starting a full-scale deadly persecution of Christian leaders.

The atheism of Karl Marx is much more radical than that of Feuerbach. The reason for this is not just that Marx was a revolutionary, but that he understands humanity not only embedded in nature and stemming from nature, but as an "active species of nature."[53] Human activity is not primarily thinking or reflection, but concrete activity and

---

48. Marx, "The Communism of the Paper *Rheinischer Beobachter*," in *On Religion* (New York: Schocken, 1964) 84.

49. Marx, "Contribution to the Critique of Hegel's Philosophy of Right" (1844), in *On Religion*, 50.

50. Marx, "Contribution," 41.

51. Ibid., 42.

52. Marx, "On the Jewish Question," in *Karl Marx: Selected Writings*, ed. David McLellan, 2nd ed. (Oxford: Oxford University Press, 2000) 51.

53. Marx, "Kritik der Hegelschen Dialektik und Philosophie überhaupt," 1:650.

this means productivity. According to Marx human history starts when humans begin "the production of the means to satisfy these needs [of everyday life], the production of material life itself."[54] This is even true for subsequent history, because individual human beings depend on the material conditions of their production.

Marx is not as materialistic as is Feuerbach, but he is convinced that humans depend totally on themselves and also forge their own history. "By producing their means of subsistence men are indirectly producing their actual material life."[55] In the same way history has a material basis, because "the whole so-called world history is nothing but a human production through human labor."[56] While humanity lives in the world and is dependent on it, humans also produce a world and thereby they have a history. Yet in contrast to Hegel, history has nothing to do with the Spirit, i.e., God, or the ideal, i.e., some supra-material values, since "history is the true natural history of humans."[57] Therefore anything abstract or anything beyond the natural, such as morals, religion, metaphysics, or any ideology and their conceptuality, have no independent existence. "They have no history, no development; but men, developing their material production and their material intercourse, alter, along with this their real existence, their thinking and the products of their thinking. Life is not determined by consciousness, but consciousness by life."[58] Consciousness therefore is an epi-phenomenon of the material basis of humanity. Since there is a basic estrangement in the societal existence of humanity, human consciousness has gone astray. The societal problems are then reflected in the wrong ideas of individual human beings, in their illusions, and their religious fantasizing.

On the human and material level, the basic problem is the division of labor which results in unjust labor conditions and the accumulation of private property (or the lack thereof) which leads to the exploitation of one human being by another. If both the division of labor and private property are abolished, humans can return to their own non-estranged communal and egalitarian existence. "The positive abolishment of pri-

---

54. Marx, *German Ideology*, in *Karl Marx: Selected Writings*, 181.

55. Ibid., 177.

56. Marx, "Privateigentum und Kommunismus," in *Werke—Schriften—Briefe*, 1:607.

57. Marx, "Kritik der Hegelschen Dialektik und Philosophie überhaupt," 1:652.

58. Marx, *German Ideology*, in *Karl Marx: Selected Writings*, 180–81.

vate property as the appropriation of human life is therefore the positive abolishment of all estrangement, the return of humanity from religion, family, state, etc. into its human, namely societal, existence."[59] Through this communal existence humans become totally human and this society of the future produces a "humanity in its whole richness of its being, a rich and deeply sensuous [*allsinnig*] humanity as its continuous reality."[60] Similar to Feuerbach, Marx showed little regard for the individual human being. All-important for him was society from which he expected that which an individual human being cannot accomplish, the production of happiness and new sustainable living conditions. Similar to Feuerbach's ideas, in which humanity becomes divinized now, society assumes the status of a new divinity. Therefore Marx, too, could not do without an absolute, though he located it within the material world.

Religion as an Earlier Stage of Human Development: Sigmund Freud

While Sigmund Freud knew that religion is too complicated to be derived from a single origin, he was convinced that "the last contribution to the criticism of the religious *Weltanschauung* was effected by psychoanalysis."[61] We should take Freud's claim at face value that his psychoanalysis made the final contribution to the criticism of religion. Both Feuerbach and Marx talked about religion as a projection. Yet for Freud this projection no longer originated from the conditions which humanity faces on this earth, but from the sickly mind of humanity at an earlier developmental stage. This meant that humans who are still religious are sick. They have not yet reached the presently available stage of human development. Freud leveled these devastating charges against the religious establishment. Yet how did he substantiate his charges?

In his book *Totem and Taboo* (1912/1913), Freud asserted that all religions can be considered as attempts to solve the same problem and then he put forth a "hypothesis which may seem as fantastic," as he him-

---

59. Marx, "Privateigentum und Kommunismus," 1:594–5.

60. Ibid., 1:602.

61. Sigmund Freud, *New Introductory Lectures on Psychoanalysis*, in *The Complete Introductory Lectures on Psychoanalysis*, trans. and ed. James Strachey (New York: Norton, 1966) 631.

self conceded.⁶² In its original state, Freud saw humanity represented by the primeval tribe in which a powerful father laid claim on all females and chased away the growing sons. One day the sons banded together, slew their father, and ate him. After the initial satisfaction of their hatred toward the father, the sons soon felt guilty and repented of their deed. This means the dead father became stronger than he had been during his life. The father was eventually represented in a totem, an inanimate or animate object which became the brothers' identification. It stood for some kind of mythological ancestral spirit which had to be treated with utmost respect. The brothers also abstained from access to the females since they once had been the sole property of the father. To strengthen this notion, the Oedipus complex was developed. As the brothers remembered the victory over the father of the clan, they celebrated a totem feast which gradually was turned into a sacrifice for the tribal godhead.

Freud concluded "that the god of each of them is formed in the likeness of his father, that his personal relationship to God depends on his relation to his father in the flesh . . . and that at bottom God is nothing other than an exalted father."⁶³ While Freud knew that his postulate of a Darwinian primeval tribe does not corroborate with ethnological research, he nevertheless stated in the conclusion of *Totem and Taboo*: "It may safely be assumed that in the beginning was the Deed!"⁶⁴ The reason why Freud stayed with this obvious contradiction is that he realized that even in our own time humanity as adults are so infantile and need protection, even when they are fully grown. "Man . . . feels he cannot relinquish the support of his God."⁶⁵ This means that even if Freud were successful in enlightening the people, they would still resort to religion to master their lives.

What is religion for Freud? Its first appearance is in totemism, the association of a group with a certain object from which it receives its identity. There a relationship of mutual respect and care was established between a human being and its totem, and a social obligation of the members of the clan towards each other and towards other tribes. Then

---

62. Sigmund Freud, *Totem and Taboo* (IV/5) trans. James Strachey (London: Routledge, 1999), 141.

63. Ibid., (IV/6) 147.

64. Ibid., (IV/7) 161, with reference to Goethe's *Faust*.

65. Freud, *Moses and Monotheism*, trans. Katherine Jones (Letchworth: Hogarth, 1939) 202.

there is animism, another constituent of religion. There the notions emerged of souls or spiritual beings, and of magic, through which the laws of the life of a soul are impressed on real things through which unpleasant things are magically warded off and pleasant things are imposed on others. When Freud turned to the Israelite religion, the religion of his own Jewish ancestors, he saw Moses as the founder of a monotheistic religion, whom he believed was rejected and murdered by the Israelites. The killing of Moses "has thus become an indispensable part of our reasoning," according to Freud, because the guilt attached to the murder led to the projection of a Messiah who was supposed to return and to bring salvation and the promised rule of the world to his people.[66]

With the turn to the Christian era, Freud postulated that the guilt consciousness over the murder of the primeval father was no longer confined to the Jewish people but had taken hold of all the Mediterranean nations. The Apostle Paul realized that the reason for our unhappiness was that we killed God the father. But we are redeemed from our guilt, because Jesus as one of us sacrificed his life to bring salvation. Therefore the death of Jesus became the religious starting point for Paul. "Original sin and salvation through sacrificial death became the basis of the new religion founded by Paul."[67] In this new religion the reconciliation with God the father is the main point, but the son who has taken sin on himself comes to stand next to God and even in place of the father. "A son-religion displaced the father-religion. As a sign of substitution the ancient totem meal was revived in the form of communion, in which the company of brothers consumed the flesh and blood of the son—no longer the father—obtained sanctity thereby and identified themselves with him."[68]

Christianity is different from Judaism since it admitted the murder of the father and expiated it. It is interesting that for Freud the actual founder of Christianity is Paul and not Christ, who according to Freud is perhaps a mythological figure.[69] Yet Christianity did not stay on the level of a spiritualized religion. It is also no longer monotheistic, but restituted again the great mother goddess, which surreptitiously made way for the many gods of polytheism. Moreover the Roman Catholic Church

---

66. Freud, *Moses and Monotheism*, 144.
67. Ibid., 214.
68. Cf. Freud, *Totem and Taboo* (IV/6) 154.
69. Cf. Freud, *Civilization and Its Discontents* (V, VIII) 69 and 100.

is "the implacable foe of all freedom of thought" and of progress to pursue the truth by employing force to suppress what it did not condone.[70] It comes as no surprise that communion for Freud is a repetition of the totem meal, albeit only in its venerative, not in its aggressive, mood. "The Christian communion, however, is essentially a fresh elimination of the father, the repetition of the guilty deed."[71]

Many religious teachings are mythologies for Freud. They are "distorted vestiges of the wish-fantasies of whole nations—the age-long dreams of young humanity."[72] They are not derived from heaven, but are projected onto heaven. Besides being a projection, religion is also strongly influenced by sexual impulses. Similar to art and social order, religion "originated in part in a contribution from the sexual instincts."[73] Perhaps, Freud surmised, perversions, which in the negative extreme are expressed as hysteria, are a remnant of the ancient sexual cults, which once were religions in the Semitic world, such as the religion of Moloch and Astarte.[74] There is also the possibility of transferring the erotic from oneself to God. To attain a happy state, religious faith sublimates one's neurotic obsession by a "diversion from sensual processes to purely spiritual ones."[75] This kind of transfer and projection is important for Freud's explanation of religion because "the vague inner perception of one's own psychic apparatus stimulates illusions of thought which are naturally projected to the outside and in a characteristic way toward the future and the beyond. Immortality, vengeance, the whole hereafter, are such depictions of our psychic interior . . . psycho-mythology."[76] The confrontation with the corpse of a loved one originated the idea of a soul and of immortality and also the first ethical command "thou shalt not kill".[77] This command was a reaction against the satisfaction of hate, which hid

---

70. Freud, *Moses and Monotheism*, 90.

71. Freud, *Totem and Taboo* (IV/6) 155.

72. Freud, "The Poet and Day-dreaming," in *Collected Papers*, trans. Joan Riviere (London: Hogarth, 1953) 4:183.

73. Sigmund Freud, "Resistances to Psycho-Analysis," in *Collected Papers*, ed. James Trachey (London: Hogarth, 1952) 5:169.

74. Cf. Sigmund Freud, *Aus den Anfängen der Psychoanalyse. 1897–1902. Briefe an Wilhelm Fliess* (Frankfurt: Fischer, 1962) 163.

75. Sigmund Freud, "From the History of an Infantile Neurosis" (IX) in *Collected Papers*, trans. Alix and James Strachey (London: Hogarth, 1950) 3:598.

76. Sigmund Freud, *Aus den Anfängen der Psychoanalyse*, 204.

77. Cf. Freud, "Thoughts on War and Death" (II) in *Collected Papers*, 4:311.

behind the mourning of a loved one. It was gradually extended to the stranger who wanted no love, and finally also to the enemy.

Religion is an attempt to master one's life, a task which is attributed to the gods. They should tame the horrors of nature, the cruelty of destiny, and especially of death, and they should compensate for the sorrows we face in this life and for the rules we must obey in our community. The gods assume more and more the role of supervising cultural rules and endowing them with divine sanction. "A store of ideas is created, born from man's need to make his helplessness tolerable and built up from the material of memories of the helplessness of his own childhood and the childhood of the human race."[78] As an inspiration as to how far humanity had advanced, Freud pointed to the infancy of humanity and to one's own childhood stage.

According to Freud, however, problems commence when religion still points to portents, miracles, prophecies, and appearances of spirits, which are reported from ancient times and from ancient manuscripts, but which have long been discovered to be the result of untamed fantasies and tendentious fraud, products of a time in which the ignorance of humanity was large and the scientific spirit was in its infancy stage. Here scientific progress becomes a threat to religion. Therefore religion for Freud is infantile and removed from reality.

But religion is not all projection. It also contains historical remembrances. Behind the assumption that God forbids people not to kill is the memory of a primeval father who was killed by the people and to whose will they themselves later subjugated. This primeval father is the original image of God. Freud also examined monotheism, the idea of one God who is held to be so powerful by the believers that they think in it exists an inkling of the eternal truth that eventually came to appear in the history of humanity. Behind this idea, there is the remembrance of one person who in primeval time appeared to be so great that this person was elevated to a godhead, accessible in the memory of humanity. This is how, according to Freud, Moses introduced to his people the notion of the one and only God.

Though religion undoubtedly had its merits in the past to help people to come to terms with their lives and the surroundings which often appeared to be threatening, the influence of religion is waning as scien-

---

78. Sigmund Freud, *The Future of an Illusion* (III) GW, trans. W. D. Robson-Scott, rev. and ed. James Strachey (Garden City, NY: Doubleday, 1964) 25.

tific reasoning increases. According to Freud "we have no other means of controlling our instinctual nature but our intelligence."[79] Religion hinders clear thinking and is a danger for the future of humanity. Therefore Freud asks us to shed our childlike ideas and progress toward maturity.

> While the different religions wrangle with one another as to which of them is in possession of the truth, our view is that the question of the truth of religious beliefs may be left altogether on the side. Religion is an attempt to master the sensory world in which we are situated, by means of the wishful world which we have developed within us as a result of biological and psychological necessities. But religion cannot achieve this. Its doctrines bear the imprint of the times in which they arose, the ignorant times of the childhood of humanity. Its consolations deserve no trust. Experience teaches us that the world is no nursery. The ethical demands on which religion seeks to lay stress need, rather, to be given another basis; for they are indispensable to human society and it is dangerous to link obedience to them with religious faith. If we attempt to assign the place of religion in the evolution of mankind, it appears not as a permanent acquisition but as a counterpart to the neurosis which individual civilized men have to go through in their passage from childhood to maturity.[80]

With what does Freud want to replace this religious illusion and this projection? His conclusion is rather sober and contrasts with the optimism of the nineteenth century. "One feels inclined to say that the intention that man should be 'happy' is not included in the plan of 'Creation.'"[81] The hope for a continuous and progressive betterment of humanity is also an illusion according to Freud. "The ideal condition of things would of course be a community of men who have subordinated their instinctual life to the dictatorship of reason. . . . But in all probability that is a Utopian expectation."[82] There is an inborn tendency in humanity towards evil, towards aggression and destruction, and therefore towards cruelty.[83] While holding that religion serves as a crutch to

---

79. Ibid., (IX) 78.

80. Freud, *New Introductory Lectures on Psychoanalysis* (XXXV) 632. Though Freud recognized that by classifying religion as illusion, this charge can neither be proved nor refuted (*Future of an Illusion* [VII] 54). He clearly attempted a "scientific" refutation.

81. Sigmund Freud, *Civilization and Its Discontents* (II) trans. and ed. James Strachey (New York: Norton, 1961) 25.

82. Freud, "Why War?" in *Collected Papers*, 5:284.

83. Cf. Freud, *Civilization and Its Discontents* (VI) 74. Joachim Scharfenberg,

master the world, Freud preferred that humanity take the future into its own hands. Therefore Freud endeavored to explain the origin of religion through anthropological and psychological constellations. Freud wanted to show how religious knowledge is gained and to contradict religion by means of enlightened reason. Thereby Freud represents "an atheistic positivism" through which religion is declared to be unable to make any contribution toward explaining reality.[84]

What shall we do, then, with the positions of Feuerbach, Marx, and Freud, the main representatives of those who charge that religion and the God phenomenon are pre-scientific attempts to come to terms with reality? Indeed, they are correct that religion goes back much further than does our modern scientific outlook. This outlook itself is largely the result of a Hellenistic spirit which seeks for symmetry, simplicity, and continuity in its explanation of the observable world. Yet to this was added the Judeo-Christian spirit which perceives the world as God's creation entrusted to humanity. Their role as steward allows humans to analyze and to explain the world as far as possible without fearing to tread on sacred ground. Modern scientific progress is hardly explainable without these twofold roots, the Hellenistic spirit and the Judeo-Christian mind.[85] Hellenism was convinced of the rationality and simplicity of the world, while the Judeo-Christian faith in one God allowed for a "secularization" of God's creation. It could be considered as no longer divine and open to human use (and abuse).

But pointing to the historical roots of our modern mindset does not refute the charges of Feuerbach, Marx, and Freud. However we can easily disclaim that modern science and the Judeo-Christian tradition were antagonistic from the very beginning. It was only in the process of the emancipation of modern science from its roots that it quite frequently turned against them as if they had contributed nothing to the rise of this prominent offshoot. Without roots science may easily find

---

Sigmund and His Critique of Religion, trans. O.C. Dean, Jr. (Philadelphia: Fortress, 1988) 120–21, notes that initially Freud believed in a continuous upward-moving progress of history, but then abandoned this optimistic notion in favor of a more pessimistic view.

84. Cf. the charge of atheistic positivism against Freud by Richard Schmid-Leupi, *Die Entwicklung des Religionsbegriffes bei Sigmund Freud* (Zürich: Zentralstelle der Studentenschaft, 1994) 116.

85. Cf. the excellent investigation by Harold P. Nebelsick, *Circles of God: Theology and Science from the Greeks to Copernicus* (Edinburgh: Scottish Academic, 1985) who convincingly demonstrates the theological roots of modern science.

itself as being suspended in midair. It is not by accident that today science looks increasingly to other disciplines for guidance and direction. Yet such longing and looking for values and direction may just reinforce the idea that we love to use crutches instead of relying on ourselves for the mastery of life.

Indeed these critics of religion were not all wrong. We must concede that religion can indeed be a projection, and often has been one. Throughout the centuries some people have justified their actions with reference to divine sanction. We may think here of the Inquisition or the Crusades on the Christian side, or the Holy War of the Moslems through which they subjugated many nations to bring them the message of Allah. Pious self-justification also applies to individual desires and wishful thinking. Many miracles which were reported never held up to careful investigation. At times even pious fraud might have been involved. When Karl Marx called religion the opiate of the people, we are reminded of the Afro-American spirituals and the yearning they express for attaining heavenly bliss in the face of a miserable this-worldly existence. Even the idea that sacrifices on earth will be compensated for by heavenly rewards went in the direction of a projection.

Freud perceptively noted not only the danger of religious fantasizing, but also that of the component of sexuality in religion. Since sexuality is a constituent of human behavior, he saw that sexuality is also an important factor in religion. Especially in monastic life, the exclusion of sexuality is supposed to further religious devotion. As Martin Luther observed, however, with many monks and nuns this did not always lead to sublimation, but often to repression. It resulted either in distorted human beings or in secretly living out one's sexual drives with concomitant guilt complexes.

It is true that religion is used to cope with reality here on earth. But the decisive question is whether religion and the God phenomenon serve as an otherworldly crutch or as a truly divine support. In the first case it is an escape mechanism that does little to contribute to the mastery of life here on earth or to shape it positively. In the second case, however, we know, as Martin Luther said, "no strength of ours can match his might! We would be lost, rejected. But now a champion comes to fight, whom God himself elected."[86] Divine assistance can be no re-

---

86. *Lutheran Book of Worship*, hymn No. 228.

placement for human activity, faith is no replacement for reason, nor reason for faith.

Even if we realize this, the lingering thought remains that Feuerbach, Marx, Freud, and company might be correct. Religion and the God phenomenon could be the result of human desires. Perhaps this was also the reason why in his later years Freud warned so strongly against giving room to the infantile fantasizing of desires, to superstitious and magic elements, and to the emergence of that which had been suppressed. Indeed, there is always the danger of lapsing into that which is religiously dubious and primarily wishful. Are religion and the God phenomenon a huge and elaborate human fabrication designed to help us through this life?

The God Delusion: Richard Dawkins

While there have always been scientists who declared themselves to be atheists, such as Frank Tipler (b. 1947) and Steven Weinberg (b. 1933), Richard Dawkins (b. 1941), professor of the Public Understanding of Science at Oxford University since 1996, has been openly crusading against a God notion and opting for a strictly naturalistic understanding of nature. To facilitate his attack on a God concept, Dawkins claims that physicists such as Albert Einstein (1879–1955) and Steven Weinberg use the term "God" only "in their special metaphorical sense" which has nothing to do with the religious use of the word.[87] These physicists will occasionally slip "into the language of religious metaphor" that has absolutely nothing to do with religion as commonly perceived.

Dawkins starts an all-out attack on faith in God, especially that of the Christian persuasion. He declares, for instance, that since "reputable biblical scholars do not in general regard the New Testament (and obviously not the Old Testament) as a reliable record of what actually happened in history," he too "shall not consider the Bible further as evidence for any kind of deity."[88] The so-called proofs for the existence of God do not prove anything for Dawkins, either. Even to posit that natural selection is God's way of achieving his creation is countered by Dawkins with ridicule. He sides with the Oxford chemist Peter W. Atkins (b. 1940), an-

---

87. Richard Dawkins, *The God Delusion* (Boston: Houghton Mifflin, 2006) 19, for this and the following quote.

88. Ibid., 97.

other avowed atheist, in dismissing such a notion as inevitably implying "a hypothetically lazy God who tries to get away with as little as possible in order to make a universe containing life."[89] According to this outlook, since natural selection would be responsible for what we have in nature today, the resulting picture is "literally God at leisure, unoccupied, unemployed, superfluous, useless." Similar to Stephen Hawking (b. 1942), Dawkins assumes that at most God would only have to lay down the initial conditions and then be reduced to inactivity.[90] This deistic notion of God results from the watchmaker analogy, a paradigm that had been quite attractive on the British Isles. It was especially promulgated by the English clergyman and philosopher William Paley (1743–1805) in his book *Natural Theology or, Evidences of the Existence and Attributes of the Deity Collected From the Appearances of Nature*. As Charles Darwin mentioned, he, too, read this book during his schooldays, but during his career as a naturalist he moved more and more away from Paley.[91] Darwin finally concluded: "Everything in nature is the result of fixed laws."[92] If we assumed that there was a supreme being that laid down these laws, Dawkins concludes, such a God would then no longer be needed and should be discarded.

As Alister McGrath (b. 1953) in his rebuttal to Dawkins objects, the concept of a watchmaker is derived from the physical aspects of the world and transferred to the biological sphere. It is "a historically contingent approach to the doctrine of creation, linked to specific historic circumstances of the eighteenth-century England, which had already been rejected as inadequate, possible even unorthodox, by many leading English theologians of the time."[93] Astute observers had noticed that to liken nature to a self-sustaining mechanism could easily lead to the notion that God was no longer needed. Dawkins' charge is therefore not

---

89. Ibid., 118, for this and the following quote.

90. Cf. Stephen Hawking, *A Brief History of Time: From Big Bang to Black Holes*, intro. Carl Sagan, ill. Ron Miller (Toronto: Bantham, 1988) 140–41.

91. For the following, cf. Hans Schwarz, "The Intelligent Design Tradition: A Response to Robert Russell," *Theology and Science* (2007) 5:102–3.

92. Charles Darwin, *The Autobiography of Charles Darwin (1809–1882)* ed. with an appendix and notes Norah Barlow (London: Collins, 1958) in *The Works of Charles Darwin*, ed. Paul H. Barrett and R. B. Freeman (London: William Pickering, 1989) 29:87.

93. Alister McGrath, *Dawkins' God: Genes, Memes, and the Meaning of Life* (Oxford: Blackwell, 2005) 52.

unfounded when it comes to eighteenth-century England; today, however, hardly anyone, whether scientist or theologian, compares nature with a mechanism. Dawkins is beating a long-dead horse.

Yet Paley did not just talk about a watchmaker. He also advocated that many items are so intricate and interlocking in their effectiveness—for instance, the different parts of the human eye—that somebody must have designed them. For Dawkins, however, the argument from design does not work, because natural selection is not design. If one admits that there is a design in nature, Dawkins contends, this "raises an even bigger problem than it solves: who designed the designer?"[94] Dawkins does not want to stop with God, as Aristotle did when he talked about a first unmoved mover. Rather, Dawkins's natural cause argument is all-pervading. He argues that "invoking a supernatural Designer is to explain precisely nothing, for it leaves unexplained the origin of the Designer. You have to say something like 'God was always there', and if you allow yourself that kind of lazy way out, you might as well just say . . . 'Life was always there', and be done with it."[95] According to Dawkins, a natural explanation (or any kind of explanation) cannot stop at a certain point. At this juncture, the theory of natural selection seems to be the most convincing explanation as to how life arrived at its present (or, in the case of extinct beings, its final) form.

According to Dawkins, nature always proceeds from the simple to the more complex. The assumption of a creator, therefore, categorically goes against his principle. Dawkins declares: "If we want to postulate a deity capable of engineering all the organized complexity in the world, either instantaneously or by guiding evolution, that deity must already have been vastly complex in the first place."[96] He continues: "The one thing that makes evolution such a neat theory is that it explains how organized complexity can arise out of primeval simplicity." Then he concludes: "The theory of evolution by cumulative natural selection is the only theory we know of that is in principle *capable* of explaining the existence of organized complexity." This means if we start with the assumption that in the beginning there were only simple compounds, then the theory of evolution is the one best explanation for the complexity of

94. Dawkins, *God Delusion*, 121.

95. Richard Dawkins, *The Blind Watchmaker. Why the Evidence of Evolution Reveals a Universe without Design* (New York: Norton, 1986) 141.

96. Ibid., 316–17, for this and the following quotes.

life we encounter today. While this thesis is acceptable in and of itself, the point of departure for Dawkins is his insistence that a deity which is already vastly complex cannot stand at the beginning. Such a notion would stand against his thesis that things in the beginning, including any deity, were simple. To put God at the beginning goes against the grain of scientific reasoning, because similarly to a child taking apart a toy, scientists always argue in the reverse manner, wanting to know how complex arrangements are devised with simple components. Therefore "the theist's answer is deeply unsatisfying, because it leaves the existence of God unexplained."[97]

Darwinian evolution by natural selection has shown "how living creatures, with their spectaculous [sic] statistical improbability and appearance of design, have evolved by slow, gradual degrees from simple beginnings. We can now safely say that the illusion of design in living creatures is just that—an illusion."[98] Dawkins then concludes: "The factual premise of religion—the God Hypothesis—is untenable. God almost certainly does not exist." Darwinian evolution by natural selection and the notion of God as a reality co-exclude each other. While McGrath points out that "some might draw the conclusion that Darwinism encourages agnosticism," Dawkins opts for the extreme: "Darwin impels us to atheism."[99] This means that he goes even further than Darwin himself, who simply admitted that all he could detect was natural causation. Here Darwin was certainly correct that one cannot scientifically prove the value of the God hypothesis. As the author of the space-time continuum, God is not an object of matter within it and therefore beyond scientific proof or disproof. But then comes Dawkins' second objection that the Designer's existence must be subject to proof. Yet God "is not one of a series of temporal contingents, each requiring explanation as in terms of a previous state."[100] When Aristotle, for instance, talks about a first unmoved mover he wants to exempt such a first cause from being part of the cause-and-effect sequence. Therefore the argument of Dawkins that nature always proceeds from simple to more complex

---

97. Dawkins, *God Delusion*, 143.
98. Ibid., 158, for this and the following quote.
99. McGrath, *Dawkins' God*, 51.
100. Anthony Kenny, "The Kingdom of the Mind," in Neil Spurway, ed., *Humanity, Environment and God. Glasgow: Centenniel Gifford Lectures* (Oxford: Blackwell, 1993) 2001.

forms and that God as a grand Designer must have been exceedingly complex would apply only if God were part of nature. Yet God is not part of anything. Creation is not an emanation of God, joined to the divine in indissoluble continuity; it was simply set forth out of nothingness. One could assume that God created an environment "within which incredibly complex entities could develop from quite simple beginnings by quite simple processes."[101]

Dawkins also sees no value in religion as such, since it takes the human mind away from the way things really are. The reason for this is his notion of faith. According to Dawkins, faith "is a state of mind that leads people to believe something—it does not matter what—in the total absence of supporting evidence. If there were good supporting evidence, then faith would be superfluous, for the evidence would compel us to believe it anyway."[102] This means faith is synonymous with being gullible. But when we consider, for instance, the disciples after Christ's resurrection, they were far from being gullible. They were initially skeptical when the women told them about the resurrected Christ (cf. Luke 24:11). Only with the evidence of the empty tomb did they believe that Christ had been resurrected.

Faith is never completely void of substantiation: it is always based on some kind of evidence. Faith is conviction that the God who has proven to be trustworthy in the past will also be trustworthy in the future. This is not essentially different from scientific statements advanced with varying degrees of trust that their "proof" of a specific point is correct. The American physicist and 1965 Nobel laureate, Richard P. Feynman (1918–88), stated: "Scientific knowledge is a body of statements of varying degrees of certainty—some most unsure, some nearly sure, but none *absolutely* certain. Now, we scientists are used to this, and we take it for granted that it is perfectly consistent to be unsure, that it is possible to live and *not* know."[103] Only at the end of time will scientists know for sure whether their assertions are true and need not be corrected on account of new evidence in the course of scientific progress.

---

101. McGrath, *Dawkins' God*, 93.

102. Richard Dawkins, *The Selfish Gene*, 2nd ed. (Oxford: Oxford University Press, 1989) 330.

103. Richard P. Feynman, *"What Do You Care What Other People Think?" Further Adventures Of a Curious Character* as told to Ralph Leigthon (New York: Norton, 1988) 245.

Yet Dawkins is beyond any uncertainty with regard to his own scientific assertions. On the other hand, Dawkins mistakes faith for being gullible and therefore wants to dispense with it.

After dispensing with the God issue, Dawkins continues to explain the origin of religion "as a *by-product* of something else."[104] This thesis shows not only how religion could survive, but also that it is not a self-sufficient entity, since its central core, God (or any kind of deity), does not pertain to reality. Still Dawkins wants to demonstrate why religion has not died out, as, for instance, the Marxists suggested it would. According to Dawkins, since religion is associated with credulity, it cannot be beneficial, and its survival must be parasitic. Some kind of parasite of the mind is inculcated at an early age, remaining with human beings as a remnant of childhood and passed on again to the next generation of children. Dawkins picks up the notion of a meme, which is some kind of "cultural gene," though in this case one of no noticeable value. We are reminded here of Freud's verdict that humanity should grow up to adulthood and shed its infantile and sickly religious garb. This may also be the reason why Dawkins associates the God notion with a "meme," using the analogy of a virus to describe its replicability and its sickly epidemic character.

Since religion has no intrinsic value, it ought to be discarded; and Dawkins sets out to do just that. The reason for discarding the God notion seems to lie in Dawkins' a priori stance as "a dyed-in-the-wool monist."[105] This persuasion informs his methodological naturalism, by which he pronounces natural selection to be exclusive and absolutistic. Naturalism thereby functions no longer as a heuristic method but has become a metaphysical declaration. As Arthur McCalla (b. 1962) explains: "Methodological naturalism abstains from making assertions about the nature of reality and instead lays down rules for discovering reliable knowledge about the universe."[106] Dawkins discards this limitation and pursues a metaphysical naturalism that rejects implicitly the existence of non-material forces or entities. While methodological naturalism is essential to science, because empirical testing rests on the lawful regularities of nature, metaphysical naturalism can only be asserted

---

104. Dawkins, *God Delusion*, 172.

105. Ibid., 180.

106. Arthur McCalla, *The Creationist Debate: The Encounter between the Bible and the Historical Mind* (Edinburgh: T. & T. Clark, 2006) 193.

and never tested. Dawkins, however, tries to extend his methodological naturalism into the metaphysical realm by claiming "if everything has a cause, God must have one too."

As previously mentioned, there is no scientific proof or disproof possible of the God phenomenon. Those who claim they can prove God's involvement in nature, such as the intelligent design movement, and those who disclaim that God has anything to do with nature and deny even God's reality, such as Richard Dawkins, transgress this boundary. This line also demarcates the limits of reason readily acknowledged by those who put forth the so-called proofs of the existence of God. We do not believe in God because we have proven God's existence—such notion of proof would contradict the notion of belief—nor do we believe in God while tacitly admitting that such belief is absurd. We believe because we trust the God whom we have experienced in our lives and who has been witnessed to us through the lives of others. That being said, we have to seek the proper place for reason in our faith in God.

TWO

Beyond Proof and Disproof

The psalmist puts it very bluntly: "Fools say in their hearts, 'There is no God'" (Ps 14:1). In antiquity it was considered foolish to deny that there is a God, because at that time most people venerated at least one god. Therefore an atheist, if there really was one, was not taken seriously. The Greek philosopher Anaxagoras (ca. 500–428 BCE), for instance, was accused of impiety, synonymous with atheism, and was forced to leave his hometown Athens, because he had declared that the sun was an incandescent stone somewhat larger than the Peloponnesus. Others were punished more severely. When Socrates was indicted for "impiety," in 399 BCE on grounds that he had corrupted the youth, neglected the gods during worship ceremonies ordered by the city, and had introduced religious novelties, he was sentenced to death and condemned to drink hemlock within twenty-four hours.

But Socrates' position and that of other "atheists" was far from being atheistic in the modern sense. What was meant by "impiety" or "atheism" in ancient Greece is spelled out by Plato in his *Laws*: A citizen commits "a serious act of impiety . . . either by establishing a shrine on private land or by sacrificing on public land to gods not included in the pantheon of the state."[1] We remember that in the early centuries of Christianity conversion to Christianity "could lead to a charge of 'atheism.' To opt for Christianity was also to opt for a religion that had no claim to acceptance by the standards of antiquity or as a national cult, such as Judaism had."[2] Since Christians did not pay tribute to the gods allowed or propagated to be venerated in the Roman Empire, they were

---

1. Plato *Laws* X, 910, in *Complete Works*, ed. with intro. and notes John M. Cooper (Indianapolis: Hackett, 1997) 1566.
2. So W. H. C. Frend, *The Rise of Christianity* (Philadelphia: Fortress, 1984) 148.

outside the legitimate cultic practices and therefore could face the death penalty. In short, religion and the adoration of higher beings was a matter of fact in antiquity.

Although it was taken for granted that there was a divine being or beings, one attempted early on to employ reason in order to demonstrate the plausibility of the existence of such a divinity. One wanted to make sure that the belief in an ultimate being rested on good reasons. The focus was not on a plurality of divine beings, but on one ultimate and all-preceding divine actor. For instance we read in Isaiah:

> Have you not known? Have you not heard? Has it not been told you from the beginning? Have you not understood from the foundations of the earth? It is he who sits above the circle of the earth, and its inhabitants are like grasshoppers; who stretches out the heavens like a curtain, and spreads them like a tent to live in; who brings princes to naught, and makes the rulers of the earth as nothing.... To whom then will you compare me, or who is my equal? says the Holy One. Lift up your eyes on high and see: Who created these? He who brings out their host and numbers them, calling them all by name; because he is great in strength, mighty in power, not one is missing. (Isa 40:21–26)

Whoever observes events in nature and human history must conclude that there is one God who is the ultimate cause of everything. From the order in nature Isaiah deduces an argument which later on was developed into one of the proofs for the existence of God.

While God was present for the Israelites in their cult and in their prayer life, God was perceived differently in the Hellenistic world. As Paul noticed in Athens, there were many gods venerated there, too (Acts 18). But it was only the poet Hesiod (ca. 700 BCE) who gave the Greeks a genealogy of the gods and who decisively shaped Greek religious mythology. The gods were understood to have similar relationships and responsibilities as humans did, though being much superior. This humanization of the deities was counteracted through the rise of philosophy in which the divine became the object matter of reflection and thereby also became far removed from any human contamination. We notice this more distanced approach in the philosophic reflections of Plato (428/427–348/47 BCE) and Aristotle (384–322 BCE) who particularly developed that which were later called proofs of the existence of God.

Developing Proofs for God's Existence:
Plato, Aristotle, and Moses Maimonides

Plato is the first to attempt to prove the existence of God. He wished to give a solid foundation for the state, so he attempted to prove "that gods do exist,"[3] because God is "the measure of all things."[4] Therefore the state and the whole order of the world rests on God. In his *Laws*, Plato asserted that there were two reasons to assume that there are gods: 1) The "earth and the sun and the stars and the universe in general, ... the wonderful procession of the seasons and its articulation into years and months" are witnesses to the gods; and 2) All "Greeks and all foreigners are unanimous in recognizing the existence of gods."[5] We notice here two "proofs" which become more elaborate in the future, the so-called cosmological proof and the proof by common consent.

In this same text, however, Plato rejected these two proofs as insufficient and advanced another argument for the existence of gods. He noted that those who deny the existence of gods assume that the basic elements of fire, water, earth, and air, and everything else that developed from these elements, owe their existence to "nature and chance" and not to "intelligent planning" or "a deity."[6] Since those who claim that these basic elements are the origin of everything, they assume that the "soul ... was derived from them, at a later stage."[7] In arguing this way, Plato contended, they reverse the correct order of origination, because, according to him "the soul came first" having been "born long before all physical things."[8]

When we look at the world, the soul is "the chief cause of all their [i.e., physical things] alterations and transformations."[9] Similar to what we hear later from Aristotle, there are two kinds of movements for Plato, one that moves others but not itself, and another kind which always moves itself and others.[10] This second kind of movement must then be

---

3. Plato *Laws* 885d, in *Complete Works*, 1543.
4. Plato *Laws* 716c, in *Complete Works*, 1403.
5. Plato *Laws* 886a, in *Complete Works*, 1543.
6. Plato *Laws* 889b–c, in *Complete Works*, 1546.
7. Plato *Laws* 891c, in *Complete Works*, 1548.
8. Plato *Laws* 892, c, a, in *Complete Works*, 1549.
9. Plato *Laws* 892a, in *Complete Works*, 1549.
10. Cf. Plato *Laws* 894b, in *Complete Works*, 1551.

the origin of all movements, a "self-generated notion," since it is impossible that if something is moved by something else, it is the origin of everything.[11] The soul is therefore the cause of all changes and of all movements and the origin of all that exists and will exist. The soul or souls which necessarily permeate everything are the lords of the heavens, the earth, and the stars, and are accorded divine status. Plato argues: "A soul or souls—and perfectly virtuous souls at that—have been shown to be the cause of all these phenomena, and whether it is by their living presence in matter that they direct all the heavens, or by some other means, we shall insist that these souls are gods."[12]

According to Plato, God is "the measure of all things" and God holds "in his hands the beginning and end and middle of all things."[13] God is not only the ruler of the world, but also the one who made everything. Therefore we read in *Sophistes*: "Divine expertise produces the things that come about by so-called nature."[14] In *Timaeus* Plato talks about a divine "Demiurge" or "craftsman" who made all the beautiful works.[15] Again, he is the one who leads things "from a state of disorder to one of order" and leads everything to be good, because God is "good."[16] Since gods "are the most beautiful and best possible" of everything that is, they never change, and therefore the "divine" is identified with "what always is."[17] While Plato attacked the cosmological argument for God's existence, he nevertheless frequently relied on it to endow his own argument with additional credibility. Order, goodness, and beauty are attributes of divine activity and are reflected in the created world.

The essential question for Plato remains why there is something and not just nothing. If everything is accidental and if everything is caused by something else, there cannot be a sufficient reason for the existence of anything. Therefore there must be something outside the cause-and-effect sequence responsible for getting this sequence started. Such an entity is not deemed accidental, but must be necessary. This is why Plato focuses on motion as that primary moment of existence

11. Plato *Laws* 894e–895a, in *Complete Works*, 1551.
12. Plato *Laws* 899b, in *Complete Works*, 1556.
13. Plato *Laws* 716c and 716a, in *Complete Works*, 1402–3.
14. Plato *Sophist* 265e, in *Complete Works*, 290.
15. Plato *Timaeus* (28a) in *Complete Works*, 1234–35.
16. Plato *Timaeus* (30a and 29e) in *Complete Works*, 1236.
17. Plato *Republic* (II.381c and X.611e) in *Complete Works*, 1020 and 1215.

rather than just on the foundational elements of nature and their creator. In linking the originator of everything to the soul, he also indicates that that which is truly the first cannot be material, it must be immaterial. In the context of polytheism, however, it was difficult for Plato to unambiguously assert one God. Therefore he prefers to abstract from the gods or the divinities to the divine. This often pantheistically sounding "divine" shines through the whole world as that which gives the created its origin, order, and destiny.

Aristotle follows very much in the wake of Plato with whom he studied for twenty years. For Aristotle the "first and most important principle ... must surely be the divine" and it is dealt with in the "best" of the "theoretical sciences" called "theology."[18] Central for Aristotle again is movement. The most perfect for him is circular motion, since it moves back into itself. It has no goal, and therefore is an eternal motion "for the body which moves in a circle is eternal and unresting."[19] Circular movement, as we can observe with the movement of the planets, has its origin in the eternal movements of the sky with its fixed stars. Since "no movement can be for the sake of itself or of another movement, ... all movements must be for the sake of the stars."[20] For Aristotle such original movement is necessarily eternal. He was convinced that "it is impossible that movement should either come into being or cease to be; for it must always have existed."[21] In short, movement is eternal and continuous and its preferred mode is circular.

Aristotle reasoned that if movement in its totality is eternal, the original movement of the sky of the fixed stars must also be eternal, because from it all other movement originates. Yet the sky of the fixed stars is not the first unmoved mover which Aristotle wanted to penetrate, because there is something which moves the fixed star-sky. This sky is at the same time "moved and moves."[22] If something is moved there must be a reason or a cause for that movement, because that which is moved is moved by necessity by something else. There must be something that moves that which is moved. Consequently Aristotle must go to some-

18. Aristotle, *Metaphysics* (xi.1064a37–b2) in *The Complete Works of Aristotle*, ed. Jonathan Barnes (Princeton: Princeton University Press, 1984) 2:1681.
19. Aristotle, *Metaphysics* (xii.1073a31f.) in *Complete Works of Aristotle*, 2:1696.
20. Aristotle, *Metaphysics* (xii.1074a26f.) in *Complete Works of Aristotle*, 2:1697.
21. Aristotle, *Metaphysics* (xii.1071b6f.) in *Complete Works of Aristotle*, 2:1693.
22. Aristotle, *Metaphysics* (xii.1072a25) in *Complete Works of Aristotle*, 2:1694.

thing else that really moves, but is not moved by something else. Being the prime mover "there is no need of another."[23]

Why should there be some first unmoved mover? Aristotle adduced two reasons: 1) It is impossible that there is an infinite regress from one cause to another because "in an infinite series there is no first term." 2) The first must be also the most perfect because if the most perfect changed, "change would be change for the worse."[24] Aristotle concludes that one must assume a first origin, "one mover, the first of unmoved things, which being eternal will be the principle of motion to everything else."[25] Everything else is ordered toward this primal origin, which means that the "eternal movement must be produced by something eternal and a single movement by a single thing."[26] Since Aristotle conceives this prime mover as a singular cause, Plato's wavering between the deities and the divine is overcome.

However, Aristotle had some difficulties in explaining how an unmoved mover can move something else, since the motion of the movement would necessarily subject it to change. Therefore he attempted to solve the problem by adducing analogies. As a solution, he proposed moving by intention, in the way a lover "produces motion by being loved."[27] "The first mover, then, of necessity exists; and in so far as it is necessary, it is good, and in this sense a first principle. For the necessary has all the senses—that which is necessary perforce because it is contrary to impulse, that without which the good is impossible, and that which cannot be otherwise but is *absolutely* necessary."[28] This first unmoved mover, this pure reality, Aristotle called "God."[29] It is the origin and the first of everything since the divine is the first and the highest. It is also that toward which all reality is oriented. It is the origin on which "depend the heavens and the world of nature" and this divine power which "holds together the universe."[30] Since this original mover is the orienting

---

23. Aristotle, *Physics* (viii.256a15–20) in *Complete Works of Aristotle*, 1:428, for this quote and the following.

24. Aristotle, *Metaphysics* (xii.1074b26) in *Complete Works of Aristotle*, 2:1698.

25. Aristotle, *Physics* (viii.259a13f.) in *Complete Works of Aristotle*, 1:433.

26. Aristotle, *Metaphysics* (xii.1073a27f.) in *Complete Works of Aristotle*, 2:1696.

27. Aristotle, *Metaphysics* (xii.1072b3) in *Complete Works of Aristotle*, 2:1694.

28. Aristotle, *Metaphysics* (xii.1072b10–13) in *Complete Works of Aristotle*, 2:1694–5.

29. Aristotle, *Metaphysics* (xii.1072b31) in *Complete Works of Aristotle*, 2:1695.

30. Aristotle, *Metaphysics* (xii.1072b14) and *Politics* (vii.1326a32) in *Complete*

force within the universe and that which holds everything together, it is not surprising that, similar to Plato, Aristotle equated that which is divine with reason, because there is nothing that is more perfect, more divine, and more elevated than divine reason itself. This divine reason then "thinks (since it is the most excellent of things), and this thinking is a thinking on thinking."[31] This means that divine reason takes no cues from somewhere else, but is itself the cue for everything else. God is understood here as a living reason which endows everything with reality, a notion which later impacted the Christian understanding of God as creative reason.

In Aristotle the cosmological argument for God's existence, namely that there is this first cause which is equated with God, and the teleological argument, namely that everything is ordered toward God, attain prominence. While early Christian theologians such as Augustine (354–430) and Origen (185–254) borrowed directly from Platonic philosophy in advancing arguments for God's existence, medieval theology no longer had direct access to the intellectual treasures of antiquity. The geographical expansion of Islam thwarted such direct contact and at the same time preserved and furthered the insights of Hellenistic philosophy, as witnessed by Islamic philosophers, such as Averroes (1126–1198) and Avicenna (ca. 980–1037), who in turn influenced Christian theology.

Yet one should not forget Jewish theologians, such as Moses Maimonides (1135–1204), who advanced the arguments for God's existence in dialogue with both Muslim and Hellenistic, especially Aristotelian, thinking. In his massive treatise *The Guide of the Perplexed* (1190) Maimonides showed that the early Islamic philosophers assume that the world is created, while the Aristotelian philosophers contend that the world is eternal. He concluded:

> The world cannot but be either eternal or created in time. If it is created in time, it undoubtedly has a creator who created it in time. For it is a first intelligible that what has appeared at a certain moment in time has not created itself in time and that its creator is other than itself. Accordingly the creator who created the world in time is the deity. If, however, the world is eternal, it follows necessarily because of this and that proof, that there is

---

Works of Aristotle, 2:1695 and 2105.

31. Aristotle, *Metaphysics* (xii.1074b33ff.) in *The Complete Works of Aristotle*, 2:1698.

> an existent other than all the bodies to be found in the world; an existent who is not a body and not a force in a body and who is one, permanent, and sempiternal; who has no cause and whose becoming subject to change is impossible. Accordingly he is a deity. Thus it has become manifest to you that the proofs for the existence and the oneness of the deity and of His not being a body ought to be procured from the starting point offered by the supposition of the eternity of the world, for in this way the demonstration will be perfect, both if the world is eternal and if it is created in time.[32]

Maimonides shows here that if the world has been created, God exists, and, if the world is eternal, God exists, too. Therefore whether the world has been created or is eternal, God exists.

In the introduction to part 2 of *The Guide of the Perplexed* Maimonides introduced twenty-six premises, all of which are taken from Aristotle. He needed them to establish his arguments for God's existence in the first chapter of this part. In premise 25 Maimonides quoted Aristotle saying: "Matter does not move itself," and he concluded: "This therefore is the capital premise calling for an inquiry concerning the existence of the Prime Mover."[33] In chapter 1 of part 2 he immediately started with this premise saying: "It follows necessarily from the twenty-fifth premise that there is a mover, which has moved a matter of that which is subject to generation and corruption so that it received form. If now it is asked: What moved this proximate mover?—it follows of necessity that there exists for it another mover either of its own species or of a different species ... now this does not go to infinity."[34] According to Maimonides, eventually we refer the movement back to the movement of a sphere that again can only be moved through a body or something immaterial outside of it or through a power in it. An external body, however, cannot be the reason for the movement of the sphere, since a body must always be moved by something else so that we would have to continue the causal nexus to infinity. An immanent power cannot be the reason for movement either, since all powers within a sphere are necessarily finite, and finite powers cannot affect that which exists forever.

---

32. Moses Maimonides, *The Guide of the Perplexed*, trans. with an intro. and notes Shlomo Pines, intro. essay Leo Strauss (Chicago: University of Chicago Press, 1963) 181f.

33. Ibid., 239.

34. Ibid., 243.

Therefore the ultimate reason for a movement of each sphere and the body within it must be an external immaterial being, i.e., God. "Now this is the deity, may His name be sublime; I am referring to the first cause moving the sphere."[35]

The second argument goes like this: "Supposing that there exists a thing composed of two things and that one of the two things exists separately outside this composed thing, it follows necessarily that the other thing also must exist outside the composed thing."[36] He explained this sequence in line with Aristotle saying that many things are composed of a mover and a moved. According to his premise he concluded: "Now we find that there exists a thing that is moved and does not at all cause to move; this is the last of the moved things. It follows accordingly that there must exist a mover that is not moved at all; this is the first mover."[37]

The third argument again follows Aristotle saying that there is no doubt that there are existent things. For these things there are three possible alternatives: 1. "No existents are subject to generation and corruption."[38] 2. "All of them are subject to generation and corruption." 3. "Some of them are subject to generation and corruption whereas others are not." While Maimonides found the first alternative absurd, since there are things that are subject to generation and corruption, he also found the second alternative absurd because if all things would be subject to generation and corruption, then it could be that everything ceases to exist and nothing could be brought to existence any more. Since we perceive, however, that things are existent, "there must be a certain existent that is not subject to generation and corruption. Now in this existent that is not subject to generation and corruption, there is no possibility of corruption at all; rather, its existence is necessary, not possible." Again, this entity which necessarily exists is equated with the deity.

The fourth argument in Maimonides started with the observation that we constantly see things "that are in potentia and pass into actuality. Now everything that passes from potentiality into actuality has something outside itself that causes it to pass."[39] Since this sequence of cause and effect cannot continue forever, "one must come to something that

---

35. Ibid., 246.
36. Ibid.
37. Ibid., 247.
38. Ibid., for this and the following quotes.
39. Ibid., 249, for this and the following quotes.

causes the passage from potentiality to actuality, that is perpetually existent in one and the same state, and in which there is no potentiality at all. . . . Now the being that is separate from matter, in which there is no possibility whatsoever, but that exists in virtue of its essence, is the deity."

At the beginning of chapter 2 Maimonides summed up the result of his arguments: "Thus it has become clear to you that the existence of the deity, may He be exalted—who is the necessary of existence that has no cause and in whose existence in respect to His essence there is no possibility—is proved by cogent and certain demonstrations, regardless of whether the world has come into being in time after having been nonexistent, or whether it has not come into being in time after having been nonexistent. Similarly, demonstrations prove that He is one and not a body, as we have set forth before."[40]

If Maimonides thought he had really proven the existence of God, that would have been the end of the arguments for the existence of God, since the matter would have been settled. Yet the opposite is the case. As we see especially in the medieval tradition in the West, proofs for the existence of God enjoyed tremendous popularity. The main lines of argumentation were laid out, such as the issue of the transition between potentiality and actuality, the cause-and-effect sequence, and the order in nature which Maimonides emphasized through his reference to the spheres of the universe.

Five Main Arguments for God's Existence

There have been many proofs of the existence of God. Thomas Aquinas (ca. 1224–1274) alone recommended eleven different proofs and he rejected or abandoned thirteen more, because he found them inappropriate to his task of ascertaining God's existence.[41] Yet there are five proofs that seem to have gained prime importance in the attempt to verify intellectually the ground of faith. The first one we want to introduce and which is still fascinating today, especially among philosophers, is the so-called ontological argument. It was most prominently advanced by the great theorist of early scholasticism, Anselm of Canterbury (1033–1109).

---

40. Ibid., 252.
41. According to John Clayton, "Gottesbeweise II. Mittelalter," in *TRE* 13:732.

The Ontological Argument

"Anselm's argument for the existence of God in the *Proslogion* is one of the most enduring texts in the history of philosophy."[42] Anselm of Canterbury wrote his *Proslogion* (1077–8), or *Address* from the point of view of a believer. He wrote: "For I do not seek to understand in order to believe but I believe in order to understand."[43] God is already presupposed by him. Since Anselm wanted to understand what he believed his whole argument has an apologetic slant. He wrote concerning God:

> Indeed we believe You to be something than which nothing greater can be thought. Is there, then, no such nature as You, for the Fool has said in his heart that God does not exist? But surely, when this very Fool hears the words 'something than which nothing greater can be thought,' he understands what he hears. And what he understands is in his understanding, even if he does not understand [judge] it to exist. Indeed for a thing to be in the understanding, is different from understanding [judging] that this thing exists.[44]

Anselm wanted to make someone who doubts God's existence understand who God is. Once such a person has fully understood who God is, that person has no choice but to admit God's existence, because "without doubt, something than which a greater cannot be thought exists both in understanding and in reality." If God is the most perfect being, this perfection includes that God must exist both in thought and in reality.[45]

This is the point where most of the criticism set in against Anselm's approach. Anselm seemed to consider existence (in reality) as a property of God in analogy to other properties of God.[46] By definition existence

---

42. So M. J. Charlesworth, *St. Anselm's Proslogion with a Reply on Behalf of the Fool by Gaunilo*, trans. with an intro. and philosophical commentary (Notre Dame: University of Notre Dame Press, 1979) 3.

43. Anselm of Canterbury, *Proslogion* I, in *Anselm of Canterbury*, ed. and trans. Jasper Hopkins and Herbert Richardson (Toronto: Edwin Mellen, 1974) 1:93.

44. Anselm of Canterbury, *Proslogion* II, in *Anselm of Canterbury*, 1:93–94, for this and the following quote.

45. These two issues have been raised by Robert Brecher, *Anselm's Argument. The Logic of Divine Existence* (Brookfield, VT: Gower, 1985) 114–15.

46. Cf. Charles Hartshorne, "What Did Anselm Discover?" in *The Many-Faced Argument: Recent Studies on the Ontological Argument for the Existence of God*, ed. John Hick and Arthur C. McGill (New York: Macmillan, 1967) 321–33, for a good treatment of the problems involved in Anselm's argument.

in reality belongs to the idea of the most perfect being. In his *On Behalf of the Fool*, Anselm's contemporary Gaunilo of Marmoutier had already objected that such a procedure is illegitimate. He attempted to show this with the example of the idea of the most perfect island that is supposed to exist somewhere, though nobody has ever encountered it. Gaunilo argues that according to Anselm's logic, this island must exist both in understanding and in reality, since it is claimed to be the most excellent island.[47]

More than five centuries later, in his *Critique of Pure Reason* Immanuel Kant (1724–1804) objected in a similar way, stating that in the ontological argument the logical and the real predicates are being confused. Unlike omnipotence or omniscience, *being* is not a real predicate, i.e., an attribute of an animate or inanimate object. Therefore the transition from existence in thought to existence in reality cannot be accomplished by simply according God the predicate "being" to make God perfect. Kant illustrated his objection with the example of a hundred coins. "A hundred actual thalers do not contain the least more than a hundred possible thalers. . . . In the state of my assets, however, there is more in the case of by a hundred actual thalers than in the case of the mere concept of them (i.e., their mere possibility)."[48] The actual existence of the thalers is thus not contained in thinking of them but has to be added to such thought. However, both Gaunilo and Kant did not seem to listen to the rest of Anselm's argument.[49]

Anselm was well aware that God's existence in reality is different from the existence in reality of excellent islands or of a hundred thalers. God's existence is not of a possible but of a necessary kind. Anselm argued that there are things that can be conceived of as either existing or not existing. But these things cannot be God. If God could be conceived of as not existing, existing things would be of higher quality than God and he would not be that, than which nothing greater can be thought. Anselm affirmed: "Therefore, Lord my God, You exist so truly [really]

---

47. Gaunilo, *A Reply on Behalf of the Fool* (6) in *Anselm of Canterbury*, 1:119.

48. Kant, *Critique of Pure Reason* (A599, B627). Unified Edition, trans. Werner S. Pluhar, intro. Patricia Kitcher (Indianapolis: Hackett, 1996) 584.

49. Cf. Charles Hartshorne, *Anselm's Discovery: A Re-examination of the Ontological Proof for God's Existence* (Lasalle, Il: Open Court, 1965) 302, where he emphasizes the necessity to re-examine Kant's rejection of the theistic proofs of the existence of God. However, Hartshorne seems to go beyond Anselm in attempting to arrive at the ontological argument without Anselm's unquestioned premise of faith in God's existence.

that You cannot even be thought not to exist. And this is rightly the case. For if any mind could conceive of something better than You, the creature would rise above the Creator and would sit in judgment over the Creator—an utterly preposterous consequence."[50] Again Anselm did not consider his line of argument as an actual proof of God's existence, because he left open the possibility that one can deny God's existence in reality. He realized that people differ considerably in their understandings of God and thus the notion of God can be understood inadequately. For a person with an inadequate understanding of God it does not naturally follow that God exists also in reality. But someone who thoroughly understands that God is that which nothing greater can be conceived, "surely understands (*intelligit*) that God so exists that He cannot even conceivably not exist." Since he felt that he was one of those, Anselm concluded his investigation saying: "I thank You, good Lord, I thank You that what at first I believed through Your giving, now by Your enlightening I so understand."[51] It becomes evident that Anselm's argument is not a proof in the traditional sense of the word, since it presupposes already a stance of faith concerning God's very existence and nature.

Karl Barth (1886–1968) who vehemently rejected the attempts of theologians to bolster the credibility of the Christian faith with any kind of "proofs" for God's existence eloquently stated that it "goes without saying that for him [Anselm] the Existence of God is given as an article of faith."[52] And he summed up the matter well by saying that according to Anselm "God gave himself as the object of his knowledge and God illumined him that he might know him as object. Apart from this event there is no proof of the existence, that is of the reality of God."[53] The question, however, must be asked whether the presupposition of the Christian God that Anselm assumed is actually necessary for the ontological argument. In other words, need one be a Christian in order to understand who it is whom we call God?[54]

50. Anselm, *Proslogion* (III) 94–5.

51. Ibid. (IV) 95.

52. This was pointed out by Karl Barth, *Anselm: Fides Quaerens Intellectum. Anselm's Proof of the Existence of God in the Context of his Theological Scheme*, trans. Ian W. Robertson (London: SCM, 1960) 78.

53. Barth, *Anselm*, 171.

54. Charles Hartshorne, for instance, in his introduction to *St. Anselm. Basic Writings*, trans. S. W. Deane, 2nd ed. (Lasalle, IL: Open Court, 1962) 19, intimates that Anselm's theory of the contingency and necessity of God, if carefully reflected upon

The French philosopher René Descartes (1596–1650) seems to have omitted the Christian presupposition of the ontological argument and proceeded on strictly philosophical grounds. In his *Meditations Concerning First Philosophy* (1641) he outlined two ways of arriving at God. In the third *Meditation* he first wondered why we have the idea of God. He was sure that this idea cannot proceed from us. The name God implies a "substance" that is "infinite, independent, omniscient, omnipotent," and by which I myself and everything else have been created. Descartes assumed that "all these attributes are such that, the more diligently I consider them, the less they seem able to originate from me alone. Accordingly, . . . it must be concluded that God necessarily exists."[55] Of course, Descartes remembered that he defined God as infinite substance. Since he considered humans a finite substance, humans could have apprehended the idea of the infinite substance by negating the finite. But Descartes disclaimed that one could arrive at an adequate understanding of an infinite substance through such negative causal inference. Descartes suggested that "there is more reality in infinite substance than in the finite substance, and hence that the perception of the infinite is somehow prior to me to that of the finite—that is, the perception of God is in some way prior to the perception of my very self."[56] It is only through God's perfect and infinite nature that I realize my imperfection and my finitude. Thus the idea of God is the most completely true, the most completely clear and distinct of all ideas that are in me. Or to put it in Paul Tillich's terminology: God as the ultimate reality exists by necessity, and because of its ultimate reality it imparts to us our own reality and existence.

In his fifth *Meditation* Descartes followed even more closely Anselm's argument, yet without reference to him. He argued that though one cannot think of a mountain without a valley it does not follow that valleys and mountains must exist. Our thinking only indicates that mountain and valley, whether existent or non-existent, are inseparably conjoined with each other. However, Descartes asserted, "From the fact that I cannot think of God except as existing, it follows that existence is

---

could carry us "well beyond his type of philosophy and theology."

55. René Descartes, *Meditations Concerning First Philosophy* (3.74) in *The Essential Writings*, trans. with intro. and concordance John J. Blom (New York: Harper, 1977) 211.

56. Ibid. (3.76), 212.

inseparable from God, and therefore that he truly exists."[57] Of course, Descartes knew that God's necessary existence might be brought about by my thinking it as necessary. But the surprising fact is, we hear Descartes say, that we cannot think of God as lacking existence, i.e., to think of this sovereignly perfect being as devoid of complete perfection. Descartes admitted that one cannot think a triangle either except to think that the sum of its three angles are not greater than two right angles and that its greatest side subtends its greatest angle. But these necessary assertions of its essence leave it open whether a triangle exists at all. This, however, is different with God. Though we think of him and his essence as clearly and distinctly as of the said triangle, Descartes asserted that we "cannot think of any other thing, except God alone, to whose essence existence pertains."[58] Thus there is nothing more evident than that there is a God, that is to say, a sovereign being, and that of all beings God alone has existence as appertaining to God's essence. Descartes did not suggest that at all times we must conceive of the idea of God. Yet each time we allow it to occupy the mind, we find ourselves necessarily constrained to ascribe to God all perfections, including that of existence.[59] This conclusion, however, is the weak point in Descartes' argument.

In recent times fewer and fewer people seem to feel compelled to think the idea of God, because for an increasing number of people the world makes good sense without ever thinking of God. Yet Descartes was not yet aware of this rapidly growing sentiment. This is substantiated by his own concluding remarks after having "proved" the existence of God. Descartes reasoned:

> The certainty and truth of every science depends solely upon the cognition of the true God, so that until I came to know him I could know nothing perfectly about anything else. But now, indeed, innumerable things concerning not only God himself and

---

57. Ibid. (5.119), 227.
58. Ibid. (5.120), 228.
59. Norman Kemp Smith, *New Studies in the Philosophy of Descartes. Descartes as Pioneer* (London: Macmillan, 1952) 306, has pointed out very convincingly that according to Descartes only in the case of God, "God and existence are inseparable in thought," while for all other contents of thought existence is not a necessary attribute. Thus it is not us who impose upon God the necessity of existence, but God himself exists by the very necessity of being God.

other intellectual things, but also concerning that entire corporeal nature that is an object of pure mathematics.[60]

For Descartes God still served as the guarantor of our and the world's reality. Yet at least since Isaac Newton (1642–1727) scientists became more and more used to explaining nature's phenomena without reference to God. While Newton was deeply interested in theological issues and understood God to be the one who created the world and rules over it with sovereign authority, he was convinced that we must detect nature and its laws by observation alone.[61] Newton was the first to establish a self-consistent and self-sufficient celestial physics, free from an all-embracing God-relatedness, and free from an all-embracing relatedness to humanity, yet without sliding into atheistic materialism. Newton, and all the representatives of classical physics after him, "started from the assumption that one can describe the world without speaking about God or ourselves."[62] The laws of nature describe relations between specific natural phenomena that are then generalized as mathematical concepts and are applied to explain other natural phenomena.

It is not only the autonomy of modern science that makes the world look so self-contained that the notion of a most perfect being outside or above the world is no longer an existential, but at the most a theoretical issue. We must remember that both Anselm and those following his train of thought made the transition from thought to reality. Exactly that transition has been violently attacked by Feuerbach and his adherents claiming that God is a projection, a figment of the human mind. We encounter still another dilemma with the ontological argument. If God is really something than which nothing greater can be thought, God is totally self-sufficient and a "something." Such God has no personal qualities and looks rather anemic. How can this abstractly deduced God then be identical with the personal God of the Judeo-Christian tradition? Is it not more persuasive to conclude that God is aloof to our personal histo-

---

60. Descartes, *Meditations Concerning First Philosophy* (5.125), 230.

61. Cf. Michael John Petry, "Newton, Isaac," in *TRE* 24:427, in his concluding remarks.

62. Werner Heisenberg, *Physics and Philosophy: The Revolution in Modern Science* (New York: Harper, 1958) 80–81. Cf. also Werner Heisenberg, *Physics and Beyond. Encounters and Conversations,* trans. A. J. Pomerans (New York: Harper, 1972) 82–84, where he thematizes the relation between science and religion.

ries and destinies and uninvolved with our world? Perhaps other arguments for God's existence give this "theoretical God" more life-blood.

The Cosmological Argument

We have already been introduced to the cosmological argument through Plato and Aristotle. In modernity the cosmological argument came to prominence with Thomas Aquinas who absorbed Aristotelian philosophy and neo-Platonism in his studies. This inspired him to prove the existence of God by focusing on the causality which is at work in the empirical world. Thomas Aquinas wrote an extensive *Commentary on the Metaphysics of Aristotle*, and in his *Summa Theologiae* (1266–1273) he introduced the so-called five ways to prove God's existence. How strong his dependence on Aristotle is, we can glean from his *Summa Contra Gentiles*. There he attributes all his proofs of God's existence to Aristotle, except for the last one where he refers to the Greek theologian John of Damascus (ca. 650–prior to 754) and the Muslim scholar Averroes, themselves influenced by Aristotle.[63] But the impetus to concern himself with arguments for God's existence seems to be derived from biblical sources. Thomas wrote: "The truths about God which St. Paul says we can know by our natural powers of reasoning—that God exists, for example—are not numbered among the articles of faith, but are presupposed by them. For faith presupposes natural knowledge, just as grace does nature and all perfections that which they perfect."[64] According to Thomas "faith needs a sure foundation in reason."[65] Therefore as a presupposition for faith Thomas introduces the arguments for God's existence. According to him, "there are five ways in which one can prove that there is a God."[66] Since, as we have noted, there are more than five ways in his own writings, he presented in his *Summa Theologiae* a selection of the proofs he feels are most persuasive.

According to his own understanding, Thomas started with the most obvious proof, the one that is based on change. We observe that some things in the world are in process of change. Anything that is in process

---

63. Thomas Aquinas, *Summa Contra Gentiles* (1:13.35), trans. with intro. and notes Anton C. Pegis (Notre Dame, IN: University of Notre Dame Press, 1955) 1:96.

64. Aquinas, *Summa Theologiae* (1a.2.2.ad1), Blackfriars edition, 2:11.

65. Cf. John Clayton, "Gottesbeweise II. Mittelalter," 13:735.

66. Aquinas, *Summa Theologiae* (1a.2.3r) 2:13.

of change is being changed by something else. If it could change itself, it would already contain actually that within it toward which it moves. Since it is still moving toward something, it can only potentially contain the goal toward which it moves, and the actuality must be caused by something outside. In other words, in order to change something, the cause of change always comes from outside of the object to be changed. Though we can push back the chain reaction of cause and effect further and further, we must stop somewhere, otherwise there would be no first cause of change, and, as a result, no subsequent causes. If we excluded the possibility of a first cause of change, which is not changed by anything else, then there would be no intermediate causes, which are caused by something prior to them and, in turn, cause something subsequent to them. Thomas now postulated such a first cause as God.

Thomas's second argument concerning the existence of God goes very much like the first one, and is based on the nature of causation. Thomas claimed: "In the observable world causes are found to be ordered in series; we never observe, nor ever could, something causing itself, for this would mean it preceded itself, and this is not possible."[67] Thomas assumed that such a series of causes and effects must stop somewhere where it reaches a first cause, for again, if there were no first efficient cause, there could be no intermediate causes and thus no causation at all. Again Thomas equated this first cause with God.

Thomas's third argument is somewhat different and is based on the distinction between what must be by necessity and what need not necessarily be. Thomas observed that in our experience things can be or cannot be; there is no necessity about their existence. Yet if everything were like this—that it springs up and then dies away—then once upon a time there was nothing. "But if that were true there would be nothing even now, because something that does not exist can only be brought into being by something already existing." From the fact that there are things now Thomas concluded that not everything is of the quality that it could be or could not be. In other words, "there has got to be something that must be."[68] This necessary thing cannot owe the necessity of its existence to something else, but owes it to itself and thus in turn causes other things to be. Again Thomas equated this first necessary cause of existence with God.

67. Aquinas, *Summa Theologiae* (1a.2.3r) 2:15.
68. Ibid.

Thomas's fourth argument again is somewhat different and is based on the gradation observed in things. Thomas stated that some things are found to be more good, more true, more noble, and so on, and other things less. All these comparative terms describe approximations using a superlative, the best, the truest, the noblest, and so on. The things which contain all these superlatives are the things most fully in being. We might expect that Thomas would now employ the ontological argument and claim that the one thing most perfect must by necessity exist. But he again uses a cosmological argument and works with the assumption of a first cause: When many things possess a common property (e.g., varying degrees of goodness), then the one most fully possessing it can cause others to participate in it. If such causative superlative would not exist, there would not be these properties. Therefore Thomas concluded that there is something "which causes in all other things their being, their goodness, and whatever other perfection they have. And this we call 'God.'"[69]

All these cosmological "proofs" of the existence of God boil down to the observation that no finite being thus far observed has the cause of its existence in itself. Therefore the conclusion is reached that there must be an infinite being which is the cause of all finite beings and of itself. Yet is such a conclusion justified on logical or phenomenal grounds? Immanuel Kant, one of the keenest critics of all proofs of God's existence, answered with an emphatic "No!" He did not take the issue as lightly as the British philosopher and sceptic Bertrand Russell (1872-1970) who simply stated: "If everything must have a cause, then God must have a cause. If there can be anything without a cause, it may just as well be the world as God. . . . There is no reason why the world could not have come into being without a cause; nor, on the other hand, is there any reason why it should not have always existed."[70] Kant, however, rightly called the cosmological argument the one that "carries with it the strongest persuasion not only for the common but also for speculative understanding."[71] Yet Kant also demonstrated the limits of the cosmological argument in his fourth antinomy of pure reason, i.e., valid statements which oppose each other. Kant showed that neither on the basis of experience nor on

---

69. Ibid. (1a.2.3r) 2:17.

70. Bertrand Russell, *Why I Am Not a Christian and Other Essays on Religion and Related Subjects* (New York: Simon & Schuster, 1957) 6-7.

71. Kant, *Critique of Pure Reason* (A604, B632) 587.

the basis of pure reason alone can it be decided whether there is a supreme cause of the world or whether such a cause is non-existent.[72]

In his actual criticism of the cosmological argument Kant again affirmed that to infer a cause from observing the contingent only applies to the observable world, but it has no meaning whatsoever outside this world.[73] Thus the principle of causality must be restricted to our observable world. Kant recognized that in the cosmological argument this principle is precisely employed to enable us to advance beyond the observable world. Yet he objected that any inference from an impossibility of an infinite series of causes to a first cause is not justifiable within the world of experience, and it is still less justifiable beyond this world in a realm into which this series can never be extended. Kant therewith emphasized that our experience and logic are confined to the realm in which we live, to our space-time continuum. There is no way logically to transcend this realm and attain any degree of certainty. Kant also reminded us of the dilemma that we had faced with the ontological argument when he stated that the logical necessity of a prime cause does not necessitate its reality. Yet Thomas offered a fifth way of proving the existence of God which, to some extent, runs like the cosmological argument, though in the opposite direction, and is usually associated with the teleological argument.

The Teleological Argument

Just like the cosmological argument, the teleological argument starts with observation, namely that there is beauty, harmony, and expediency in the world. Thomas wrote:

> An orderedness of actions to an end is observed in all bodies obeying natural laws, even when they lack awareness. For their behaviour hardly ever varies, and will practically always turn out well; which shows that they truly tend to a goal, and do not merely hit it by accident. Nothing however that lacks awareness tends to a goal, except under the direction of someone with awareness and with understanding; the arrow, for example, requires an ar-

---

72. Ibid. (A452ff., B480ff.) 479–81.
73. Ibid. (A609f., B637f.) 591–92.

cher. Everything in nature, therefore, is directed to its goal by someone with understanding, and this we call 'God'.[74]

Though Thomas argued here with the necessity of God as the prime cause, the focus is on the governance of the world, or divine providence, which leads the world toward a certain goal. Again, this argument has a long history. Already in Greek antiquity, the amazing interconnectedness in both the animate and inanimate world led inquiring spirits, such as Anaxagoras, to the assertion that there must be a world intelligence that functions as the ordering power of the universe.

Even the Roman philosopher and skeptic Marcus Tullius Cicero (106–43 BCE) conceded that "there is nothing more beautiful, nothing more beneficent, more splendid to look upon or more constant in its movements," than the universe.[75] Nearly two thousand years afterwards the German biologist and neo-vitalistic philosopher Hans Driesch (1867–1941) still assumed a whole-making causality within the organic world.[76] This *entelechy*, as he called it, is not contained in space and time but acts in it. It works teleologically in transforming a mere sum of equipotentialities into the wholeness of a mature organism. Similarly it leads to restitution in lower animals, for instance, when the tail of a salamander grows back after it has been cut off. In plants the same *entelechy* leads to adaptation. When plants are removed from a warm climate and are placed into a cooler environment, they protect themselves with a hairy film. Hans Driesch considered each living organism in its indisputable wholeness as the most obvious result of this *entelechy*.

Before agreeing too readily with Driesch, we should also remember Charles Darwin's assessment of natural adaptation when he said: "I cannot think that the world, as we see it, is the result of chance; and yet I

---

74. Aquinas, *Summa Theologiae* (1a.2.3r), 2:17.

75. Marcus Tullius Cicero, *The Nature of the Gods* (III, 23) trans. Horace C.P. McGregor, intro. J. M. Ross (Harmondsworth, UK: Penguin, 1972) 202. Of course, this statement does not imply for Cicero that there must be a God or gods who have everything superbly organized.

76. Cf. Hans Driesch, "The Breakdown of Materialism," in *The Great Design: Order and Progress in Nature*, ed. by Frances Mason, intro. by Sir J. Arthur Thomson (New York: Macmillan, 1935) 288, who says: "Matter *and something else* are at work, and this 'something else' acts in a teleological, a *whole-making* way." Cf. also his Gifford Lectures, published as *The Science and Philosophy of the Organism*, 2 vols. (London: A. & C. Black, 1908).

cannot look at each separate thing as the result of Design."[77] Perceiving design and beauty in nature is only half of the truth. Immanuel Kant again seemed right in his evaluation of the teleological argument. He asserted that this proof which presents the world to us as an immeasurable stage of variety, order, purposiveness, and beauty must be mentioned with respect. "It is the proof that is oldest, clearest, and most commensurate with common human reason. It enlivens the study of nature, just as the proof itself has its existence from and acquires ever new force through this study."[78] In talking about harmony, purposiveness, and harmonious adaptation, however, this physico-theological proof, as Kant called it, only refers to the form of the world and not to its substance. If we want to prove the existence of an all-sufficient primordial being, according to Kant, we would then have to resort to the cosmological argument. Since we have already noticed that he reduces the cosmological argument to its ontological presupposition, we are not surprised when he arrives at the conclusion that the teleological argument serves only as an introduction to the ontological argument. Kant finally sums up his criticism by saying:

> The physicotheological proof of a single original being as supreme being is based on the cosmological proof thereof, but this proof in turn on the ontological proof. And since no further path besides these three is open to speculative reason, the ontological proof—from pure concepts of reason alone—is the only possible proof, if indeed a proof of a proposition so far exalted above all empirical use of the understanding is possible at all.[79]

Kant not only demonstrated the interdependence of the three arguments of the existence of God thus far reviewed, but he also pointed to a dangerous moment in the teleological argument, namely that the God therewith proved would only be a world architect.[80] This idea of a world architect received hardly any attention in the Middle Ages. As we remember, Thomas Aquinas only in his fifth and last way to prove the existence of God emphasized the goal-directedness and orderliness of nature. In the period of the Enlightenment, however, the teleological

---

77. Charles Darwin in a letter to Asa Gray, November 26, 1860, published in *The Correspondence of Charles Darwin*, vol. 8, *1860* (Cambridge: Cambridge University Press, 1993) 496.

78. Kant, *Critique of Pure Reason* (A623, B651) 603.

79. Ibid. (A630, B658) 608.

80. Ibid. (A627, B655) 606.

argument not only led to the assumption of a world architect, but even more mechanically to that of a divine watchmaker.

Leading up to the Enlightenment, the philosopher Gottfried Wilhelm Leibniz (1646–1716) already indicated this transition with his idea that God has created the best of all possible worlds. Of course, Leibniz rejected the concept that even the greatest artistic masterpieces of our limited mind could be set in parallel to the least productions and mechanisms made by divine wisdom. He also asserted that the difference between the human and the divine artifacts is "not merely one of degree, but even one of kind."[81] It follows from the perfection of the supreme author of all things that the order of the whole universe is the most perfect, and that each living entity or *monad*, as Leibniz calls it, "represents the universe according to its point of view" and that it has all its "perceptions and desires as thoroughly well-ordered as is compatible with all the rest."[82] Leibniz concludes that "this perfect agreement of so many substances which have no communication with one another can come only from their common cause."[83] Thus there is "a new and surprisingly clear proof of the existence of God."

Though Leibniz attempted to demonstrate the foresight and perfection of God, again his argument considers only half of the truth. Nature is not always so complete, so well-ordered and so expedient as Leibniz's idea of a pre-established *harmony* assumed. When the French Jesuit and paleontologist Pierre Teilhard de Chardin (1881–1955), for instance, spoke of the manifold errors and trials through which nature attained its present level, his claim coincides much better with the observable reality.

Yet the most dangerous aspect in Leibniz's argument is the idea of a *pre-established* harmony existing within creation and preordained by God. For instance, in pursuing the same idea of a pre-established harmony, the Christian apologist and Archdeacon of Carlisle, William Paley (1743–1805), a contemporary of Kant, ventured to compare the works of nature with a watch. Though he asserted that "the contrivances of nature

81. Gottfried Wilhelm Leibniz, *New System* (10), in Leibniz, *The Monadology and Other Philosophical Writings*, trans. with intro. and notes Robert Latta (New York: Garland, 1985) 309.

82. Leibniz, *Principles of Nature and Grace, Founded on Reason* (12) in Leibniz, *The Monadology*, 418.

83. Leibniz, *New System* (16) Leibniz, *The Monadology*, 316, for this quote and the next.

surpass the contrivances of art, in the complexity, subtility, and curiosity of the mechanism,"[84] it is only too tempting for minds less bound to the Christian tradition to interpret the world on a totally mechanistic basis and relegate God to the once important but now irrelevant position of the divine watchmaker. This shows us that in order to arrive at a proof of the existence of God, theologians have unintentionally furthered the argument that the world no longer needs an active God.

It is not without significance that the teleological argument is again widely debated today after the influence of neo-Reformation theology had waned with its outright rejection of a point of contact between divine revelation and the created order. The arguments here range from the blind watchmaker advanced by the British zoologist Richard Dawkins (b. 1941) who argues on the basis of accumulative selection that a divine intelligence is not needed to bring forth a created order. "Slow, gradual, cumulative selection is the ultimate explanation for our existence."[85] On the other side of the spectrum is the intelligent design argument advanced especially by evangelical theologians.[86]

The intelligent design argument has a long history going all the way back to the Greeks. Yet it achieved prominence in the two centuries following the rise of science in the seventeenth century. It spawned a whole movement in theology, the so-called physico-theology that used the newly gained advances in the natural sciences to glorify God. Pointing to these discoveries, advocates of physico-theology attempted to prove God's wisdom and grandeur. Theologians searching in nature and scientists with theological ambitions created numerous publications to demonstrate how ingeniously God had created the natural world. In Great Britain we could count among these physico-theologians Isaac Newton (1642–1727), Robert Boyle (1627–1691), and John Ray (1627–1705). John Ray's *The Wisdom of God Manifested in the Work's of Creation* was first published in London in 1691, and by the year 1846 it had already been reprinted more than twenty times. At the conclusion of his *Principia Mathematica* (1687), Newton asserted: "This most beautiful

---

84. William Paley, *Natural Theology* (I/8) reprinted in *The Cosmological Arguments: A Spectrum of Opinion*, ed. by Donald R. Burrill (Garden City, NY: Doubleday Anchor, 1967) 170.

85. Richard Dawkins, *The Blind Watchmaker* (New York: Norton, 1986) 318.

86. Cf. Uko Zylstra, "Intelligent Design Theory: An Argument for Biotic Laws," *Zygon* 39 (2004) 175–91, for details.

system of the sun, planets, and comets, could only proceed from the council and dominion of an intelligent and powerful Being."[87] Yet in his posthumously published *Dialogues Concerning Natural Religion* (1779), David Hume had already cautioned that it is never "within the reach of human capacity to explain ultimate causes, or show the last connections of any objects."[88]

Despite Hume's word of caution and inspired by the work of William Paley, Francis Henry, Eighth Earl of Bridgewater (1756–1829) left £8,000 to the Royal Society for the writing of the treatise *On the Power, Wisdom, and Goodness of God, as Manifested in the Creation; illustrating such work by all reasonable arguments*.[89] The result was twelve volumes published in London (1833–1836). The argument from design was thus alive and well far into the nineteenth century. Even Charles Darwin was thoroughly acquainted with it through Paley's writings. Through his career as a naturalist, however, he progressively moved away from design and concluded: "The old argument of design in nature, as given by Paley, which formerly seemed to me so conclusive, fails, now that the law of Natural Selection has been discovered."[90] And yet, in spite of Darwin's certainty, theologians and scientists still held on to the notion of design. For instance, the great Princeton theologian Charles Hodge (1797–1878), referring to the complicated organs of plants and animals, asked of Darwin: "Why doesn't he say, they are the product of the divine intelligence? If God made them, it makes no difference how He made them, as far as the question of design is concerned, whether at once or by a process of evolution. But instead of referring to the purpose of God, he laboriously endeavors to prove that they may be accounted

---

87. Isaac Newton, *Principia Mathematica*, trans. Andrew Motte, at the end of the "General Scholium."

88. David Hume, *Dialogues Concerning Natural Religion*, in Charles W. Hendel, Jr., ed. *Hume Selections* (New York: Scribner's, 1927) 344.

89. *The Bridgewater Treatises on the Power, Wisdom and Goodness of God as Manifested in the Creation*, Treatise III: William Whewell, *On Astronomoy and General Physics Considered with Reference to Natural Theology*, 4th ed. (London: William Pickering, 1834) ix.

90. Charles Darwin, *The Autobiography of Charles Darwin 1809–1882*, ed. with an appendix and notes Nora Barlow (London: Collins, 1958) in *The Works of Charles Darwin*, ed. Paul H. Barrett and R. B. Freeman (London: William Pickering, 1989) 29:87.

for without any design or purpose whatever."[91] Hodge did not deny evolution per se, but he rejected the idea that evolution was to be explained in natural terms instead of supernatural ones. It is precisely this concern that marks the agenda of the present-day intelligent design movement.

As Jay Wesley Richards explains: "The main difference between this argument for intelligent design and much earlier natural theology and apologetics is that it is an 'inference to the best explanation' rather than a deductive 'proof' for God's existence."[92] The proponents of the intelligent design movement focus predominantly on biological evolution and argue that Darwinian evolution is unable to account for the massive complexity of cells. Therefore the bio-chemical complexity points to the existence of an intelligent designer of organic life. "The resulting realization that life was designed by an intelligence is a shock to us in the twentieth century who have gotten used to thinking of life as the result of simple natural laws," asserts Michael Behe (b. 1952).[93] The proponents of the movement carefully avoid identifying the "intelligent designer" with God, since they are intent on having the intelligent design theory taught in public schools as an alternative to the evolutionary theory. Small wonder that most scientists see this as overstepping their competency. On strictly scientific grounds, one can never arrive at a supernatural designer by investigating the material base.[94] While also advocating a teleology, the proponents of the so-called anthropic principle are much more restrained in their claims.

The anthropic principle was first introduced by the British theoretical physicist Brandon Carter (b. 1942). Carter claimed "that what we can expect to observe must be restricted by conditions necessary for our presence as observers. (Although our situation is not necessarily *central*, it is inevitably privileged to some extent)."[95] In order for us to

91. Charles Hodge, *What Is Darwinism?* (New York: Scribner, 1874) 58.

92. Jay Wesley Richards, "Proud Obstacles and a Resonable Hope: The Apologetic Value of Intelligent Design," in *Signs of Intelligence: Understanding Intelligent Design*, William A. Dembski and James M. Kushiner, eds. (Grand Rapids: Brazos, 2001) 57.

93. J. Michael Behe, *Darwin's Black Box: The Biochemical Challenge to Evolution*, (New York: Simon & Schuster, 1996) 252.

94. Cf. Arthur McCalla, *The Creationist Debate: The Encounter Between the Bible and the Historical Mind* (London: T. & T. Clark, 2006) 190-98, who gives a brief and critical overview of the intentions and the claims of the intelligent design proponents.

95. Brandon Carter, "Large Number Coincidences and the Anthropic Principle in Cosmology," in *Confrontation of Cosmological Theories with Observational Data*, ed. M. S. Longair (Dordrecht: D. Reidel, 1974) 291.

observe the universe, we must have a privileged position in such a way that the conditions necessary for our being here must have existed. This contention led the astronomer John D. Barrow (b. 1952) and the mathematician Frank J. Tipler to advance *the anthropic cosmological principle* in three different variations. First, there is the weak anthropic principle which states: "The observed value of all physical and cosmological quantities are not equally probable but they take on values restricted by the requirement that there exist sites where carbon-based life can evolve and by the requirement that the Universe be old enough for it to have already done so."[96] The strong anthropic principle goes one step further and claims: "The Universe must have those properties which allow life to develop within it at some stage in its history."[97] Lastly, they formulated the final anthropic principle which states: "Intelligent information-processing must come into existence in the Universe, and, once it comes into existence, it will never die out."[98]

Underlying this principle and its teleological slant is our highly increased understanding of the cosmos. Scientists are now able to point out that if the fundamental laws in physics which governed the evolvement of this cosmos had only been a little different from the way they are then life, as it is today, would never have been possible. For instance, if the Big Bang had been just a tiny fraction more violent than it was, no galaxies would have formed. Contrariwise, if the Big Bang had been a little less violent than it was, the universe would have already been contracted and again no galaxies would have been possible. Also if our earth had been a little closer to the sun, as for instance Venus is, no life would be possible because of the immense heat and, on the other hand, if it had been as far away as Mars, it would have been too cold. Again, the size of our planet Earth had to be just right, not too large and not too small. Again for the presence of life it is necessary that water in its solid state is lighter than in its liquid state, something which is not true for most other items when they consolidate from liquid to solid form, such as iron, or oxygen. If water did not behave differently, the oceans would freeze from bottom to top and this means that life could not have evolved from water. All these different arrangements had to coincide for

96. John D. Barrow and Frank J. Tipler, *The Anthropic Cosmological Principle*, 2nd ed. (Oxford: Clarendon, 1987) 16.
97. Ibid., 21.
98. Ibid., 23.

life to evolve. This seems to intimate that there is a life-giving factor at the core of the whole evolutionary process.

Of course, these teleological arguments are derived from the past. Life in our universe has evolved and therefore, so the assertion, there must be certain constants that made the origin and development of life possible. We notice here a kind of circular reasoning: Things are this way because the natural laws guided things in that direction and, without these laws things would not be the way they are. The results are again twofold: "Some perceive purpose in the cosmos, and others perceive its absence—which perception is valid?"[99] Even the teleological argument does not necessitate God; at the most it can only make God's activity more intelligible.

The Moral Argument

The moral argument for the existence of God gained new recognition through Immanuel Kant. Unlike the English empiricist David Hume a generation before him, Kant did not just criticize traditional arguments for the existence of God, but advanced as his own argument that of the moral necessity of God. Yet Kant was not the first philosopher to resort to the moral argument. The Spanish physician, philosopher, and theologian Raimund of Sabund (d. 1436) earlier advocated it in his *Theologia Naturalis Sive Liber Creaturarum* (Natural Theology or the Book of the Created, 1434–1436).[100] According to Raimund humans are reasonable beings. Yet they can neither reward nor punish themselves. Thus there must be someone higher who assumes the role of distributing reward and punishment. If such ultimate retribution did not exist, human life would make no sense, since in one's personal life good and bad actions would not balance out.

In concluding his *Critique of Practical Reason*, Kant touched on the same issue when he confessed: "Two things fill the mind with ever new and increasing admiration and awe, the oftener and more steadily they

---

99. So David Wilcox, "How Blind the Watchmaker," in the interesting volume *Evidence of Purpose: Scientists Discover the Creator*, ed. John Marks Templeton (New York: Continuum, 1994) 180, which contains contributions by Paul Davies, John C. Eccles, John Polkinghorne, and Arthur Peacocke among others, and is much more restrained in its assertions than the title of the publication would indicate.

100. Raymundus de Sabunde, *Theologia Naturalis Sive Liber Creaturarum* (Martin Flach, 1501); cf. also Walter Andreas Euler, "Raimund von Sabunde," TRE 28:122–25.

are reflected on: the starry heavens above me and the moral law within me."[101] While the starry heavens show us the magnitude of the universe and our own smallness, the moral law within us endows us with dignity and personal worth. The moral law impels us to strive for the highest good in the world. But no rational being can conform in this world at any time to the moral law. Kant claimed that such perfection can only be attained through infinite progress beyond this life in life eternal. If we assume we could attain it already in this life, we either bend the moral law according to our inclinations, or we indulge in fantasizing which completely contradict our knowledge of ourselves.

Kant proceeded to show that both immortality and God must be postulated by pure practical reason. Conformity with the moral law, which is to bring about true happiness, rests on the assumption that harmony can be attained between nature, our own destiny, and the moral law within us. The latter two might be able to conform, provided that we are the author of both of them. But how can they conform with the world around us? Kant observed that since humanity is not the cause of nature "his will cannot by its own strength bring nature, as it touches on his happiness, into complete harmony with his practical principles."[102] If, however, there is a supreme cause of nature which has a causality corresponding to the moral intention of humanity, such conformity could be reached. Consequently Kant assumed the existence of God as the necessary presupposition for achieving the highest good. If there is no God, as ultimate author and coordinator of our moral drive and nature's innate possibilities, it would not make sense for us to strive for (unattainable) ultimate harmony. Kant readily admitted that the notion of God is derived from a practical need and "it can be called *faith* and even pure *rational faith*, because pure reason alone (by its theoretical as well as practical employment) is the source from which it springs."[103] This argument for God, as the purposive integrator of our yearning and the cause of the world, also shows that we are "the final end of creation," and that nature will eventually harmonize with our happiness. Kant even

---

101. Kant, *Critique of Practical Reason* (V, 161) in *Critique of Practical Reason and Other Writings in Moral Philosophy*, trans. and ed. with an intro. Lewis White Beck (Chicago: University of Chicago Press, 1949) 258.

102. Ibid. (V, 125) 228.

103. Ibid. (V, 126) 229.

asserts "that without human beings the whole of creation would be a mere desert, existing in vain, and without a final end."[104]

The idealist philosopher Johann Gottlieb Fichte (1762–1814), deeply influenced by Kant, again emphasized a moral order of the world.[105] He claimed that everyone experiences a call to duty, which is related in its content to that of everyone else's call. The originator of this call and of its unity with all other calls endows our life with direction and also guarantees the final victory of the good. While Kant still maintained that God as the purposive integrator must be perceived as a personal agent, Fichte's idealistic notion of God is clearly pantheistic. In essence it is similar to the German poet and dramatist Friedrich Schiller's (1759–1805) comment that "the world history is the world's judgment."[106] God is equated with the driving forces of the world. God is no longer the unconditioned conditioner, but the unexplainable way the world processes present themselves. Such a notion, however, indicates that the moral argument for God's existence can easily divorce itself from the Judeo-Christian faith, to the support of which it was once developed, and result in a pessimistic or at least skeptical outlook on world processes.

The Argument of Common Consent

The last argument we want to mention is the historical argument or the argument from common consent. Since its basic assertion is a phenomenological one, namely that all tribes and nations at all times revered a god or gods, it hardly indicates in its outset that it wants to lead up to the God of Judeo-Christian faith.[107] Having observed that all peoples at

---

104. Kant, *Critique of the Power of Judgment* (par. 86) ed. Paul Guyer, trans. Paul Guyer and Eric Matthews (Cambridge: Cambridge University Press, 2000) 308–9.

105. Cf. Johann Gottlieb Fichte, *Die Bestimmung des Menschen* (III) ed. with an intro. Eduard Spranger (Hamburg: Felix Meiner, 1954) esp. 134–39.

106. Friedrich Schiller in his poem "Resignation," in Friedrich Schiller, *Gesammelte Werke in fünf Bänden*, ed. Reinhold Netolitzky (Gütersloh: C. Bertelsmann Lesering, 1959) 3:394. As we can see from his inaugural lecture in Jena of 1789, "Was heisst und zu welchem Ende studiert man Universalgeschichte?" in *Gesammelte Werke*, vol. 4, esp. 95–96, Schiller was actually rather pessimistic about discerning a teleological principle according to which world history does proceed.

107. John A. O'Brien, *Truths Men Live By: A Philosophy of Religion and Life* (New York: Macmillan, 1948) 141–42, reaffirms the argument of common consent stating that the belief in God has existed among all the races from the earliest times down to

all times worship deities or higher beings of some kind, the conclusion is reached that there must be a reality behind this common attitude of humanity.

Though this argument might have sufficed in centuries past, it is no longer applicable to our own time. The clearly increasing number of people who unintentionally or deliberately reject the notion of God or of any gods is one of the most bewildering phenomena of our time. In this situation the historical argument is a very dangerous one, because it could also lead to the assumption of Freud and others that up to a certain period humanity worshipped metaphysical powers, but that through a process of maturation humanity dissolved the metaphysical world into the physical and has no longer a need for the belief in divine agents.

Living by Faith

"Since its beginnings, prominently in Greek thought, up to the present day, proofs for and against the existence of God have occupied a considerable number of the best minds of the East as well as of the West."[108] This means that there is a fascination in the human race to see whether on a rational basis one can ascertain God's existence. This very fact should make us stop and ponder the issue of God's existence anew, if we are tempted to discard the God question altogether.

Beyond this point, the opinions are split. Official Roman Catholic doctrine still holds that the proofs for the existence of God are "'converging and convincing arguments,' which allow us to attain certainty about truth."[109] Therefore the *Catechism of the Catholic Church* states: "Starting from movement, becoming, contingency, and the world's order and beauty, one can come to a knowledge of God as the origin and the end of the universe." This is in line with the declaration of Vatican I (1870–1871) "that God, the beginning and end of all things, can be

---

the present. Then he continues to demonstrate that though the advance of modern science is fatal to all polytheistic forms of religion, Christian monotheism "is necessary to supplement and complete the fragmentary interpretation of nature afforded by science." Of course, such "demonstration" of the necessity of Christian faith does not take into account that science itself can become a religion.

108. So John Clayton, "Gottesbeweise III. Systematisch/Religionsphilosophisch," in *TRE* 13:740.

109. *Catechism of the Catholic Church* (New York: Doubleday, 1995) 19, where we also find reference to Thomas Aquinas on the following page.

known with certitude by the natural light of human reason from created things."[110]

On the Protestant side, however, Kant's criticism of the proofs of God's existence left an undeniable impact. Most Protestant theologians are very hesitant to ascribe to human reason such a high faculty. But already a generation before Kant, the German pietist, philosopher, and mystic, Johann Georg Hamann (1730–1788) had pointed out that a God whom we can grasp with our reason and whom we can penetrate with our mind is no God.[111] Any proof of God's existence would mean either that God is on an equal basis with us, i.e., part of our world, or that we are on an equal basis with God, i.e., not confined to our world. Though Hamann's observation is basically right, he forgets that whenever we speak of God we are unable to grasp God completely. This inability to approach God necessitates that we use approximations or anthropomorphisms in our God language. Even when we confess that God has disclosed God's self to us in Jesus Christ, we admit that Jesus is God in *human* form but not in God's own divinity. Moreover, would it not be feasible that God is also apprehended to some extent to people outside of Jesus Christ? Is Vatican I wrong when, upholding the natural knowledge of God, it quoted Paul's Letter to the Romans saying: "For the invisible things of him, from the creation of the world, are clearly seen, being understood by the things that are made" (Rom 1:20)?[112] Even Paul seems to concede at this point that God can be known to some degree by natural reason.

But what can human reason actually ascertain? Whether Thomas Aquinas or Anselm of Canterbury, whether Plato or Aristotle, they all thought that they had proven beyond reasonable doubt that God is. If there is God, however, God cannot exist like you and me or even like a

---

110. Heinrich Denzinger, *The Sources of Catholic Dogma*, trans. R. J. Deferrari (St. Louis, MO: B. Herder, 1957) 443, which is more affirmative than the statement quoted above.

111. Cf. Johann Georg Hamann in a letter of February 18, 1786, in which he says: "For if it is fools who say in their heart, 'There is no God,' those who try to prove his existence seem to me to be even more foolish" (reprinted in Ronald Gregor Smith, *J.G. Hamann. 1730–1788. A Study in Christian Existence. With Selections from His Writings* [New York: Harper, 1960] 253). Cf. Walter Leibrecht, *God and Man in the Thought of Hamann*, trans. James H. Stam and Martin H. Bertram (Philadelphia: Fortress, 1966) esp. 33–34, where he refers to the hiddenness of God according to Hamann.

112. Denzinger, *Sources of Catholic Dogma*, 443.

tree or a mountain. God does not exist as something that stands forth and is clearly discernible. The Danish philosopher of religion Søren Kierkegaard (1813-1855), for instance, claimed: "I do not believe that God exists, but know it."[113] And the theologian Paul Tillich (1886-1965) asserted in a similar way: "God does not exist. . . . To argue that God exists is to deny him."[114] To avoid the danger that God's existence is in some ways likened to our own, one often talks about the being of God. God is, but does not exist. Since medieval theologians such as Thomas or Anselm used the Latin medium and Plato and Aristotle the Greek language, they naturally talked about God's being (ontology) and that God is (*esse*), but not that God exists (*existere*). Therefore the charge that they proved something which does not apply to God would not hold. Nevertheless, we should ask: What kind of God did they assert?

Both Plato and Aristotle talked about a first unmoved mover. Later on one focused on a world architect or at the most a creator and perfector of the world. But a world architect or the first unmoved mover can at best push the button to get everything started or lay out the initial conditions according to which the world runs its course. This kind of God the French scientist and lay theologian Blaise Pascal (1623-1662) called the God of philosophers who is vastly different from the God of Abraham, Isaac, and Jacob.[115] The latter was the God who called Abraham to a new land and blessed him and his descendants.

Why would theologians even bother with a God whose greatest contribution was to lay down the initial conditions? When we consider the apologetic slant that Anselm pursued, we get the notion that his arguments are employed to show the plausibility structure of the God phenomenon. Anselm then concluded that there are indeed good reasons to assume that there is God. Then there is also the doxological function through which reason is employed to demonstrate the God phenom-

---

113. Søren Kierkegaard, *Concluding Unscientific Postscript to Philosophical Fragments*, ed., trans., intro. and notes, Howard V. Hong and Edna Hong (Princeton, NJ: Princeton University Press, 1992) 2:54.

114. Paul Tillich, *Systematic Theology* (Chicago: University of Chicago Press, 1951) 1:205.

115. Cf. Blaise Pascal, *Pensées* (VIII, 556) in *The Provincial Letters, Pensées, Scientific Treaties. Great Books of the Western World* (Chicago: Encyclopaedia Britannica, 1952) 271, where Pascal contrasts the God "of heathens and Epicureans" with "the God of Abraham, the God of Isaac, the God of Jacob, the God of Christians, [who] is a God of love and of comfort."

enon as far as it is apprehensible by reason. "Proofs" of the existence of God, however, were hardly ever intended as a means of double-checking whether God is really there. They always imply a prior faith decision, even if it is one of "pure rational faith" as in Kant's moral argument. The one who sets out to "prove" is already convinced that there is "someone" to prove. If we want to confine ourselves to a neutral ground prior to faith or prior to unbelief, then Kant's critique of the first three arguments must be heeded and our result would be the ambivalent position of Kant's antinomies of pure reason. It is there that Kant demonstrated that as soon as we leave the ground of faith or unfaith and argue about something beyond sense experience (God, immortality, etc.) we can "prove" the pros and the cons of the argument with equal validity.

In conclusion, we can say that God is beyond proof and disproof. Regardless of how intensely Feuerbach, Marx, and Freud emphasized that God is only a figment of the human mind, there is nothing that turns their claims into actual disproofs of God. Conversely, all the natural knowledge of God is derived from an interpretation of nature or from certain premises that are again beyond proof. A careful reading of Romans 1 should have made this clear, because Paul stated with regard to the pagans: "For what can be known about God is plain to them, because God has shown it to them. Ever since the creation of the world his eternal power and divine nature, invisible though they are, have been understood and seen from the things that he has made" (Rom 1:19f.). This means that the natural knowledge of God with which reason is concerned is not as natural as one might think. God has given that knowledge to us and therefore we are able to see God in and through nature. But such seeing is not unambiguous, as Paul also noted when he wrote: "And their senseless minds were darkened" (Rom 1:21). There is always a certain ambiguity and therefore none of the proofs are real proofs. They are arguments in favor of God while the critics argue to disclaim God. Therefore our acceptance of the God phenomenon rests on faith—faith guided by reason.

PART II

Discerning the God among the gods

Since we have realized that those who disclaim that there is a God or some kind of powers beyond and above us are as much believers as those who assert the opposite, it is clear that the God issue must be investigated further. Who or what is that which is believed to be beyond ourselves and which is worshiped in many different ways? Can we trace the origin of this veneration and thereby also its development or is it something that is intrinsically tied to our own existence? Moreover, does it make any difference how we conceptualize this transcendent phenomenon? We have even more reason to investigate the God phenomenon in more detail, since the prognosis which Dietrich Bonhoeffer made in a Nazi prison cell in 1944 has not come true. He stated that we are approaching a totally religionless age, since the world "has come of age" and no longer needs religion as a crutch to master its life.[1] If anything, there is "a return of religion."[2] Therefore we are still confronted with the enigma of religion.

---

1. Dietrich Bonhoeffer, *Letters and Papers from Prison*, rev. ed., ed. Eberhard Bethge (New York: Macmillan, 1967) 170.

2. So Falk Wagner, "Religion II: Theologiegeschichtlich und systematisch-theologisch," in *TRE* 28:523.

THREE

The Enigma of Religion

Contrary to the predictions made by some followers of Karl Barth after World War II that Christianity is waiting at the deathbed of the world's religions to see them wilt away, the world's religions have made an astounding comeback.[1] In many European countries as well as in North America, the multi-confessional scene has become "enriched" by a multi-religious mix. Where once there were only churches and church steeples, there are now mosques, minarets, and temples representing the different religions of the world. Moreover there are numerous religious movements, not just the more "traditional" ones, such as the Hare Krishna and Scientology, but a multitude of spiritual, mystic, occult, theosophic, and meditative cults. Their leaders often make demands on their followers and call for a kind of obedience which mainline churches would never dare to ask from their believers. All of the above can claim to be a religion, but what sort? Perhaps we get closer to a proper understanding of religion if we attempt to define what we mean by it.

Defining Religion

The Roman philosopher Cicero explained the term "religion" as being derived from *relegere* (to choose or to read again) and standing in contrast to *negligere* (to neglect).[2] Cicero meant that we should carefully consider what the gods want from us. He concluded that the obligatory

---

1. Cf. Hendrik Kraemer, *The Christian Message in a Non-Christian World*, 3rd ed. (Grand Rapids: Kregel, 1956) 140, who claimed that the only point of contact between the Christian faith and the world's religions "is the disposition and the attitude of the missionary."

2. Marcus Tullius Cicero, *The Nature of the Gods* (II/72) 152-53.

veneration of the gods is met if we follow the cultic precepts, especially with regard to sacrifice and the interpretation of the portents. Cicero understood this kind of veneration of the gods as *religio*.

Early Christianity took over this *religio* concept and amended it for its own purposes. Though initially the cultic veneration of God was accepted, the Christian convert and writer Lactantius (ca. 250–ca. 325), who is sometimes called "the Christian Cicero," held the term religion to be derived from *religare* (to fasten or to bind to). It expresses the fact that "we are fastened and bound to God by this bond of piety" since God is our creator whom we know and follow.[3]

The North African theologian and bishop Augustine (354–430), though in complete agreement with Lactantius, described religion as a gift of God that reminds our soul "of its original and perfect nature."[4] Religion requires cultic devotion to God and the duty to serve him appropriately. Augustine therefore distinguished between "true religion," in which one adores "one God alone" and serves this God "with complete dedication," and "a multiplicity of divinities" each having different duties and functions.[5] The adoration of one God alone, of course, refers to God as the Father of Jesus Christ. This means that religion can be a Christian phenomenon, but it also can refer to the veneration of other gods.

Especially with regard to our present society in which large segments seem to have nothing to do with religion we must note another important distinction in viewing religion. One can distinguish between the sacred (temple, cult, worship) and the profane or secular (originally meaning that which lies outside the temple, or is concerned with pursuits that have nothing to do with a specific religious cult). This distinction points to the difference between a transcendent deity or deities and everything else, or between the creator and the created. But what appears at first glance to be a good working definition does not do justice to all religious perspectives. For instance, pre-literate religions as we meet them in the tribal religions of the Native Americans, in the religion of the Australian Aborigines, or among the tribes of Papua New Guinea before the advent of Christian missionaries, do not distinguish

3. Lactantius, *The Divine Institutes* (IV, 28) trans. M. F. McDonald, in *FaCh*, 49:318.

4. Augustine, *Of True Religion* (X, 19) in *Augustine: Earlier Writings*, trans. with an intro. J. H. S. Burleigh, The Library of Christian Classics (Philadelphia: Westminster, 1953) 235. Cf. also ibid. (LV, 111–12) 281–82.

5. Augustine *City of God* XIX, 17 (Garden City, NY: Doubleday, 1958) 464.

between the profane or secular and a transcendent sphere. Religious customs and rituals permeate all of life. Everything is religiously colored. For instance, how to treat the environment, how to marry, or what to do with the dead. In Islam too there is no actual distinction between the secular and the sacred, or rather between state and religion. This is the reason why in many Islamic countries there is an unbashed pressure to introduce the *Shariah* (the religious law) as the law of the country.

A more inclusive definition of religion is advanced by the historian of religion Winston King (1907–2000), who writes: "Religion is the organization of life around the depth dimensions of experience—varied in form, completeness, and clarity in accordance with the environing culture."[6] While order and organization are certainly indicative of religion, the question is what is meant by "depth dimensions of experience." While love and hatred, anger and disgust are such depth dimensions of experiences, they are rarely indicative of religion. Furthermore when King talks about the organization of life in accordance with the environing culture, he leaves the impression that the environing culture is something separate from religion or that it impacts religion. Throughout history, however, religion has always impacted the environing culture and even adopted some of its features. For instance, the Hellenization process of Christianity was not an adulteration of the gospel, but a necessary step taken to permeate and transform the culture so that the Christian message could be propagated in the Hellenic medium of language and thought.

The definition of Paul Tillich, which he applied to the object of theology, is more persuasive for us. According to him religion is that which becomes "a matter of ultimate concern for us . . . [and this ultimate concern] is that which determines our being or not-being."[7] Religion is something that involves people not casually, but existentially. It is ultimately a matter of life and death. All peace and well-being here and in the hereafter depend on our right appropriation of religion. Friedrich Schleiermacher (1768–1834), the father of modern theology, sensed this well. In his youthful work *On Religion: Speeches to Its Cultural Despisers* (1799) he contended against Enlightenment rationalism that religion is

---

6. Winston L. King, "Religion," in *The Encyclopedia of Religion*, ed. Mircea Eliade (New York: Macmillan, 1987) 12:286.

7. Paul Tillich, *Systematic Theology* (Chicago: University of Chicago, 1951) 1:12 and 14.

more than right knowledge and right action. Religious life arises for him from our relationship to the universe. While "metaphysics and morals see in the whole universe only humanity as the center of all relatedness," religion "wishes to intuit the universe, wishes devoutly to overhear the universe's own manifestations and actions, longs to be grasped and filled by the universe's immediate influences in childlike passivity."[8] Against the anthropocentrism of the philosopher Immanuel Kant, Schleiermacher affirmed that we are part of a larger whole which opens itself to us.

Moreover Schleiermacher contended that "a person is born with the religious capacity," a notion which is furthered by Schleiermacher's observation of "the longing of young minds for the miraculous and supernatural."[9] Religion must be cultivated in communion between a person and the universe. But religion also has a social element, because the more passionately something moves a person, the stronger is the urge to communicate that to others.

Schleiermacher also considered world religions outside of Christianity, and showed that religion is present in a definite form because the intuition of the universe is only possible in a definite way. While the individual fragments which we encounter in the plurality of denominations results from a misunderstanding, since the Christian religion is basically one, the plurality of religions is rooted in the essence of religion. No one can possess religion completely, since a human being is finite and religion is infinite. Each religion must organize itself "in manifestations that are rather different from one another."[10] While denominations need not differ significantly from each other, the case is different with religions. According to Schleiermacher it is here that we encounter different aspects of that which makes up religion.

Schleiermacher emphasized against Kant that "religion's essence is neither thinking nor acting, but intuition and feeling."[11] But he did not want to suggest that thinking and acting have nothing to do with religion. Schleiermacher emphasized: "Religion shows itself to you as the necessary and indispensable third next to those two, as the natural counterpart, not slighter in worth and splendor than what you wish of

---

8. Friedrich Schleiermacher, *On Religion: Speeches to Its Cultural Despisers*, trans. and ed. Richard Crouter (Cambridge: Cambridge University Press, 1996) 22–23.

9. Ibid., 59.

10. Ibid., 97.

11. Ibid., 22.

them. To want to have speculation and praxis without religion is rash arrogance."[12] First, some kind of experience that there is something beyond ourselves must be experienced which Schleiermacher calls religion. But this experience precedes human reflection and action. Almost in Barthian fashion Schleiermacher wanted to ascertain that we first acknowledge that something occurs with us, to which we respond.

Since the religious experience, as an existential encounter with the ultimate, leads to action and reflection, the latter two should not be excluded from religion. To avoid Feuerbach's charge of projection, we should heed the sequence. First experience, then action and reflection. For instance, when the prophet Isaiah became aware of a presence of the living God (Yahweh) in the temple, he cried out: "Woe is me! I am lost, for I am a man of unclean lips, and I live among a people of unclean lips; yet my eyes have seen the King, the Lord of hosts!" (Isa 6:5). The encounter with the Holy One made Isaiah aware of his mortality and sinfulness. Similarly, according to the legend, Prince Gautama had several encounters with the fleetingness of life which made him realize his own finitude. Then he changed his life and eventually became the Buddha. This pattern appears to be the foundation of religion. Through religious activities we attempt to overcome any improprieties which threaten our future. Religious activities devoted to delivering us from anything or anyone who might prevent us from communion with those powers over us are religion's response to these threats.

Origin and Destiny of Religion

Approximately five thousand to six thousand years ago, humanity first started to entrust its thoughts and feelings to written documents. But the total history of humanity, which must be considered when we talk about the origin of religion, is at least a hundred times older. There are, for instance, the magificent cave paintings from Altamira in northern Spain, which might be interpreted as some kind of summons for hunting magic. One could argue that these paintings, dating approximately from 30,000 to 10,000 BCE, might then be religious only in a secondary way, being attempts to secure life on earth through magic. But religion is seen much more clearly when we regard the human destiny beyond this

---

12. Ibid., 23.

life. From its earliest time onward humanity was concerned not just with this life, but also with life after death.

The paleontologist Karl J. Narr (1921–2009) therefore writes:

> It is only from the Middle Paleolithicum onward that we know about funerals which, in their way, partly testify to the protection of the dead and, most likely, also to the provisions of food and tools offered for the dead and partly also for binding the deceased. Regardless of what the case may have been, loving care for the deceased or fear of the dead, it witnesses to the faith in a continuance of life after death in some form or other . . . But even in earlier times (e.g. the Peking Man) there are indications that skulls or parts of skulls were separately preserved which we may explain by the idea of a further connection and a continuation of action after (for our conceptuality, physical) death in some form or other.[13]

Narr says the human beings he is talking about are "in principle fully developed human beings," which means the transition must have been made from animal to humanity. In a similar way the paleo-historian Jakob Ozols (b. 1922) states: "Though it may sound surprising, the oldest religious expression of early humanity accessible to us is the faith in a nonmaterial form of soul indwelling humanity."[14]

Behind the customs Narr tells us about is perhaps the belief in some kind of general animism. It developed in the last Ice Age to a shamanism which, at least in northeast Asia, has continued into the beginning of the twentieth century. According to shamans, there is a little figure of shadowy existence which can neither be grasped nor wounded with common weapons. This is the actual life of a person. Without this little figure the person is helpless and sick.

> After death, this shape of the soul separates from the body and leads its own life largely independent of the body. Yet it continues to return to the skeleton, especially to the skull, to rest there.

---

13. Karl J. Narr, "Beiträge der Urgeschichte zur Kenntnis der Menschennatur," in *Neue Anthropologie*, ed. Hans-Georg Gadamer and Paul Vogler (Stuttgart: DTV, 1973) 4:31–32 and 37. Cf. also John Hick, *Death and Eternal Life* (New York: Harper & Row, 1976) 55–56, in his section on "primitive man." Hick states that humanity is unique in knowing that it is going to die but at the same time denies it and hopes for a life beyond (cf. 55).

14. Jakob Ozols, "Über die Jenseitsvorstellungen des vorgeschichtlichen Menschen," in *Tod und Jenseits im Glauben der Völker*, ed. Hans-Joachim Klimkeit (Wiesbaden: Otto Harrassowitz, 1978) 14.

> When a person is alive it leaves the body only at night or in extraordinary situations, such as sudden fright, severe disease or in special conditions such as trance or ecstasy. This shape of the soul should not remain absent for long. If it does not return soon, the person falls sick, it is exposed to many dangers and with a longer absence of this shape of the soul the person must even die.[15]

There is an actual duplicate of every person which resides in the body. Ozols also explains that drilling small holes into skulls of persons who are still alive may have been attempts to help this shape of the soul enter and leave the skull without problems. For the same purpose there exist holes in coffins made of stone.

We can see from Stone Age paintings that the souls of the dead no longer belong to this world. They have their own realm of life in the beyond, a shadow world that was already considered a matter of fact for people living in the Ice Age. Since the skull is so important, we need not be surprised that we have burials of skulls only, and since animals were not thought to be that different from people, even the skulls of some animals were ritually buried. For prehistoric persons the concept of life after death was determined primarily by the conviction of an immortal shape of the soul. "This conviction has remained the most important part of religions until the most recent times. It is evidently shaped by the concept of events in dreams, but also by other events. The state without protection and participation during sleep has led to the assumption that this shape of the soul is the actual life and the protective power of the person."[16] The recognition of an *anima* (spirit) residing in a human person which can move to different places, especially during sleep, as one may naively conclude from dreams about things that are far away, was expanded to the idea that this *anima* leaves the body forever at death and continues to exist somewhere else. This notion of a spirit residing in a human being leads us immediately to the animistic theory of the origin of religion.

Animistic Theory

In 1871 in his epoch-making work *Primitive Culture*, the English anthropologist Sir Edward Burnett Tylor (1832–1917) suggested animism

15. Ibid., 15.
16. Ibid., 35.

as the origin of humanity's religion.¹⁷ Animism, he claimed, concerns itself with souls of individual creatures, capable of continued existence after death or after the destruction of the body, and with other spirits upward to the rank of powerful deities.

> Spiritual beings are held to affect or control the events of the material world, and man's life here and hereafter; and it being considered that they hold intercourse with men, and receive pleasure or displeasure from human actions, the belief in their existence leads naturally, and it might almost be said inevitably, sooner or later to active reverence and propitiation. Thus Animism, in its full development, includes the belief in souls and in a future state, in controlling deities and subordinate spirits.[18]

Primitive or rather pre-literate people, Tylor asserted, were wrestling with two groups of questions: First, what makes the difference between a living body and a dead one? And second, what are those human shapes that appear in dreams and visions? Pre-literate people reached the solution that two things belong to a person, a life and a phantom. They are both closely connected with the body, and at death life leaves the body forever. The phantom, however, did not leave, because even during a person's lifetime it had been separable from the body and could appear to people distant from the body. Tylor suggests that at a later stage primitive people combined life and phantom as manifestations of one and the same soul. The personal soul is a shadowy human image, causing life and thought in the individual; it animates, conferring personal consciousness and volition of its bodily owner, past or present, and leaving the body far behind, it is able to flash swiftly from place to place.

Tylor then expanded "the general scheme of Animism . . . to complete the full general philosophy of Natural Religion among mankind."[19] Spirits are regarded as personified causes, and "the idea of souls, demons, deities, and any other classes of spiritual beings, are conceptions of similar nature throughout, the conceptions of souls being the original ones of the series." For Tylor the conception of the human soul developed into the characters of good and evil demons, and finally ascended to the rank

---

17. Sir Edward Burnett Tylor, *Religion in Primitive Culture* (New York: Harper, 1958) 9–10.

18. Ibid., 10–11.

19. Ibid., 194–95, for this and the following quote.

of deities. He concluded that in considering the nature of the great gods of the nations in whom the vastest functions of the universe are vested,

> it will still be apparent that these mighty deities are modeled on human souls, that in great measure their feeling and sympathy, their character and habit, their will and action, even their material and form, display throughout their adaptations, exaggerations and distortions, characteristics shaped upon those of the human spirit.[20]

This animistic explanation of the origin of religion proved very attractive. Deities are patterned according to elementary human experiences and serve as a pre-scientific explanation of the world. Perhaps pre-literate religion could have originated in this way. But one wonders if such a religion could have developed into a full-fledged polytheism or even monotheism. At the most, animism can lead to ancestor worship, as seen in Confucianism, in Roman and Greek religions, and in many religions in Africa.[21] Yet veneration of the spirits of ancestors usually occurs parallel and not antecedent to the worship of regular deities. Thus the line of development proposed by Tylor rests on shaky ground.

Pre-animistic Theory

In 1900 the cultural anthropologist Robert R. Marett (1866–1943) published an essay with the title "Pre-animistic Religion" in which he suggested that pre-literate religion is "at once a wider, and in certain respects a vaguer, thing than 'the belief in spiritual beings' of Tylor's famous 'minimum definition.'"[22] However, Marett did not want to advance the idea that there was once a pre-animistic era in the history of religion, void of animism, but nevertheless filled with religion of some kind. While he agreed with Tylor that animism was a primary condition of religion, he claimed that there were other conditions not less primary.

---

20. Ibid., 333–34.

21. Rudolf Otto, *The Idea of the Holy: An Inquiry into the Non-rational Factor in the Idea of the Divine and Its Relation to the Rational*, trans. John W. Harvey (New York: Oxford University Press, 1958) 119, denies the possibility of even this development. He objects: "Even in itself this entire theory of an ostensible attribution of 'soul' or the principle of animation to everything is a mere fabrication of the study."

22. So in retrospect R. R. Marett in the preface to his book, *The Threshold of Religion* (London: Methuen, 1929) viii.

In some cases, he suggested, animistic interpretations had even been superimposed on what previously had been non-animistic. He proposed that in pre-literate religions there is a binary compound consisting of a "taboo" element and a "mana" element. The taboo element is predominantly negative in its action, being applied to many facets of the world of ordinary happenings. The mana element, however, is mainly positive in its action, being applied to "something transcending the ordinary world," something wonderful and awesome.[23] Marett did not want to replace Tylor's animistic theory with the introduction of a taboo-mana complex. He suggested that mana comes close to "the bare designation of that positive emotional value which is the raw material of religion, and needs only to be moralized—to be identified with goodness—to become its essence."[24]

Marett actually advanced a dynamistic understanding of a religion where pre-literate humanity encounters a general impersonal power which must either be warded off (taboo), or which can be used to attain supernatural effects (mana). Though the phenomena of taboo and mana certainly exist, we wonder if the personal power(s) underlying them are ever thought of as existing independently of these manifestations in persons or things which are considered taboo or containing mana. It is also difficult to explain convincingly how the belief in taboo and mana can ever develop into the belief in godly powers. It seems that Marett's theses lend themselves much more easily "to explain the origin of magic," than of religion in general.[25]

Though Marett disagrees with James Frazer's idea that magic is the "primitive's" way to explain the world in a pre-scientific form,[26] he seems to share with him the conviction that magic develops into religion (according to Frazer, religion is the step between magic and scientific reasoning). But religion and magic seem to be equally basic to human existence. Magic is the understanding that humanity can attain or at least gain influence upon the powers which control its life. In religion, however, humanity feels dependent upon such powers. Both, the feeling of dependence upon such power(s) and the assumption that humanity can

23. Ibid., xxviii.
24. Ibid., xxxi.
25. This objection is rightly raised by Hans-Joachim Schoeps, *The Religions of Mankind*, trans. Richard and Clara Winston (Garden City, NY: Doubleday, 1966) 8.
26. Cf. Marett, *Threshold of Religion*, 73.

exert influence upon them, are co-existent in "primitive religions" and did not develop from each other.[27] Perhaps Marett should have heeded more his own insight that "the first chapter of the history of religion remains in large part indecipherable."[28]

Original Monotheism

While the pre-animistic and animistic theories of the origin of religion clearly suggest an evolutionary concept of our religious development, the idea of original monotheism proceeds the opposite way. Though already advanced by critics of Tylor, such as the Scottish novelist Andrew Lang (1844–1912) in his book *The Making of Religion* (1898), the thesis of original monotheism gained its systematic form through the work of the ethnologist and Roman Catholic missionary of the Society of Divine Word, Wilhelm Schmidt (1868–1954). He claimed in a twelve-volume investigation on the origin of the idea of God (*Der Ursprung der Gottesidee*: 1912–1955) that the belief in an all-powerful highest being stood at the beginning of all religious development. Through a process of degeneration this belief was lost and humanity developed a mythology with many gods and spirits. "The results of this, both moral and social, were anything but desirable, leading to extreme degradation and even to the deification of the immoral and antisocial. The principal cause of this corruption was that the figure of the Supreme Being was sinking further and further into the background, hidden behind the impenetrable phalanx of the thousand new gods and daimones."[29] Schmidt argues that this development was necessitated by the increasing human specialization through which humans needed special gods for their special enterprises. Finally Jesus Christ taught humanity again to believe in the heavenly Father. Wilhelm Schmidt also claims that the belief in this highest God can still be traced in pre-literate religion. Australian aborigines, African

---

27. Gustav Mensching, *Die Religion. Erscheinungsformen, Strukturtypen und Lebensgesetze* (Stuttgart: Curt E. Schwab, 1959) 134, rightly emphasizes the close interdependence of magic and religion in pre-literate religion that makes it impossible to assert priority for one or the other.

28. Marett, *Threshold of Religion*, viii.

29. Wilhelm Schmidt, *The Origin and Growth of Religion: Facts and Theories*, trans. H. J. Rose, 2nd ed. (London: Methuen, 1935) 289.

bushmen, as well as Mongols and many culturally isolated tribes believe in a singular highest god.[30]

Though Schmidt's theory sounds convincing, the notion of such a highest being, undoubtedly present among most pre-literate people, is often very vague. Many times the high god receives no special cultic attention, in contrast to spirits, powers, and demonic beings. It is also very difficult to extrapolate from a present notion of such a high god to the notion of a high god in prehistoric time. Schmidt deserves great merit in confronting us with the fact that most people hold to the notion of a high god which seems to exist independently of all other religious practices. But his theory concerning the origin of religion from an original monotheism to the depravity of polytheism seems to be too closely patterned according to the creation and fall stories in Genesis 1–11 to have more than theoretical value.[31] Furthermore development, if we can talk about it as such, has also proceeded in the opposite direction. For instance, in the Greek religion Zeus was not originally a high god; only gradually he emerged as the leader of the Greek pantheon. We can learn from the example of the Greek pantheon that the concept of a high god does not need to conflict with the belief in the existence of other gods. While today most historians of religion reject the thesis of an original monotheism, they are free to admit that there does exist a worship of a supreme being among pre-literates.[32]

---

30. See especially his book, *Origin and Growth of Religion*, which is largely devoted to substantiate the notion of a high god among pre-literate people.

31. Otto, *Idea of the Holy*, 129, might be right when he calls this theory an "offspring of missionary apologetic, which, eager to save the second chapter of Genesis, yet feels the shame of a modern at the walking of Yahweh 'in the garden in the cool of the day.'" Nevertheless, Otto feels that this theory points to facts "which remain downright riddles, if we start from any naturalistic foundation of religion—whether animism, pantheism, or another."

32. Cf. Gerhardus van der Leeuw, *Religion in Essence and Manifestation: A Study in Phenomenology*, trans. J. E. Turner (New York: Harper Torchbooks, 1963) 1:161. The remark of Schoeps in his otherwise excellent study, *The Religions of Mankind*, 9, that the Dutch scholar van der Leeuw and others have argued "that the concept of a single God is a latecomer in the history of religions," is somewhat misleading. Van der Leeuw certainly agrees with the existence of a worship of a supreme being among pre-literates while rejecting the idea of an original monotheism.

The Mother Goddess

Rosemary Radford Ruether (b. 1936) wrote in her book *Sexism and God-Talk* (1983): "From archaeological evidence one can conclude that the most ancient human image of the divine was female. From Paleolithic to Neolithic times and into the beginnings of ancient civilization, we find the widely diffused image of the Goddess without an accompanying male cult figure."[33] Ruether sees two central myths emerge in the ancient Near Eastern world that relate to God and Goddess in different ways. "One is the myth of the dying and rising God-king, his rescue and marriage with the Goddess."[34] There is, for instance, the Isis-Osiris myth in Egypt, where Osiris is slain and Isis then comes to his rescue raising him from the dead. Ruether concludes: "The resurrection of the king culminates in his marriage to the Goddess, who thereby elevates her human husband to divine status and places him on the throne."[35] According to Ruether the other great myth which emerged in Sumer is the Marduk-Tiamat story. In this Babylonian creation myth the young god Marduk slays the sea goddess Tiamat and out of her body creates the world. Ruether states: "The old Goddess comes to represent the powers of chaos, which are defeated by the new powers of order. . . . That Tiamat is . . . indeed the primary matter out of which all things emerge, the matter within which Marduk himself stands as orderer, becomes evident."[36]

Indeed goddesses play an important role in antiquity. Mother goddesses are present virtually everywhere as we can deduce from the archaic figurines of female goddesses discovered in Asia and Europe. There is the goddess Inanna venerated in ancient Uruk (Sumeria) as the queen of heaven and earth and the goddess of love, later identified with the goddess Ishtar. This goddess of Semitic origin is the queen of love and fertility.[37] But then in Egypt we have the earth-god Geb, "a primordial god" who has "male gender," according to the Egyptologist Siegfried Morenz (1914–1970) in contrast to earth-goddesses in other regions.[38]

---

33. Rosemary Radford Ruether, *Sexism and God-Talk: Toward a Feminist Theology* (Boston: Beacon, 1983) 47.

34. Ibid., 49.

35. Ibid., 50.

36. Ibid., 50–51.

37. So Peter Gerlitz, "Muttergottheiten," in *TRE*, 23:499, in his informative article, who provides an extensive bibliography.

38. Siegfried Morenz, *Egyptian Religion*, trans. Ann E. Keep (Ithaca, NY: Cornell University Press, 1973) 261.

In the Greco-Roman environment we encounter the *Magna Mater* (the great mother), Kybele, an import from Phrygia, part of present-day Turkey, who is called "the mother of the gods" by the Greek poet Euripides (ca. 480–406 BCE).[39] In India among the Dravidian original population we can also detect the importance of mother goddesses. We can see them depicted in ancient artifacts of the so-called "Indus valley civilization," and then there is the cult of Shiva, a god who can be regarded as "the great Lord," but then also comprising "the male and female principle" as the "ambivalent primal mother."[40] Then there is Durga "the cardinal mother-goddess of India" who originally hails from the mountains of India and her dark offshoot Kali.[41] While Kali is cruel and bloodthirsty, Durga is more a *Magna Mater*. "The great goddess has different relevancy depending on her function: At the same time she is creator, preserver, and destroyer. In the history of the world she causes chaos and then creates again an empire in which law and order rule. This *ambivalence* is the special characteristic of the Indian mother goddess."[42]

The widespread occurrence of mother goddesses and of earth goddesses associated with the fertility of the ground led to the idea that there was originally a matriarchy prevalent among humanity from which these mother goddesses evolved in contradistinction to the male sky god. The Swiss anthropologist and lawyer Johann Jacob Bachofen (1815–1887) in his 1861 book, *Das Mutterrecht (A Study of the Religious and Juridical Aspects of Gynecocracy in the Ancient World*[43]) claimed that in ancient cultures there existed a maternal order or matriarchy as an early social order followed by a stage of promiscuity which then was supplanted by a patriarchy of male dominance.[44] This theory proved to

---

39. Euripides, *Helen*, in *Aeschylus, Sophocles, Euripides, Aristophanes: Great Books of the Western World* (Chicago: Encyclopaedia Britannica, 1952) 310.

40. So Heinrich von Stietencron, "Hinduismus," in *TRE* 15:349, and Jan Gonda, *Die Religionen Indiens*, vol. 2: *Der jüngere Hinduismus* (Stuttgart: W. Kohlhammer, 1963) 206–7, who talks about an "androgynous deity." Also Jack Finegan, *The Archeology of World Religions* (Princeton, NJ: Princeton University Press, 1952) 127, who refers here to "effigies of a mother goddess."

41. Sukumari Bhattacharji, *The Indian Theogony: A Comparative Study of Indian Mythology from the Vedas to the Puranas* (Cambridge: University Press Press, 1970) 168, 174, quote on p. 165.

42. Gerlitz, "Muttergottheiten," 501–2.

43. Lewiston, NY: Edwin Mellen, 2003.

44. Cf. the introduction to Bachofen's *Mutterrecht* (Mother Right) as reprinted in *Myth, Religion, and Mother Right. Selected Writings of J.J. Bachofen*, trans. Ralph

be very influential on ethnology especially since it suggested an evolutionary development en vogue in the nineteenth century.

While there is no doubt that mother goddesses were widely venerated, modern anthropologists and historians of religion deny that a strictly matriarchal society ever existed, and with it a cult of a mother goddess as the starting point of religion. In ancient times there was a high infant mortality rate and no social support system for people except the family and here especially one's offspring. Human fertility as shown with the birth-giving woman then was essential for survival. Therefore mother goddesses played an important role in the life of the people since they seemed to ensure survival. Yet often they were also ambivalent since birth and growing-up was far from assured with modern medical assistance still unknown. But "a 'primitive' archaic matriarchy cannot be substantiated either by history of religion or by ethnology; it is a myth."[45] However, goddesses have played and continue to play an important role in many religions. We see this especially well in ancient Israel where archaeologists have unearthed naked female figurines in many regions, perhaps depicting the Canaanite fertility goddess Astarte. Asherah, another female goddess, may even have been regarded as Yahweh's consort by some of the early Israelites.[46] Yet Asherah may also have been understood as mediating Yahweh's blessings, as one can conclude from some inscriptions.[47] While people evidently needed such a female identification figure the official Israelite cult vehemently denounced such veneration as idolatry.[48]

Manheim (London: Routledge, 1967) 71.

45. So rightly Peter Gerlitz, "Muttergottheiten," 502, and James J. Preston, ed., *Mother Worship. Theme and Variation*, 2nd ed. (Chapel Hill: University of North Carolina Press, 1983).

46. See more about this in the careful treatment of "The Origins of Israelite Religion," P. Kyle McCarter, Jr., in *The Rise of Ancient Israel*, ed. Hershel Shanks (Washington, DC: Biblical Archaeology Society, 2002). Cf. also the extensive discussion by William G. Dever, *Did God Have a Wife? Archaeology and Folk Religion in Ancient Israel* (Grand Rapids: Eerdmans, 2005) esp. 176–208, where he discusses all relevant scholarship to this point.

47. See Othmar Keel-Christoph Uehlinger, *Gods, Goddesses, and Images of God in Ancient Israel*, trans. Thomas H. Trapp (Minneapolis: Fortress, 1998) 278.

48. Ruether, *Sexism and God-Talk*, 56, is half-right when she claims: "The Goddess is not so much eliminated as she is absorbed and put into a new relationship with Yahweh as her Lord." While Yahweh also shows female features, the guardians of the official Israelite cult made sure that Asherah never became Yahweh's consort. Yahweh alone

PART II: DISCERNING THE GOD AMONG THE GODS

It Began with Drugs

A pioneer in deciphering the Dead Sea scrolls, the English philologist John Allegro (1923–1988) advanced a very daring thesis concerning the origin of religion. Because of the wide attention it received, his proposal should at least be mentioned here. In his books *The Sacred Mushroom and the Cross* (1970) and *The End of a Road* (1970) he claimed that religion can be explained as originating from orgiastic drug and fertility cults. Yahweh, for instance, "was himself a fertility deity, whose worship by real or simulated sexual intercourse and related rituals was an original part of the cult."[49] According to Allegro, the Greek god Zeus and the Hebrew God Yahweh derive their name from a common linguistic source which he finds in ancient Sumer, which was located between the Tigris and Euphrates Rivers.[50] All the names for god, such as Zeus, Yahweh, and even Allah, mean "the sperm of heaven." Religion is born out of a sense of weakness in the face of a largely hostile environment. Humanity was looking for something beyond itself and beyond its environment, namely to the sky, for something to tap as a creative power. From the sky then comes the creative sperm (water) which impregnates the earth and makes earth yield its crops. Even in the name Jesus/Joshua, Allegro finds this fertility emphasis, because he claims the name means "'the semen that heals' or 'fructifies,' the god-juice that gives life."[51] Thus Christianity, like all other religious manifestations of the Near East, was derived from a fertility cult first celebrated in ancient Sumer. Allegro points to Sumer, part of present-day Iraq, because there humanity first started to entrust its thoughts to written words. This means for him that Sumer encompasses humanity's whole (unwritten) history of thought.

But how is this fertility religiousness related to drugs? Allegro discovers the clue in the red-capped *Amanita muscaria* or toadstool. This

---

is God and needs no companion whether male or female. Mark S. Smith, *The Early History of God. Yahweh and Other Deities in Ancient Israel*, 2nd ed., foreword Patrick D. Miller (Grand Rapids: Eerdmans, 2002) xxxii, states "the data marshalled in support of the goddess [Asherah] in this period [monarchic Israel] are more problematic than advocates have suggested."

49. John M. Allegro, *The End of a Road* (New York: Dial, 1971) 9.

50. See his "proof" in John M. Allegro, *The Sacred Mushroom and the Cross. A Study of the Nature and Origins of Christianity within the Fertility Cults of the Ancient Near East* (London: Hodder & Stoughton, 1970) 215–16 n. 1.

51. Allegro, *End of a Road*, 23.

mushroom contains in its cap several powerful drugs which can give users effects varying from light euphoria, extreme physical violence, or almost supernatural strength. According to Allegro, "some users have reported having the illusion of traveling vast distances over space and time, floating free of their bodies, and enjoying unaccustomed spiritual perceptiveness."[52] Allegro finds striking similarities between the effects of this holy plant, as it was called from the earliest times onward, and the prophetic experiences in the Old Testament, even the appearance of the Son of Man in Rev 1:13–16. This mushroom, with its upshooting stem and red canopy, even seems to depict sexual copulation. Since mushrooms grow especially well after storms, the thought naturally followed that the heavenly deity must have brought about this miraculous fertility. This means for Allegro that Israelite cult and mythology, Yahweh worship, patriarchal legends, Exodus from Egypt, and so on are without historical value. They relate merely to fertility-drug cults and were only later "historized." Theology was made "to hang upon the actions and words of their legendary characters as real people."[53] A similar phenomenon can be observed with the Christian faith. In Allegro's eyes "religion is part of growing up."[54] Though maturation is a painful process, Allegro observes that "if the world survives to adulthood, the new road that stretches ahead promises far greater opportunities for the fulfillment of man's spiritual potential than could any of the old religions. At least he will be able to call his world his own."[55] Thus Allegro asks for freedom from the crumbling confinements of religion.

While the judgment might be true that Allegro's hypothesis "is unlikely to cause many sleepless nights in the theological faculties,"[56] Allegro's observations do deserve some attention. We agree with Allegro that fertility cults play a major role in religions. This was true for the Canaanite Astarte cult in Israel's neighborhood as well as for the ancient mystic-orgiastic Cybele cult. Yet to reduce all religions to fertility cults overstates the point. It would have been good for Allegro not to confine his observations to the ancient Near East. Buddhism, for instance, would

52. Ibid., 32.
53. Ibid., 9.
54. Ibid., 178.
55. Ibid., 184.
56. So rightly John C. King, *A Christian View of the Mushroom Myth* (London: Hodder & Stoughton, 1970) 11.

be very difficult to explain on the basis of a fertility cult. While humanity's anxiety and fear are certainly conducive to a religious apotropaic attitude, as we will see, there are other basic characteristics of religion. Finally, we must also admit that drugs can play a role in religions, as for instance, with certain native American tribes, the Peyote cult or, for instance, wine being served with certain sacred meals. We should also mention the ecstatic experience, as in speaking in tongues, a phenomenon which can be learned, but is occasionally associated with intoxication (cf. Acts 2:13). To reduce everything in religion to these causes only, is a reductionism which does not do justice to religious phenomena, even in instances where these causes can be detected. With Allegro it also becomes clear that for him the explanation of the origin of religion is an attempt to show that religion is a relic of the past and does not fit into our present time. This sentiment has been shared quite often during the last two centuries. We want to name here only a few of its most prominent representatives.

A Relic of the Past?

The French philosopher August Comte (1798–1857) became a founder of positivism through his six volume *The Positive Philosophy* (1830–1842). Postulating three stages in the progressive history of humanity Comte also predicted which course religion should take: (1) The first stage Comte assumed is the theological or fictitious phase in which humanity conceives of the events in nature as dependent upon the will of higher personal forces. These forces are first thought to be embodied in objects of nature (a period of fetishism), then in God's rule over larger areas of nature (polytheism), and finally in one God who is thought to rule the whole world (monotheism). The human mind directs itself thereby mainly to the inner nature of being and to the first and final causes of the phenomena humanity observes. (2) In the second phase of human development, the metaphysical or abstract period, humans replace the anthropomorphism of the first period by more abstract forces, such as powers, inner natures, or souls. (3) It is not until the third, scientific or positive phase, that humanity recognizes its limitations by giving up the search for the origin and hidden causes of the universe, and for the knowledge of final causes of phenomena. By a well-combined use of reasoning and observation, humanity endeavors to discover the actual laws of phenomena.

Comte did not want to do away with religion, because he saw "the need of a spiritual power."[57] But he was convinced that "Monotheism in Western Europe is now as obsolete and as injurious as Polytheism was fifteen centuries ago. The discipline in which its moral value principally consisted has long since decayed."[58] Monotheism supplies no field for the imagination and it never sincerely promoted the pursuits of practical life. However, there is another religion which replaces monotheism. Comte claimed: "Positivism becomes, in the true sense of the word, a Religion; the only religion which is real and complete; destined therefore to replace all imperfect and provisional systems resting on the primitive basis of theology."[59] In this new religion "Love, then is our principle; Order our basis; and Progress our end," as Comte wrote.[60] For positivism humanity is the "only true Great Being" and "the highest progress of man and of society consists in gradual increase of our mastery over all our defects, especially the defects of our moral nature."[61] Reason will be brought to its right use in helping humanity towards self-perfection. "Positive religion brings before us in a definite shape the noblest of human problems, the permanent preponderance of Social feeling over Self-love."[62] In this system, the goddess of reason which had been decreed at the height of the French Revolution is received into positivism, now a philosophic and religious system. Comte reiterates here the creed of the nineteenth century, faith in humanity and in human progress, a faith that claimed it could dispense with transcendent forces.

The Scottish cultural anthropologist James G. Frazer (1854–1941) is best known through his voluminous work, *The Golden Bough* (3rd ed., 12 vols., 1911–1915). Similar to Comte, he also distinguished three phases in human development, magic, religion, and science. Frazer treated the beliefs of the ancient Greeks and Romans from a philosophical, evolutionary point of view, as if they were "pre-literates." They re-

---

57. Auguste Comte, *A General View of Positivism*, trans. J. H. Bridges, official centenary ed. (New York: Robert Speller, 1957) 84.

58. Ibid., 442.

59. Ibid., 365.

60. Ibid., 355.

61. Ibid., 365 and 362.

62. Ibid., 441.

sembled in general and in detail other "pre-literate" societies even of more modern times. Though he never mentioned "the name of Jesus," it was clear to him that Christianity, too, "shares this imperfect (because irrational) understanding of the universe" of these societies.[63]

In *The Golden Bough* Frazer established his thesis concerning religion, reiterated in many other places, that there is "the movement of the higher thought, so far as we can trace it, . . . from magic through religion to science."[64] In magic humanity depends on itself to meet the difficulties and dangers of daily life. It believes in a certain established order of nature which it can, however, manipulate. As this fails, religion sets in to explain natural phenomena as being regulated by the will, the passion, or the caprice of spiritual beings which are like humans though vastly superior. As this proves unsatisfactory too, finally scientific reasoning sets in. Frazer concluded: "In the last analysis magic, religion, and science are nothing but theories of thought; and as science has supplanted its predecessors, so it may hereafter be itself superseded by some more perfect hypothesis."[65]

In other publications Frazer was less hesitant to draw parallels to the Christian religion. For instance, in *Man, God and Immortality: Thoughts on Human Progress* (1927) he initially arrived at a very appropriate definition of religion when he wrote: "By religion, then, I understand a propitiation or conciliation of powers superior to man which are believed to direct and control the course of nature and of human life. Thus defined, religion consists of two elements, a theoretical and a practical, namely, a belief in powers higher than man and an attempt to propitiate or please them."[66] These powers from whom conciliation is sought are understood as personal agents. Next to these natural personified phenomena one also worships the dead since one believes that "the dead retain their consciousness and personality" and "that they can powerfully influence the fortunes of the living."[67] Then Frazer contended that the birth of

---

63. So Robert Ackerman, "Frazer, James G.," in *The Encyclopedia of Religion*, ed. Mircea Eliade, 5:416, where he makes extensive reference to *The Golden Bough*.

64. James George Frazer, *The Golden Bough: A Study in Magic and Religion*, abridged ed. (New York: Macmillan, 1979) 824.

65. Ibid., 825–26.

66. James George Frazer, *Man, God and Immortality: Thoughts on Human Progress*, rev. ed. (London: Macmillan, 1927) 297.

67. Ibid., 302.

Christ is superseded by the nativity of the sun, and that the Phrygian god Attis coincides and resembles in his destiny the definite resurrection of Christ. He concluded that "taken altogether, the coincidences of the Christian with the heathen festivals are too close and too numerous to be accidental."[68] This meant for Frazer that Christianity did not just replace the religions of Greece and Rome, but that the major tenets of the Christian faith were developed to facilitate such replacement.

Frazer distinguished three kinds of gods. The first are inferred by humanity from observing surrounding nature, the second are recognized by virtue of certain extraordinary mental manifestations in oneself or in others. Finally humanity worships "the deified spirits of dead men. To judge by the accounts we possess not only of savage and barbarous tribes but of some highly civilized peoples, the worship of the human dead has been one of the commonest and most influential forms of natural religion, perhaps indeed the commonest and most influential of all."[69] Again, in this threefold distinction of the gods the reference to Christianity—a worship of a dead Jesus—is implicit rather than explicit. Yet Frazer left no doubt that religion is a thing of the past and therefore he as an anthropologist could classify and compare the various religious features. Humanity had progressed from the magic via the religious to the scientific sphere. As Frazer admitted, that may not even be the final stage of development. Again, evolutionary concepts rule supreme. This meant for Frazer as it did for Comte, that religion is only a transitory phenomenon.

The American pragmatist philosopher William James (1842–1910) did not go along with this kind of evolutionary thinking and, in contrast to any scientific skepticism contended: "Anything short of God is not rational, anything more than God is not possible."[70] For James faith was not obtained by a sacrifice of the intellect, but through careful reflection on the world.

In addressing the issue of whether there is a God, James took recourse to pragmatism.[71] In so doing he did not introduce a new proof for

---

68. Ibid., 334.

69. James George Frazer, *The Belief in Immortality and the Worship of the Dead*, The Gifford Lectures 1911–1912 (London: Macmillan, 1913) 1:23–24.

70. William James, *The Will to Believe and Other Essays in Popular Philosophy* (London: Longmans, Green, 1921) 116.

71. So Edward C. Moore, *American Pragmatism: Peirce, James, and Dewey* (New

the existence of God, but tried to prove "that we have a right to believe that God exists and to act as though religion were true."[72] The reason for this is twofold: Since we cannot decide the truth of religion on intellectual grounds but nevertheless must decide it, we have a right to make a conclusion on emotional grounds, and if we prefer to believe then we have a right to do so. Secondly, "since religion might be such that it cannot become true unless we believe it, we have a right to believe it, and to act accordingly."

In his Gifford Lectures, entitled *The Varieties of Religious Experience: A Study in Human Nature* (1901/1902), a series that was established to present lectures in the defense of "natural religion," James used the occasion to vigorously defend religion. He contended that religious life includes the following beliefs:

1. That the visible world is part of the more spiritual universe from which it draws its chief significance;

2. That union or harmonious relation with that higher universe is our true end;

3. That prayer or inner communion with the spirit thereof—be that spirit "God" or "law"—is a process wherein work is really done, and spiritual energy flows in and produces effects, psychological or material, within the phenomenal world.[73]

Yet in the light of other sciences and of general philosophy James realized that the science of religion cannot decide whether such beliefs can be considered true. Most likely the conclusion is that such beliefs are an anachronism, belonging to a past age.

In this situation James referred to the world of our experience, since it consists of an objective and a subjective part. While the objective part is "the sum total of whatsoever at any given time we may be thinking of, the subjective part is the inner 'state' in which the thinking comes to pass."[74] This inner state James claimed "is our very experience itself; its reality and that of our experience are one." This means that

---

York: Columbia University Press, 1961) 116–17.

72. Ibid., 129, for this and the following quote.

73. William James, *The Varieties of Religious Experience. A Study in Human Nature* (London: Longmans, Green, 1928) 485.

74. Ibid., 498–99, for this and the following quote.

reality and our experience go together even to the point that the internal belief produces the external object. While usually an internal belief follows the discovery of an external object, there can also be an exception to that meaning "that here the external object can only follow on the internal belief."[75] This was exactly the point of contention between James and the scientific proponents of materialism. They had no internal belief. Therefore the missing external object corroborated their internal disbelief.

James concluded: "Whatever it may be on its *farther* side, the 'more' with which in religious experience we feel ourselves connected is on its *hither* side the subconscious continuation of our conscious life. . . . The theologian's contention that the religious man is moved by an external power is vindicated, for it is one of the peculiarities of invasions from the subconscious region to take on objective appearances, and to suggest to the Subject an external control."[76] This religious power is not something that we control because whatever we experience from that side is opened to us as a gift. For Christians this supreme reality is God. As James stated:

> We and God have business with each other; and in opening ourselves to his influence our deepest destiny is fulfilled. The universe, at those parts of it which our personal being constitutes, takes a turn generally for the worse or for the better in proportion as each one of us fulfills or evades God's demands. As far as this goes I probably have you with me, for I only translate into schematic language what I may call the instinctive belief of mankind: God is real since he produces real effects.[77]

Appealing to the instinctive beliefs of humanity, as James did, can become dangerous, once these beliefs change and the claim is made that God no longer produces any real effects. This is at least what the God-is-dead theologians claimed more than half a century later. James employed reason because he wanted to get away from irrationalistic access to religion, both with regard to its defenders and of those who reject it. Instead he appealed to the inner side of humanity. The reason for this was that "reality would always be a mystery to human understanding."[78]

---

75. So Moore, *American Pragmatism*, 129.

76. James, *Varieties of Religious Experience*, 512–13.

77. Ibid., 516–17.

78. So Gerald E. Myers, *William James: His Life and Thought* (New Haven: Yale University, 1986) 447.

Yet for James God and humanity are part of the same universe. God is not absolutely infinite and, furthermore, we are called into cooperation with God.[79] James overcame the bifurcation between God and humanity and showed that our efforts do indeed count. Such an approach is especially noticeable when we look at how religion expresses itself. There is hardly anything that cannot take on a religious dimension.

Basic Concepts in the World of Religions

Both the term "religion" and the very study of religions for the sake of knowledge and comparison is typically Western. Largely it is an outgrowth of the Enlightenment which provided a more distanced approach to one's own religion, i.e., the Christian faith and concomitantly the possibility to compare it with other religions. Even the basic concepts for that study evolved in the West, although their historic origin may be in other places. The large variety of religious expressions in our world go hand in hand with a vast variety of means through which religious activities are expressed, not to mention a multitude of objects toward which these religious exercises are directed.

Means and Objects of Religion

As James Frazer has shown, religion is foremost concerned about salvation.[80] Humans conduct religious exercises to be saved from certain dangers, such as violent death by the elements of nature, from disease and wild animals, or from any needs. Many of these items are covered for Christians in the prayers of the church when the faithful pray for people in all their different conditions of life and implore God to bring everything to a good end. Salvation from these destructive and life-impairing or evil forces usually extends to the realm of this world and also to life beyond. It includes both this life and the hereafter. Prayer is a religious activity, or a sacred action. Sacred actions always contain an

---

79. For further details cf. Edward C. Moore, *American Pragmatism*, 133–34.

80. This is true for all religions. While salvation is conceived of quite differently in the various religions one cannot claim with Joseph M. Kitagawa, *The History of Religions. Understanding Human Experience* (Atlanta, GA: Scholars, 1987) 34, that in "positive religion . . . there is no enlightenment, deliverance, or salvation in the usual sense of the term."

element of order and often follow a ritual pattern which usually becomes standardized. They may involve reciting or chanting certain words, bowing or kneeling, making offerings of various kinds, and even dancing. The Christian liturgy may serve as good example of ritual actions.

While religion is not confined to a certain locale, in all religions there are special religious areas or structures that are set apart, such as the house altars in Greco-Roman times, churches, mosques, and synagogues, and other holy places. One does not enter these areas in a casual manner, but often acknowledges this special place, either through removal of footwear, prayers, making the sign of the cross, bowing or kneeling, silence, preparatory fasting or special ablutions. Once these preparations are made, some places are accessible to everyone, while other places are restricted to certain people, such as the priest or other specially designated persons.

Religion is always upheld by a community of adherents. Membership may be ethnically restricted as in the Israelite religion, or even gender based such as the predominantly male Mithras cult in the ancient Roman Empire. In literate societies the religious communities use sacred writings which usually comprise the reported words of holy people of the past, such as prophets, or of the founder of a certain religion, such as Buddha, or even of the God to whom this religion is dedicated, such as in the Qu'ran. Often these writings contain mythical elements, such as creation myths, myths about savior figures, or myths concerning the end of the world. These myths, which also are existent in pre-literate religions and societies, have important explanatory functions. In narratives or symbols they express that which is fundamentally indescribable, namely the absolute beginnings of the world or ultimate realities. Myth should not be understood as something that is false or that did not occur, but it enunciates something which can only be expressed indirectly.

Religion is not restricted to a particular aspect of human life or of human activity. It pertains to the totality of human existence. All of the senses are involved as one goes through certain rituals in cultic devotions, reads divine texts or words inspired by the divine, is summoned to certain acts and responses by prophets or holy people, and encounters the religious object through special phenomena, such as unusual events which are called miracles or signs of the divine. One can also have visions and auditions through which the divine is mediated. By approaching the object of religion in these various ways, one can be very sober and have faith in the validity of one's experiences, or one can attempt to communicate in a state of utter ecstasy, often enhanced through the use of stimulants. The approach can also be one of extreme inwardness as in mystic devotion and result in meditation and opening up for the divine descent.

These various ways are all intended to lead to one goal, the understanding that one's existence is now freed from bondage and that salvation is closer than it was before. This is partly shown in the responses to the encounter with religious objects. These responses again involve the entire human existence. Often they are of a symbolic nature and result in cultic acts such as sacrifice, dramatic actions, dances, songs, and music, and other audible responses, as well as taking the form of prayer and adoration. The whole ethical sphere must also be included in the religious scene and can be understood as both means and result of the approach toward the object of religion. But what is this object of humanity's religious activities?

The possibilities we encounter are plentiful. The object of religious activities can be thought of as a plurality of powers, such as ghosts, demons, or angels. It can consist of supreme powers, such as gods, or simply an impersonal god as in Platonic philosophy. Sometimes only one supreme being is made the sole object of religious activities. In most cases, however, the objects of religion do not coincide with the objects of religious acts, because there seems to be a dialectic relationship between the sacred (object of religion) and the profane (means and object of religious acts). In other words the objects in nature become transparent for the actual object of religion. For instance, when a stone becomes the object of cultic devotion, this stone does not cease to be a stone or a profane object, but for those to whom this stone reveals itself as sacred, "its immediate reality is transmuted into a supernatural reality."[81] Thus the Ka'bah in Mecca, the cultic center of Islam, is just a granite building. Yet it can become the manifestation of something much more important than this unassuming edifice. This is even more true of the Black Stone at the Ka'bah which again for the Muslim is much more than just a meteorite.

---

81. Mircea Eliade, *The Sacred and the Profane: The Nature of Religion*, trans. W.R. Trask (New York: Harcourt Brace, 1959) 12.

The dialectic between the actual object of religion and the means and object of religious acts and the ensuing problematic can also be illustrated by the veneration of icons in the Eastern Orthodox tradition. There was a long struggle in the East whether icons could be used as means of devotion fearing that such use might detract from the actual worship of God and would foster the worship of the created instead of the Creator. As John of Damascus states, it was decided: "Everything, therefore, that is dedicated to God we worship, conferring the adoration to Him."[82] Adoration is for God only, veneration or worship, however, can also be accorded to that which is used to adore God. This distinction between veneration and adoration while helpful also indicates a problem. That which is venerated or worshiped can easily though wrongly be exchanged for that to whom alone adoration belongs. Religious activities can easily be misguided.

John of Damascus also tells us: "The honor rendered to the image passes over to the prototype."[83] The icon or the object of religious acts is not an end in itself. It is transparent so that we are able to reach the actual object of our devotion. There are many other objects that can assume this "dual" character, such as mountains, trees, water, animals, stars, thunder, fertility, and even such undifferentiated objects as earth and fire. The orders of nature must also be included, such as the lunar month, the week (still referred to in the context of Easter as Holy Week), the solar year and its main seasons, especially summer and winter.

We agree with the anthropologist Bronislaw Malinowski (1884–1942) when he says that to the "primitive" all is religion, "that he perpetually lives in a world of mysticism and ritualism."[84] Hearing Martin Luther (1483–1546) say that "worship is not restricted to one or two kinds of activities, or to one or two professions, but it is part of all activities and professions,"[85] we wonder if the all-inclusiveness of religion is only true for "the primitive." If religion pertains to human existence as a whole, it is futile to exclude any aspect from it, or to claim that through their maturation people emancipate certain aspects of their lives from

---

82. John of Damascus, *Exposition to the Orthodox Faith* (XI) in *NPNF SS*, 9:80.

83. Ibid. (XI) 9:88.

84. Bronislaw Malinowski, *Magic, Science and Religion and Other Essays*, intro. Robert Redfield (Garden City, NY: Doubleday, 1954) 24.

85. Martin Luther, *Kirchenpostille* in *WA* 10:1/1,413.7–9 in his exposition of Luke 2:37.

the religious sphere. Thus it is extremely difficult, if not hopeless, to define clearly the objects and the means of religious activities, especially in functioning as a disclosure of the sacred. The whole human reality is potentially open to the disclosure of the object of religious devotion and similarly it can be used as a means to approach or to respond to the object of religious devotions.[86] This all-inclusiveness of religion is especially well expressed in the notion of one supreme God.

One Supreme God

The discovery that most religions hold to the idea of one God, or to put it in more neutral terms, of one supreme being, came as quite a surprise to many interested in the world's religions. The notion of a high god, if it would prove to be an integral part of pre-literate religion, would shatter the idea of a gradual evolution from animism to polydemonism, polytheism, and finally to monotheism. Of course, one can always argue that the concept of a high god is the result of missionary teaching, since the missionaries came in contact with pre-literate tribes and conveyed this prevailing concept.[87] But, as we noted, Wilhelm Schmidt adduced enough evidence proving that the belief in a high god is so universal among all the peoples of the simplest cultures, that it can no longer be discarded as an echo of missionary teaching or as an irrelevant fragment of mythology. Even the idea, at one time proposed, that this highest being is a *Deus otiosus,* a god who originally created the world and who is regarded as its creator but who then withdrew and no longer cares about the world, is difficult to maintain.[88] On the contrary, often this highest being is believed to have instituted the ceremonies of worship or is the object of worship and even of sacrifice. It is also remarkable that outside

---

86. At this point we want to confine ourselves simply to pointing out the diversity of the means and objects in religion. For further information, cf. the helpful book of W. Richard Comstock, *The Study of Religion and Primitive Religions* (New York: Harper, 1972) esp. 28–72. Comstock distinguishes between myth and ritual in religion, both being highly symbolic, and then defines religion as symbolic expression. Of course, this leaves the question open as to what or who is symbolically expressed.

87. Andrew Lang, *Magic and Religion* (London: Longmans, Green, 1901) esp. 15–45, vehemently disclaims this possibility in citing considerable evidence that excludes the influence of missionaries. Cf. also Nathan Söderblom, *The Living God: Basal Forms of Personal Religion,* with a biographical intro. Yngve Brilioth (Boston: Beacon, 1962) 21–22; and Bronislaw Malinowski, *Magic, Science and Religion,* 23.

88. So Geo Widengren, *Religionsphänomenologie* (Berlin: Walter de Gruyter, 1969) 53.

the prescribed rites, the individual spontaneously turns to the high god when in trouble or when its mind is uplifted.

Often the high gods are regarded as culture heroes, as all-fathers, or as creators. This main quality enables them to give answer to the question about origin and cause, and distinguishes them from spirits, souls, and gods. Naturally they are placed in and identified with such prominent localities as sun, moon, or thunder. But the Swedish historian of religion and archbishop Nathan Söderblom (1866–1931) asserts that they are not derived from nature or from human life but that "they constitute a presentiment of the Creator."[89] Yet we wonder if such an evaluation can be justified. We have seen in Wilhelm Schmidt's thesis of an original monotheism that the Judeo-Christian faith served for him as the glasses through which he perceived and evaluated the world of religion. We are far from standing on neutral ground ourselves knowing that even the vantage point of a dispassionate spectator shows a certain engagement. However, we realize that some observations connect the idea of a highest being much closer with human nature.

The Italian historian of religion, Raffaele Pettazzoni (1883–1959), for instance, maintains that the notion of a supreme being springs from our "existential needs."[90] Similar to Söderblom, he rejects the idea that the phenomenology of the supreme being, i.e., how the supreme being shows itself, is exhausted "by the alternatives of a Supreme Being who is creator of the world" and therefore a candidate for gradual inactivity, "and a Supreme Being who is omnipresent and omniscient with the explicit vocation to interventionism."[91] Though many supreme beings, such as the Roman Jupiter or the Greek Zeus, are celestial beings, the notion of a supreme being does not just lead to the concept of a celestial being. "For many peoples the Supreme Being is not the heavenly Father, but the Mother Earth."[92] Pettazzoni goes on to assert that: "Behind the Mother Earth there is a long tradition of agricultural matriarchal civilization. The Heavenly Father is the Supreme Being typical of the nomads

---

89. Söderblom, *Living God*, 22.

90. Raffaele Pettazzoni, "The Supreme Being: Phenomenological Structure and Historical Development," in *The History of Religions. Essays in Methodology*, ed. Mircea Eliade and Joseph M. Kitagawa, preface Jerald C. Brauer (Chicago: University of Chicago, 1959) 60.

91. Ibid., 63.

92. Ibid., 64–66, for this and the following quotes.

who live on the products of their herds; the herds live on the pastures, and these in their turn depend on rain from the sky." In more remote times, prior to agriculture and the breeding of livestock, Pettazzoni surmises, the supreme being was the Lord of the animals and the success of the hunt depended upon him. Therefore he concludes that the notion of the supreme being is always connected with that which is vital to human existence. Existential anxiety about daily living is "the common root in the structure of the Supreme Being, but this structure is historically expressed in different forms: the Lord of animals, the Mother Earth, the Heavenly Father."

Though we agree with Pettazzoni's existential emphasis, we doubt that the historic progression implied in his argument can be verified. Why, for instance, did the Israelites not abandon their "sky God" Yahweh, and adopt the earth or fertility god Baal when they abandoned their nomadic existence and settled down in an agricultural setting? Though transition from the Lord of animals to a sky god and to an earth god may have some merit, there does not seem to be a necessity for a people to abandon one concept of a highest being in favor of a different one when they attain a "higher" cultural level.

As does Pettazzoni, the Swedish historian of religion Geo Widengren (1907-1996) emphasizes the primal notion of a highest being which determines human destiny and is beyond bad and good. He even regards this idea of a highest being as an "original feature in the concept of god."[93] Widengren demonstrates that the belief in one god as the creator and Lord of our existence is accepted in most religions whether they originated in Australia, Africa, America, Asia, or in Europe. Since pre-literate and tribal religions are still widespread in Africa, we need not wonder that Widengren finds his main proof for the highest being in African religions.[94] He is not as narrow as Pettazzoni in his description of the supreme being by confining his relevance mainly to the creation of the world and to the provision of food. Though the god gives rain and provides or withholds fertility, Widengren sees in him also "the Lord over life and death and the one who gives well-being or who sends sickness."[95] Occasionally the god is even regarded as the judge of humanity's doings. Thus this highest being, as the Lord over life

---

93. Widengren, *Religionsphänomenologie*, 129.
94. Cf. ibid., 47-49.
95. Ibid., 52-53.

and fertility, determines in decisive ways the existence of society and of the individual.

If the high god has such all-encompassing function the question of the manner in which the multitude of other gods and powers are related to this high god almost necessarily arises. Widengren offers a very plausible explanation in connecting the different qualities and functions that these other powers and deities enjoy with their origin. There is first of all a group of deities that result from a specialization or absorption process of the high god. Often the high god is attributed specialized functions, such as Jupiter with lightning. However, gradually this function may gain such momentum that it becomes an independent god while the god originally associated with it becomes suppressed in this context. Often the place of adoration can also become a second name for a high god, such as Zeus Elymnios, which means Zeus who is worshipped on the mountain Elymnion. Sometimes other gods which have been worshipped for a long time, perhaps even former high gods, lose power and are gradually regarded as followers of the new emerging high god. For instance, in Greek religion Hades, a god of the underworld, is introduced as a brother of Zeus. Yet Homer can call Hades "the underground Zeus,"[96] thereby indicating that Zeus is the supreme god.

A second group of gods is clearly associated with nature, such as gods of the earth, mountains, rivers, trees, and springs.[97] With extreme caution Widengren suggests that they could be understood as derivatives of a pantheistically conceived high god. But the belief in a pantheistic high god presupposes a great deal of abstraction at an early stage in the history of humanity. Hence, contrary to Widengren's suggestion, it might be more satisfactory simply to refer here to the experience of, and dependence upon, nature and to understand these gods of nature as expressions of humanity's fear of powers against which people were relatively helpless.

Finally, Widengren mentions a group of gods who function as mediators between humanity and the highest god. Here is the place of the "culture hero," as for instance Prometheus in the Greek religion.[98] Prometheus' evaluation, however, oscillates between the description by Hesiod (ca. 700 BCE) a bringer of civilization as well as woe, and the

---

96. So Schoeps, *Religions of Mankind*, 123.

97. Cf. for the following Widengren, *Religionsphänomenologie*, 125–27.

98. Ibid., 89–92.

insight of the Greek dramatist Aeschylus (525/24–456/55 BCE) that he prevents the threatening destruction of humanity, as decreed by Zeus. Enabling humanity to survive, Prometheus introduces all the arts and sciences. This shows that the cultural hero can either be a trickster or a salvation-bringing mediator. In both cases humanity understands itself at the mercy of higher powers.

Regardless of the form in which it may appear, religion always seems to imply the belief in a supreme god. Since this belief has as its ultimate concern human destiny, and to a lesser degree the destiny of all beings, we might not be far off in regarding this belief as a primordial human notion. There is someone who ultimately controls our future, someone to whom humans attempt to relate.

Holiness or Insanity?

Considering the attributes conferred upon the one supreme god, it becomes clear that such a being cannot be approached in a casual way. Consequently, in his classic *The Idea of the Holy* the German historian of religion Rudolf Otto (1869–1937) pointed out that holiness is a basic experience of all religion. As creatures humans feel dependent. Recognizing their dependence they are overwhelmed by their own nothingness, in contrast to that which is supreme above all creatureliness.[99] The feeling of dependence, stemming from the status as creature ensues from an experience of the numinous. Where the presence of the numinous is not felt, there can be no feeling of dependence and creatureliness. Being confronted with the numinous, there is "the feeling of personal nothingness and submergence before the awe-inspiring object directly experienced."[100] This awe-inspiring confrontation is not just a negative experience, because we also sense the majesty and power with which we are confronted. We realize our own impotence and nothingness by the haunting presence of a "superpower." This power is not like a threatening object; it contains energy, will, and movement. Otto shows that the dynamic of the holy can be encountered on the level of the demonic as well as on the level of the "living" God.[101] Understandably this power could easily be perceived as something threatening. But Otto emphasizes that

---

99. Cf. for the following Otto, *Idea of the Holy*, 10–11.
100. Ibid., 17.
101. Ibid., 23.

it contains a polarity between the awe-inspiring and fascinating. The numinous not only puts us in our creaturely place; it also allures and captivates us. In other words, we cannot escape it, since it is both "the daunting and the fascinating."[102]

Many Old Testament passages can be quoted to illustrate holiness as a basic concept of religion as Rudolf Otto shows. For instance, on the flight from his brother, Jacob had the dream of an encounter with angels and even with Yahweh. When he awakened, he reacted in typical religious fashion: "He was afraid, and said, 'How awesome is this place! This is none other than the house of God, and this is the gate of heaven'" (Gen 28:17). But admitting his awe and recognizing Yahweh's superior power is not the full story. Jacob did not simply run away in fear, as someone might run away from a threatening enemy. He was drawn back to this place, erected a stone, and poured oil on it. In other words, the experience of awe drove him to recognize the superior power in a cultic act. We could also cite Moses' encounter with the burning bush. When Moses discovered the bush, he was fascinated by the unusual phenomenon of a burning bush that did not burn up. But right away Yahweh put him in his place and demanded that Moses show respect to God's majesty by taking off his sandals, for the ground on which he stood was holy (Exod 3:5).

These examples demonstrate that it would be a gross misunderstanding to follow the Latin proverb *timor fecit deos* (fear created gods) and conclude that humanity creates gods as an expression of the existential fear or anxiety that dwells in it. The opposite is true. Because humanity has the experience of holiness as something awe-inspiring and fear-causing, it feels existentially insecure. Its basic anxiety always presupposes outside itself a cause of this anxiety. For instance, Isaiah did not feel a certain anxiety or fear and then conclude that he had better follow Yahweh, but because he sensed that Yahweh had called him he expressed his basic existential inadequacy (Isa 6:5). Thus a religious person is not someone who has certain existential deficiencies, but rather is someone "to whom something is holy."[103] This sentiment seems also to be substantiated by psychology.

The Swiss psychologist and psychiatrist Carl Gustav Jung (1875–1961), for instance, suggested that the essential processes of religious

102. Ibid., 31.
103. Söderblom, *Living God*, 21.

life take place not in the spirit, in feelings, or in reason, but in the unconscious. This unconscious or psychic realm, however, is "far removed from all human volition and influence."[104] Jung fully agreed with Otto in saying that the numinous is "a dynamic existence or effect, not caused by an arbitrary act of will. On the contrary, it seizes and controls the human subject, which is always its victim rather than its creator. The numinosum is an involuntary condition of the subject, whatever its cause may be."[105] In following Jung it seems impossible to explain the experience of the numinous as a figment of the human mind or as a projection of our (known) desires.

We remember that in *The Varieties of Religious Experience* William James had already claimed before Jung that the subconscious is mediating between nature and the "higher region." He feels that the subconscious can be analyzed by the scientist as well as safeguarded by the theologian who asserts that a religious person is moved by an external power. Such external power, however, is not disjunctive with the visible world, since "the visible world is part of a more spiritual universe from which it draws its chief significance."[106] James suggests that union or harmonious relation with that higher universe is our true end. In his pragmatic optimism we hear little of humanity's alienation from the "higher world." Consequently he states that each religious attitude in its diversity is but a "syllable in human nature's total message, it takes the whole of us to spell the meaning out completely."[107] In contrast to the positive connection between the human psyche and religion as expressed by Carl Gustav Jung and William James, we remember that another prominent representative of psychoanalysis, Sigmund Freud, attacked religion rather vehemently.

According to Freud religion is largely projection and "a large portion of the mythological conception of the world which reaches far into the most modern religions, *is nothing but psychology projected to the outer world.*"[108] The unclear inner perceptions of our own psychic

---

104. Hans Schaer, *Religion and the Cure of Souls in Jung's Psychology*, trans. R. F. C. Hull (London: Routledge, 1999) 62–63.

105. Carl Gustav Jung, *Psychology and Religion* (New Haven, CT: Yale University Press, 1938) 4.

106. James, *Varieties of Religious Experience*, 485.

107. Ibid., 487.

108. Sigmund Freud, *Psychopathology of Everyday Life* in *The Basic Writings of*

apparatus incite illusionary thinking, which then is projected into the world around us, and characteristically also into the future and into the beyond. Immortality, vengeance and the whole hereafter were labeled by Freud as projections of our psychic interior and as psychomythology.[109] Freud suggested that myths could very likely be regarded as "distorted vestiges of wish-fantasies of whole nations" and as age-long dreams of humanity in its infancy stage.[110] Freud claimed that myths did not originate in heaven but on earth, and were in turn projected into heaven.[111] Even the gods are largely human creations. Humanity ascribed to them everything that seemed unreachable or forbidden. Humanity projected into them "all human characteristics—along with the crimes they prompt."[112] Psychologically speaking, the belief in a personal God is ultimately nothing but the belief in an elevated father and mother image and this desire for the "grand sublimations of father and mother" leads to religion.[113] Hence Freud surmised that the roots of the need for religion are in the parental complex. "At bottom God is nothing other than an exalted father."[114] Of course, Freud knows that this theory cannot account for the existence of mother goddesses. But this does not prevent Freud from arriving at the devastating conclusion that religion is nothing to take seriously. It is only a developmental stage of humanity which must be left behind.

Freud's theory resembles somewhat Feuerbach's idea that religion is a projection of human desires, and it is easy to understand that it en-

---

Sigmund Freud, trans., ed., and intro. A. A. Brill (New York: Random House, 1938) 164.

109. Cf. Sigmund Freud, *Totem and Taboo* (III/1) 77, with reference to W. Wundt.

110. Sigmund Freud, *The Poet and Day-Dreaming* in *On Creativity and the Unconscious: Papers on the Psychology of Art, Literature, Love, Religion*, sel. with an intro. Benjamin Nelson (New York: Harper, 1958) 53.

111. Sigmund Freud, "The Theme of the Three Caskets" (I) in *Collected Papers*, trans. Joan Riviere (London: Hogarth, 1953) 4:245.

112. Sigmund Freud, "Obsessive Acts and Religious Practices" in *Collected Papers*, trans. Joan Riviere (London: Hogarth, 1950) 2:35.

113. Sigmund Freud, *Leonardo da Vinci and a Memory of His Childhood* in *The Standard Edition of the Complete Psychological Works of Sigmund Freud*, ed. James Strachey (London: Hogarth, 1957) 11:123. Of course, Freud is right when he claimed that for children God is often a projection of the parental image. But does this qualify the notion of a personal God as mere projection? Cf. also Freud, *Totem and Taboo* (IV/6) 148.

114. Freud, *Totem and Taboo* (IV/6) 147.

gendered considerable discussion.[115] Unlike Feuerbach, however, Freud claimed that this projection originated from the sickly mind of emerging humanity and could be traced back to some rather simple motifs, such as the murder of the ancestoral father, the Oedipus complex, and totemism as the beginning of human culture. Scholars in the history of religion like Wilhelm Schmidt found it easy to prove that these theories could not be made to agree with the material adduced by ethnology.[116]

However, Freud's approach is not as negative towards religion as it seems at first glance. Freud's investigation shows us first, that there is a definite analogy between religious and pathological phenomena, perhaps indicating a certain interdependence between them. But we question Freud's assumption that this discovery has thereby unearthed the origin of all religious phenomena.[117] Secondly, Freud has shown, for instance in his treatise on the totem animal, that symbols can point to the birth of idols. But again, is this all? Can psychoanalysis prove that this is all there is to symbols? Hardly. Symbols are not just fantasies that should be overcome and abolished. They also "give rise to thought"; thought about the ultimate meaning of life.[118] This brings us to the final, critical point. In his failure to recognize the ambiguity contained in that which he analyzes, religion becomes for Freud all projection, all desire, and all wrong.[119] However, historians since Wilhelm Dilthey (1833–1911) have cautioned us that understanding means living with that which is to be understood. In his analyses of the human psyche Freud is too much the "objective" observer to tolerate ambiguity. While attempting to show us how reality really is, he distorts it and presents us with only part of it. In so doing he forces us to distinguish between sickness and saintliness,

---

115. Cf. Dietrich Rössler, "Freud, Sigmund," in *TRE* 11:580–82, with regard to his impact on theology which he, however, finds limited.

116. According to Kasimir Birk, *Sigmund Freud und die Religion* (Münsterschwarzach: Vier-Türme-Verlag, 1970) 88–90.

117. Cf. Paul Ricoeur, *Freud and Philosophy: An Essay an Interpretation*, trans. D. Savage (New Haven, CT: Yale University Press, 1970) 533, where he affirms that psychoanalysis has no way to prove whether religious phenomena simply result from obsession and whether faith is merely consolation stemming from the childhood pattern.

118. So Ricoeur, *Freud and Philosophy*, 543.

119. Arthur Guirdham, *Christ and Freud: A Study of Religious Experience and Observance* (London: Allen & Unwin, 1959) 57, rightly cautions us in connection with Freud against intellectual systems that explain all things too neatly. "The human mind is not a computing machine and mathematics is, after all, not a form of truth but the ultimate abstraction."

and between idol and symbol. In other words, he unintentionally tells us that even the holiness of God does not prevent us from constructing and using God according to our own desires. This can be especially observed with the concepts of mana and taboo which are also central to the idea of holiness.

Mana, Magic, and Taboo

We have already encountered the concepts of "mana" and "taboo" in the pre-animistic theory of Robert Marett. Since they, together with the concept of magic, are rather wide-spread if not universal on the religious scene, they will now receive more extensive treatment. "Mana" is a word in the Melanesian languages, perhaps imported from Polynesia, and denotes a supernatural invisible power that usually rests in a strong person, such as a chief or a medicine man, and which can also be imparted to animals, plants, and stones.[120] The belief in a power inherent in animate and inanimate objects, which can be transferred to other persons and other objects, is characteristic of most religions. The Old Testament provides us with many examples of the concept of mana. However, there mana usually does not rest in a strong person, but is absorbed in God's holiness. For instance, the Old Testament tells us that Yahweh commanded the Israelites to use the ashes of the red heifer for a cultic cleansing ritual (Num 19:9). The idea that Yahweh's spirit can be imparted to Moses and then in turn to other persons points in a similar direction. Yet the understanding that Yahweh can again withdraw his empowering spirit indicates that in the Israelite religion this mana or power is never thought of as existing independently from Yahweh. The example of King Manasseh who practiced soothsaying and sorcery (2 Chr 33:6), however, reminds us that the Israelites did not always follow this thinking. More than once were they tempted to make use of this power in a way independent of Yahweh's will. Then they acted in analogy to magic practices, common to most religions, especially on a tribal level.

Magic betrays the belief in mysterious powers that when tapped in their proper way bring inevitable and predictable results. Yet "magic is not born of an abstract conception of universal power, subsequently applied to concrete cases."[121] Each type of magic originated in its own

120. Cf. Schoeps, *Religions of Mankind*, 13–14.
121. Malinowski, *Magic, Science and Religion*, 78.

situation and represents the spontaneous reaction of humanity to a particular situation. Magic is a ready-made ritual act and belief "with a definite mental and practical technique which serves to bridge over the dangerous gaps in every important pursuit or critical situation."[122] Since it shows human anxiety and is at the same time a means to overcome it, magic bears a very close affinity to religion. Even modern human beings who are convinced of a rational mastery of their own existence and who discard both "primitive superstition" and religious ties, still maintain their magical inclination. Amulets, talismans, and mascots are almost omnipresent; in the form of charms they dangle from bracelets, from rearview mirrors, and are worn around the neck. Quite often, however, they are no longer symbols of transcendent powers but have become idols of secular humanity.[123]

The idea of taboo is related to the concepts of mana and magic and is associated with the idea of holiness. The term *taboo* perhaps comes from the Polynesian *tapu* meaning to mark exceedingly or to mark out as forbidden. It was first introduced into the English language by Captain James Cook (1728-1779) who noticed its use on the Tonga Islands in 1777. Again we find many analogies to the idea of taboo in the Judeo-Christian religion. Most well-known to us are the Old Testament laws concerning clean and unclean which unmistakably imply the taboo concept. But again these *tohoroth* laws are closely related to Yahweh, as the one who decreed certain things as clean and others as unclean. If people transgress these laws, they are excluded from the community and from communion with Yahweh until purification is obtained (Lev 5:2ff). In most religions taboos are also concerned with the dead and their places of rest, with women during their menstrual flow, during pregnancy, and

---

122. Ibid., 90.

123. Gustav Mensching, *Die Religion*, 134-35, introduces a very helpful nomenclature when he distinguishes between two kinds of magic, "a religious and a profane." According to Mensching the profane magic, to which secular people adhere, has nothing to do with religion but rather with superstition. Cf. also Carl Heinz Ratschow, *Magie und Religion* (Gütersloh: C. Bertelsmann, 1955) esp. 148-50, who points out that in magic there exists a feeling of union which is widely lost today *(unio magica)* whereas religion betrays a historical consciousness and strives to regain this union which it feels is lost for humanity. It makes us wonder, however, why modern humanity is often tempted to return to a non-historical state, either in deliberately renouncing history and by living in a kind of counterculture, or implicitly through total neglect of historical realities. Should this indicate that humanity is not as far removed from a belief in magic than it assumes it is?

in childbirth; often the bride and groom are taboo until the wedding day, and certain places, such as a temple, or certain days, for instance festivals or the new moon day, are covered by taboo rules. In this manner taboo can serve to set aside certain objects that are not accessible for average persons or it can simply warn people about negative influences from demons and spirits, as in the case of the deceased. In other words, taboo is used to protect human life against possible danger arising from that which is experienced as beyond human capability. Most peoples also have some kind of buffer zone in the institution of divine kingship. While ordinary people thereby escape the danger of coming into too close contact with these powers beyond their control, they still have access to them through their royal representatives.

Divine Kingship

The idea of the divine kingship gained very dubious fame in Old Testament studies, especially through its most prominent advocates, the Scandinavian Old Testament scholars Sigmund Mowinckel (1884–1965) and Ivan Engnell (1909–1964). They attempted to understand the whole Israelite religion as having originated from one spiritual center, which they saw located in the enthronement festival of Yahweh.[124] For example Engnell suggested that the idea of the divine kingship was prevalent throughout the ancient Near East. Therefore, the Israelite understanding of Passover, the Feast of Booths, the belief in the resurrection, messianism, and even essential features of the idea of religion were derived from this pattern. But it seems that the history of the Israelite religion is more complicated and many-faceted than Engnell suggested.

Many scholars even deny that a festival of the enthronement of Yahweh ever existed. The German Old Testament scholar Georg Fohrer (1915–2003), for instance, pointed out that an identification of God and king, which such a festival presupposes, is an unacceptable thought for Israel. Unlike other religions, in the Israelite religion the king is never

---

124. Sigmund Mowinckel, *Psalmenstudien*, vol. 2: *Das Thronbesteigungsfest Jahwäs und der Ursprung der Eschatologie* (Amsterdam: P. Schippers, 1961) and Ivan Engnell, especially in his doctoral dissertation, *Studies in Divine Kingship in the Ancient Near East*, 2nd ed. (Oxford: Blackwell, 1967). For further discussion cf. Hans Schwarz, *Eschatology* (Grand Rapids: Eerdmans, 2000) 28-30.

thought of as God's representative, far less God's embodiment.[125] Yet we should not overlook that "it is a common concept throughout the Near East that the god, or high god, was the king of the state or polity."[126] While Israel could not totally extricate itself from this socio-cultural and religious context, for Israel this divine kingship could only be attributed to Yahweh. For instance, "the Enthronement Psalms deal with Yahweh's accession to his royal throne and exercise of royal power over the divine council, creation and Israel." As we can gather from 1 Sam 8:4–9 there was initially even a tension between Yahweh's kingship and Israel's desire to have an earthly king. The kings in Israel were under Yahweh's lordship, being anointed by God. If they displeased God they could be rejected (cf. 1 Sam 15:10). But Yahweh made with David's house "an everlasting covenant" (2 Sam 23:5, and cf. 2 Samuel 7), a covenant that had consequences far beyond the Israelite covenant community. We remember that Jesus had been called king (Luke 19:38) and "was descended from David according to the flesh" (Rom 1:3).

We need not be surprised that in Israel the king enjoyed an elevated status. For instance, we read in the Mishnah Sanhedrin, i.e., the initially orally transmitted teaching of the Jewish supreme legal court: none is allowed to ride the king's horse, "and none may sit on his throne and none may make use of his sceptre. None may see him when his hair is being cut or when he is naked, or when he is in the bath-house."[127] These rules do not just express due respect for the kingly authority. Though in Israelite thinking the king is nothing apart from his election and sustenance by Yahweh, these rules make us aware that even for Israel the king is not just a human figure.

The exceptional role of the king is much more emphasized in other cultures. There the king mostly enjoys a fairly independent position and is often regarded as divine by virtue of his own office or by descent.[128] For instance, until 1945 the Japanese Emperor was considered to be son

---

125. So Georg Fohrer, *History of Israelite Religion*, trans. David E. Green (Nashville: Abingdon, 1972) 142–45 and 204–5.

126. So Keith W. Whitelam, "King and Kingship," in *The Anchor Bible Dictionary*, 4:43, for this and the following quote.

127. Mishnah Sanhedrin 2:5, in Herbert Danby, *The Mishnah*, trans. from the Hebrew with intro. and brief explanatory notes (London: Oxford University, 1933) 385. Cf. also to this passage Schoeps, *Religions of Mankind*, 17.

128. For the following cf. Schoeps, *The Religions of Mankind*, 17–8; and Widengren, *Religionsphänomenologie*, 369–71.

of the sun and was considered to be actual god, on whom the welfare of the state depended. Until the mid nineteenth century the Japanese Emperor was not even allowed to leave his palace, since someone might see him and thereby desecrate his holiness. Later, when he was allowed to leave his palace, people had to turn their backs to him for the same reason. Very interesting also is a custom in ancient Rome where the king was not allowed to mingle with other people or touch the ground with his feet, for fear that he would make the people or the ground he touched sacred; he had to be carried in a sedan-chair. The idea that the king is not permitted to touch the ground with his feet is also very wide-spread among African tribes. Often the tribal chief can only walk as far as a carpet or an animal skin extends. Traces of this practice can be found in the famous red carpet treatment for foreign dignitaries and, in a more "sacred" fashion, in the custom that, until a generation ago, the Pope was carried to mass audiences, that everyone has to bend the knee before him, and that his seat was always elevated above the rest of the people. We are also reminded of the idea of sacred kingship when we hear that according to English tradition the king or queen is anointed with oil on the day of his/her coronation.

The king did not just enjoy certain privileges through his divine status. Often the idea of sacred kingship could also imply dangerous aspects for the king. In ancient Mexico, for example, the Aztec rulers had to swear during their coronation ceremony that they would permit the sun to shine, that they would give rain to the clouds and command the earth to bear fruit. One can easily imagine the consequences for the king if nature did not meet the expectations expressed in his oath. Similarly, in certain tribes the custom is reported that the king (chief) is killed or kills himself once his physical power diminishes, since his intercessory and protective power is then believed also to be waning away.[129] Thus those who mediate the ultimate holiness are themselves subject to fear and trembling as well as engendering it in their subjects.

At the end of our chapter we have hardly lifted the veil from the enigma of religion. We have seen that religion is constituent of human history and in one way or other also of human existence. In contrast to scenarios from various sides which want to tell us that religion is on the way out, that people want to master their own lives, religion is very

---

129. So Friedrich Heiler, *Erscheinungsformen und Wesen der Religion*, 2nd ed. (Stuttgart: W. Kohlhammer, 1979) 368.

much alive and perhaps as vigorous as ever. There is also not one convincing theory that explains how religion originated. The main reason for the pervasiveness of religion and for the futility to explain it (away) is that it permeates virtually every facet of human life. All secular endeavors notwithstanding, people always accompany their activities with religious symbols, e.g., wearing cross necklaces or checking their horoscope. Even if people would disclaim that they put any relevance in these actions, they indicate that religious "observances" are still a part of their lives. Therefore we want to turn now to the more structured expressions of religion as they show themselves in the great religions of humanity to see whether these religions and the God experienced in them makes a difference in the lives of the faithful.

FOUR

Deciphering the Religious Landscape

Confronted as we are with a multitude of religious concepts and having realized how difficult it is to define religion or even trace its origin, it comes as no surprise that no one religion is like another. Even if we agree with the often-uttered statement that we all believe in the same God, this God is understood very differently by the various religions. This claim becomes even more accurate when one considers the wide ethnic scope of religions and their adherents. There are, for instance, religions that include only one ethnic group. Hinduism is basically still today the religion of India or of Indian people living in other countries. Only a minute minority of Hindus are of non-Indian origin. Similarly, the religion of Islam was initially an Arab religion. Even the conquest of other countries was not executed in the attempt to convert their inhabitants, though after centuries of Muslim control in North Africa only traces of the Christian population remain. Most of the Christians there converted to Islam because of the subtle or overt pressure exerted on them as "infidels." There are also pre-literate or tribal religions that serve as the religion of certain tribes and clans. Such a tribal religion may be implied in Joshua's ultimatum to the Israelites: "Now if you are unwilling to serve the Lord, choose this day whom you will serve, whether the gods your ancestors served in the region beyond the River, or the gods of the Amorites in whose land you are living; but as for me and my household, we will serve the Lord" (Josh 24:15). Joshua acknowledged that the ancestors of Israel served other gods, but claimed Yahweh for himself and his family. We may assume that this kind of tribal arrangement is the first step in humanity's religious development.

Prehistoric and Tribal Religions

To chart the development of tribal religions, we must go back at least 60,000 years and then steadily advance along an unbroken line to present. The Paleolithic Era (at least from 100,000 BCE onward), the Neolithic Era (ca. 6000–3200 BCE), the Bronze Age (3200–1200 BCE), and the Iron Age (1200–600 BCE) are all key periods in this progression. However, since prehistoric archaeology is to a large extent accidental, and since its discoveries are wordless, the discovered cultic and ceremonial artifacts, sites, pictures, symbols require considerable interpretation. There is therefore a large degree of conjecture, and conclusions are often reached only by comparing the prehistoric religious remains with parallels in contemporary tribal religions. Having acknowledged this "opaqueness" of prehistoric documents, historian of religion Mircea Eliade (1907–1986) is certainly right when he counters the skepticism of some scholars: "*Homo faber* was at the same time *Homo ludens, sapiens, and religiosus.*"[1]

Though many questions remain unanswered, we have some significant insights into the religious practices and beliefs of these ancient people. For instance, archeologists have uncovered human burial sites dating from the middle Paleolithic period onward, and beginning with the upper Paleolithic period there is a growing richness and diversity to the goods found in these graves. There was also the practice of "second burials," meaning that the bodies were cremated and the skulls subsequently buried in a ritual way. The Neolithic period bears witness to megalithic graves composed of huge boulders, but we do not know whether these hero-like burials indicated the emergence of an ancestor cult. Middle Paleolithic burial sites reveal evidence of sacrifices, suggesting offerings to the dead. In the Neolithic period alone do we find signs of human sacrifice.

When it comes to pictorial expression such as cave paintings or engravings on bones, the primary subjects are animals. Human beings are rarely depicted, and when so, they are often endowed with animal attributes such as bird-like features. Some paintings of animals include piercing their bodies, perhaps indicating magic for hunting. Statuettes depicting the male body are uncommon, but there is an abundance of

---

1. Mircea Eliade, *A History of Religious Ideas*, vol. 1: *From the Stone Age to Eleusinian Mysteries*, trans. Willard R. Trask (Chicago: University of Chicago Press, 1978) 8.

female statuettes related to fertility. In fact, goddess worship seems to be prevalent in ancient tribal cults. Judging from archaeological finds, we can safely say that "the religion of Old Europe was polytheistic and dominated by female deities. The primary goddess inherited from the Paleolithic [Era] was the Great Goddess, whose functions included the gift of life and increase of material goods, death-wielding and decrease, and regeneration. She was the absolute ruler of human, animal, and plant-life, and the controller of lunar cycles and seasons. As giver of all, death wielder, and regeneratrix, she is one and the same goddess in spite of the multiplicity of forms in which she manifests herself."[2] The worship of such a supreme deity at a very early stage in human religious development appears inconsistent with the notion of a pre-deistic worldview where personal gods or demons were still unknown and only the actions of sacred powers existed, expressed through concepts of *mana* and *taboo* and accessed through totems, holy objects, and magic rites.[3] This fairly sophisticated outlook of human destiny led Malinowski, not without justification, to regard wizards and witches as specialists who from earliest time onward handled the art of magic, and to claim simultaneously that the sphere of religion had always been accessible to everyone.[4]

We should also not forget that pre-historic religion did not suddenly die out but continues today in the tribal religions of Africa, Asia, or certain parts of the Americas. Though often suppressed by official monotheistic religions, features of these pre-historic religions live on, even if only in folklore and fairy tales. The Great Goddess can appear as the fate involved with childbirth that foretells the length of life, or she takes the guise of the White Lady who represents death. Folklore and fairy tales serve as the corporate memory of ancient times, though now these goddesses are often demoted to mere witches or fairies. But there is another more immediate link with the past, especially when we look at sacred sites. Pagan temples in ancient Rome were converted to Christian churches, and monasteries or pilgrimage churches throughout Central Europe stand on the foundations of pre-historic sanctuaries or

---

2. So declares Marija Gimbutas, in the insightful article "Prehistoric Religions: Old Europe," in *The Encyclopedia of Religion*, 11:511. We should note here that the Americas were not yet populated by humans at this time.

3. Contrary to Paul Radin, *Primitive Religion: Its Nature and Origin* (New York: Dover, 1957) 300–302.

4. Malinowski, *Magic, Science and Religion*, 88–89.

holy sites situated by rivers or exposed hills. Jerusalem also comes to mind: the first and the second temple replaced a pagan Jebusite shrine, only to have the Muslim Dome of the Rock built atop their foundations, in turn. The story of King David purchasing the thrashing floor of the Jebusite Araunah (2 Sam 24:21) to build an altar emphasizes that this was a legitimate place for Israelite devotion.[5] Similarly, some Muslims today firmly contend that there are no Jewish or Israelite artifacts to be found on the Temple Mount. The name of the venerated deity may change, but the location remains the same. If there is a continuity of the people, ethnic or otherwise, some traces of the earlier cults may find their way into subsequent incarnations. This shows that, more than a bond of folklore and fairy tales, there is unbroken continuity in religion itself from the pre-historic to the present.

It is difficult to prove the frequent claim that pre-historic religion and present tribal religions are truly primitive, be it in their cosmology or in their perception of human destiny. It is also difficult, if not outright impossible, to show a strict development common to these earliest forms of religious expression. And it is just as unwarranted to affirm that religion emerged specifically out of magic as it is to claim that "magic very definitely preceded religion."[6] We have a similar dilemma concerning the origin of pre-historic "monotheism." High gods emerge in an amazing manifoldness in pre-historic and tribal religions as creators, cultural heroes, great goddesses, sky gods, and lords of the animals. One may rightfully conclude that these deities represent "the highest form that abstract thinking assumed among any aboriginal peoples."[7] But it

---

5. Cf. Volkmar Fritz, "Tempel II," in *TRE*, 33:48, who emphasizes this point.

6. It is unclear why Paul Radin, *Primitive Religion*, 75, asserts on the one hand that magic very definitely preceded religion, while rejecting on the other hand the idea that "religion grew specifically out of magic." Both are so closely intertwined that it is next to impossible to prove either a genetic or a historical priority.

7. Ibid., 266. We agree with Radin that religion cannot be understood apart from life and from the vicissitudes of the economic order in which it is so intimately embedded. Yet we wonder whether Radin's approach does justice to the religions of the "primitives." Radin is still tempted to relegate "primitive" religion to an archaic phenomenon of the past. The question here is of eminent importance, whether certain cultures and societies allow only for certain religious phenomena or whether religious phenomena might in part be responsible for a specific development of cultures and societies. If the latter is true as, for instance, Max Weber on a sociological level and, to some extent, E. E. Evans-Pritchard, *Theories of Primitive Religion* (Oxford: Clarendon Press, 1965) 112, on a religious anthropological level assert, then religious phenomena may also in part

is erroneous to perceive high gods as developments of the spirits and "souls" of animism and polydemonism, or to see in them the influence of higher religions. Animism, polydemonism, polytheism, and the manipulation of magic are not threatened by the appearance of high gods; this is apparent in monotheistic religions where many of these features still exist in one way or other, especially among the adherents, even if such presence is not officially condoned. It seems that all the concepts present in pre-historic and tribal religions—high gods, mana, taboo, magic, animism, polydemonism, and even polytheism—gradually led to, and to some extent already represented, a personal understanding of God as the governor of human existence and of the world around us.

It is also fairly safe to maintain that no religion prior to 800–500 BCE was more than a tribal religion. Beginning with this era, which the German philosopher Karl Jaspers (1883–1969) called the pivotal age of history, we can trace the emergence of universal religions that extend beyond their original tribal confinements. It is hardly mere coincidence that within this barely three-hundred-year period a Deutero-Isaiah, a Buddha, a Lao-tsu, a Zoroaster, and even a Homer and Plato stimulated the spiritual life of humanity. It was during this epoch that modern humanity emerged, having felt a solidarity in the basic understanding of its ultimate concerns that made it break through the tribal barriers.

Polytheistic Religions

Polytheistic religions, meaning the worship of several or many gods, seem to provide a transitional link between tribal religions and monotheism. In the history of Latin America, Africa, Papua New Guinea, and many other places where tribal religions have rapidly been supplanted by the Christian faith, this transition came too abruptly. New religions such as cargo cult and voodoo emerged, and messianic pretenders with a clearly polytheistic persuasion arose.[8] Yet the concept of "polytheism",

---

"transcend" the cultures and societies in which they appear. Therefore Mircea Eliade is right when he mentions that, whatever their contribution to the advance of science and technology might have been, the real genius of the "primitives" was not expressed on this level. "Their creativity was expressed almost exclusively on the religious plane." Mircea Eliade, "On Understanding Primitive Religions," in *Glaube, Geist, Geschichte: Festschrift für Ernst Benz zum 60. Geburtstage am 17. November 1967*, ed. Gerhard Müller and Winfried Zeller (Leiden: Brill, 1967) 504.

8. For a good survey of the African scene, cf. Marie-Louise Martin, *The Biblical*

per se, arose out of the Christian tradition as a term originally used to denigrate pagan religions. For instance, Origen (185–254) talked about "atheistic polytheism" or polytheistic atheism.[9] Nowadays polytheism is often considered as a step in religious development either toward monotheism or as a degeneration thereof. Yet polytheism remains a fully independent entity, neither an erosion of monotheism nor a religious stepping-stone on the way to monotheism.

Polytheistic religions exist in their own right and can be very different from each other, as, for instance, Greek polytheism is distinct from the Mayan religion in Meso-America. But most of them share a core of common characteristic. While we may assume that there were polytheistic features in pre-historical religions, we encounter polytheism primarily "in more advanced cultures."[10] These cultures show an increased division of labor, social stratification, and political structures. In the past polytheism flourished in the Greek city states, in the Mesopotamian kingdoms and empires of Sumeria, Assyria, and Babylonia, in Egypt, and also in Meso-America and Peru, not to mention India.

Diversified human activities led to a more diversified and discrete understanding of the powers surrounding humanity. There is a change from a more dynamistic and demonistic understanding of transcendent powers to a more anthropomorphic one. Human beings apparently began to distinguish more clearly between the area of the power's responsibility and the power itself. In Greek religion, in Shamanic religion, and to some extent even in the Israelite religion, we detect a polydemonistic background with a plurality of object-residing powers and a subsequent emergence of more detached powers.

As soon as these powers were understood to be removed enough from the traditional empowered objects, they were clothed in anthropomorphic gowns. In Greek antiquity, for example, Xenophanes (ca. 580–ca. 490 BCE) remarked that humanity pictures its gods according to its own likeness. Consequently, he reprimanded Homer and Hesiod

---

Concept of Messianism and Messianism in Southern Africa (Morija, Basutoland: Morija Sesuto, 1964) esp. 158–60. Cf. also G. C. Oosthuizen, "The Task of Africa's Traditional Religion in the Church's Dilemma in South Africa," in Jacob K. Olupona, ed., *African Spirituality. Forms, Meanings and Expressions* (New York: Herder & Herder, 2000) 278, who states that there are 6,000 African Independent Churches, implying that European Church structures do not serve the needs of the Africans.

9. Origen, *Against Celsus* (III, 73) in *ANF* 4:493.
10. Zwi Werblowsky, "Polytheism," in *The Encyclopedia of Religion*, 11:436.

for patterning the gods too much according to human weaknesses.[11] Nevertheless, there is a big difference between these gods and human beings, because the gods are immortal. While humanity is considered to have the potential to attain divinity, as we see with the Roman emperors, human beings and gods are not identical. Gods can assume human shape, as in the Hindu concept of avatars, or they can exist in human manifestations. But they can always slip back into their godhead and therefore sometimes fool humans as to their real identity. And yet humans and gods are also related, as Hesiod tells us when he wrote that "the gods and mortal men sprang from one source."[12] Yet another Greek poet, Pindar (522/518–after 446 BCE), set the record straight when he claimed: "One is the race of men, one is the race of gods, and from one mother do we both derive our breath; yet a power that is wholly sundered parteth us: in that the one is naught, while for the other the brazen heaven endureth as an abode unshaken for evermore."[13] As with humanity, gods also have their origins and their history. For instance, in contrast to the biblical God, a history-making God as opposed to these gods of history, the Greek gods have their family relations, love affairs, and offspring.

The emergence of the godheads' distinct anthropomorphic features went hand in hand with their increasing specialization. This can best be observed in Roman religion, where many gods were characterized by special adjectives, such as Jupiter, the thrower of thunder, or Fortuna, the goddess of luck. The gods assume a more functional role, similar to that of the saints in Roman Catholicism, where the function of one saint can differ from one region to another. The multitude of gods was often believed to operate under one godhead, such as the Greek Olympic gods under Zeus, or the later Roman gods under Jupiter, the god of the

11. Xenophanes of Colophon (21:16, 11, and 12) says: 16. "Aethiopians have gods with snub noses and black hair, Thracians have gods with grey eyes and red hair" . . . 11. "Both Homer and Hesiod have attributed to the gods all things that are shameful and a reproach to mankind: theft, adultery, and mutual deception." 12. "They have narrated every possible wicked story of the gods: theft, adultery, and mutual deception." Cf. Kathleen Freeman, *Ancilla to the Pre-Socratic Philosophers: A Complete Translation of the Fragments in Diels, "Fragmente der Vorsokratiker"* (Oxford: Blackwell, 1956) 22.

12. Hesiod, *Works and Days* (108) ed. T. A. Sinclair (Hildesheim: Georg Olms, 1966) 15, cf. also the comments by Sinclair.

13. Pindar, *Nemean Odes* (6:1–5) in *The Odes of Pindar Including the Principal Fragments*, intro. and trans. John Sandys (Cambridge: Harvard University Press, 1961) 369.

Emperor. Sometimes the cooperation of this polytheistic high god with specialized gods resembles a monarchic or a city-type of government.

As we have seen from the fate of the Greek philosopher Socrates and that of the early Christians, this kind of "monotheistic" polytheism was highly exclusive. If one doubted or rejected the legitimacy of the pantheon venerated by a certain group of people, the group often counteracted with persecution or even capital punishment. This shows us that polytheism already portrayed the factor of exclusiveness. However, this did not introduce a static feature into polytheistic religions. Characteristics of one god could easily be merged with those of another god, and even new gods could be introduced. The Roman Jupiter, for instance, could be identified with the Greek Zeus, or the Roman Minerva with the Greek Athena, and the Persian fertility goddess Magna Mater Cybele could make her successful debut on the imperial Roman religious scene of without her adherents facing any problems.

Yet, paradoxically, polytheism can also become monotheistic without ceasing to be polytheistic, as the German Egyptologist Siegfried Morenz (1914–1970) tells us. For instance, in Egyptian mythology "Amon, the primordial god, is said to be 'the only One who made himself into millions.' For in this case the unity of the primordial god is nevertheless preserved by the fact that the hymnist praises the one God even though he has developed to the point of infinite multiplicity."[14] Here we might also recall Amenophis IV, Akhnaton (ruled as king 1353–1336 BCE), who left no place for the countless deities in the Egyptian pantheon but decreed that "the person of the sun-god alone was deemed a worthy object of religious belief." Besides these monotheistic trends in a clearly polytheistic religion, Morenz also points to "Egyptian trinities ... whereby the gods were created out of the primordial god at the decisive initial moment, and so formulating a 'trinity of becoming', comprising the primordial One and the first pair of gods so begotten."[15] For Morenz this does not indicate that there was an evolution toward monotheism in the Egyptian religion, rather, this single divine unity "was seen as that primordial 'power' which existed before the gods and which later took

---

14. Siegfried Morenz, *Egyptian Religion,* trans. Ann E. Keep (London: Methuen, 1973) 146, for this and the following quote.

15. Ibid., 145.

individual shape."¹⁶ This means that the various gods were seen as manifestations of what is ultimately one divine principle.

This would also coincide with the monist or non-dualist doctrines, or with Mahayana Buddhism, where there is no god or divine being, just emptiness, nothingness, and Nirvana. Yet "all monistic—even non-theistic—views on the higher and more sophisticated doctrinal levels notwithstanding, a *de facto* functional polytheism can continue to exist among the masses of devout believers."¹⁷ This is not only true for Hindus or the ancient Egyptians who overcame Akhnaton's monotheism, but also for "the ordinary Buddhist (and even the Buddhist monk) . . . [who relate] to the many Buddhas and *boddhisattvas* that in fact constitute the Buddhist pantheon like a polytheist to his gods." This means that ordinary people need this kind of access to the ultimate through more accessible anthropomorphic embodiments, similar to the way many devout Roman Catholics prefer the cult of the saints to approach the one God for their everyday needs.

When we come closer to our own time, polytheism no longer seems to be compatible with the enterprising spirit of modern humanity. It might be tempting to point to "founders" of world religions such as Moses, Buddha, Jesus, Mohammed, and Zoroaster, and claim that it was in fact their passionate proclamation of the power of one god who brooks no rivals that officially marked monotheism's emergence. But we must also remember the contrary evidence of Homer and Hesiod, who decisively formed Greek polytheism rather than a monotheistic religion. Although monotheism presupposes a prior polytheism, the latter does not always evolve into the former. For instance, after the advent of Moses, there was a decidedly monotheistic tendency in Israel's official religion. However, Israel's neighbors, evidently untouched by this inclination, continued to favor their specific blend of polytheism.

When we consider the cultural and technological drive exhibited by those nations most clearly influenced by monotheism, we wonder whether we can deny that we are confronted with a progress caused by spiritual factors. Admittedly, Greek and Roman polytheism led to a very high level of culture, too. But the intrinsic mood demonstrated by Greek and Roman philosophy was not one of optimism but of pessimism.

---

16. Morenz, *Egyptian Religion*, 150.

17. Werblowsky, "Polytheism," in *The Encyclopedia of Religion*, 11:439, for this and the following quote.

Again we must refer to Xenophanes, who had already discovered that the Greek gods looked much like deified men and that these gods were subject to the destiny of the world.[18] Stoic heroism best describes the earth-denying yet earth-bound fate of humanity. The only continuity is provided by the eternal recurrence of the constant, by the ever-moving celestial spheres. But there could never be anything new under the sun, only reconfigurations of already existing facts. Affirming the identity of creator, sustainer, and savior, monotheism can be much more progressive, since God not only provided the beginning, but also sustains the present and urges humanity toward the future goal.

It is no surprise that in many regions of the world polytheism was superseded by monotheism, be it of the Christian or the Muslim kind. This did not mean that the host of deities were totally abolished. While they no longer existed according to orthodox teaching, they often recurred in subservient functions as saints. Monotheism, too, as Israelite history shows, emerged only gradually. There was first *monolatry*, meaning the exclusive worship of only one god without denying the existence of others. Archeological findings such as the Astarte figurines in Palestine or replicas of the Sacred Bull bear witness to this fact. The people's hesitance to abolish these gods completely proved to be the continuous lament of the great prophets of Israel, such as Amos or Micah. These other gods ultimately lost out, but it took centuries to happen. What was the reason for the eventual acceptance of monotheism?

Monotheistic Religions

Monotheism, the faith that there is only one god, is usually associated with the Jewish, Christian, and Islamic religions. As we have seen, however, monotheistic tendencies have long been present in human religious history. While the theory of an original monotheism holds little credence, "research in recent years has it made clear that a great many primal or archaic peoples have conceptions of a high god who is creator of the world, has supreme authority over other gods and spirits, and pre-

---

18. Xenophanes (21:13) in Kathleen Freeman, *Ancilla to the Pre-Socratic Philosophers*, 22. Xenophanes (22:23 and 24) himself suggests abandoning the idea of gods and believing in just one God who sets everything in motion and who is "not at all like mortals in body or in mind." However, his notion does not yet imply monotheism. Cf. Kathleen Freeman, *The Pre-Socratic Philosophers: A Companion to Diels*, "Fragmente der Vorsokratiker" (Oxford: Blackwell, 1956) 97–99.

sides over human morality."[19] We have noted that Plato stressed the unity of the good and identified it with a god understood to be perfectly good, changeless, and the maker of the best possible world. Aristotle, too, followed him in that idea with the concept of a prime unmoved mover. In Egyptian religion, too, we have noticed the emphasis on Amenophis IV's proclamation of the sun disk, Aton, as the only god that exists, naming himself Akhnaton, the one devoted to Aton. Yet this kind of "monotheism" was of short duration, since after the death of Amenophis IV the priests again reverted to the earlier plurality of gods.

Hinduism, too, is characterized by a monistic tendency in its Advita or non-dualistic thought, where Brahman is the unifying divine principle of everything. Also Krishna as the Avatar, i.e., the "incarnation," of Vishnu can be put forth as the supreme god, declaring that "no other higher thing whatsoever exists."[20] Yet even with this official recognition of the one highest being, people still worship their particularistic gods. Even Buddhism can be regarded as an essential monism. In Amida Buddhism or Pure Land Buddhism, Amida Buddha or the Buddha of love is considered supreme and is worshipped exclusively; or, in Hinayana Buddhism, everything is focused on Nirvana as the unifying goal of everything. We should also think of Zoroastrianism, a religion that had considerable impact on exilic Judaism. It advocated only one god, Ahura Mazda, who created only good things and is good, just, and moral. Zoroastrianism wanted to overcome the then-prevalent polytheism of its environment. But there remained a dualism of Spenta Mainyu, the good spirit, and Angra Mainyu, his evil counterpart, destined to struggle with each other throughout history until the good finally prevails.

Three religions are generally held to fully express monotheism: Judaism, Christianity, and Islam. Whereas Christianity emerged from Judaism, Islam arose against the background of the polytheism of the ancient Near East and assimilated facets of both Judaism and Christianity. Even in the religion of Israel, we find no strict monotheism, per se; only the ever clearer realization that there is one true God, Yahweh. The other gods do not amount to much. For a long time the people of Israel still worshipped in the high places and had their own idols (cf. Micah 1:5, 7).

19. So Theodore M. Ludwig, "Monotheism," in *The Encyclopedia of Religion*, 10:69.

20. *The Bhagavad Gita* (7.7) trans. and interpreted Franklin Edgerton (New York: Harper, 1964) 38.

Yet later Judaism reveals an unqualified monotheism, based on the Decalogue where the first commandment reads: "I am the Lord your God, who brought you out of the land of Egypt, out of the house of slavery; you shall have no other gods before me" (Exod 20:2f.). The other foundation of Israelite monotheism is the Shema Israel, the "Hear, O Israel: The Lord is our God, the Lord alone" (Deut 6:4). With this affirmation "all other forms of polytheism are excluded. There is only *one* God and no other."[21]

While the Canaanite fertility god Baal or the female fertility goddess Asherah could be divided into several local gods or goddesses (Judg 3:7), the God of Israel could not be divided. God was not a local god who was confined to a certain abode, not even to Jerusalem, as Ezekiel witnessed when "the God of Israel" appeared among the exiles "by the river Chebar" (Ezek 10:20). The Israelites therefore were admonished: "Hear, O Israel: The Lord is our God, the Lord alone. You shall love the Lord your God with all your heart, and with all your soul, and with all your might" (Deut 6:4ff.). The Shema Israel ("Hear, O Israel") is the basic confession of the Jews, as early Jewish historian Flavius Josephus (37/38–ca. 100 CE) attests: "Let everyone commemorate before God the benefits which he bestowed upon them at their deliverance out of the land of Egypt, and this twice every day, both when the day begins and when the hour of sleep comes on."[22] The Shema Israel, with other texts, is also written on parchment and enclosed in the mezuah, a small metal cylinder attached to the right doorpost of Jewish homes. These texts are also enclosed in the phylacteries or *tefillin*, bound on the forehead and on the left arm at hours of prayer. It is not only the memory of what God has done for the Israelites that makes this creed so important for Judaism. The unity of the Godhead as creator, preserver, and redeemer distinguishes God from the created. In the conclusion of his treatise on the *Creation of the World*, the Jewish philosopher Philo of Alexandria (d. ca. 45 CE) says that Moses (i.e., the Pentateuch) taught us that

> the Deity has a real being and existence; . . . God is one; . . . the world was created; . . . the world also which was thus created is

---

21. So Esther Starobinski-Safran, "Monotheismus III—Judentum," in *TRE*, 23:249.

22. Josephus, *Jewish Antiquities* (IV.212) in *The New Complete Works of Josephus*, trans. William Whiston, commentary Paul L. Maier (Grand Rapids: Kregel, 1999) 156.

one, since also the Creator is one; . . . God exerts his providence for the benefit of the world.[23]

Once the plurality of holy powers and beings was understood to be absorbed into only one God, it facilitated the worship of only one God, for none of the gods or holy powers could claim to be neglected. Moreover, it opened the possibility of a thoroughgoing desacralization of the world, since the world was considered as God's residence, at most. It certainly could not be equated with his being. The world was understood as created by God and no longer experienced as something sacred in its own right. People could now dare to subdue, i.e., exercise stewardship over, the earth and all the powers contained therein. The one God is the divine originator and grantor of all facets of life. This meant that the God who provides this life also supervises its present course and establishes its final goal. Nothing equated with change is divine, and therefore God too cannot be associated with transitoriness. God can sovereignly decree the movement of history toward a final goal envisioned by God. History is now freed from the cyclic pessimism prevalent in the polytheistic religions of Greece and India, a pessimism engendered by the great wheel of existence or the seasonal rhythm of birth and decay. History is endowed with divinely sanctioned linear progressiveness. In other words, the monotheism ensuing from the cradle of Israelite religion enables history to have a definite starting-point, a definite course, and a definite goal. But monotheism has no built-in mechanism that would necessarily lead to an upward slanting progression in which humanity plays a dominant role. If the one God assumes too much the position of an all-determining power through which each facet of human life is ruled, and if God refuses to endow human activities with responsible freedom, then monotheism can also lead to human passivity.

Its global presence and significance notwithstanding, Judaism has basically remained an ethnic religion. However, there are two other strands of monotheism, Islam and Christianity, which transcended their ethnic origin and have become world religions in the true sense of the word. To these two, we would like to add another religion, Buddhism. It is usually not considered monotheistic but monistic, meaning that it explains the whole world from one ultimate principle. Yet Buddhism in its various facets is a world religion, and, similar to the other two

23. Philo, *On the Creation of the World* (61) in Philo Judaeus, *The Essential Philo*, ed. Nahum N. Glatzer (New York: Schocken, 1971) 40.

monotheistic religions, it provides a unified perspective on human life, its destiny, and the surrounding natural world.[24] Though we do not want to present an extensive portrait of these three religious traditions, we would like to elucidate at least their most significant monotheistic or monistic features, especially with regard to how they evoke a human response to their religious precepts or the commands of the deity. With regard to Christianity, it should be obvious that it cannot be presented without considering its Judaic and Israelite roots.

Submission (to God): Islam

From the Arabic root *slm*, meaning "to be in peace, to be an integral whole," comes *islam*, meaning "to surrender to God's law and thus to be an integral whole," and *muslim*, "a person who so surrenders."[25] These definitions show us in a nutshell the religious conviction of Islam: if one wants to maintain order and wholeness, one must accept God's law. While nature obeys God's law automatically, humanity ought to obey it by choice. It is therefore no surprise that in the *Qur'an*, the holy book of the Muslims, Islam is described as "the creational law of God according to which He created man with the quality of choosing right or wrong."[26]

Historically speaking, Islam originated in the early seventh century on the Arabian peninsula in what is now Saudi Arabia, assimilating both Arab and Judeo-Christian elements.[27] But the *Qur'an* states in Sura 4: "O believers, believe in God and His Messenger and the Book He has revealed to His Apostle, and the Books revealed before."[28] The message of Islam is contained in the *Qur'an* which God recited to his messen-

---

24. Huston Smith, *Forgotten Truth: The Common Vision of the World's Religions* (San Francisco: Harper SanFrancisco, 1992) 55, alerts us that in Buddhism nirvana is "the Infinite which is all-inclusive."

25. Fazlur Rahman, "Islam: An Overview," in *The Encyclopedia of Religion*, 7:303.

26. *Qur'an* 30:30 (cited according to *Al-Qur'an. A Contemporary Translation*, trans. Ahmed Ali [Princeto, NJ: Princeton University Press, 1994]).

27. Jewish and Christian presence was quite significant in this area and Mohammed was well aware of it. Even his title "Mohammed," meaning "the one to be highly praised" was originally a Christian messianic attribute. Cf. Karl-Heinz Ohlig, "Wir müssen uns wehren—Appell für eine neue Islamwissenschaft," in *Homiletisch-Liturgisches Korrespondenzblatt—Neue Folge*, 24:173, and the enlightening article by Anton Schall, "Islam I," in *TRE* 16:316f.

28. *Qur'an* 4:136.

ger. God did not reveal himself, but revealed a book to Mohammed (ca. 569–632 CE), who is not just a prophet like Isaiah or Amos, but *the* prophet and thereby "the seal of the prophets." The God portrayed in the *Qur'an* is a transcendent, all-powerful God who is also merciful. No creature can share in God's divinity. Similarly to Gen 1, we hear in the *Qur'an* concerning God's creative power: "When He wills a thing He has only to say: 'Be!' and it is."[29] Since whatever God creates has an orderly nature, humanity must also follow that order. Even miracles are not in high esteem, since they would interrupt the orderly fashion of things. Therefore the *Qur'an* talks about "showing one's deeds," since the last judgment will focus upon individual performance.[30] There is also a judgment in history which comes upon nations and communities on the basis of their total performance, because "those of Our creatures who are good will in the end rule the earth."[31]

Since Mohammed declared: "I believe in whatever Scripture God has revealed,"[32] Muslims cannot claim salvational exclusivity, but "whoever believes in God and the Last Day, and whosoever does right, shall have his reward with his Lord, and will neither have fear nor regret."[33] Salvation can also come through other "book religions." Consequently, Jews and Christians were recognized as "people of the Book," and so were Zoroastrians, Hindus, and Buddhists. But they are not equal to Muslims. They had to pay a tax for not being Muslims and Muslims are prohibited from having social exchange or intermarriage with these groups unless the "unbeliever" becomes a Muslim, or, in the case of non-Muslim women, their children become Muslims. That the Muslims stay in the right religion is safeguarded through the law of apostasy. While not spelled out in the *Qur'an*, this law states: "That a Muslim apostate should be given three chances to repent and in the case of nonrepentance must be executed."[34] While a non-Muslim can become a Muslim, since this is the only true religion, a Muslim is not allowed to fall away from the right faith. Since non-Muslims are inferior, a non-Muslim is also forbidden from bringing evidence against a Muslim in a criminal

---

29. *Qur'an* 36:82.
30. *Qur'an* 99:6–8.
31. *Qur'an* 21:105.
32. *Qur'an* 42:15.
33. *Qur'an* 2:62.
34. Rahman, "Islam: An Overview," 7:321.

case. Though this law is still adhered too in most countries in which Muslims enjoy the majority, such as Egypt or Pakistan, it is neither sanctioned by the *Qur'an* nor by the *Sunnah* (arab. "custom"), a collection of sayings and ways of conduct of Mohammed, collected later in the ninth century and compiled as the *Hadith* ("communication") which has normative value. These later developments of the Muslim law, however, leave no doubt that if one is a Muslim, meaning one who follows God's (Allah's) law as spelled out in the *Qur'an* and in subsequent traditions, such a person can do no wrong, because that person follows God and his dictates. Even the state should ideally foster the Islamic law, because this way the fulfillment of God's will is assured.

The call for the introduction of the *Shari'a*, the Islamic legal code, in countries with a clear Muslim majority is only consequential according to the self-understanding of this religion. In the twentieth century in many countries with a Muslim majority, perhaps as a consequence of the colonial experience, Muslim and non-Muslim enjoyed nearly equal individual rights; since the 1980s, however, the application of the *Shari'a* was given increased consideration. In a constitutional amendment of 1980 in Egypt, for instance, we read in article 2: "The Islamic Shari'a is the main source of legislation."[35] Though in Egypt this change largely remained only on the books, continuous Islamistic pressure could lead to an Islamic codification of the law.

Ideally, the whole life of the Muslim is determined by the *Shari'a* (the way) or the body of regulations which make up Islamic religious law. It contains all the prescriptions of Allah which pertain to human actions, and it stands so high in rank that it has been said that "Allah did not reveal himself but he mediated only his law."[36] Early Islam did not even distinguish between law and religion. Therefore theology does not dominate Islamic scholarship, but rather "the study and explication of the Law."[37] Since all aspects of life fall under the religious sphere, the *Shari'a* contains prescriptions concerning religious and cultic duties as well as

---

35. As quoted in Bernard Botiveau, "The Law of the Nation-State and the Status of non-Muslims in Egypt and Syria," in *Christian Communities in the Arab Middle East: The Challenge of the Future*, ed. Andrea Pacini (Oxford: Clarendon, 1998) 123 n. 28.

36. Annemarie Schimmel, "Der Islam," in Friedrich Heiler, *Die Religionen der Menschheit in Vergangenheit und Gegenwart* (Stuttgart: Reclam, 1959) 819.

37. John Alden Williams, *Islam* (New York: George Braziller, 1961) 92.

juridical and political rules. All actions are divided into five categories:[38] obligatory, not obligatory but recommended, neutral or permitted, not forbidden but reprehensible, and forbidden. For instance: it is obligatory to wash oneself before prayer; it is recommended to start with the right side; it is permitted that warm or cold water be used; and it is forbidden that someone touches the water beforehand. Furthermore, the actions are evaluated according to their validity or invalidity. Of course, most of these laws are already contained in the *Qur'an* (meaning "recital"), the sacred book of Islam.

There are two main types of texts in the *Qur'an*: those which are clear and definite and those which could have more than one meaning. The texts which are clear and definite cover basic beliefs, such as belief in Allah and the last day. They also contain information concerning the origin of the law. When it comes to these texts, there is no freedom of interpretation. As to the texts which could have more than one meaning, they "are concerned with subsidiary aspects of Islam, but not its fundamentals, and have given rise to a plurality of Muslim theories and attitudes which are more or less personal points of view and are far from being obligatory."[39] Here clear reasoning is required. Since reasoning can go in different ways, there arose a diversity of religious and civil practice among Muslim believers.[40] Yet the *Qur'an* remains the inviolable foundation of faith and the code of legislation. Since there are items contained in the *Qur'an* that can have more than one meaning, we also have to consider the *Sunnah* or custom that declares "the legislation given by the Prophet on matters not specifically detailed in the *Qur'an*, and traditions based on the actions and utterances of Muhammad as a human being."[41] The value of the *Sunnah* lies in the fact that it expounds specific aspects of the general principles of the *Qur'an*, either by example of action or by adding certain ceremonies not expressly described in the *Qur'an*. For

---

38. Cf. for the following "Shariah," in Cyril Glassé, intro. Huston Smith, *The Concise Encyclopedia of Islam* (San Francisco: Harper SanFrancisco, 1991) 361.

39. Cf. for the following Mahmud Shaltout, "Islamic Beliefs and Code of Laws," in *Islam—The Straight Path. Islam Interpreted by Muslims*, ed. Kenneth W. Morgan (New York: Ronald, 1958) 88.

40. Cf. Mohammad Hashim Kamali, "Law and Society: The Interplay of Revelation and Reason in the Shariah," in John L. Esposito, ed., *The Oxford History of Islam* (Oxford: Oxford University Press, 1999) 110, for more information.

41. Shaltout, "Islamic Beliefs," 134.

instance, the *Qur'an* enjoins prayer, but the *Sunnah* tells how prayer is to be performed.

Then there is the *Hadith*, the "account" or "report" that relates the deeds and utterances of the Prophet as reported by his companions. But not everything contained in the *Hadith* actually goes back to Mohammed; often its various strands were simply developed in order to support the traditions of various groups within Islam. It serves as a basis of law within Islamic jurisprudence. Through critical studies of the *Hadith*, one is able to establish and maintain the historical continuity between the Prophet's lifetime and the present by concluding what Mohammed "might have said had he been asked."[42] Finally, there is discretion employed in the communal consultations concerning issues not specifically covered in the *Qur'an* and the *Sunnah*, and there is the private discretion of the individual to decide through independent thinking. Both kinds of discretion are "not binding for anyone" except the individual(s) who use(s) them.[43]

Though the numerous legal codes contained in the *Shari'a* are based on the idea that Allah speaks and commands while the believer submits and obeys, obedience is not merely passive or servile. Muslim theologians assert that "Muslims conceive of their religion as a community which says 'Yes' to God and His world, and the joyful performance of the Law, in most areas of the Islamic world, is looked on as a positive religious value."[44] When we consider the creed, the first of the five pillars of Islam (the others being daily prayers, fasting, giving of alms, and the pilgrimage to Mecca), which is always contained in the first section of the law, we find not only the confession of Allah, of the last day, and of the resurrection, but also of Allah's predetermining will. This is a clear indication of how the tension between free will and determinism contained in the *Qur'an* itself has traditionally been resolved.[45] As Abu Hanifa (d. 767) says in his last will: "We confess that the predetermining of good and evil is all from Allah."[46] So we read in Sura 87.2f. of Allah,

---

42. So Williams, *Islam*, 88.

43. Shaltout, "Islamic Beliefs," 140.

44. Williams, *Islam*, 93.

45. For the discussion on free will and determinism, cf. L. Gardet, "Al-Kada' wa'l-Kadar" (i.e., the Decree of God) in *The Encyclopedia of Islam: New Edition*, 4:365–367.

46. *A Reader on Islam. Passages from Standard Arabic Writings Illustrative of the Beliefs and Practices of Muslims*, ed. Arthur Jeffrey (Gravenhage: Mouton, 1962) 343.

"Who creates and proportions, Who determines and directs." Allah determines all facets of human life. Hence it is impossible to render any actions in the world as profane: the important Judeo-Christian distinctions between church and state, between the ecclesiastical and worldly spheres, are absent from the Muslim vocabulary.[47]

One way of breaking out of this almost overbearing dominance of Allah over human life was found in Sufism. Having its roots in the more mystic strands of the *Qur'an,* this ecstatic movement gained supreme importance from the end of the ninth century onward by molding the attitude toward life in individual Muslims, especially those in rural areas. To some extent it symbolizes the victory of the common person "over the earthly mighty and the learned professors and scholars," representatives of the all-embracing law.[48] A sufi is a person whose heart is empty of attachment to anything other than Allah. Through submission to Allah comes faith and awareness of Allah.[49] Under Sufism common people managed to live in a world of ideas and emotions of their own construction. The movement received considerable criticism from orthodox Muslims because of its "need to submit to the authority of charismatic men who claimed a special relationship to Allah through ecstasy."[50] But deep mystical experiences of Allah remain rare in Islam, and its mystical and ecstatic elements made Sufism suspect of embracing outside influences such as Christian monasticism. Ultimately it provided

---

Some Muslims, however, object to a deterministic view of God. Syed Ameer Ali, *The Spirit of Islam: A History of the Evolution and Ideals of Islam. With a Life of the Prophet* (London: Chatto & Windus, 1964) 403, for instance, asserts that in contradiction to the stern fatalism of the pre-Islamite Arabs, the teachings of Islam advocate the idea of human volitional liberty. Yet in the light of the *Qur'an* itself, this assertion is difficult to maintain.

47. Cf. Shafik Ghorbal, "Ideas and Movements in Islamic History," in *Islam—The Straight Path,* 43.

48. Ghorbal, "Ideas and Movements," 66; cf. also Reynold Alleyne Nicholson, *Studies in Islamic Mysticism* (Cambridge: Cambridge University Press, 1967) 78, who rightly claims that the *wali,* or saint, bridges the chasm that the *Qur'an* and scholasticism have set between humanity "and an absolutely transcendent God."

49. Cf. the helpful Intro by Sheik Ragip Robert Frager al Jerrahi in *Essential Sufism,* James Fadiman and Robert Frager, eds. (San Francisco: Harper SanFrancisco, 1997) esp. 3–10.

50. Ron Greaves, *Aspects of Islam* (Washington, DC: Georgetown University Press, 2005) 133.

no actual stimulus for progressive mastery of the world, especially with its re-emphasis on conformity with the *Shari'a*.

Traditional Muslim education did not provide much hope for a creative intellectual movement. It consisted mainly of memorizing prescribed texts, especially the *Qur'an*, and studying the same material generation after generation.[51] But there were important Islamic achievements in the area of philosophy, mathematics, chemistry, and medicine.[52] It is interesting that, for instance, in the Ottoman or Turkish "Empire", many scholars among the ruling elite participated in orders that combined a relatively strict adherence to Islamic law with an active participation in Sufi brotherhoods as a way of emphasizing the importance of Islamic piety within society.[53] This means that one adhered to the law but was then allowed freedom for other pursuits. This is consistent with the Arab philosopher Ibn-Rushd (lat.: Averroes; 1126–1198), who made a tremendous impact on Christian theology. He developed a system of twofold truth, allowing him on the one hand to show conformity to Islamic traditionalism while on the other hand pursuing his philosophic insights unhindered. According to Ibn Rushd, "there is one truth for philosophers, which is philosophy, and another for the masses, which is religion."[54]

In the last few centuries, however, there has been a renewed emphasis on the progressive dynamism of the *Qur'an* teachings. Muhammad Ibn Abd al-Wahhab (1703–1792), for instance, returned to the *Qur'an* and the traditions of early Islam while revolting against the stifling results of a strict application of the *Shari'a*.[55] The movement engendered by him known as Wahhabism has been most influential in the Arab countries and in India during the last two centuries: it was instrumental in abolishing veneration of saints and of their tombs and restoring a strict adherence to the *Qur'an* and the *Sunnah* of the Prophet. These efforts almost completely wiped out Sufism and its veneration of saints on the Arab peninsula. Wahhabism is an Islamic renewal movement pressing

---

51. Ghorbal, "Ideas and Movements," 70–71.

52. Schimmel, "Der Islam," 840–41.

53. John Obert Voll, "Foundation for Renewal and Reform. Islamic Movements in the Eighteenth and Nineteenth Centuries," in Esposito, ed., *Oxford History of Islam*, 512.

54. "Ibn Rushd," in *Concise Encyclopedia of Islam*, 175.

55. For the following, cf. Greaves, *Aspects of Islam*, 198.

for the total Islamization of society. In the early nineteenth century, Wahhabism took over Medina (1805) and Mecca (1806), destroying all places that it considered heretical. "Wahhabi authors tend to describe the history of their movement in general, and with regard to the 20th century in particular, as an almost unremitting success story."[56] This demonstrates the attractiveness of a doctrinaire worldview. It shows its pernicious influence in the present anti-Western Jihadist movement that declares holy war against non-Muslims. For two centuries it has been Saudia Arabia's dominant faith. In its austere form it insists on a literal interpretation of the *Qur'an*, and it condemns all who do not practice its particular form of Islam as heathen and enemies. This radical intolerance can lead to violent Jihad, as in the case of Osama bin Laden.

Muhammad Ikbal (1876–1938), the spiritual father of Pakistan, deserves mention along these lines.[57] Rather than embracing a literalist intolerance, his approach was just the opposite. Being exposed to Western education in England and Germany, he recognized that dynamic Islamic thinking had been repressed for centuries by a strict dogmatism and covered over by pantheistic mysticism. Ikbal, in turn, advanced the idea that the *Qur'an* is a doctrine destined for further and higher development. Thus he understands humans as God's administrators in this world who are compelled to develop their personality in steady combat with the powers of evil and who will finally attain perfect personhood. Of course, we notice that this is not exactly *Qur'an* teaching. It contains a good sense of Western idealistic philosophy and also shows that Nietzsche's concept of the superman was not foreign to Ikbal. The person most responsible for establishing a modern Muslim country on the Indian subcontinent after Ikbal's death in 1938 was Pakistan's first governor-general (1947–1948), Mohammad Ali Jinnah (1876–1948). Yet Jinnah was not a very religious person, and he died before a constitution for Pakistan could be adopted. The 1956 and 1961 constitutions then mandated the creation of an Advisory Council of Islamic Ideology. When Fazlur Rahman, a member of that Council and the director of the Central Institute of Islamic research, questioned some of the contemporary beliefs and practices, he angered the traditionalists so much that he was forced to resign his position in 1968. Upon receiving death threats,

---

56. W. Ende, "Wahabiyya," in *Encyclopedia of Islam: New Edition*, 11:46.

57. Cf. for the following Annemarie Schimmel, "Ikbal, Muhammad," in *The Encyclopedia of Islam: New Edition*, 3:1058.

he and his family emigrated from Pakistan, and he served as Professor of Islamic thought from 1969–1988 at the University of Chicago.[58] In the following decades Pakistan moved away from its earlier modernist ideals and again appealed to more traditional Islamist views.

Which direction is Islam going? Is it becoming more focused on itself, thereby establishing itself as a religion which strictly regulates every facet of life? Or does it open itself up to self-critical reflection? A look at the more immediate past may provide some clues.

The mighty Ottoman Empire once controlled North Africa, Egypt, Mesopotamia, and large parts of the European Balkans, including the shores of the Black Sea, serving as a bulwark of Islam against Western Christendom. It disintegrated as a result of World War I (1914–1918), and from its remnants Mustafa Kemal Atatürk (1881–1938) founded modern Turkey as a secular state. It was thought that these drastic changes might also effect the end of Islam as a world religion. Especially in the last half century, however, Islam has made a remarkable comeback, not only in Africa but also in many other countries. It is now the second largest world religion, comprising more than one billion adherents. Even in the U.S. it made inroads, especially among those of the African-American community who felt mistreated by traditional Christianity. Some of these joined the ranks of the Black Muslims (The Nation of Islam), especially noted for their concern for the black prison population.

The Iranian Revolution against Shah Mohammed Reza Pahlavi's (1919–1980) policies of imposed Westernization occurred in 1979. Just ten years earlier, the revolutionary regime of Colonel Muammar al-Qaddafi (b. 1942) in Libya was established. There are mosques now in Hong Kong, Germany, and many other countries, often funded through the oil revenues of Saudi Arabia. Western ways of living are shunned, and many younger women again accept the veil, a custom that had declined just a generation ago. The call for Islamic *Jihad*, the holy war against the infidels, meaning non-Muslims, is declared in some quarters, and terrorism such as the September 11, 2001, attack under Osama bin Laden has ensued. Many factors contribute to these new fundamentalist or conservative tendencies. There is a rapidly increasing population among

---

58. Cf. Th. Emil Homerin, "The Modernization of Islam," in Jacob Neusner, ed., *Religious Foundations of Western Civilization. Judaism, Christianity, and Islam* (Nashville: Abingdon, 2006) 528f.

Muslims due to the notion that the production of numerous offspring is divinely sanctioned. Economic development cannot keep up with the mushrooming population, and the consequence is widespread unemployment, especially among younger people. This in turn breeds discontent, and it is easy to attribute the blame for the malaise to outside forces. The West, present in these regions through multi-nationals and the mass media, is especially perceived as a secular threat for Islam. Whatever truth there might be to this perception, the question must be asked of Islam: does it allow for enough freedom to overcome its intrinsic legalism? Can it provide an incentive for its believers to master their lives without resorting to fatalist extremism or easy scapegoats?

As Fazlur Rahman elaborates, at present "there exists a total vacuum of Islamic intellectualism and a proliferation of modern secular institutions." These are not integrated into the conservative social milieu and therefore do nothing to change the basic outlook of society.[59] The fact that Muslim modernist scholars have spent a large part of their teaching and writing careers in the West is more than mere coincidence: they have more freedom there to carry out their research and to express their opinions concerning Islam and Muslim societies. In Muslim nations, Islamic militants have targeted scholars like Fazlur Rahman who express modernist views and whom they deem to be apostates.

Another prominent victim of dogmatic extremism is Abu Zeid (b. 1943). In 1993, Nasr Hamed Abu Zeid, professor at the University of Cairo, was accused of committing apostasy and blasphemy in his scholarship on Qur'anic exegesis. His fault lay in claiming "that the Qur'an should be read and understood in terms of its historical context in seventh-century Arabia."[60] A militant group accused him of apostasy and even pressed for the annulment of his marriage on the premise that a Muslim woman cannot be married to an apostate. They also wanted him executed. Following a second death threat from an associate of Osama bin Laden, Abu Zeid and his wife fled to the Netherlands, where he teaches Islamic History at the University of Leiden.

---

59. Cf. Fazlur Rahman, "Islamic Modernism: Its Scope, Method, and Aleternatives," in Jacob Neusner, ed., *Religious Foundations of Western Civilization*, 548. In this essay he also outlines how intellectuals cope in today's conservative Islamic societies by either being silent, by double-speaking and double-writing, or by advocating reform through tradition.

60. Homerin, "Modernization of Islam," 570.

Whether freedom or repression will eventually win remains undecided. Yet there could be hope. As Fazlur Rahman steadfastly contends: we must candidly and without inhibitions discuss what Islam requires of Muslim believers today. "The entire body of the *Shari'a* must be subjected to fresh examination in the light of the Qur'anic evidence. A systematic and bold interpretation of the Qur'an must be undertaken."[61] Rahman goes on to emphasize that such an enterprise should not be a projection of subjective ideas, be they liberal or traditionalist, but it must follow a strict methodology. But are the fears of the results of such an endeavor too great on both sides of the fence?

The emphasis on Allah's prescripts certainly provides an ordered outlook on life and the world around us. Furthermore, it promotes a sense of community that is often missing in the individualistic West. But it can also lead to a lack of initiative or engender fatalistic extremism. If the emphasis, however, would shift from Allah's all-powerfulness to his infinite mercy, people might be more apt to respond to that mercy with actions of gratitude for the mercy they have received. Service need not be enslavement, but can lead instead to initiative, resourcefulness, and adaptation. It remains to be settled whether this option, also contained in the *Qur'an*, will gain the upper hand. Perhaps the invitation in the *Qur'an* "O People of the Book, let us come to an agreement on that which is common between us, that we worship no one but God,"[62] might be a good starting point for both Jews and Christians to join Muslims in the service of the one God. It could further mutual respect and cooperation and thereby advance the unity of humankind.[63]

Attaining Understanding: Buddhism

Since Buddhism is focused on attaining understanding, it may not be classified as a religion in the proper sense of the word. Yet we should remember the story of Philip and the Ethiopian in the Book of Acts. When Philip joined the court official of the Ethiopian queen Candace, Philip asked him: "Do you understand what you are reading?" (Acts 8:30) Understanding is essential if one does not want to follow precepts

---

61. Fazlur Rahman, "Islamic Modernism," 543.

62. Qur'an 3:64.

63. Cf. also Hans Schwarz, "Foreword," to Chellain Lawrence, *Jesus as Prophet in Christianity and Islam: A Model for Inter Faith Dialogue* (Delhi: ISPCK, 1997) xviiff.

blindly; yet Buddhism asks for more than mere intellectual understanding. The Sanskrit/Pali word *buddha* means "one who has awakened," and the Sanskrit/Pali term *buddhi* means "intelligence" and "understanding." This indicates that someone who has awakened from his or her existential slumber has come to understanding or attained insight. Therefore the term *buddha* is not the proper name of Buddha but denotes an individual who has attained this quality of insight. In India the designation *buddha* has had a wide circulation among various religious traditions. It was bestowed as a title on those who had attained transforming and liberating insight into the nature of reality. There have been many buddhas of different times and places, as Buddhist literature attests.

The so-called "historical Buddha lived sometime during the period from the sixth through the fourth centuries" BCE.[64] We remember that this was an especially fertile time for religion. "The future Buddha was born as a princeling, named Siddhattha (Sanskrit: Siddhartha) in the Gotama clan among a people known as the Sakkas, who dwelled near the present-day border of India and Nepal."[65] He renounced his royal upbringing and his family life, studied with various spiritual teachers, and first practiced asceticism. He subsequently rejected an ascetic lifestyle in favor of moderation. Finally he achieved spiritual insight after a night of spiritual struggle beneath a tree at a place now known as Bodhgaya. He proclaimed his newly attained insights to a small group of disciples in an animal park near Benares and spent the rest of his life giving spiritual instruction to his ever-growing body of disciples and to the public, as well. When he died at age eighty-one, he already had a large following which had become a well-organized community, the Sangha. There are a few items in the story of his life that may point to historical facts, such as that he married and had a child, or that a more ascetically inclined cousin seriously challenged his leadership of the community. Yet these historical items remain incidental to the teachings of Buddha and of Buddhism.

Buddhism today is the sum total of what Buddhist adherents have said, done, and held dear through the centuries. Though this allows for considerable diversity, there are some ordering or integrative factors.

---

64. According to Frank E. Reynolds and Charles Hallisey, "Buddha," in *Encyclopedia of Religion*, 2:321.

65. According to L. S. Cousins, "Buddhism," in *A New Handbook of Living Religions*, ed. John R. Hinnells (Oxford: Blackwell, 1997) 374–76.

Important here is, first of all, what the founder of Buddhism, Gautama, purportedly taught, and how that teaching has unfolded over the centuries. Then there is the monastic organization, the Sangha, whose historical continuity provides a focal point for Buddhist practice and the persistence of Buddhist thought and values.

Buddhism originated around the fifth or fourth century BCE in a small community as a sectarian movement within the dominant Hindu religion. It received a big boost when the Indian Emperor Ashoka (273–231 BCE) of the Mauryan dynasty, who ruled the greater part of South Asia, turned to Buddhism in his abhorrence of war. The king became strongly committed to spread the Buddhist teachings.[66] He worshipped at Buddhist shrines, enlarged Buddhist monuments, went on Buddhist pilgrimages, and formally expressed adherence to the Sangha. Yet this official acceptance of Buddhism lasted only a short while in India. Within fifty years after his death, the Buddhist-oriented Mauryan dynasty collapsed (186 BCE) "and was replaced by the Śunga dynasty, more supportive of Brahmanic Hindu traditions."[67] Today, there are very few Buddhists left in India, but there are other countries where Buddhism is the state religion, such as in Sri Lanka, Myanmar, and Thailand.

All Buddhist traditions recognize the four noble truths, which according to (Theravada) tradition Buddha delivered to his five original disciples on the occasion of his enlightenment. These four noble truths "constitute a 'middle way' between rigorous asceticism and sensual indulgence."[68] There are two focal points: craving to hold that which is impermanent, and not knowing that this orientation cannot yield satisfaction. Buddha proclaimed:

> This, monks, is the noble truth of *dukkha* ("suffering"): birth . . . , old age . . . , disease . . . , dying . . . , association with what is not dear . . . , separation from what is dear . . . , not getting that which is wished for. . . . And this, monks, is the noble truth of the uprising. . . . This craving, which is characterized by repeated existence, accompanied by passion for joys, delighting in this and that; that is to say, craving for sensual desires, craving for existence, craving for cessation of existence. And this, monks, is the noble truth of cessation . . . complete dispassion and cessation

---

66. Cf. L. S. Cousins, "Buddhism," 378, and see for the following quote.

67. Frank E. Reynolds and Charles Hallisey, "Buddhism: An Overview," in *Encyclopedia of Religion*, 2:339.

68. John Ross Carter, "Four Noble Truths," in *Encyclopedia of Religion*, 5:403.

of craving, abandonment, rejection, release of it, without attachment to it. And this, monks, is the noble truth of the path . . . leading to the cessation . . . just this Noble Eightfold Way; that is to say, proper view, proper intention, proper speech, proper action, proper livelihood, proper effort, proper mindfulness, proper concentration.[69]

The first noble truth is the understanding that all life is suffering, exemplified by birth, old age, and disease. The one who attains this insight is already an *arhat*, a perfect saint. The second noble truth is the understanding of the cause of suffering. The craving for life which is fed by perceptions and feelings leads to suffering and to rebirth. Thus we must abolish this cause by eliminating four fundamental evils: sensual desire, the desire to be, wrong beliefs, and ignorance. The third noble truth lies in the insight of how to attain cessation of suffering, which, as a result of the cessation of craving for life, enables us to end the cycle of rebirth and reach Nirvana. Finally, the fourth noble truth, as given above, is the eightfold way leading to the cessation of suffering and thereby achieving Nirvana. It consists of actual instructions for arriving at the goal outlined in the first three truths. Important here is that human action is not disassociated from the intention that constitutes it. It is assumed that actions constituted by good intentions will lead to good and pleasant results, while actions constituted by bad intentions will lead to bad and unpleasant results. Beyond these ethical precepts there is also a mental discipline to be followed which includes Yoga exercises, control of breathing, fasting, and mystic concentration.

It is obvious for Buddhists that Buddha did not come into the world for the first time in the sixth century BCE. Like everyone else, he had undergone many rebirths, experiencing the world as an animal, a human being, and a god. "During his many rebirths, he would have shared the common fate of all that lives. A spiritual perfection like that of a Buddha cannot be the result of just one life. It must mature slowly throughout the ages."[70] This conviction shows us two characteristic

---

69. As quoted more extensively in Carter, "Four Noble Truths," 5:402–3.

70. Edward Conze, *Buddhism: Its Essence and Development*, preface Arthur Waley (New York: Harper Torchbook, 1959) 35. Jagadish Kashyap, "Origin and Expansion of Buddhism," in *The Path of the Buddha. Buddhism Interpreted by Buddhists*, ed. Kenneth W. Morgan (New York: Ronald, 1956) 3, states too that the term "Buddha" is not a proper name but an honorary title applied to one who has reached the very peak of transcendental wisdom through the practice of the ten great spiritual perfections in

teachings of Buddhism, the idea of reincarnation and the idealization of Buddha. Reincarnation was already a basic tenet in the Hindu religion out of which Gautama came. Through the *karma* or total result of our existence on earth, our life is continued in a new reborn form as animal, human, or god, and thus the *samsara,* or the whirlpool of existence, never ceases.

The idealization of Buddha is already present in Hinayana ("Small Vehicle") Buddhism, but it is more prevalent in Mahayana ("Great Vehicle") Buddhism. This idea is enhanced through the concept of a Bodhisattva ("enlightenment being"). "A Bodhisattva is a future Buddha" who attempts to realize the ideals of being Buddha and who strives "for the enlightenment of other sentient beings."[71] Mahayana alone envisions all its followers to become Bodhisattvas, and it seeks to persuade everybody to become like Buddha, since Buddha himself wished to help all creatures and bring them to full enlightenment. Hinayana, however, is content that an adherent become an *arhat* or saint, because an *arhat* should strive only for its own enlightenment and liberation. This is one of the basic differences between the two main branches of Buddhism, Hinayana, also known as Theravada, meaning "the School of the Elders," and Mahayana. Besides these, there is a third kind of Buddhism, esoteric or Tantric Buddhism, which seems to have originated in Eastern India around the third century CE and is now found in Tibet and as Shingon Buddhism in Japan. It uses incantations (*mantra*) and burned offerings (*homa*) to relate humanity to the supra-worldly forces or deities.[72]

Primitive Buddhism persisted for the first 100 years after Buddha's death, whereupon Hinayana Buddhism succeeded and remained prevalent until around 100 CE.[73] It remains today the main religion in Sri Lanka, Myanmar, Thailand, Laos, and Cambodia. Around 100 CE Mahayana Buddhism emerged, and both strands coexisted for the next 200 years. Finally, Mahayana prevailed for another 200 years until both

---

numberless births during an incomprehensible length of time. "A Buddha is not a person but is rather a personality evolved through the accumulation of spiritual qualities. The cumulative forces of virtues and perfections finally bring forth a Buddha, a superman, in the world" (3).

71. Beatrice Lane Suzuki, *Mahayana Buddhism: A Brief Outline,* foreword Christmas Humphreys (New York: Collier, 1963) 65–66.

72. For details, cf. Alex Wayman, "Esoteric Buddhism," in *Encyclopedia of Religion,* 2:472–82.

73. Cf. for the following Beatrice Lane Suzuki, *Mahayana Buddhism,* 22–23.

came into conflict with Indian orthodoxy. Nowadays Mahayana prevails over Hinayana in China, Tibet, Korea, and Japan. Since Hinayana is more concerned about individual enlightenment, it is best represented in Buddhist monasticism. Mahayana, however, is more interested in universal enlightenment and attempts to be a missionary folk religion. While adherents of Mahayana freely admit that Hinayana may have preserved more the letter of Buddha's teachings, they insist they have better captured its spirit, and they concede that both strands are rooted in primitive Buddhism. Their respective names, Mahayana ("great vehicle") and Hinayana ("small vehicle"), express the idea that the larger vehicle is able to carry all beings to salvation while the smaller can carry only a few. The names convey the feeling that, while Mahayana can encompass Hinayana, the opposite is not the case. Yet both forms strive for the same goal, the attainment of nirvana.

Nirvana is not simply void, as one might assume. It means first of all the extinction of all passion for life, similar to the extinction of a flame through cessation of fuel. It is also the state in which all evil passions are subdued and uprooted. Here the mind regains its original purity and grace, altogether free from worries and other annoyances. The latter understanding of nirvana can even be equated with *samsara*, the wheel of life. It is then no longer a transcendental entity to be reached after death, or after the cycles of death and birth have ceased. In living a life of eternal becoming, we already are nirvana. "All that we need do, therefore, is to find ourselves."[74] While Hinayana is more interested in the negative, world-denying side of nirvana, Mahayana conceives of nirvana more positively as a pure and undefiled reality which stands by itself. While nirvana has no cosmological functions, it comes close to "the attributes of the Godhead as they are understood by the more mystical tradition of Christian thought."[75]

Apart from the major division between Mahayana and Hinayana, there are many Buddhist sects, each of them emphasizing one aspect of Buddhism. Zen, for instance, emphasizes self-control, discipline, and simplicity; Shin, gratitude and brotherhood of life; Nichiren, a nationalistic viewpoint and sacrifice; and Shingon, symbolism, ritualism, and

---

74. Suzuki, *Mahayana Buddhism*, 49. For a good introduction to Western interpretations of nirvana cf. Guy Richard Welbon, *The Buddhist Nirvana and Its Western Interpreters* (Chicago: University of Chicago, 1968).

75. Conze, *Buddhism: Its Essence and Development*, 39.

art. Despite these variations, Buddhist thought as a whole always strives for tolerance and inclusiveness. And the ideal sect is one that attempts to harmonize tradition with a progressive spirit.

At first glance, Buddhism appears pessimistic and world-negating. According to Buddhist thinking, it is already futile to spend thoughts on the idea of a personal creator of the universe, because the purpose of Buddhist doctrine is to release beings from suffering and not to speculate on the origin of the world. Yet it is wrong to assume that Buddhist thought would result in radical pessimism. Though it reflects a complete disillusionment with the world as it is, it shows an extreme sensitivity to pain, suffering, and any kind of turmoil, and it is totally dedicated to the alleviation of these evil causes.[76] Buddhists also insist that the object of Buddhist life is not negation but a search for freedom from ignorance and reincarnation, since partial knowledge leads to wrong deeds or to evil *karma*. Nevertheless, we wonder whether a Buddhist scholar such as Beatrice Suzuki (1878–1939) is right when she asserts that "Buddhist life is an open war on bondage, slavery, and attachment of all kinds."[77]

As with Islam, there has been a revival of Buddhism, mining the richness of both the monastic order and of Buddhist writings. Education is promulgated, and Buddhist universities offer the same spectrum of learned disciplines as non-Buddhist counterparts. There has also been an attempt to develop Buddhist forms of contemporary political and social ideologies. "Buddhist interpretations of nationalism and national responsibility, Buddhist conceptions and justifications of democracy, and Buddhist versions and justification of socialism have been developed."[78] We may think here of the experiment to develop a Buddhist socialism in Sri Lanka through Sirimaro Bandaranaike (1916–2000), the world's first woman prime minister (1960–1965; 1970–1977; and 1994–2000).

---

76. Cf. H. Saddhatissa, *Buddhist Ethics: Essence of Buddhism* (London: Allen & Unwin, 1970) especially his chapter on "Sanctions of Moral Conduct: The Precepts," 87–112. One cannot but notice the similarity between the Judeo-Christian tradition and Buddhist ethics as far as basic precepts are concerned. Cf. also Gunapala Dharmasiri, *Fundamentals of Buddhist Ethics* (Antioch, CA: Golden Leaves, 1989) esp. the appendix: "Buddism and the Modern World" (25–39) where the author shows analogies to psycho-therapeutic techniques of Victor Frankl.

77. Suzuki, *Mahayana Buddhism*, 75. Such an "aggressive" attitude, however, seems to be incoherent with the principles laid out in the four noble truths.

78. Frank E. Reynolds and Robert Campany, "Buddhist Ethics," in *Encyclopedia of Religion*, 2:503.

There are also very progressive Buddhist sects. One example is the currently and quickly expanding Japanese sect Soka Gakkai founded in 1930 by a Tokyo school teacher as the Value Creating Educational Society. Tsunesaburo Makiguchi (1871–1944), the founder, based the Society's program on a combination of the teachings of the Buddhist sect Nichiren Shoshu and his own theory of value. He held that "*there are three values: beauty, benefit, and goodness.*"[79] The purpose of life is found in the pursuit of happiness through the attainment of the three supreme virtues, which are accessible only by faith in the teachings of Nichiren.[80] The goal of the believer is to promote this type of Buddhism as the only true kind. In 1995 Soka Gakkai had a membership of more than 8.1 million families in Japan and its own political party (the Komeito, i.e., Clean Government Party) which, in the 1986 national elections, won ten percent of the votes and seats in the Diet.[81] However, within Buddhism such a world-affirming movement is still an exception, and it does not change the overall picture, namely that for Buddhism humans are strangers on earth.[82] Their task is to regain the state of perfection which was theirs

---

79. Nichiren Shoshu is one of the many sects based on a reinterpretation of Buddhism by the thirteenth century Japanese religious leader Nichiren. Shoshu means "true religion" or, as the followers of Soka Gakkai prefer to say, "true Buddhism." Adherents of Nichiren Shoshu hold Nichiren to be the true Buddha, replacing Siddharta Gautama. For a critical introduction to Soka Gakkai, especially in its historical dimension, cf. Noah S. Brannen, *Soka Gakkai. Japan's Militant Buddhists* (Richmond, VA: John Knox, 1968) quote on 137.

80. Cf. Kiyoaki Murata, *Japan's New Buddhism. An Objective Account* of *Soka Gakkai* (New York: Walker/Weatherbill, 1969) 17.

81. Figures from Karel Dobbelaere, *Soka Gakkai. From Lay Movement to Religion*, trans. Olivier Urbain (Salt Lake City: Signature, 1998) 17: and Daniel A. Metraux, *The History and Theology of Soka Gakkai: A Japanese New Religion* (Lewiston, NY: Mellen, 1988) 134.

82. In our attempt to understand the progressive spirit of Soka Gakkai, we should not forget the special character of Japanese Buddhism as an imported religion. It was amalgamated with native beliefs and initially it was primarily used for practical (ethical) ends (cf. E. Dale Saunders, *Buddhism in Japan: With an Outline of Its Origins in India* [Philadelphia: University of Pennsylvania Press, 1964] 261–63). The rise of a number of new syncretistic sects or religions based on ideas drawn indiscriminately from Christianity, Shinto, and Buddhism also indicates a certain dissatisfaction of society with religion as it attempts to adjust itself to the problems of modern (Western) civilization. We might not be wrong to consider Soka Gakkai with its "largely pragmatic and Kantian" persuasions (James Allen Dator, *Soka Gakkai. Builders of the Third Civilization: American and Japanese Members* [Seattle: University of Washington Press, 1969] 9) as an attempt to cope with a foreign civilization while still striving to preserve

before they fell into this world. Thus self-denial can be adapted to highly political and capitalistic endeavors, such as the rebirth of Japan after World War II. Yet our modern technological civilization originated and is sustained through a different spirit. It regards humanity as born for this earth, and it advocates self-preservation and continual progress as its highest goals. The earth is our home and our task is to treat it as such.

In spite of this fundamental difference, the Judeo-Christian faith, out of which the progressive spirit of our present technological civilization emerged, and Buddhist thought show some striking parallels, even interdependencies. Most well-known is the fact that Siddharta Buddha's conversion story was introduced to the West by Christian pilgrims and was rather popular in the Middle Ages as the story of Barlaam and Josaphat. Though both names, Barlaam and Josaphat, are only a disguise for Bodhisattva, they made their way into the Christian calendar for saints as Saint Barlaam and Saint Josaphat, being identified as an Indian prince and a merchant respectively.[83] Of course, this incident deserves attention only as a historical curiosity.

Of more serious nature, however, is the fact that at virtually the same time as Christianity emerged, Buddhism underwent a radical reform of its basic tenets which made it more similar to Christianity than it had ever been before.[84] Lovingkindness and compassion, subordinate virtues in older Buddhism, became stressed more and more and moved right into the center of Buddhist religion. Then we hear of compassionate beings, Bodhisattvas, who sacrificed their lives for the welfare of all. They remind us of Christ's sacrificial death and of his command that we should become like him, i.e. sacrifice our lives for others. Furthermore,

---

some of its own cultural and religious heritage. We are surprised to hear Dator, *Soka Gakkai*, 140–41, say that in contrast to the "Americans," the Japanese do not seem to be a "religious people." Should this mean that the renunciation of its religious heritage was the price that Japan had to pay to become the most "Western" of all "Far Eastern" countries?

83. See Wolfgang Philipp, *Die Absolutheit des Christentum und die Summe der Anthropologie* (Heidelberg: Quelle & Meyer, 1959) 69–70; cf. *Butler's Lives of the Saints*, ed. Herbert Thurston and Donald Attwater, vol. 4 (New York: P. J. Kenedy, 1956) 432–33, for further information on the historic development of this story "about two saints who never existed."

84. Cf. for the following penetrating studies by Edward Conze, *Thirty Years of Buddhist Studies. Selected Essays* (Columbia, S.C.: University of South Carolina Press, 1968) 48–50, who points out these striking phenomena without attempting to draw any conclusions.

the concept of Amida, the Buddha of Eternal Light and Infinite Life, originated as a savior figure infinite in love, wisdom, and power, again clearly resembling Christ.[85] Though Amida as the object of faith evidently comes close to Christ, Buddhists are quick to show that, unlike Christ, Amida is mercy itself and does not judge or suffer for our sins. A crucified or judging Christ is an impossible thought for Buddhism.[86]

Nevertheless, the fact is striking that Mahayana Buddhism, which is so analogous to Christianity and which is much more adaptable to Western thought, emerged in the period almost immediately following the rise of Christianity. Hinayana is not completely exempted from analogies to the Christian faith, either. Though it rejected the idea of a savior, since everyone must save oneself and no one can save another, in the third century CE it developed the concept of Maitreya, the coming Buddha.[87] This sudden interest in "eschatology" seems rather strange, even foreign, to primitive Buddhism. It should also be noted that the two Indian regions in which Mahayana Buddhism made its first appearance, the South of India and the Indian Northwest, were geographically in contact with the Mediterranean cultures. This has been shown in recent years through findings of huge hoards of Roman coins and by the art represented in these regions. It is also remarkable that, contrary to Hinayana, Mahayana demonstrates an openness to foreign, non-Indian influences.[88] As Edward Conze (1904-1979) has shown, there are even occasional close verbal coincidences between Christian and Mahayana Scriptures. But there is an even more serious affinity.

---

85. Amida Buddhism is also called Pure Land Buddhism, because through faith in the celestial Buddha (Amida) one can enter the Pure Land in which one can attain nirvana. This kind of Buddhism, a branch of Mahayana Buddhism, is especially popular in Japan.

86. Conze, *Thirty Years*, 46; and Daisetz Teitaro Suzuki, *Mysticism: Christian and Buddhist* (New York: Harper, 1957) 136, who says: "Christianity, on the other hand presents a few things which are difficult to comprehend, namely, the symbol of crucifixion. The crucified Christ is a terrible sight and I cannot help associating it with the sadistic impulse of a psychically affected brain." Cf. also for the concept of Amida, Suzuki, *Mahayana Buddhism*, 63-64.

87. Cf. for the following Conze, *Thirty Years*, 38 and 49-50.

88. Daisetz Teitaro Suzuki, *Outlines of Mahayana Buddhism*, prefatory essay by Alan Watts (New York: Schocken, 1963) 5, mentions too the external and internal forces acting in the body of Buddhism to produce the Mahayana system by absorbing and assimilating all the discordant thoughts with which it came in contact. Yet he does not elaborate on these forces and influences.

Christian mystics with their negative theology and their concepts of God as ground of being, as nothingness, and as naked Godhead, and the Buddhist concept of nirvana, bear very close resemblances. Buddhism can be justifiably regarded as a special form of mysticism in which the goal of salvation, oneness with nirvana, is basically identical to the goal of the Christian mystic, oneness with God.[89] One might also be tempted to assume that both forms strive for the same kind of world-negating self-redemption. Yet exactly at this point there emerges a decisive difference. While researching the teachings of the German theologian and mystic Meister Eckhart (1260–1328), the German historian of religion Rudolf Otto (1869–1937) discovered that Eckhart's mysticism is "colored by the Christian teaching of justification and permeated through and through by the influences of its origin, by Christian conceptions, without which it would be an almost empty contraption."[90] This emphasis on justification stemming from the experience and knowledge of God's saving activity is totally missing in Buddhist mysticism. The Japanese Buddhist scholar D. T. Suzuki (1870–1966) describes the situation most eloquently when he says:

> What a contrast between the crucifixion-image of Christ and the picture of Buddha lying on a bed surrounded by his disciples and other beings; non-human as well as human! Is it not interesting and inspiring to see all kinds of animals coming together to mourn the death of Buddha?[91]

Suzuki very sensitively noticed the fundamental difference between Christ dying vertically on the cross and Buddha passing away horizontally. The former provided the possibility of reconciliation with God, who is above and beyond ourselves, whereas Buddha showed us ways and means to attain harmonious unity with all being.

Another striking analogy, the one between Buddhist monasticism and the world-denying form of Christian monasticism is still unresolved. Nevertheless, we must ask ourselves to what extent mysticism and monasticism, even of the Christian persuasion, are essential components of Judeo-Christian faith. Though mysticism is always related to a particular religion and cannot survive apart from it, it is a

---

89. Philipp, *Die Absolutheit*, 61.

90. Rudolf Otto, *Mysticism East and West: A Comparative Analysis of the Nature of Mysticism*, trans. B. L. Bracey and R. C. Payne (New York: Collier, 1962) 216.

91. Suzuki, *Mysticism*, 137.

phenomenon common to many religions and occurs in Islam as well as in Judaism (as Kabbalah) and in Christianity. Because of its esoteric, individualistic character, its representatives have often come into conflict with their religious authorities. Their goal is always the same: the liberation of humanity, or of its inner core, from the earthly situation of doom, and salvation of its whole being through union with absolute and pure primal Being, or God. Monasticism, though also very widespread among most world religions, is more flexible in its attitude toward the world and may be either extremely esoteric and world-withdrawn, as with early Christian monasticism in Egypt, or very world-involved and often extremely casuistic, as the Jesuits have been at times.

The recent attractiveness of Buddhism for many people in the West rests on the middle path, neither being obsessed with life, nor rejecting it. Therefore meditation exercises "in order to find oneself" are attractive for many people who feel they are driven to rush through this world, thereby losing themselves and the value of life. According to his life and teachings, Buddha has attained insight into right living. Yet what is the goal of this living? It is very similar to that of Stoic philosophy: to find a niche where one can live comfortably without being crushed by the forces of this world.

The Christian outlook is quite different, because Christians believe in a redeemer who on the one hand provides a goal, heaven or eternal bliss, and who on the other hand is also the creator, the one who gave this world its origin and who provides its present destiny. While Christians, too, should pursue a middle path, the reason for doing so is not to attain life eternal. As Paul affirmed, Christians are already a new creation. This new creation, this new quality of life, should therefore be activated in such a way that the present world is transformed into a semblance of what we aspire to, namely God's kingdom. The Judeo-Christian tradition appreciates and affirms life in this world without neglecting the fact that its goal is the hereafter. The Israelite religion emerged when the Israelites left the desert and settled down in a cultured land, and Christianity spread when Christian missionaries ventured into the cities of the Roman Empire. Judeo-Christian faith is both world-affirming and God-relying. Its focus is not only on the life to come but also on the world in which we live.

As we will see later, the Judeo-Christian faith is neither a faith where we submit ourselves and our actions to an all-powerful God nor a faith where we assume we can attain a right understanding, and therefore master on our own the problems we might encounter in this world. Rather, the Judeo-Christian faith is based on God's action which summons us to an appropriate response. As we see in Abraham's experience (Genesis 12), God paves the way, and therefore we can follow. God acts and we react. What, then, are the other great religions of the world as seen from a Christian perspective? Are they just different ways to the same goal?

FIVE

Copernican versus Pre-Copernican Evaluations

Prior to the suicidal destruction of the World Trade Center in New York on September 11, 2001, many people in the West believed that we basically worship the same God, but with different names, be it Jehovah, Allah, or simply God. But with this and other terrorist attacks committed in the name of Allah, such a simplified equation of diverse religious traditions came under severe scrutiny. Is a god, for whom suicide bombers sacrifice their own lives and take with them other innocent lives of men, women, and children, really the same god in whom Christians believe, who in Jesus Christ sacrificed his human embodiment once and for all for the wrong doings of the world and therefore abolished any further human sacrifice?

Even if we surmise that such attacks are either done out of despair or are the result of a warped human mind, they are executed in the name of the one God. Should we then conclude that our understanding of God is the sole correct one? Such indiscriminate rejection of all other religious traditions is unjustified. We remember that atrocities have also been committed in the name of the Christian God. For instance, the Inquisition advanced the idea that one should destroy the body of a heretic so that at least his or her soul would not end up in destruction. Then there were the forced conversions of native populations in South America in the name of Christ. The wholesale rejection of other religious traditions, as advanced by some followers of Karl Barth in the twentieth century, also lacks the backing of the New Testament. Paul, for instance, called Abraham, the Jewish patriarch, an "example of faith" (Rom 4:12). He certainly did not do this believing that Abraham's religion was all wrong. On the contrary, Paul attempted to demonstrate a continuity amid all discontinuity, and even a historical priority of the

Old Testament over the New (cf. Romans 9–11). Paul, however, was not only appreciative of his Old Testament heritage. In his famous speech on the Areopagus in Athens, Paul is proclaiming to the Athenians the God whom they "worship as unknown" (Acts 17:23). This is the line the Apologists of the Early Church followed when they were confronted with a multitude of religions which all claimed some kind of revelation.

A Common Knowledge of God

The first and most biblical argument of the Apologists was that of the *logos spermatikos*. It contained the conviction that the preexistent logos, "implanted in every race of men," enabled pagan thinkers like Socrates already to see dimly what came later to be clearly perceived through the revelation of the incarnate logos in the person of Jesus.[1] Since the prologue of the Gospel of John shows us that this logos had already been present at the creation of the world, the Apologists concluded that it had been present too in the history of Israel, and even to some degree in paganism. The Stoics, the poets, and the historians each "spoke well in proportion to the share he had of the spermatic word."[2] Now that the seminal logos had become incarnate in the person of Jesus Christ, those under his guidance could find the fuller meaning of these intuitions. Thus the logos prepared the advent of the Christian self-disclosure of God and bridged the gulf between Christianity and the religions which Christianity encountered in the Greco-Roman world.

Another quite common method for the Early Christian Apologists was to assert that the truth contained in paganism had come from the Old Testament.[3] This argument had already been advanced by Jewish writers, such as Philo (b. ca. 15/10 BCE) and Josephus (37/38–ca. 100), when they traced various Greek doctrines to a biblical origin. Yet in attacking the pagan rituals bishop Ambrose of Milan (339–397) demonstrated that the argument from antiquity should not be slavishly followed, since "there is no shame in passing to better things" if they be-

---

1. Justin Martyr, *The Second Apology for the Christians. Addressed to the Roman Senate* (8) in *ANF*, 1:191.

2. Ibid. (13) 193.

3. Cf. for further details Jaroslav Pelikan, *The Christian Tradition. A History of the Development of Doctrine* (Chicago: University of Chicago Press, 1971) 1:33–34.

came available.[4] This leads to the third very interesting argument, that of accommodation. Christian Apologists suggested that God had accommodated himself to human weakness in the Old Testament. God had not yet fully disclosed God's true self. This allowed them to explain the parallels between Jewish and pagan rites of sacrifices as steps of God's pedagogical action leading up to God's self-disclosure in Jesus Christ. This reasoning expresses God's love in moving humanity along from paganism via Judaism to the Christian faith. Most of these arguments have been variously employed throughout the centuries and applied to the relationship between Christian faith and other religious traditions.

Following tradition, the reformer Martin Luther (1483–1546) also affirmed a twofold knowledge of God, explaining it as "the general and the particular."[5] The general knowledge has been placed by God into the human heart, attested to by natural law, affirmed by human reason, and again through philosophy. Though some people such as Epicureans and atheists try to deny the awareness of such a god, "they do it by force and want to quench this light in their hearts. They are like people who purposely stop their ears or pinch their eyes shut to close out sound and light. However, they do not succeed in this; their conscience tells them otherwise."[6] In his exposition of Jonah, Luther emphasized: "Such a light and such a perception is innate in the hearts of all men; and this light cannot be subdued or extinguished."[7] If pagans, for instance, called on their gods whom they really believed possessed a divine nature, then this demonstrates that "they have this manifestation about Him in themselves."[8] All religions, therefore, testify to the existence of a powerful and divine being. So is it that humans are naturally aware that their existence is limited and dependent on something or someone else. We are neither responsible for our own existence nor do we fully control it. "Because of a natural instinct, the heathen also . . . know that there is a supreme deity."[9] Luther makes frequent reference to Rom 1:19ff., a pas-

---

4. Ambrose, *Letters* (188) in *NPNF SS*, 10:418.

5. Martin Luther, *Lecture on Galatians*, in *LW* 26:399.

6. Martin Luther in his exposition of Jonah 1:5, *Lectures on Jonah*, in *LW* 19:54.

7. Martin Luther, *Lectures on Jonah*, in *LW* 19:53. The Epicureans, named after the Greek philosopher Epicurus (ca. 341–270 BCE) were known for their fearlessness before the gods and their pursuit of happiness.

8. Martin Luther, commenting on Rom 1:19, *Lectures on Romans. Glosses and Scholia* (1515–16) in *LW* 25:9.

9. Martin Luther, on Gen 17:7, *Lectures on Genesis*, in *LW* 3:117.

sage he draws on when he contends that "they have a natural knowledge of God." This natural knowledge of God, according to Luther, we encounter first in the law, then through reason, and finally in philosophy.

For example, the knowledge of God gained through the Ten Commandments is shared by all people. "The knowledge contained in the Law is known to reason," explained Luther.[10] "For to have a God is not alone a Mosaic law, but also a natural law, as St. Paul says (Rom. 1:20), but the heathen know of the deity, that there is a God. This is also evidenced by the fact that they have set up gods and arranged forms of divine service, which would have been impossible if they had neither known or thought about God. For God has shown it to them."[11] Hence the Ten Commandments, according to Luther, belong to the category of general or natural knowledge of God, and indeed blend together with this knowledge in many ways. The natural law, which is found in its purest form in the Ten Commandments, demands the honoring of God in the first table (according to Roman Catholic and Lutheran counting, the first three commandments) and requires the love of one's neighbor in the second table (the fourth through tenth). Since God has engraved the natural law equally in the hearts of all people, we are able to know God and what God wants us to do through the natural law. For these reasons, Luther viewed reason and philosophy as originally good gifts from God that enable us to know much about God. Especially in his book *The Bondage of the Will* (1525) Luther stressed that reason is able to say some things about God. "For all men find these sentiments written on their hearts and acknowledge and approve them (though unwillingly) when they hear them discussed: first, that God is omnipotent, not only in power, but also in action (as I have said), otherwise he would be a ridiculous God; and secondly, that he knows and foreknows all things, and can neither err nor be deceived."[12]

However, Luther was very skeptical of human reason in theological matters, since he knew that humans can quickly find a reasonable argument that allows them to justify their own actions and thereby avoid doing God's will. Likewise, he also held philosophy to be too speculative

---

10. Martin Luther, on John 1:18, *Auslegungen des ersten und zweiten Kapitels Johannis in Predigten*, in WA 46:667, 10–11.

11. Martin Luther, *Against the Heavenly Prophets in the Matter of Images and Sacraments*, in *LW* 40:96–97.

12. Martin Luther, *The Bondage of the Will*, in *LW* 33:191.

for it produced many claims about God that Luther felt clearly contradicted Scripture. Of course, we must concede here that Luther would not talk about autonomous human reason as it evolved during the Enlightenment period, but reason always guided by God. Luther writes: "One cannot comprehend God, yet one senses God's presence, for God lets himself be seen and known by one and all and reveals himself as a benevolent creator who acts for our good and gives us all good things. This is testified to by the sun and moon, heaven and earth, and all the fruits that grow from the earth."[13] Nevertheless, knowledge of God based on reason does not stand on firm ground because, as Luther well knew, people do not want to believe that God punishes sin, and therefore they prefer to follow their own thinking. They tend to compromise this knowledge and speculate about God through their own rational reflections. The God-given knowledge is often distorted through human highhandedness and leads to idolatry, that is, to the following of other gods rather than the true God.

Philosophy, too, which Luther uses almost interchangeably with reason, turns its attention to the created order and recognizes the one who rules the world. It knows that there is a first mover and a highest being, as Plato had already shown. Yet the will of the creator remains hidden from reason, for humans are so blindfolded by their sinful self-centeredness that they cannot see the world as it really is. While the Platonists came to the conclusion through their speculations that God is spirit and rules the world and is the ground of all that is good in the natural order, they were so blinded by the sovereignty and majesty of God's works that in their search for God they did not recognize him. Why God made things the way he did and why God rules in the way he does are questions for which the philosophers have no answers.

The speculative knowledge of God produced by philosophy also fails in the end because it addresses the pure majesty of God, which is beyond human comprehension. According to Luther, speculative philosophy seeks to reach from the here and now to the beyond. As Immanuel Kant later demonstrated, such an attempt is futile because God cannot be reached from a human starting point. While Luther admitted that speculative philosophy is able to discern some things about God, he contended that it often becomes lost in abstract speculation. Therefore all natural knowledge of God is ambivalent, on the one hand

13. Martin Luther, "Tischrede," no. 6530, in *WATR* 6:20,19-29.

attaining true insight in God's very being, but often distorted through our predilections of how we would want God to be.

For Christians there is another way to know God, through God's self-disclosure in Jesus Christ. According to Luther, this way is far to be preferred, because "there is a vast difference between knowing that there is a God and knowing who or what God is. Nature knows the former—it is inscribed in everybody's heart; the latter is taught only by the Holy Spirit."[14] While natural knowledge could be compared to theoretical knowledge, the special knowledge in Jesus Christ is existential knowledge, because there we know what God has in store for us and how he feels about us. We experience God's love in the existential knowledge through Christ. Therefore Luther can reject natural knowledge saying: "It is extremely dumb to want to know him. Therefore one should cling to the Word."[15] This means that Luther admitted that the same God had disclosed God's self to all people. Therefore all people knew about God. Religions are expressive of God and God's will toward humanity. Yet Luther emphasized that in the Christian faith there is a plus. While all other knowledge about God is "outside knowledge," only the knowledge through God's self-disclosure in Jesus Christ reveals something about God's "heart" and in this way is existential knowledge.

This is also the position of the reformer John Calvin (1509–1564) who wrote in his *Institutes*: "God himself has implanted in all men a certain understanding of his divine majesty."[16] Therefore Calvin concluded that religion is not an arbitrary invention, though "clever men have devised very many things in religion by which to inspire the common folk with reverence and to strike them with terror."[17] Yet "it is utterly vain for some men to say that religion was invented by the subtlety and craft of a few to hold the simple folk in thrall by this device and that those very persons who originated the worship of God for others did not in the least believe that any God existed."[18] If Calvin had not lived in the sixteenth century, one could think that he wrote this in direct rebuttal to Feuerbach's claim of religion being a projection of the human mind or

---

14. Martin Luther, commenting on Jonah 1:5, *Lectures on Jonah*, in *LW* 19:55.

15. Martin Luther, *Predigten über das 5. Buch Mose*, in *WA* 28:608, 8–9.

16. John Calvin, *Institutes of the Christian Religion* (I.3.1) ed. John T. McNeill, trans. Ford Lewis Battles (Philadelphia: Westminster, 1960) 1:43.

17. John Calvin, *Institutes* (I.3.2) 1:45.

18. Calvin, *Institutes* (I.3.2.) 1:44.

to Marx's idea that it was a device to subjugate and exploit the masses. Religion, indeed, has some credibility, since it includes knowledge of God.

Similarly to Luther, Calvin emphasized that God manifests God's self in the created works, and in governing the universe. This divine wisdom is for everybody to see. Even history witnesses to the providence of God and his creation attests to divine wisdom. Calvin refers here implicitly to authors of antiquity such as Cicero and Seneca.[19]

Just like Luther, Calvin showed that God gave to humanity an actual knowledge accessible in Scripture. He wrote that despite this natural knowledge:

> it is needful that another and better help be added to direct us aright to the very Creator of the universe. It was not in vain, then, that he added the light of his Word by which to become known unto salvation; and he regarded as worthy of this privilege those whom he pleased to gather more closely and intimately to himself. . . . Not only does he teach the elect to look upon a god, but also shows himself as the God upon whom they are to look. He has from the beginning maintained this plan for his church, so that besides these common proofs he also put forth his Word, which is a more direct and more certain mark whereby he is to be recognized.[20]

Very similarly to Luther he emphasized that the knowledge through God's self-disclosure in Jesus Christ is existential knowledge towards salvation and is not as ambiguous as the outside knowledge. It is important for Calvin that this existential knowledge is reserved for the elect, indicating differently from Luther that God designed a plan from the very beginning that includes our individual destinies. It was evident for both Luther and Calvin that though God's knowledge was present among all people, salvation was only possible through the encounter with God as God disclosed himself in the Judeo-Christian tradition. The position advocated by Luther and Calvin has been repeated far into the twentieth century with various modifications.

Karl Barth (1886–1968) gave this position a radical twist by juxtaposing humanity's religions and the Christian faith. Barth claimed that especially since Schleiermacher at the beginning of the nineteenth cen-

---

19. Cf. Calvin, *Institutes* (I.5.2) 1:53 nn. 5 and 6.
20. Calvin, *Institutes* (I.6.1) 1:69-70.

tury, Christian theology had turned more and more into an anthropology. Therefore Feuerbach was right when he claimed that theology had to be dissolved into anthropology.[21] In contrast to this anthropological turn, Karl Barth declared that as theologians we are summoned to talk about God. This talk is different from talking in a raised voice about humanity. "The Gospel is not a religious message to inform mankind of their divinity or to tell them how they may become divine. The Gospel proclaims a God utterly distinct from men."[22] Of course, Barth admits that God's revelation is present in a world drenched with religion, but this does not mean that revelation is the affirmation of religion. "Religion is unbelief."[23] It is the one great concern of godless humanity. The divine reality offered and manifested to us in revelation is replaced in religion "by a concept of God arbitrarily and wilfully evolved by man. . . . It is the attempted replacement of the divine work by a human manufacture."[24] In religion we do the talking instead of God; we take something for ourselves instead of accepting a gift. We reach out and venture to grasp at God instead of letting God act on our behalf. Because religion is this reaching out and grasping at God, it is opposed to revelation and it is "the concentrated expression of human unbelief." While revelation is God's self-offering and self-manifestation through which God wants to reconcile us to Godself, through religion we try to come to terms with our own lives, to justify and sanctify ourselves.[25] But God does not condone this human self-redemptive attitude.

According to Barth the real crisis of religion is revelation, since there the whole religious process is reversed. God comes down to us and we no longer venture to come to terms with God on our own. Since Christian faith has at its foundation God's self-disclosure, "the Christian religion is the true religion."[26] Revelation is a strictly Christian phenomenon, because "the Christian religion is the predicate to the subject of

---

21. Cf. Karl Barth in "An Introductory Essay" to Ludwig Feuerbach, *The Essence of Christianity*, trans. George Eliot, foreword H. Richard Niebuhr (New York: Harper, 1957) esp. xx–xxi.

22. Karl Barth, *The Epistle to the Romans*, trans. from the 6th edition by E. C. Hoskyns (London: Oxford University, 1963) 28.

23. Karl Barth, *Church Dogmatics*, 1:2: *The Doctrine of the Word of God*, trans. G. T. Thomson and H. Knight (New York: Charles Scribner's, 1956) 299.

24. Ibid., 1:2:302–03, for this and the following quote.

25. Cf. ibid., 1.2:307–309.

26. Ibid., 1.2:326.

the name of Jesus Christ" and through the name Jesus Christ it becomes the true "religion."[27] The adjective "Christian" thereby can never express "a grasping at some possession of our own. It can only be a reaching out for the divine possession included in this name."[28] In other words, the name of Jesus Christ is the one thing that "is really decisive for the distinction of truth and error" among religions.[29] The name of Jesus Christ does not stand for our own accomplishment, as do the divine projections in the world religions, but it stands for God's own doing. "Christ is not the king chosen by us; on the contrary, we are the people chosen by him."[30] The relationship between the name "Jesus Christ" and the Christian "religion" is not to be reversed.

With this understanding of the Christian faith, Barth can easily disregard Feuerbach's observation that, like any other religion, Christianity is a projection of the human mind. For Barth such an accusation is absolutely inadequate, since Christianity is the direct opposite of a projection. However, he concedes that if limited to the religious sphere, Feuerbach was not wrong. Religion is a kind of projection. Barth observes an immanent questionableness of religion, since religion is never more than a reflection of what humanity is and has. While atheism points to the futility of these projections, it cannot rid itself from its own inherent religious attitude. Atheism becomes a new religion, in which humanity is again convinced that it can master its own existence. A similar pattern is followed by mysticism, since, in a less revolutionary way, there the being of God is assumed to be dependent on humanity's existence.

Karl Barth is certainly right that both in the Christian faith and in the world's religions there are many aspects which result from human preferences or even imaginations. But it is problematic if one categorically juxtaposes the Christian faith and other religions. Contrary to what Paul had done in his famous speech on the Areopagus in Athens when he used the altar to the unknown god as his point of contact with the religions in Athens, there is nothing positive left in the world religions which could be used as a point of contact with the Christian faith. It comes as no surprise that historians of religions who followed the line of

---

27. Ibid., 1.2:347.
28. Ibid., 1.2:349.
29. Ibid., 1.2:343.
30. Otto Weber, *Karl Barth's Church Dogmatics,* trans. Arthur C. Cochrane (Philadelphia: Westminster, 1953) 54.

thinking of Karl Barth, such as Hendrik Kraemer (1888–1965) from the Netherlands, had no appreciation of the world's religions whatsoever.

In his book *The Christian Message in a Non-Christian World*, Kraemer emphasized the dissimilarities between the various religions and the Christian faith and called the world religions misdirected and mainly great human achievements. The only legitimate point of contact between them is "the disposition and the attitude of the missionary."[31] Kraemer claimed that this is not done out of a feeling of superiority, but for Christ's sake and for the sake of the people involved. Implied here is that these religions are an offense to Christ and without Christ these people will be eternally lost. Therefore the answer through the centuries has been to bring people to Christ so that they can attain salvation.

At least since the middle of the twentieth century with the newly won independence of former Western colonies and the resurgence of the world's religions, there are no signs that the world will be won over to Christ. To the contrary, in the twentieth century alone, there have been more Christian martyrs than in the first four centuries altogether when there were the so-called persecutions of the Christians under Roman Emperors such as Nero (emp. 54–68) or Diocletian (emp. 284–305). Since people, for instance in India, are no longer under the tutelage of a Western "Christian" nation, their dominant environment is Hindu. To break out of such an environment means to forfeit all the economic and kinship ties that go with such an environment. Therefore one usually foregoes an actual conversion, though at heart and in one's private practice, one shows allegiance to the Christian faith.[32] Moreover, Christianity no longer enjoys the protection of the former colonial powers. As a minority in non-Western countries, Christianity does not want to jeopardize its good standing with the majority religion and therefore does not encourage large-scale conversions. This new situation necessitates a reconsideration of relating the Christian faith to the world's religions.

---

31. Hendrik Kraemer, *The Christian Message in a Non-Christian World*, 3rd ed. (Grand Rapids: Kregel, 1956) 136 and 140. In a later publication, *Religion and the Christian Faith* (Philadelphia: Westminster, 1956) where he gave an excellent survey of the different approaches to relate the Christian faith and the world religions, Kraemer attempts to modify his approach. Yet despite his candid and refreshing evaluations of the positions portrayed, his own position is hardly more appreciative of the world's religions than in his earlier book (cf. 31 and 44, 9–50).

32. Cf. Herbert E. Hoefler and his study of the population in Madras, *Churchless Christianity* (Madras: Gurukul Theological College, 1991).

Symptomatic of this changing sentiment is the evolving theological perspective from the historian of religion Ernst Troeltsch to the theologian Paul Tillich (1886–1965) on the Protestant side, and the deliberations of Vatican II (1962–1965) on the Roman Catholic side. We turn now to these views.

Moving Beyond the Dialectic

Ernst Troeltsch (1865–1923), professor of theology at the University of Heidelberg, and subsequently professor of philosophy in Berlin, comes from the history of religions school and is one of the founders of the historicist approach to religion. He stated the agenda of historicism in his 1898 essay "Historical and Dogmatic Method in Theology": "The historical method itself, by its use of criticism, analogy, and correlation, produces with irresistible necessity a web of mutually interacting activities of the human spirit, which are never independent and absolute but always interrelated and therefore understandable only within the context of the most comprehensive whole."[33] This means that historical criticism treats its sources critically, it looks for analogies, and then tries to correlate analogies, antecedent and subsequent movements, and ideas. Not one idea or movement on the religious scene is totally independent and absolute. The same, however, must also be said for the results of historical research, since they too are placed in an ever-expanding horizon.

Troeltsch was not satisfied with historicizing, psychologizing, and relativizing everything connected with religion, a procedure which disclaimed religion's validity. He rightly saw that "this very process cuts off our access to all that is normative and objective, and therefore leads to an increasing yearning for the absolute—precisely for religion."[34] Religion for him is not to be explained away because "religion is a constitutive part of historical existence."[35] Religions are part of our historical existence which change with us and with history. How such changes occur in one particular religious tradition Troeltsch showed in his massive two-volume work, *The Social Teaching of the Christian Churches* (1911).

---

33. Ernst Troeltsch, "Historical and Dogmatic Method in Theology," in Ernst Troeltsch, *Religion in History: Essays*, trans. James Luther Adams and Walter F. Bense (Minneapolis: Fortress, 1991) 15.

34. Troeltsch, "On the Question of the Religions A Priori," in *Religion in History*, 34.

35. Troeltsch, "Christianity and the History of Religion," in *Religion in History*, 77.

Troeltsch not only described religious movements, he also asked what they amount to and what ultimately motivates them in a religious sense. Thereby he did not adhere to the positivistic theory according to which "one knows to begin with what religion is and what it can only be: namely, an intellectual error of the primitive mentality which has managed to survive so long because of its great importance for social cohesion and its connection with the human need for happiness."[36] On the other hand he does not want to agree with an idealistic interpretation of religion which sees in religion "a qualitatively individual and creative power of spiritual life."[37] He wants to adopt a position between these various theories that, on the one hand, are represented by Kant and Hegel and their followers, and Auguste Comte and his school on the other. Troeltsch offered the results of these deliberations in his book *The Absoluteness of Christianity and the History of Religions* (1901) where he asserted:

> Christianity must be understood not only as the culmination point but also as the convergence point of all the developmental tendencies that can be discerned in religion. It may therefore be designated, in contrast to other religions, as the focal synthesis of all religious tendencies and the disclosure of what is in principle a new way of life. . . . Christianity is the culmination point not despite but in terms of its particularity and distinctive features, and on this basis the goal of religion undergoes decisively new determinations.[38]

Troeltsch is historian enough to know that history does not stand still and therefore "it cannot be proved with absolute certainty that Christianity will always remain the final culmination point, that it will never be surpassed." Troeltsch also concedes that in every living religion there is a power at work that provides genuine deliverance from guilt, grief, and earthly life.[39] Troeltsch checks his universalistic ideas by pointing out that Christianity is unlikely to be surpassed as the way of

---

36. Troeltsch, "Religion and the Science of Religion," trans. Michael Pye, in Ernst Troeltsch, *Writings on Theology and Religion*, trans. and ed. Robert Morgan and Michael Pye (London: Duckworth, 1977) 85.

37. Troeltsch, *Writings on Theology*, 86.

38. Troeltsch, *The Absoluteness of Christianity and the History of Religions*, intro. James Luther Adams, trans. David Reid (Richmond, VA: John Knox, 1971) 114–15, for this and the following quote.

39. Cf. ibid., 126.

attaining deliverance from the human predicament and loving fellowship with God.

When Troeltsch wrote his first lecture for his intended visit to Great Britain in 1923, he entitled it "The Place of Christianity Among the World Religions." He wanted to indicate how his thoughts had developed since his 1901 publication *The Absoluteness of Christianity*.[40] Now Troeltsch went a decisive step further and pulled together his analysis of religion and culture and recognized that a religion always depends upon the intellectual, social, and national conditions which provide the context in which religion exists. This means for Christianity that although it was once a Jewish sect, it "has become the religion of all Europe."[41] Christianity stands or falls with European civilization because it has entirely lost its oriental character and become Westernized and Hellenized. "Our European conceptions of personality and its eternal, divine right, and of progress towards a kingdom of the spirit and of God, our enormous capacity for expansion and for the interconnection of spiritual and temporal, our whole social order, our science, our art—all these rest, whether we know it or not, whether we like it or not, upon the basis of this deorientalized Christianity."

With this assertion Troeltsch recognized Christianity as the seminal ground for the Western way of life. Therefore it is not surprising when Troeltsch stated: "The only religion we can endure is Christianity, for Christianity has grown up with us and has become a part of our very being."[42] Then he continues to assert: "Christianity could not be the religion of such a highly developed racial group if it did not possess a mighty spiritual power and truth; in short, if it were not, in some degree, a manifestation of that Divine Life itself." Religion experienced in this way can then obtain a criterion of validity, but, as he assured, only its validity for us in the West. For other racial groups, who live under entirely different cultural conditions, the divine life may express itself in a very different way.

Now Troeltsch no longer claimed the absolute superiority of Christianity as he had twenty years earlier. He only stated a unity of

---

40. Troeltsch, "The Place of Christianity Among the World Religions," in Ernst Troeltsch, *Christian Thought: Its History and Application*, ed. with an intro. Baron Friedrich von Hügel (New York: Meridian Living Age, 1957) 36.

41. Ibid., 54, for this and the following quote.

42. Ibid., 55, for this and the following quote.

religion saying: "As all religion has thus a common goal in the Unknown, the Future, perchance in the Beyond, so too it has a common ground in the Divine Spirit ever pressing the finite mind onward towards further light and fuller consciousness, a Spirit Which indwells the finite spirit, and Whose ultimate union with it is the purpose of the whole many-sided process."[43] Troeltsch affirmed here a common goal for all religions and also a common ground. While the common ground had already been affirmed by Luther, Calvin, and many others, a common goal, namely salvation, was a major change.

Another item was perhaps even more important. Because of his contextual work Troeltsch noticed that not only the socio-cultural context influenced religion, but that religion made a decisive impact on this context. This means that religion transforms the culture in which it finds itself. He rightly claimed that Western culture is inexplicable and indefensible without the Judeo-Christian input. Often, however, the Western gown of the Christian faith is seen to be more a hindrance than an asset in its dialogue with other religions.

As did Troeltsch, the British historian Arnold Toynbee (1889–1975) also discerned a common ground and a common goal of all religions. But he thought little of religious particularities. Toynbee abandoned a Christocentric view of the Christian faith and stated that all the living higher religions should subordinate their traditional rivalries in order to reflect on their common ground. Toynbee finds this common ground first of all in human nature which is basically self-centered and which has succumbed to original sin. "The call to wrestle with Original Sin is the challenge in response to which all higher religions have arisen."[44] Toynbee regards it as hardly accidental that the higher religions, as we know them today, all made their appearances within a period of less than a thousand years of one another. He assumed that it was the same human nature, with which we are confronted today, that evoked the higher religions. Thus the higher religions have common ground in the permanence and universality of human nature and in the present state of the world. Higher religions also share a common aim, namely to emancipate individual souls so that they can glorify God and enjoy him

---

43. Ibid., 61.

44. Arnold Toynbee, *Christianity Among the Religions of the World* (London: Oxford University, 1958) 85–86.

forever. Since the major religions address themselves to all, this aim is not reserved for a privileged minority.

However, Toynbee saw two main obstacles which prevent Christianity from recognizing these common denominators in other higher religions and from being recognized by those other religions themselves. First, Toynbee suggested that Christianity should clearly distinguish between its message and Western civilization through and in which it usually presents the Christian message. With this suggestion, Toynbee touched on that which is demanded by many missiologists today, an indigenization of religion. He claimed that often the Western garb hindered others from adopting Christianity.[45] Of course, it is questionable whether one can disassociate a particular form of religion so easily from its cultural environment. Toynbee's law of inverse operation, in which he suggested that "the circumstances favorable to spiritual and to secular progress are not only different but are antithetical," does not prove the case.[46]

We admit that religions often make their appearance and spread most rapidly when civilizations are in an unstable state. However, there is a clear dependence of Western progress on the Judeo-Christian faith. Without the progressive spirit of this faith, Western civilization would have been bound to a similar pessimistic cyclic pattern as are all other civilizations.[47] Thus one could predict that if missionaries had not exported their Western perspective along with the Christian faith, the Christian faith alone would be sufficient to transform the cultural and religious milieu of the respective missionary scene. Even in the West the Germanic and Greco-Roman context with its highly deterministic and fate-governed view on things was gradually transformed. If it had been otherwise, the Christian faith would have lost its transformative power. Of course, we do not want to imply that missionaries should advance a neo-colonialistic or imperialistic stance with regard to the religio-cultural milieu in which they work. Neither should they become

---

45. Cf. ibid., 92–93.

46. Arnold Toynbee, *A Study of History* (London: Oxford University, 1961) 7:701.

47. Karl Löwith, *Meaning in History* (Chicago: University of Chicago Press, 1957) 19, expressed this point well when he wrote: "It seems as if the two great conceptions of antiquity and Christianity, cyclic motion and eschatological direction, have exhausted the basic approaches to the understanding of history. Even most recent attempts at an interpretation of history are nothing else but variations of these two principles or a mixture of both of them."

advocates of a modern secular spirit, since, as we have seen, this spirit is only indirectly related to the Christian faith. While missionaries can never be effective unless they are able to understand the worldview of the people to whom they minister and unless they are able to relate the Christian message to their context, they dare not leave the impression that acceptance of the message would make no difference to the life and living of the listeners.

Second, Toynbee observed that many in the East and West reject Christianity because of its allegedly arrogant spirit. Consequently we should "try to purge our Christianity of the traditional Christian belief that Christianity is unique,"[48] because out of the belief in its uniqueness follows its exclusive-mindedness and its intolerance. Toynbee did not want Christianity to renounce the idea that its own convictions are right and true. It should recognize, however, that all higher religions are also in some measure revelations of that which is true and right. Higher religions differ in the content and in the degree of the revelation that has been given to humanity through them. And they also differ in the extent to which this revelation has been translated into practice by their followers. But Toynbee claimed that all religions "are light radiating from the same source from which our own religion derives its spiritual light."[49]

Toynbee also mentioned that in six major religions, Buddhism, Hinduism, Zoroastrianism, Islam, Judaism, and Christianity, the greatest spiritual presence has a personal aspect. According to Toynbee this "personal aspect is a bond of unity which transcends the differences between their views of what the personal aspect is."[50] Though looking for a common ground, Toynbee rejected all syncretistic endeavors, since such artificial religions would fail to capture the imagination, the feelings, and the allegiance of humanity. He wanted religions to retain their historic identities, while becoming more and more open-minded and open-hearted towards one another. However, Christianity "should continue to preach these [Christian] truths and ideals to the non-Christian majority of our fellow human beings" and give practical examples of it in action.[51] Toynbee also touched on the essence of the Christian faith

---

48. Toynbee, *Christianity Among the Religions of the World*, 95.

49. Ibid., 100.

50. Toynbee, *An Historian's Approach to Religion* (London: Oxford University, 1956) 274.

51. Toynbee, *Christianity Among the Religions of the World*, 105.

when he named three points in the Christian faith which he wanted to be furthered: 1. The proclamation of the saving history of God in the life of Jesus Christ. 2. The conviction that human beings ought to follow the example that God has set in the history of Jesus Christ. 3. The enactment of this conviction in one's own life. When we disregard Toynbee's universalistic attitude, he seemed to have captured the essence of the Christian faith and he rightly scolds Christianity for its often unjustified arrogance.

Remembering our brief survey of the world's religions, we wonder whether there is as much similarity between the Christian faith and these religions as Toynbee suggested. While Toynbee is highly idealistic and reductive in correlating the Christian faith with other religions, he is certainly correct that there can be more cooperation and dialogue between the Christian faith and the world's religions than there is at the present. One should, however, not forget that the initiatives for such dialogue have always come from Christian quarters, be it through the Vatican on the Roman Catholic side or the World Council of Churches on the Protestant side. This also indicates that one assumes from the Christian perspective more common ground between the world's religions and the Christian faith than has previously been admitted. This opinion is also shared by Paul Tillich.

In volume 3 of his *Systematic Theology* Paul Tillich (1886–1965) still emphasized the necessity for mission. Since the "Spiritual Community" should include all of humanity there needs to be an expansion of the churches. Yet Tillich cautioned: "The purpose of missions as an institutionalized function of the church is not to save individuals from eternal condemnation—as it was in some pietistic missions; nor is the purpose cross-fertilization of religions and cultures. The purpose of mission is rather the actualization of the Spiritual Community within concrete churches all over the world."[52] This means that Tillich neither opted for some kind of syncretism, be it of religions or cultures, nor of saving people, but to actualize the spiritual community throughout the world. Tillich also knew how difficult it is to separate the Christian message from a particular culture within which it is proclaimed. There is no abstract Christian message. Nevertheless, the Spiritual Presence is the

---

52. Paul Tillich, *Systematic Theology*, vol. 3: *Life and the Spirit. History and the Kingdom of God* (Chicago: University of Chicago Press, 1963) 193.

most important thing and therefore a missionary has to communicate that Presence and not his or her particular background.

Since Tillich believed that the universal logos is present throughout the world, he wrote: "It is most important for the practice of the Christian ministry, especially in its missionary activities toward those both within and without the Christian culture, to consider pagans, humanists, and Jews as members of the latent Spiritual Community and not as complete strangers who are invited into the Spiritual Community from outside."[53] Again, he would affirm with the Reformers that God is present outside the Christian faith and that the invisible church is not synonymous with the visible church but can also be larger. Therefore one cannot treat the people outside the church as ignorant pagans. Yet the church as the manifestation of the Spiritual Community, imperfect as it may be, "still has a missionary task of bringing people into a manifest relationship with the New Being, who is Jesus the Christ."[54] This includes bringing adherents of other religions into the Christian church, enabling them to become Christians.

In the Bampton Lectures for 1962, presented in the fall of 1968 at Columbia University, at practically the same time when Tillich's third volume of his *Systematic Theology* was in the making, he described the relation between Christianity and the world religions as "profoundly dialectical."[55] On the one hand he called Christianity all-inclusive and universal, and on the other hand he saw its ultimate criterion in the concreteness in Jesus as the Christ. The appearance and reception of Jesus of Nazareth as the Christ is the event on which Christianity is based and it provides in human history the decisive self-manifestation of the source and aim of all being. Tillich did not opt for religious syncretism, since this would rob a particular religion of its concreteness and at the same time of its dynamic power.[56] He did not want a victory of one religion either, since this would impose one particular answer on all other particular answers. Only in breaking through one's particularity can one

---

53. Ibid., 3:155.

54. So Terance Thomas, ed., Paul Tillich, *The Encounter of Religions and Quasi-Religions* (Lewiston: Edwin Mellen, 1990) xv, in his enlightening analysis of Tillich's struggle with the world's religions.

55. Paul Tillich, *Christianity and the Encounter of the World Religions*, foreword Krister Stendahl (Minneapolis: Fortress, 1994 [1963]) 32.

56. Cf. ibid., 61.

experience the Spiritual Presence in other expressions of the ultimate meaning of human existence and engage in a fruitful critical dialogue.[57] Tillich, of course, justified this dialogic situation in which he said the Christian faith finds itself, since the universal logos, at work in the world at large, and the incarnate logos, manifesting itself in the church, its traditions, and its present reality, correspond with each other.[58]

Tillich is aware "that Christianity must acknowledge that it is a religion and as a religion stands under the judgment of the Protestant principle, the same judgment with which it judges all other religions. On the other hand, Christianity must manifest that in the Christ, particularly in the Cross of Christ, it has a principle which transcends religion, which is the end of religion. In this tension Christianity stands."[59] Again, this statement and the following is from a presentation on "Christian and Non-Christian Revelation" that Tillich made in 1961. It was there that he further stated: "Revelatory experiences underlie all religions. There is not an exclusive Christian revelation. If that were the case, it could not even have been received by man." An exclusive Christian revelation would be so unique that humanity would have no categories in which to phrase it. It would be elusive and no longer containable in human form. But even contained in earthen vessels, we cannot simply ask people to accept the Christian revelation. Tillich explained:

> Were I a missionary, I would not approach the Japanese people and say, as I did not in my many speeches and discussions, "become a Christian, become a Methodist, or Lutheran, or Roman Catholic, or whatever you want." That might happen voluntarily of course. But I would say, "We don't want to bring you another religion. We want to point to a criterion which is the criterion over and against all religions, including our own. If you accept this criterion, you may judge yourselves as much as you judge us and perhaps we can unite in the acceptance of this criterion, because this criterion is nothing other than the majesty of the divine or holy itself over against any particular form in which it appears."

---

57. Cf. ibid., 78–79.

58. Cf. Tillich, *Systematic Theology*, vol. 1: *Reason and Revelation. Being and God* (Chicago: University of Chicago Press, 1951) 28.

59. Tillich, "Christian and Non-Christian Revelation," in *Encounter of Religions and Quasi-Religions*, 72–73, for this and the following two quotes.

This means that Tillich did not give up on the centrality of the Christ event. However, he did not want it to be confused with any particular denominational expression. At the same time he knows that it can only be apprehended in that kind of particularistic expression.

Even in his last public lecture, "The Significance of the History of Religions for Systematic Theology," delivered on the evening of October 12, 1965, Tillich did not stray from this path. He claimed though that "there are revealing and saving powers in all religions" and that

> there may be—and I stress this, there *may* be—a central event in the history of religions which unites the positive results of those critical developments in the history of religion in and under which revelatory experiences are going on—an event which therefore, makes possible a concrete theology that has universalistic significance.[60]

Tillich was much more hesitant than Troeltsch had been to assert that there is actually a central event in the history of religions as a unifying factor. He only conceded that there may be this possibility. He also refrained from spelling out in speculative fashion what this "central event in the history of religions" might be. Roman Catholic theologians, especially in the wake of Vatican II (1962–1965) were less restrained to name that central event. This, of course, was due to the "Declaration on the Relationship of the Church to Non-Christian Religions" of Vatican II.

Already in 1964, a year prior to the official promulgation of the *Declaration*, Pope Paul VI (1897–1978) set up a Secretariat for Non-Christian Religions, the aim of which was "to create a climate of cordiality between Christians and followers of other religions, to dissipate prejudice and ignorance, especially among Catholics, and to establish fruitful contact with members of other religions concerning questions of common interest."[61] This indicates a new climate which no longer juxtaposes the Christian faith and non-Christian religions. This is underscored in the *Declaration* where we read: "For all peoples comprise a single community, and have a single origin, since God made the whole

---

60. Paul Tillich, *The Future of Religion*, ed. Jerald C. Brauer (New York: Harper, 1966) 81. In this essay Tillich does not tire in emphasizing the importance of the world religions for systematic theologians. This is a much needed emphasis.

61. According to *The Documents of Vatican II*, Walter M. Abbott, gen. ed. (New York: America, 1966) 660 n. 1.

race of men dwell over the entire face of the earth (cf. Acts 17:26). One also is their final goal: God. His providence, His manifestations of goodness, and His saving designs extend to all men (cf. Wis. 8:1; Acts 14:17; Rom. 2:6–7; 1 Tim. 2:4) against the day when the elect will be united in that Holy City, ablaze with the splendor of God, where the nations will walk in His light (cf. Apoc. 21:23f.).″[62]

The Second Vatican Council affirmed here that all of humanity forms one community. Humanity has one origin and one destiny, and in the eschaton will be united again in and with God. The document specifically singles out Hinduism, Buddhism and Islam. Especially with the latter it wants to leave behind the many quarrels and hostilities of the past to strive for mutual understanding. The Council therefore declares: "The Catholic Church rejects nothing which is true and holy in these religions."[63] It also affirms that though these religions are quite different from the Christian faith, both in practice and teaching, nevertheless they "often reflect a ray of that Truth which enlightens all men." The faithful are exhorted by the Council "through dialogue and collaboration with the followers of other religions . . . [to] promote the spiritual and moral goods found among these men, as well as the values in their society and culture." It is no surprise that here religious freedom is unambiguously affirmed as well as the need to cooperate with other religions and to affirm whatever positive contributions they make to society. The Declaration also makes overtures to the Jewish community, no longer talking about the need of their conversion to Christianity, but affirming the common roots and even the necessity of common biblical and theological studies.

Pope John Paul II (1920–2005) gave the rapprochement with other Christian religions added impetus, when in his first encyclical letter of 1979 he asked why followers of non-Christian religions can make Christians ashamed through their firm beliefs. He then recommended activities that facilitate a "coming closer together," for instance, "through dialogue, contacts, prayer in common, investigation of treasures of human spirituality."[64] In a speech in 1981, he summoned all Christians to

---

62. "Declaration on the Relationship of the Church to Non-Christian Religions" (1) in *The Documents of Vatican II*, 660–61.

63. "Declaration on the Relationship of the Church to Non-Christian Religions" (2) 662–63, for this and the following two quotes.

64. As quoted in Jacques Dupuis, "Interreligious Dialogue in the Church's

a commitment to dialogue with the believers of other religions "so that mutual understanding and collaboration may grow; so that moral values may be strengthened; so that God may be praised in all creation."[65] The stance of Pope John Paul II is not simply pragmatic. The coming together with other religions also serves a doxological function, that all of humanity may honor its creator with one voice.

A few years later (1984), John Paul II affirmed: "God is the Father of the entire human family; Christ has joined every person to Himself; the Spirit works in each individual. Therefore, dialogue is also based on love for the human person as such . . . and on the bond existing between culture and the religions which people profess."[66] We are not only referred here to the work of God as the originator and facilitator of the human journey. There is specific mention of the work of the spirit in each human individual and that Christ has joined every person to himself. This means that whether recognized or not, the triune God is present, in the whole world, including in every religion. Because of this triune presence, John Paul II explained: "Authentic dialogue becomes witness and true evangelization is accomplished by respecting and listening to one another."

This positive appreciation of non-Christian religions was immediately picked up on by Karl Rahner (1904–84), the premier Roman Catholic theologian of the twentieth century.[67] Starting with Paul's insight that non-Christians do not know God and yet worship him (Acts 17:23), Rahner is free to admit "that God is greater than man and the Church."[68] Though we should be firm toward all non-Christian religions, we should at the same time be humble and tolerant. There is no doubt for Karl Rahner that Christianity is the absolute religion, intended for all people. He claims that "Christ and his continuing historical presence in the world (which we call 'Church') is *the* religion which binds man

---

Evangelizing Mission," in René Latourelle, ed., *Vatican II. Assessment and Perspectives. Twenty-five Years After (1962–1987)* (New York: Paulist, 1989) 3:251.

65. As quoted in ibid., 3:252.

66. As quoted in ibid., 3:253, for this and the following.

67. Cf. Karl Rahner, "Christianity and the Non-Christian Religions," in *Theological Investigations*, vol. 5: *Later Writings*, trans. Karl H. Kruger (Baltimore: Helicon, 1966) 115–34.

68. Ibid., 134.

to God."⁶⁹ Yet he affirms that a non-Christian religion too contains supernatural elements arising out of the grace which is given to all as a gratuitous gift on account of Christ.

Without denying the error and depravity contained in it, Rahner asserted: "A non-Christian religion can be recognized as a *lawful religion*."⁷⁰ Such concession to the validity of non-Christian religions witnesses to the fact that God is present outside the limits of the visible church. It also suggests that every human being is really and truly exposed to the influence of divine, supernatural grace which offers an interior union with God and which demands a decision toward this grace which is reflected in the non-Christian attitude towards his "lawful" religion. Rahner understands by lawful religion "an institutional religion whose 'use' by man at a certain period can be regarded on the whole as a positive means of gaining the right relationship to God and thus for the attaining of salvation, a means which is therefore positively included in God's plan of salvation."⁷¹ This means that the religions outside and prior to Christianity are not regarded as illegitimate from the very start, but as quite capable of having positive significance. A member of a non-Christian religion is not labeled a mere non-Christian, but someone "who can and must be regarded in this or that respect as an anonymous Christian."⁷² That person already has some knowledge, however distorted, of God's grace and truth. The transition between Christian and non-Christian, or between Christians and Christendom itself, is then no longer expressed in terms of an absolute *either-or*, but in a gradual *more or less*. In his *Foundations of Christian Faith*, Rahner no longer used the term "anonymous Christians," a term which caused a lot of controversy. But he still affirmed that "in this Spirit of his he [Christ] is present and operative in all faith."⁷³

Rahner's stand excludes a conversion in the traditional sense as the goal of missionary activity. In most cases the goal would rather be an explicit self-realization of one's hitherto anonymous Christian existence and an ever growing awareness of God's grace and truth. Two

69. Ibid., 118.
70. Ibid., 121.
71. Ibid., 125.
72. Ibid., 131.
73. Karl Rahner, *Foundations of Christian Faith. An Introduction to the Idea of Christianity*, trans. William V. Dych (New York: Crossroad, 1990) 318.

big questions, however, emerge in listening to Rahner's thoughtful and persuasive approach: 1) Did not Jesus' proclamation and that of the early church lead first to a decision and then to a continuous growth in grace and truth, while Rahner's approach proceeds in the opposite direction? There is a growth in grace and truth but no longer a necessary decision. 2) Does not Rahner's approach by avoiding a clear distinction between Christian and non-Christian faiths, lead to a sliding scale of Christianity in which one is never really certain whether one is already on the side of those who are saved? The latter reservation is amplified through Rahner's remark that one reason for missionary activity is that "the individual who grasps Christianity in a clearer, purer and more reflective way has, other things being equal, a still greater chance of salvation than someone who is merely an anonymous Christian."[74]

The Swiss theologian Hans Küng (b. 1928) taught in the Roman Catholic faculty at the University of Tübingen until he got into trouble with Rome for his modernistic tendencies and was removed from that faculty. He was then appointed to a professorship for ecumenical theology outside of that faculty and remained at Tübingen. Küng at once picked up on the new approach of Vatican II toward other religions. His major concern is with the countless millions outside Christianity who are no longer considered to be poor heathen, but rather are modern people in industrialized countries with great and ancient cultures, such as in India and Japan. He does not find the dialectic approach satisfying, because it ultimately labels world religions as an expression of unbelief and godlessness. He does not feel either that the traditional Roman Catholic stance, which asserts that there is no salvation outside the church, still applies to our present problems concerning world religions. He finds the fact affirmed by Vatican II "that men can be saved outside the Catholic Church."[75]

Nevertheless, Hans Küng initially assumed a dialectic position in which he argues on the one hand that though the world religions contain truth concerning the true God, they are in error. They are "an expression of estrangement from God and from him whom the gracious God has sent, and who is not only light but *the* Light, not only truth but *the*

---

74. Rahner, "Christianity and the Non-Christian Religions," 132.

75. Hans Küng, *Freedom Today*, trans. Cecily Hastings (New York: Sheed & Ward, 1966) 121.

Truth."⁷⁶ But Küng concedes on the other hand that "the world religions do, though in error, proclaim the truth of the true God." Though they are far from God he is not far from them. They may flee from the true God but they are graciously held by one who is their God too. Thus the grace of the true God can witness itself even through false gods, and one can trace the image of the true God even through its misplaced and disassociated features. Küng, however, goes far beyond his initial dialectic approach when he adopts a concept of the universal presence and grace of God to suggest that while the church is the "extraordinary" way of salvation, the world religions are the "ordinary" way of salvation for non-Christian humanity.

> God is the Lord not only of the special salvation history of the Church, but also of that other salvation history: the universal salvation history of all mankind. This universal salvation history is bound up with special salvation history in a common origin, meaning and goal, and is subject to the same grace of God.

With this highly universalistic approach, Küng goes well beyond Vatican II. Though it was asserted at Vatican II that the Roman Catholic Church rejects nothing that is true and holy in other religions, Küng can hardly find backing in Vatican II when he surmises that "*every* world religion is under God's grace and can be a way of salvation: whether it is primitive or highly evolved, mythological or enlightened, mystical or rational, theistic or non-theistic, a real or only a quasi-religion. Every religion can be a way of salvation and we may hope that every one is."⁷⁷ Still, these assumptions do not abolish for Küng the uniqueness of the Christian faith. Küng finds that this radical universalism is grounded, centered and made concrete in Jesus Christ, in whom God has spoken for all humanity in a unique way. Without this concretization, Küng claims, we would not know that God's love includes all people, that God desires all people to be saved, and that he gave Jesus Christ as a ransom for all (1 Tim 2:4–6). Therefore, Küng does not want the church to stop bearing witness to Jesus Christ in the sight of the world religions, to cease with the proclamation, declaration, and exposition of his gospel.⁷⁸ But Küng insists that the church should also function as the true "vanguard

---

76. Ibid., 139–40, including the following two quotes.
77. Ibid., 147.
78. Cf. ibid., 155.

of humanity," a living invitation and a joyful challenge to the people of the world religions.[79] He reminds us too that we should have a more relaxed attitude towards the traditional "saving of souls" as the exclusive function of the church, discovering that the salvation of humanity does not depend on us, since it is already accomplished in Jesus Christ.

While Küng has written on many different topics and knows how to engage his large readership, he has more recently paid attention again to the dialogue with other world religions, though from a more ethical, if not to say, pragmatic perspective. *Ecumene*, he claims, is not just the community of the Christian churches, but in its original meaning it signifies the whole inhabited earth, which implies the community of the great religions of the world.[80] In a project on a global ethos (*Global Responsibility: In Search of a New World Ethic*), he seeks to develop an ecumenical theology for peace. His contention is: "no human life together without a world ethics for the nations; no peace among the nations without peace among the religions; no peace among the religions without dialogue among the religions."[81] It is easy to see that with his thoughts he is again inspired by some arguments advanced by Pope John Paul II. Yet his global ethos goes beyond the Pope's stand on global solidarity. The question remains to be seen whether an ethos can be developed beyond what Martin Luther already advanced, namely that the Ten Commandments are given by God through reason and therefore are obligatory for all of humanity to ensure its survival.

It is not without significance that Roman Catholic theology can more easily adopt a positive understanding of the world's religions even to the point of asserting that there is saving grace in them. It does so without sliding into the path of liberalism, which reduces religious diversity to the assertion that behind all the religious phenomena there is just one god. Inspired by Vatican II and Pope John Paul II, Roman Catholic theology approaches other religions in a Trinitarian, if not to say Christocentric fashion. The triune God is operative throughout the world and therefore also in other religions. This provides both the possibility of affirming a saving grace in them and also of accepting in them that which is good and salutary for human survival and human solidar-

---

79. Ibid., 160.

80. Cf. Hans Küng, *Global Responsibility. In Search of a New World Ethic*, trans. John Bowden (New York: Crossroad. 1991) 76.

81. Ibid., 138.

ity. There is also a move that goes in a very different direction, no longer asserting a triune God operative in the world, but claiming a Copernican revolution in correlating the Christian faith with other religions.

The official Roman Catholic Church, however, clearly rejected the idea that salvific figures in other religions can be seen as parallel and complementary to Christ. In 2000, the Congregation for the Doctrine of the Faith, under the leadership of its prefect, Joseph Cardinal Ratzinger, now Pope Benedict XVI (b. 1927) issued the declaration "Dominus Iesus: On the Unicity and Salvific Universality of Jesus Christ in the Church." It states: "4. The Church's constant missionary proclamation is endangered today by relativistic theories which seek to justify religious pluralism, not only *de facto*, but also *de iure* (*or in principle*)." Then it continues to assert the definitive and complete character of the revelation of Jesus Christ. Therefore no complementarity can be found in other religions. At the same time, it is recognized "that there are some elements in these texts which may be *de facto* instruments by which countless people throughout the centuries have been and still are able today to nourish and maintain their life-relationship with God" (no. 8).

Cardinal Ratzinger could then admit that in the world religions we can find a secret working of God behind them. "Through the other religions God touches man and brings him onto the path. But it is always the same God, the God of Jesus Christ."[82] The important point here is the Christocentricity. God is at work even through other religions, but it is the God who in fullness can only be known through Jesus Christ. The caution against a religious pluralism was also voiced by John Paul II when he stated: "It is wrong to consider the church as the path to salvation equal to those of other religions."[83] As prefect of the Congregation for the Doctrine of Faith Cardinal Ratzinger identified "the theology of religious pluralism as the number one enemy of the faith."[84] While at least for the present pope the issue of religious pluralism is also tied

---

82. Joseph Cardinal Ratzinger, *Salt of the Earth: The Church at the End of the Millennium. An Interview with Peter Seewald*, trans. Adrian Walker (San Francisco: Ignatius, 1997) 259.

83. John Paul II, "Not All Religions Are Equal," in *Ecumenical News International: Bulletin* (February 9, 2000) 24.

84. John L. Allen, Jr., *Pope Benedict XVI: A Biography of Joseph Ratzinger* (New York: Continuum, 2000) 241, where on the following pages he gives examples of Roman Catholic theologians who got in trouble with the Congregation over the issue of religious pluralism.

to the unique position of the Roman Catholic Church, one should not overlook that religious pluralism with regard to the world's religions diminishes the universal salvific activity of Christ. It comes as no surprise that in order to accommodate a pluralistic position a call is made for a Copernican revolution.

A Copernican Revolution

The British philosopher of religion John Hick (b. 1922), among many other prestigious assignments, taught from 1979 to 1992 at the Claremont School of Theology in Claremont, California. He was the editor of the 1977 publication *The Myth of God Incarnate* and concerned himself more than many others with the place of the Christian faith among the world's religions. In an article, "Jesus and the World Religions," in *The Myth of God Incarnate,* Hick makes first a direct attack on Christology. He claims that aspects of the traditions about Jesus have been fused with human hopes and desires so that a great work of art resulted, giving credence to Feuerbach's projection thesis. He writes: "Buddhology and christology developed in comparable ways. The human Gautama came to be thought of as the incarnation of a transcendent, pre-existent Buddha as the human Jesus came to be thought of as the incarnation of the pre-existent Logos or the divine Son."[85]

Hick does not want to downgrade Jesus to an ordinary human being, but considers him as "a man of God, living in the unseen presence of God, and addressing God as *abba,* father. His spirit was open to God and his life a continuous response to the divine love as both utterly gracious and utterly demanding."[86] This means that Jesus had a very intensive God-awareness to which he complied. Yet, Hick interjects,

> if the Christian gospel had moved east, into India, instead of west, into the Roman empire, Jesus' religious significance would probably have been expressed by hailing him within Hindu culture as a divine Avatar and within the Mahayana Buddhism which was then developing in India as a Bodhisattva, one who has attained to oneness with Ultimate Reality but remains in the

---

85. John Hick, "Jesus and the World Religions," in John Hick, ed., *The Myth of God Incarnate* (Philadelphia: Westminster, 1977) 169.

86. Ibid., 172.

human world out of compassion for mankind and to show others the way of life.[87]

The dogmatic conceptuality of Jesus' significance was therefore totally accidental and synonymous with what happened to Buddha in Mahayana Buddhism.

Hick disclaims that Jesus was literally God incarnate, that by his death alone humanity can be saved, and only by responding to him humanity can attain salvation, i.e., life eternal. If such were true, Hick objects, the large majority of the human race would not be saved. Hick finds such exclusivism at odds with the understanding of a loving God and father of all humanity. He contends that theologians therefore have developed notions, for instance that devout persons of other faiths may be Christians without knowing it, or be anonymous Christians or belong to an invisible church, etc. But as well intentioned as these theories are, "in the end they are an anachronistic clinging to the husk of the old doctrine after its substance has crumbled."[88] All salvation "is the work of God. The different religions have the different names for God acting savingly towards mankind."[89]

The life of Jesus was only one way in which God has savingly acted, but the ultimate reality has also acted in a saving way in other forms. This does not make the Christian faith superfluous for other religions, because "the specifically Christian gift to the world is that men should come to know Jesus and take him into their religious life—not to displace, but to deepen and enlarge the relationship with God to which they have already come within their own tradition." Hick calls for a "Copernican revolution" in our understanding of religions. No longer is Christianity at the center of the universe of faith, while the other religions are judged according to their nearness or distance from it. Rather God is at the center, and we must see "both our own and the other great world religions as revolving around the same divine reality."[90]

Hick has reiterated over and over again his Copernican revolution in theology, away from the Christianity-centered universe of faith to a

---

87. Ibid., 176.
88. Ibid., 180.
89. Ibid., 181, for this and the following quote.
90. John Hick, *The Second Christianity* (London: SCM, 1983 [1968]) 82.

God-centered universe.[91] According to Hick, God is the sun from whom all light and life originates and whom all religions reflect in their own ways. Hick hypothesizes that God, the ultimate divine reality, in what Karl Jaspers called the axial period (ca. 800–500 BCE), revealed his presence and will to humanity "through a number of especially sensitive and responsive persons."[92] These people in turn gave rise to the different world religions, according to the history, culture, language, and climate of their particular time and place.

Hick suggests that the differences between the variant forms of religious experience in thought should not be played down, but one should realize "that the great world faiths embody different perceptions and conceptions of, and correspondingly different responses to, the Real or the Ultimate from within the major variant cultural ways of being human."[93] This means that fascinating differences but also a basic complementarity exist between the religious traditions. According to Hick, "salvation consists in human beings becoming fully human, by fulfilling the God-given potentialities of their nature."[94] This gradual growth is "a slow and many-sided process" which is not just reserved for Christians but open for everyone. The Christian tradition is only one of a plurality of contexts of salvation within which the transformation of human existence from self-centeredness to God-centeredness is occurring. It can no longer be claimed, since the empirical evidence stands against it, that "Christianity constitutes a more favorable setting for this transformation than other traditions."[95] We must be much more modest in our claims. As Christians "we can revere Christ as the one through whom we have found salvation, without having to deny other points of reported saving contact between God and man. We can commend the way of Christian faith without having to discommend other ways of faith. We can say that

---

91. Cf. John Hick, *God and the Universe of Faiths* (London: Collins, 1977) 131.

92. Cf. John Hick, "Whatever Path Men Choose Is Mine," in *Christianity and Other Religions. Selected Readings*, ed. John Hick and Brian Hebblethwaite (Philadelphia: Fortress, 1980) 182–83.

93. Hick, *Second Christianity*, 86.

94. Hick, *Second Christianity*, 79, for this and the following quote.

95. Hick, *Disputed Questions in Theology and the Philosophy of Religion* (London: Macmillan, 1993) 85.

there is salvation in Christ without having to say that there is no salvation other than in Christ."[96] Apparently Christ is one voice among many.

How does Hick arrive at such a positive evaluation of the world's religions? There is first of all his self-deemed Copernican revolution. Hick contends that a pre-Copernican claims that Christianity is at the center of the universe of faith, while the Copernican stand maintains that God is at the center. However, we have seen from the deliberations of Vatican II that the Council already claimed that God is at the center, although understood to be the triune God, and therefore intimately connected with the Christian faith. It is clear that Hick operates with a reduced Christology or has eliminated Christology. He also collapses the divine spirit with God and therefore can see the same trans-Christian god being operative throughout the world and in all religions. Important for Hick is also that each religion is a mixture of the influence of the divine spirit and of specific human traditions so that religions are culturally conditioned responses to the presence of the divine spirit.[97] Consequently Hick can arrive at a positive evaluation of the world religions, since they are human responses to the same divine spirit.

According to Hick, the divine spirit or the divine logos has been at work as long as there has been humanity and is still at work today as the various religious traditions increasingly interact with each other. Hick does not see himself as being unfaithful to the revelation of God's limitless love in Jesus when he conceives of this as only one particular disclosure of a universal reality. On the contrary, Hick feels he is taking "the universal reality of God's love seriously," since that love is extended to humanity in a multitude of ways.[98] Hick understands a Christian not as someone who conceives of Christ as the one in whom God disclosed himself in an unsurpassable way, but "as one who affirms one's religious identity within the continuing tradition that originated with Jesus."[99] There is no longer an ontological truth-claim to be affirmed in terms of exclusivity, but a relational one in terms of affinity. There is no singular revelation, but a multivalent one, and the world's religions "are culturally-conditioned human responses to God's revelation."[100] Jesus is

96. Hick, "Whatever Path Men Choose," 186.
97. See for the following Hick, *Second Christianity*, 88–89.
98. Hick, *Second Christianity*, 92.
99. Hick, *Disputed Questions*, 55.
100. So correctly Gregory H. Carruthers, *The Uniqueness of Jesus Christ in the*

not *the* human face of God as if there were no others, but a human face alongside others but not in competition with them.

For Hick religions are "expressions of the diversities of human types and temperaments and thought forms."[101] For instance, Christian ideas have been formed within the intellectual framework provided by Greek philosophy, and the Christian church was molded as an institution by the Roman Empire and its systems of laws. "The Catholic mind reflects something of the Latin Mediterranean temperament and the Protestant mind something of the northern Germanic temperament."[102] Similar observations can be made about the other religions of the world. For Hick religion is not just a cultural phenomenon. It certainly is a way of life, but he states, "we must insist that religion involves knowledge of God."[103] In the various forms of religious experience we have human encounters with the divine reality, and there are on the other hand theological doctrines or theories which humans have developed to conceptualize the meaning of those encounters.

While Hick is correct that each religious tradition "has constituted its own unique mixture of good and evil," he strongly asserts the non-absoluteness of Christianity.[104] Yet with regard to a lively dialogue with other religions he concedes: "We live amidst unfinished business; but we must trust that continuing dialogue will prove to be dialogue into truth, and that in a fuller grasp of truth our present conflicting doctrines will ultimately be transcended."[105] Hick can only advance hope and not much more except the assurance "that each of the great streams of faith within which human life is lived can learn from the others."[106] Indeed, by studying other religions one can always learn about one's own. Yet Hick must face the question why for such a gain one needs unilaterally to

---

Theocentric Model of the Christian Theology of World Religions: An Elaboration and Evaluation of the Position of John Hick (Lanham, MD: University Press of America, 1990) 41.

101. John Hick, "The Outcome: Dialogue into Truth," in John Hick, ed., *Truth and Dialogue: The Relationship between World Religions* (London: Sheldon, 1974) 142.

102. Ibid., 141.

103. Ibid., 148.

104. Hick, "Non-Absoluteness of Christianity," in John Hick and Paul Knitter, eds., *The Myth of Christian Uniqueness. Toward a Pluralistic Theology of Religions* (Maryknoll, NY: Orbis, 1987) 30.

105. Hick, "The Outcome: Dialogue into Truth," 155.

106. So John Hick, *God Has Many Names* (Philadelphia: Westminster, 1982) 136.

dismantle the Christian truth claim. Perhaps what is hidden behind the whole approach of Hick is that from the Judeo-Christian angle we have formed a historical consciousness, which makes us aware "of the historico-cultural limitation of all knowledge and religious beliefs, and the difficulty, if not impossibility, of judging the truth claims of another culture or religion on the basis of one's own."[107] While the Judeo-Christian tradition, at least in its Western form, has faced the Enlightenment, and consequently developed a historical consciousness that makes it critical of itself and of others, such historical consciousness is largely missing in other religions. There are no critical editions of the sacred writings of other traditions promulgated from within their fold, and therefore the dialogue, though certainly needed, is usually offered from the Judeo-Christian side.

Many people share Hick's sentiment that we must reconsider the Christian claim of the uniqueness of the Christian faith. We could refer here to historians of religions, such as Wilfred Cantwell Smith (1916–2000) and Raimundo Panikkar (b. 1918) as well as the Indian theologian Stanley J. Samartha (1920–2003) or the American liberation theologian Rosemary Radford Ruether. A most forceful and influential advocate of religious pluralism, however, has been Paul Knitter (b. 1939), a Roman Catholic theologian who from 1975 till his retirement in 2002 had been professor of theology in the religion department of Xavier University. Already in his PhD dissertation at the Protestant Theological Faculty of the University of Marburg, Knitter urged for a "truly dialectical attitude" toward other religions in order to overcome the negative attitude concerning the possibility of salvation in these religions.[108] Progressing on this path, Knitter stayed with this agenda of a pluralistic theology of religions.

In 1963 Willem A. Visser't Hooft (1900–1985) claimed in a publication with the title *No Other Name*:

> The New Testament is not unmindful of the fact that this concentration of the whole history of salvation in one single individual does not fit into the accepted categories of Jews and Greeks, of religion and philosophy. But it considers this central truth so essen-

---

107. So correctly Paul Knitter in his "Preface" to *The Myth of Christian Uniqueness*, ix.

108. Cf. Paul Knitter, *Towards a Protestant Theology of Religions: A Case Study of Paul Althaus and Contemporary Attitudes* (Marburg: N. G. Elwert, 1974) 231–32.

tial that it cannot be stated too often or too emphatically. In every part of the New Testament, in every stage of the early tradition, we find that the coming of Jesus has completely transformed the human situation. Man's eternal destiny depends on his decision concerning the relation to this one Jesus of Nazareth.[109]

As Visser't Hooft pointed out, the Christian faith did not emerge on an island. There were many other competing religions, and some of them were well established. Nevertheless, the Christian faith claimed the uniqueness of Jesus Christ as savior. This was not understood in terms of excluding the rest of humanity from salvation. On the contrary, others were to be invited to be members of the benefits of Christ's salvific activity.

Barely twenty years later, Knitter put a big question mark behind this book title when he published *No Other Name? A Critical Survey of Christian Attitudes Toward the World Religions*. In this publication Knitter contends that the name of Jesus Christ implies a language of personal commitment rather than ultimate truth. He proposes a "theocentric model" of Christology and asserts a relational uniqueness for Jesus in which Jesus is unique in his relationship with us, and therefore is neither normative nor exclusive.[110] Knitter finds this theocentric Christology justified, since Jesus' original message was theocentric too. After Jesus' death and resurrection the focus shifted from a theocentric to a Christocentric approach, since the proclaimer became the proclaimed. Yet "Jesus gave us no christology."[111] However, he seemed to feel and claim a special intimacy with God, a special sonship, and he had a deep awareness of God as his father which was in line with the Jewish tradition.

When the New Testament writers expressed their conviction that Jesus is exclusive or at least normative, saying that there is "no other name" by which one can be saved (Acts 4:12) or that Jesus is the "only begotten Son of God" (John 1:14), then one has to understand these claims, according to Knitter, in their historical and cultural context. In the classicist culture of that time, something had to have unchanging

---

109. W. A. Visser't Hooft, *No Other Name: The Choice between Syncretism and Christian Universalism* (Philadelphia: Westminster, 1963) 96.

110. Cf. Paul Knitter, *No Other Name? A Critical Survey of Christian Attitudes toward the World Religions* (Maryknoll, NY: Orbis, 1985) 171–72.

111. Paul Knitter, *No Other Name?*, 174.

and normative qualities in order to be true and reliable.[112] Moreover, given the prevailing Jewish eschatological and apocalyptic thought patterns, it was natural that Christians should interpret their experience of God in Jesus as final and unsurpassable. Furthermore, we must consider the minority status of the Christians within the larger Jewish community and within the vast Roman Empire. To defend itself the Christian community needed clear identity and total commitment. The doctrinal language that we encounter in the New Testament and which sets forth an exclusive and normative Christology should therefore be called "survival language"; it was necessary for the survival of the community. By defining Jesus Christ in absolute terms, by announcing him as the one and only savior, the early Christians cut out for themselves an identity different from that of all their opponents or competitors. "Such language also evoked a total commitment that would steel them in the face of persecution or ridicule."[113] Since this context is not the same as our contemporary context, Knitter concludes, we can return to a theocentric Christology that is non-normative and non-exclusive.

Knitter eventually moved beyond the non-normative and non-exclusive to actual pluralism. As he claims, this shift was especially the experience of the "unbelievable and sometimes overwhelming religious richness ... and a multitude of religions which since centuries had lived there [i.e., in India] and communicated with each other (on a practical level)."[114] For Knitter the starting point of the transformation for his convictions is threefold: first, his experience with various religions living together in one and the same locality, then his deep empathy for the validity of other religious traditions, and finally his own Christian faith which he is not willing to abandon. Therefore he wants to foster a dialogue maintaining "the richness of pluralism without allowing it to disintegrate into the pap of relativism."[115] In order to attain such dialogue, Knitter claims that one must adopt a hermeneutics of suspicion, being hermeneutically suspicious of our given Christian positions concerning

---

112. For the following see Paul Knitter, *No Other Name?* 182-83.

113. Paul Knitter, *No Other Name?*, 184.

114. So Paul Knitter in his enlightening autobiographical remarks in Paul F. Knitter, *Horizonte der Befreiung. Auf dem Weg zu einer pluralistischen Theologie der Religionen*, ed. Bernd Jaspert (Frankfurt am Main: Otto Lembeck, 1997) 22.

115. Knitter, "Toward a Liberation Theology of Religions," in *The Myth of Christian Uniqueness*, 181.

outsiders, because too often interpretations of Scripture and formulations of doctrine become ideology, "a means of promoting one's own interests at the expense of someone else's."[116]

Knitter suggests that we perhaps should give up the search or the claim of a "common ground" which different religions share. It may not even be true that we strive for the same in all religions or even have the same God. If we attempt to establish or distill a common essence or center, "we all too easily miss what is genuinely different, and therefore what is genuinely challenging or frightening, in other religions."[117] It may even be that there is not *one* ultimate behind all the world religions, but several ultimates. Against such radical pluralists as John Cobb or Raimundo Panikkar, Knitter is not yet willing to give up completely a common starting point or a common ground. But he shifts the commonality from the *theos*, the divine, to the *soteria*, to salvation. To do this he comes back again to his earlier publication, *No Other Name?*, where he talked about a survival language. This survival language, according to Knitter, is actually an action language. According to Knitter, Jesus "was called 'one and only' or 'only begotten', not *primarily* to give us definite theologico-philosophical statements, and not *primarily* to exclude others, but rather to urge the action or practice of total commitment to his vision and way."[118] This means that the supposedly ontological language is actually a praxis-oriented language. Jesus wants to call us to action. Therefore in the center of faith is not the issue of ontology, but of activity. This shift in emphasis goes together with Knitter's increasing concern for global responsibility, a notion which also shows the influence of Hans Küng and his global ethos.[119]

Knitter's publication *No Other Name?* is indicative of a larger movement that urges the reconsideration of the claim of Christ's uniqueness. Even evangelicals are concerned about this sentiment, since they have admittedly "made it ridiculously easy for liberals to attack classical theology (in particular, its christology). Scholars such as John Hick have been

---

116. Ibid., 182.

117. Ibid., 184.

118. Ibid., 196.

119. Cf. Paul Knitter, *One Earth Many Religions. Multifaith Dialogue & Global Responsibility*, preface Hans Küng (Maryknoll, NY: Orbis, 1995) but also his autobiographic remarks in *Horizonte der Befreiung*, 23, where he mentions his "friend and colleague Hans Küng" and his project "global ethos."

making mincemeat of us, arguing all too convincingly that Evangelicals have nothing to contribute to the discussion of religious pluralism."[120]

The standpoint of the evangelicals is not as uniform as one might think. First, there is the restrictive view that all the unevangelized will be damned. Then there is the more inclusive position that salvation is universally accessible. This view is held by most evangelicals, but, as John P. Sanders (b. 1956) in his comprehensive study *No Other Name* has shown, it can be further broken down into three positions.[121] One group affirms that God will send the message to any person who seeks him out, and they maintain that "only those who hear about and accept Christ from a human agent before death will be saved." A second group affirms that "all people have an encounter with Jesus at the moment of death." Finally, there are proponents of eschatological evangelism, who "maintain that death is not final and that the unevangelized encounter Christ after death." If salvation is no longer contingent upon accepting Christ as one's savior during one's life here on earth, then, the argument often goes, this effectively undercuts "the urgency of proclaiming the gospel of salvation through faith in Jesus. Christ."[122] Sanders has thought through the issue of the necessity for evangelism and gives four cogent reasons in favor of it.[123]

> 1. The first and most obvious reason is that Jesus commanded us to go and preach the gospel to all people. . . . 2. Motivation for missions also arises from the desire to share what we cannot hold inside ourselves, to share with others the blessings we have received. . . . 3. The Bible indicates that God wants to bring the fullness of eternal life into the lives of all people *now*. . . . 4. Finally, proponents of the wider-hope perspective are motivated to missions by the fact that the spiritual warfare that the prophets, apostles, and our Lord engaged in is not finished. The forces of evil still affect human affairs horribly.

---

120. So Clark H. Pinnock, foreword to John P. Sanders, *No Other Name: An Investigation into the Destiny of the Unevangelized* (Grand Rapids: Eerdmans, 1992) xiv.

121. See for the following, including the quotations from ibid., 282.

122. This even seems to be implied in the position of James A. Scherer, "Missiological Naming: 'Who Shall I Say Sent Me?'" in *Our Naming of God: Problems and Prospects of God-Talk Today*, ed. Carl E. Braaten (Minneapolis: Fortress, 1989) 111, who also pointed out the juxtaposition of Visser 't Hooft's and Knitter's publications.

123. Sanders, *No Other Name*, 284-85.

Indeed, it would be a strange idea that the salvation of other people depends on our effectiveness, on our spreading the gospel. As Sanders has pointed out, we proclaim salvation in and through Christ not in order to be a helpmate in God's salvational activity but because of the impact the gospel of Jesus Christ has upon us. Evangelicals still insist that Christ in one way or other is the source of salvation, whether in this life, at death, or beyond death.

The inclusiveness of Christ as the salvific aim for all people has also been promulgated by some representatives of process thought. John Cobb (b. 1925), for instance, asserts "that for us Christ is the Way that excludes no Ways."[124] Cobb brings together the notion of the logos and of Christ in claiming "'Christ' is therefore a name for the Logos. No statement can be made about Christ that is not true of the Logos. But 'Christ' does not simply designate the Logos as God as the principle of order and novelty. It refers to the logos as incarnate, hence as the process of creative transformation in and of the world."[125] While in the classical Greek understanding, the logos stood for the world order, through Christ the logos for Cobb has become immanent or incarnate in the world of living things and especially of human beings. Since God as logos is present in the world, he is present and felt in all events. This divine immanence is the creative transformation of the world, urging on to maximum incorporation of elements from the past into a new synthesis. "To what extent the new aim is successful, to that extent there is creative transformation. This creative transformation is Christ."

According to Cobb, Christ as the power of creative transformation can be discerned in Jesus. This does not mean that Jesus is immediately named the Christ, because it leaves open "the possibility that Jesus is to be seen alongside hundreds of other creative transformers who have fashioned our history."[126] If Jesus is in a more significant sense the Christ, then he must have advanced creative transformation more than these others. While the structure of existence is far from what Jesus had in view, his words do indeed contribute to creative transformation in the hearer. One can see that "they are the occasion for the realization

---

124. John B. Cobb Jr., *Christ in a Pluralistic Age* (Philadelphia: Westminster, 1975) 22.

125. Ibid., 76, for this and the following quotation

126. Ibid., 107.

of Christ within the hearer."[127] For those who did not hear him, so the conclusion would go, Jesus is not the Christ. Since Christ is at work throughout the world, the eventual goals must be similar. Cobb shows this in trying to wed together the Buddhist notion of a post-personal existence and the Christian goal that goes beyond a fully developed personal individualization. "That Christianity and Buddhism could each be so transformed by the internalization of each other as to move toward a future unity is an image of hope in a time of fragmentation."[128]

Cobb goes even beyond that in trying to wed together Paolo Soleri's vision for the city of God, Whitehead's understanding of the kingdom of heaven, and Pannenberg's affirmation of the biblical doctrine of the resurrection. All these images of hope point toward a transcendence of separate individuality in full community with other people and with all things. "In this community the tensions between self and Christ decline, and in a final consummation they would disappear. This is the movement of incarnation."[129] Christ is the way that excludes no other ways, since he is intrinsic to all ways.

We could now cite many other positions in relating the Christian faith and other world religions. But the issues and options would remain the same. Our world has become smaller. We no longer live in splendid isolation, neither with regard to nationality and race, nor with regard to religion. This cohabitation necessitates dialogue and cooperation. It also necessitates that we look at ourselves and ask to what extent our Christian faith is not only expressive of a certain culture, the Judeo-Christian tradition, but has become victim of a certain culture, be it German or Latin American, male-dominated or liberationist. Through dialogue we also become increasingly aware that not everything that we assume to be Christian does indeed carry Christ's imprint. It may often be expressive of our own preferences or neglects. The earthen vessels of which Paul spoke when he talked about God's self-disclosure are very real. How can we then discern the God amid all the real or imagined manifestations of the divine?

---

127. Ibid., 110.
128. Ibid., 220.
129. Ibid., 258.

A Decisive Difference: Jesus the Christ

In adequately determining the relationship between revelation encountered in the Christian faith and in the world religions, it would be a gross oversimplification to abstract from all historical peculiarities and to look for a common denominator. Unlike philosophical truth, existential truth is always embodied in historical forms and is never found in abstract ideas. Hence a strictly phenomenological approach is unable to do justice to the intricacies of history.[130] For instance, Zeus and Yahweh are both phenomenologically speaking high gods, but they bear hardly any other resemblance to each other. It is very difficult to maintain on strictly empirical grounds that all religions converge toward a common goal. The very fact that pre-literate religions, polytheism, and monotheism coexist on the same time level, and to some extent even in the same religion, makes it also difficult to talk about a religious progression in the usual evolutionary sense. Since the major religions are world religions and therefore universalistic, they have incorporated many heterogeneous elements and assimilated them into their own traditions during their individual historic evolvement and expansion. Often these adoptions and adaptations were even made from other world religions.[131] Thus our search for understanding the world's religions has led us to discover certain common elements, and also a remarkable interchange between religions, in part fostered by the increasing amalgamation of humanity. The common elements we discover should therefore not make us overlook the distinctiveness and peculiarity of the different religious traditions.[132] The common elements often have little to do with

---

130. Cf. the excellent essay by Wolfhart Pannenberg, "Toward a Theology of the History of Religions," in *Basic Questions in Theology: Collected Essays*, trans. George H. Kehm (Philadelphia: Fortress, 1971) vol. 2, esp. 75, where he states that the more the phenomenology of religion "abstracts from the historical particularity of its material, the less it is able *empirically* to distinguish between superficial and essential mutualities."

131. Cf. the relationship between Buddhism and Christianity, or even more evident, between Islam and the Judeo-Christian tradition. Wolfhart Pannenberg, "Toward a Theology of the History of Religions," 86-88, has shown especially convincingly the influence of other traditions upon the development of Christianity.

132. This is the problem with an approach through religious phenomenology as Huston Smith presented it in *Forgotten Truth: The Common Vision of the World's Rekligions*, 118. While correctly presenting the commonality among the world's religions, he forgets the distinctiveness, when he claims that he primordial outlook of the world's religions is "vertical," even subsuming under it the Christian hope in the Kingdom of God, and contrasting it with the "modern version of hope" which is emphatically historical."

an actual commonality but might be the result from "borrowing" either from a common source or from each other.

Does this generous "borrowing" indicate that all religions will gradually overcome their distinctive claims for salvation and merge into one religious body of global dimensions? There is no indication of the emergence of one universal religion.[133] Even an overtly syncretistic religion such as Buddhism only adapts heterogeneous elements into its body of tradition, but is by nature unwilling to submit its tradition to other truth claims. Contrary to Toynbee's conviction, it is not a peculiarity only of the Christian faith to assert with utmost conviction the truth claim of its own religion. We should remember that in most countries in which the Christian faith is the majority religion, Christianity is no longer a state religion. Since the French Revolution, a disestablishment of the Christian faith has occurred in virtually every country. In countries, however, where other religions have a decided majority, there is often an emergent religious nationalism. If these other religions hold their own, should we simply admit that each religion has its own view of truth and is co-equal with other religions? Such a position is usually rejected by most religions. Whether Buddhism, Hinduism, or Islam, each religion claims that it has *the answer* for this life and the hereafter. How should we then attain a proper correlation between these different truth claims?

Since neither believers nor unbelievers can by their own volition abandon their own position to assess objectively the religious scene, the best way for adequately evaluating the relationship between the Christian faith and other religions concerning their understanding of revelation is to look for a criterion within our own tradition while being mindful that we can never obtain a "neutral" or "objective" position. With this limitation we could conclude from our Judeo-Christian stand: If revelation means God's self-disclosure, such self-disclosure would occur most effectively in an actual I-thou encounter. Such an encounter is confirmed by the paradise stories in Genesis. But in relegating the encounter with God to paradise, the biblical writers tell us that an I-thou encounter is no longer a possibility for us.

---

133. Cf. Friedrich Heiler, "Versuche einer Synthese der Religionen und einer neuen Menschheitsreligion," in *Die Religionen der Menschheit in Vergangenheit und Gegenwart*, 877-89, who gives a good survey of significant attempts to create one world religion. He realizes that these attempts arise from the feeling of a basic unity of all religions. Yet he does not think that this unity can be attained.

As we will discuss more extensively later, the God-disclosive history of the Judeo-Christian faith is of much more modest beginnings. First Yahweh was encountered through dead objects, in theophanies in a burning bush and at Mt. Sinai. Of course, God's self had to interpret the meaning of these events. Eventually God used prophets, such as Moses, Amos, or Isaiah to disclose Godself to Israel. At a later stage we encounter God's disclosure through the medium of the written word, the Torah, and finally, though not accepted by all Jews, the Christian message that God's self-disclosure occurred through God's embodiment in Jesus of Nazareth. Not incidentally, this incarnation of God in an actual person is introduced as an analogy to the ideal paradisiacal time (cf. John 1). Yet it is not a repetition of the past. Paul, for instance, understood Jesus as the Christ not as a parallel but as an antithesis to Adam, the first human being.[134] In so doing, Paul wanted to show that that which we were initially unable and unwilling to do, to live in conformity and community with God, is now being accomplished through Jesus, the human face of God. As a real person Jesus was able and willing to live in conformity and community with God until his very end. Since Jesus achieved this goal in our interest, or *pro nobis*, we can envision such a goal for ourselves through faith in Jesus the Christ. Moreover, the achievement of this goal can already be anticipated proleptically. The future can be approached with confidence, since the ultimate future, eternal union with God, has already been secured for us through the Christ event.

Virtually all religions acknowledge that the discord we experience in our existence cannot be mended by ourselves.[135] While some religions such as Islam are very explicit that we need divine guidance to attain salvation, others, such as Buddhism, are more subdued in affirming that we are ultimately dependent on higher powers. However, the life of Buddha, as it is narrated in many legends, shows that it was a conversion experience which let him renounce his princely life. Moreover, the enlightenment he attained was again something that came to him from

---

134. Cf. Howard N. Wallace, "Adam," in *The Anchor Bible Dictionary* (New York: Doubleday, 1992) 1:64, who points out the analogy and the contrast between Adam and Christ as portrayed by Paul.

135. This has been forcefully advanced by Huston Smith, *Forgotten Truth*, 143, when he claims that the modern notion of progress contains not actual hope. Only religion does present hope because we are assured that "at death man is ushered into the unimaginable expanse of reality no longer fragmentary but total." Then follows judgment and union or communion with the Infinite.

outside himself. The necessity of such an input from the outside is the central claim which virtually all religions share with the Christian faith.

In Jesus the Christ, the Christian faith claims that humanity encounters the culmination of a God-disclosive history which evolved and grew over the centuries. This self-disclosure occurred in a human being who was not just understood as one divine self-manifestation among others, but *the* divine self-manifestation. Therefore as a sign of their identity the early Christian community chose the sign of the fish, in Greek ICHTHYS, the abbreviation for *Jesous Christous Theos Hyios Soter*, or in English, Jesus Christ, Son of God, Savior. The apostles were called fishers of people (Mark 1:18), pulling people out of the mire of this world, putting them on firm ground, and giving them a perspective for the future. This positive outlook on the world gained through a new life was facilitated by the faith that Jesus represented and gave people access to the God who created the whole world and sustained them in the present, and who guided them and the world to a new future. While the idea of the triune God was a later inference, the original identity was unquestioned, namely that Jesus the Christ through the power of the Spirit showed the way to God the Father.

This recognition of God as creator, sustainer, and savior had immense consequences beyond the strictly religious sphere. We are not wrong to assume that the typical Western affirmation of the world, its typical optimistic and irreversibly progressive spirit, cannot be thought of without the Judeo-Christian tradition as its source of inspiration and its sense of direction.[136] Even the Western understanding of a human being as a person with inalienable human rights is difficult to understand—as pointed out by Troeltsch—without the Christian conviction that all human beings are elected by God to live as distinctive persons in eternal conformity and communion with God the creator, and that

---

136. Cf. the thoughtful remarks by Bernard Towers, "The Scientific Revolution and the Unity of Man," in J. Robert Nelson, ed., *No Man Is Alien: Essays on the Unity of Mankind* (Leiden: Brill, 1971) esp. 166–68. Though aware that there has been science also in other cultures, Towers shows that "science, as we know it on a world-wide basis, stems directly from the culture of the Christian West" (166). He also points out that mutual suspicion and recrimination between science and the Christian faith, "have resulted from both a betrayal by Christians of their own tradition, and an ignorance on the part of many scientists of what that tradition really has to say about the world and our responsibilities to it" (168).

humanity can already now participate proleptically in this promised experience.

It would be shortsighted, however, to conclude that non-Christian religions are just a lie measured by Christian standards. It cannot be substantiated on biblical grounds that non-Christian religions do not contain any truth, that they are plagiarists in the instances in which they bear similarities to the Christian faith, and that they simply express humanity's need for God in the instances in which they differ from the Christian faith. We agree with the ecumenist and historian of religion Friedrich Heiler (1892–1967) that non-Christian religions too bear witness to the fact "that God seeks humanity,"[137] and not only that humanity seeks God. The essence of any religion, pre-literate, polytheistic, monotheistic, or Christian, is the communion of humanity with the transcendent reality. The historian of religion Gustav Mensching (1901–1978) is right when he sides with Rudolf Otto, saying that in all religions there is "a genuine possibility of an encounter with the Holy."[138] Neither the Bible nor even Luther or Calvin taught that God was confined to the Old and New Testament covenant community. Furthermore, the manifoldness of the world religions witness neither more nor less to the sinfulness of humanity in general than does denominational pluralism to the sinfulness of Christians in particular. Therefore, we must move beyond a strict dialectical recognition of a primal revelation to all people.[139] A primal notion of God to which nature, human existence, human history, and human intellect attest, does not adequately reflect the realities encountered in non-Christian religions. We have seen in our investigation of the "proofs" of the existence of God that such a notion is a philosophical abstraction and already presupposes a religious commitment. Therefore

---

137. So Friedrich Heiler, *Erscheinungsformen und Wesen der Religion*, 2nd ed. (Stuttgart: W. Kohlhammer, 1979) 563; cf. also Nathan Söderblom, *The Living God. Basal Forms of Personal Religion*, biogr. intro. Yngve Brilioth (London: Oxford University Press, 1933) 384–85, who stated that for Christian theology the history of religions is a divine self-communication.

138. So Gustav Mensching, *Die Religion: Erscheinungsformen, Strukturtypen und Lebensgesetze* (Munich: Wilhelm Goldmann, 1962) 357. Martin Buber, *The Eclipse of God: Studies in the Relation between Religion and Philosophy* (New York: Harper, 1952) 22, appropriately remarked: "The great images of God fashioned by mankind are born not out of imagination but of real encounters with real divine power and glory."

139. Cf. Paul Althaus, *Die christliche Wahrheit*, 5th ed. (Gütersloh: Gerd Mohn, 1959) 37–94, who only arrives at the notion of an *Uroffenbarung*, a primal revelation accessible to all people.

the historian of religion, Nathan Söderblom, who was also one of the pioneers of the ecumenical movement, was right when he claimed: "No religion is a product of culture, all religion depends on a revelation."[140]

We must recognize that doom can also be experienced outside the Christian faith and the certitude of salvation can also be encountered. A salvational egotism, confining salvation only to Christians, cannot be substantiated from either the Old or the New Testaments. The early church already wrestled with the question of the ultimate destiny of those who had died before Christ appeared on earth and offered salvation to humanity. When it included in its creed the phrase that Christ had "descended to the dead," many of its theologians interpreted this to imply "that those who were geographically or temporally disadvantaged and therefore unable to live their lives in conformity with Christ during their time on earth might be confronted with his offer of salvation in some other form."[141] It would be utterly incongruous with what we know about God that God would permit those countless millions to live in eternity distant from God who never during their lifetime here on earth had an actual choice to accept God as disclosed in Jesus Christ. Perhaps it was because the gospel was not proclaimed to them or that it was proclaimed to them in such a distorted way that they preferred to adhere to their native religions. How could we expect that they would have to bear the eternal consequences of the shortcomings of others? However, it borders on speculation to outline a definite way according to which those not confronted with the Christian gospel can or will be saved.

When we assert that salvation can be encountered outside the Christian faith, we do not open the doors to an everybody-may-believe-as-he-or-she-pleases attitude. There was never the slightest doubt for members of the covenant communities—Israel or the Church—that salvation would only be granted through exclusive allegiance to God within the respective covenant relationship. Wilfred Cantwell Smith has expressed the situation of those outside the Judeo-Christian tradition very accurately when he said that a Buddhist, a Hindu, or a Muslim "is saved, and is saved only, because God is the kind of God whom Jesus Christ has revealed Him to be."[142] As we will see more extensively later,

---

140. Nathan Söderblom, *The Nature of Revelation*, ed. and intro. Edgar M. Carlson, trans. Frederic E. Pamp (Philadelphia: Fortress, 1966) 42.

141. Hans Schwarz, *Eschatology* (Grand Rapids: Eerdmans, 2000) 349.

142. Wilfred Cantwell Smith, *The Faith of Other Men* (New York: Harper, 1972) 139–40.

without Jesus Christ we would never have known, though we might perhaps have guessed, that God is a God of love and compassion. We must agree here with Luther that without Christ we really do not know for sure what God is like. Thus the exclusivistically sounding statement: "I am the way, and the truth, and the life. No one comes to the Father except through me" (John 14:6), ultimately points beyond the Christian confines. It leads us to the recognition that anybody who is saved, whether Christian or non-Christian, is saved by the only possibility of salvation, namely the anguish and love of God shown to us in Jesus Christ. Consequently, the New Testament command: "Go therefore and make disciples of all nations, baptizing them in the name of the Father and of the Son and of the Holy Spirit" (Matt 28:19), does not lose its urgency. But the recognition of the salvability of non-Christians would prevent us from the strange notion that their salvation depends on us and our effectiveness. It would free us from the responsibility of having to win "victories" on the missionary "battlefield" to assure the salvation of humanity. Instead, like Paul, we could state what we share in common with the non-Christian religions and then proceed to the joyful proclamation of God's self-disclosure in Jesus Christ.

While we must admit that non-Christians can be saved, we should not embrace them in pseudo-sisterly love or confuse them and us by calling them anonymous Christians. We have noticed that even in pre-literate religions there is a notion of a high god. But we also realize that only in monotheistic religions is the disclosure of God experienced in a definite personal I-thou encounter. For the Christian faith the culmination of this disclosive process, however, seems to come in Jesus the Christ, the one God in human form. We have also seen that the understanding that God calls and humanity responds is present in the religious experience of non-Christians. Nevertheless, they still put prime emphasis on humanity's ritual, legal, or devotional obedience as being constitutive for God's activity.[143] Yet we will see that the Judeo-Christian

---

143. Cf. the interesting essay by Carl Heinz Ratschow, "Die Religionen und das Christentum," *Neue Zeitschrift für Systematische Theologie und Religionsphilosophie* 9 (1967) 126, who mentions that the decisive difference between Christian faith and the non-Christian religions lies in the fact that according to Christian faith mortification of humanity is *consecutive* to God's offer of salvation, whereas in non-Christian religions mortification is always *constitutive* for obtaining salvation. While he may overstate the point the significant issue is whether God's redemptive activity is largely constitutive for or largely resultant from human activity.

tradition emphasizes just the opposite, the total primacy of God's invitation to salvation out of which humanity's response follows.

A religion, including the Christian faith, "is not primarily a system of doctrines."[144] It is a faith "'community' with its beliefs, laws, customs, penetrating not only what is usually associated with the 'religious' domains but also the 'profane' realms of communal and individual life." Therefore Christian proclamation will and must also include the practical and the anthropological. An adequate elaboration of the common ground and the differences between Christian and non-Christian religions presupposed in any effective proclamation, necessitates a dialogue. But again a dialogue dare not become a one-way street. Instead, in dialogue not only should we learn more about someone else's faith, we should also become more aware of our own religious peculiarities, thereby having a stimulating effect on our life attitude. For instance, in a dialogue with Buddhists Christians would become more aware of their unique understanding of God's solidarity with humanity through the suffering in Jesus Christ. But we might also wonder whether the Christian aggressive attitude toward nature, which is missing in Buddhism, is really in accord with God's command to subdue the earth. The greatest contribution of any such dialogue would probably be measured by the degree to which it challenges, clarifies and perhaps even modifies our Christian ideas and practices. This means that Christians cannot enter such a dialogue with the idea that they cannot learn anything positive in their encounter with non-Christian religions.

While God's self-disclosure in Jesus Christ is illuminative for the Christian understanding of the non-Christian religions, they in turn form the larger horizon within which the Judeo-Christian tradition finds its appropriate place and testing ground. Raimundo Panikkar is right when he demands a truly dialogical approach which presupposes "that nobody has access to the universal horizon of human experience."[145] Perhaps we should remind ourselves of Paul's own precept: "Not that I have already obtained this or have already reached the goal; but I press on to make it my own, because Jesus Christ has made me his own" (Phil

---

144. So rightly Joseph M. Kitagawa, *The History of Religions: Understanding Human Experience* (Atlanta: Scholars, 1987) 266, in his helpful four points to be observed in an interfaith dialogue.

145. Raimundo Pannikkar, "Sunyata and Pleroma: The Buddhist and Christian Response to the Human Predicament," in *Religion and the Humanizing of Man*, ed. James M. Robinson (Waterloo, Ontario: Council on the Study of Religion, 1973) 77.

3:12). Then the task of the Christian Church, so eloquently expressed by the Methodist ecumenist J. Robert Nelson (1920–2004), might possibly be accomplished "to make more credible the historic claims which it preaches concerning its role in the ultimate reconciliation of mankind."[146]

"Religion is the foundation of culture and determines the forms of culture," the way we view family, state, economic order, art, and science.[147] This means that each religion has its own way of informing the life of its adherers. At the same time, however, we notice a phenomenon called globalization which is driven mainly by economic factors and attempts to impose on all of humanity, regardless of their religious or non-religious affiliation, similar patterns of conduct. Whether one works for a multinational corporation in India, Germany, or Sierra Leone, whether one is a Hindu, Muslim, or Christian, the standards for working in these corporations are virtually identical. The same is true for using the products of these multinationals. If one pilots a Boeing airplane, procedures are standardized regardless of the pilot's national or religious affiliation. Since globalization impacts our everyday life to an ever greater degree, from the fruit we eat, to the clothes we wear, and the gadgets we use to communicate with each other, religion is more and more relegated to the fringes of our life and has become an extremely private matter. Globalization results in an increasing secularization of all facets of life. This is even true for religion in that it often becomes a watered down buffet table of beliefs, in which particularities and absolute claims are shunned. Often religion has become success-oriented as a means to make us feel good and to provide us with God's "blessings."

We encounter the paradoxical situation that, on the one hand, religion enjoys increasing popularity, not only through religious nationalism, but also through the increasing awareness by people that they need a spiritual base from which to order their lives. On the other hand, most noticeably in the urban environment, life proceeds as if religion were virtually non-existent. Through its emphasis on one God distinct from the created world, the Judeo-Christian tradition facilitated a desacralization of the world, while at the same time maintaining its transparency for the sacred, for God as the creator, sustainer and redeemer. But the

---

146. J. Robert Nelson, "Signs of Mankind's Solidarity," in *No Man Is Alien*, 13.

147. This has been pointed out very well by Owen C. Thomas, ed., *Attitudes Toward Other Religions: Some Christian Interpretations* (London: SCM, 1969) 2.

modern process of secularization tends to be strictly mono-dimensional. It allows for no dialectic between the creator and the created, but focuses only on the created under the aspect of the material. The resultant practical materialism threatens to undermine the spiritual impact of every religion and will have dangerous results in the long run.

Finite humanity always needs and searches for an ultimate foundation upon which it can place its trust and from which it can obtain guidance for conducting its life. The new practical materialism, however, attempts to take over the spiritual direction once provided by religion. How threatening and destabilizing this move has become, shows itself, for example, in the Japanese context. In line with the Confucian religious tradition the employer was regarded as a kind of patriarch, who looked out for the well-being of the employees who in turn pledged their whole energies for the success of the company. However, due to economic constraints, lifelong employment is no longer assured and one faces sudden lay-offs. Here the whole fabric of society is threatened. Many other examples could be adduced that show that this kind of emphasis on the material increases dehumanization instead of furthering the human good.

The Judeo-Christian tradition cannot let this materialistic globalization continue unquestioned. While witnessing to the one God who is the creator and sustainer of all, globalization can be affirmed as a good pointer to the unity of the world and of its humanity even in observing similar standards of conduct. But we are mindful of Jesus' caution against the temptation of materialism: "One does not live by bread alone" (Matt 4:4). Since globalization regards the material without its relationship to its creator, the direction and purpose of globalization remain within the realm of the material and includes the maximizing of material returns, expansion to crowd out competitors, and improving the efficiency of all processes. Again we should laud the efforts not to squander our resources and the attempt to reap the highest benefits. But the workers who enable the productive process do not come into focus as human beings. They are considered as material to increase productivity or as a hindrance to that effect. If, however, human beings are living beings, as the creation accounts assure us (cf. Gen 2:7), we cannot leave out the life-giving spirit. There must also be a depth dimension, a spiritual side, to the material basis of globalization.

Lest we evolve into a world civilization without humanness and without a sense of direction beyond progress for progress' sake, we must remind the forces behind this globalization movement that its progressive drive is plagiarized from the Judeo-Christian tradition. Since this process hurts humanity through the exclusive emphasis on the material, this process cannot retain its vitality unless it opens itself to the original Judeo-Christian understanding of humanity as a finite being endowed with infinite value. Moreover, we must caution other religions that they, too, will be endangered by this rampant practical materialism. The nationalistic resurgence of these religions will only render lip service to the spiritual dimension of humanity. But it will not exert any formative influence on the lives of the faithful. Even where there has been a reversal to traditional values, such as in Iran, the people become dissatisfied with the old ways and pressure their leaders to join the globalization movement. Therefore those coming from the Judeo-Christian tradition must not cease to offer to people everywhere, in America and Europe as well as in Asia and in Africa, a frame of reference within which they can understand, modify, and integrate the practical materialism of this globalization movement. To accomplish this task we need an adequate understanding of who this God is who is encountered in the Judeo-Christian tradition.

PART III

The God Who Entrusts

So far we have only alluded to the intrinsic monotheistic structure of the Judeo-Christian understanding of God and to the emphasis on the human response to God's initiative in the salvational process. We have also mentioned that these characteristics induced a world-affirming mood and led to a thorough-going desacralization of the world which allowed humanity to domesticate the world. It is now time to elaborate on these two points.

In both creation accounts we notice the charge that God gives humanity: first, with the words: "Fill the earth and subdue it; and have dominion over the fish of the sea and over the birds of the air and over every living thing that moves upon the earth" (Gen 1:28), and then, according to the Yahwistic creation account: "The Lord God took the man and put him in the garden of Eden to till it and keep it" (Gen 2:15). This means that humanity is supposed to be the caretaker of God's creation. Through human alienation from God, however, history became tainted with human deviation from God's precepts. But there is also the affirmation that ultimately there will be a new creation in which any alienation and separation will be overcome. History is not the working out of human plans and ideas. Ultimately it is God's plan to lead the world's history to its final fulfillment. At the end stands the vision: "See, the home of God is among mortals. He will dwell with them as their God; they will be his peoples, and God himself will be with them; he will wipe every tear from their eyes. Death will be no more; mourning and crying and pain will be no more, for the first things have passed away" (Rev 21:3f). In order to bring this tremendous change about, God has to be the Lord of history. This is the way God showed himself from the very beginning of the Judeo-Christian history.

SIX

The Lord of History

In his magisterial investigation, *The Quest of the Historical Jesus: A Critical Study of Its Progress from Reimarus to Wrede* (1906), Albert Schweitzer (1875-1965) claimed:

> There is either the eschatological solution, which at one stroke elevates to genuine history the Marcan account as it stands, with all its disconnectedness and inconsistencies; and there is, on the other hand, the literary solution, which regards the incongruous dogmatic element as interpolated by the earliest evangelist into the tradition and therefore deletes the messianic claim from the historical life of Jesus altogether. *Tertium non datur* [there is no third way possible].[1]

A similar *either-or* has often been posed with regard to the Old Testament. Either it is a literary composition, implying that it is of little historical value, or indeed it narrates history. Yet already the alternative which Schweitzer posed overstated its case. While the eschatological solution has been widely adopted with regard to Jesus, nevertheless many scholars realized how strongly the New Testament authors depicted this eschatological position from their own peculiar historical, and thus necessarily theological, perspective. The same is true of the Old Testament. We are not confronted there with a relatively short piece of history, at the most one hundred years as in the New Testament. If we start with Abraham, Isaac, and Jacob, and end with the latest prophetic writings, we span nearly two millennia. It is understandable that the earliest history is almost fading into the background, while the history adjoining the New Testament stands out much more clearly.

---

1. Albert Schweitzer, *The Quest of the Historical Jesus*, first complete ed., ed. John Bowden (Minneapolis: Fortress, 2001) 302.

In the past, archaeology has often been used to give more credence to a historical reconstruction of the Israelite history. Yet archaeology has also shown that Israel's past was much more diverse than the Old Testament authors want to make us believe. The reason for this is not surprising, since the authors of Scripture were not objective researchers in the modern sense. They were rather existentially involved interpreters of the history they witnessed or that was related to them. Given therefore "its selective and theological tendencies, the biblical text cannot be regarded as an objective, let alone sufficient, account of Israel's past."[2]

As far as we know, all the Old Testament documents were recorded in post-exilic times. Therefore the question remains, and perhaps can never be satisfactorily answered, to what extent these texts give us accurate information about the ancient Israelites. Whether the historicity of the patriarchal traditions, the Exodus event, or the figure of Moses can be maintained is a highly controversial issue. We cannot expect any help from archaeology either. As William Brown (b. 1958) emphasizes: "Yet the simple fact remains: archaeology can neither confirm nor disconfirm the deliverance of a band of Asiatic slaves from Pharaoh's mighty hand."[3] While we will perhaps never know what really happened in Israel's earliest history, we must acknowledge that there is a certain view of that earliest history portrayed in the Old Testament. Some aspects of this history may be highly colored; other aspects, however, are rather candid and even sobering. When we look through the Old Testament, we notice, for instance, that there are many "names" for God, such as Elohim, Yahweh, El Shaddai, El Elyon, El Bethel, or simply El, the general Semitic word for "god." The main term for God in Hebrew, however, is Elohim. It can denote either God as a proper name or a god or gods, and even the gods. The various functions of this term indicate that the term is not strictly reserved for the Israelite God.

But the term Yahweh never denotes any given god, but rather only the God who is the God of Israel (Exod 5:1). "Even though the Old Testament is unanimous in asserting that for Israel the name Yahweh was first revealed at the time of Moses, nevertheless the Yahweh cult can have roots which in the history of religions go back much further

---

2. So William P. Brown in his helpful "An Update in the Search of Israel's History," in John Bright, *A History of Israel*, intro. and appendix William P. Brown, 4th ed. (Louisville: Westminster John Knox, 2000) 466.

3. Ibid., 469–70.

(among the Kenites?)."⁴ But Israel did not always know God by his proper name Yahweh. For instance, when Moses was sent to Israel's rescue, he wondered how he should introduce the God who had been with Israel's ancestors. The answer is clear: It is Yahweh who was with Israel's ancestors and who will now rescue Israel from the Egyptian oppression (Exod 3:13f.). It is not a "new" god who is introduced to the Israelites.⁵

The One Who Is with Us: The God of Abraham, Isaac, and Jacob

Further evidence of the later emergence of the name Yahweh is strangely enough given by the youngest source of the Pentateuch, the priestly writer, a source usually named P which emphasizes cultic and priestly practices. In both Gen 17:1 and Exod 6:2-3, the writer affirms that God did not reveal himself to the patriarchs with his proper name, Yahweh; for them he is still known as El Shaddai or God Almighty.⁶ In the Israelite religion the proper name for God, Yahweh, is of later date and its appearance is closely connected with Moses. This coincides with the finding that only from the time of Moses onward do we find proper names that are compounds of the proper name Yahweh.⁷ But who then is this anonymous God of Israel's ancestors? While more and more extrabiblical sources can be adduced to cover the period of Israel's earliest history, many of these items are only indirectly related to that history, therefore making a reconstruction always somewhat hypothetical. Yet since Albrecht Alt's epoch making work *The God of the Fathers* (1929), it has at least become clear that the patriarchal stories in the book of Genesis are not mere fairy tales. Rather they give us valuable information about the actual worship performed by historic persons, such as

---

4. Gerhard von Rad, *Genesis: A Commentary*, rev. ed., trans. John H. Marks (Philadelphia: Westminster, 1976) 113, in his exegesis of Gen 4:26.

5. Cf. Cornelius Houtman, *Exodus*, trans. Johan Rebel and Sierd Woudstra (Kampen: Kok, 1993) 1:366, in his exegesis of Exod 3:13.

6. Cf. von Rad, *Genesis*, 193, in his exegesis of Gen 17:1, who mentions that, in the theology of P, God's revelation as El Shaddai "designates a definite and, moreover, a temporary stage of God's revelation to the patriarchs." Cf. also Martin Noth, *Exodus, A Commentary*, trans. John S. Bowden (Philadelphia: Westminster, 1962) 61, in his exegesis of Exod 6:2-3.

7. This was pointed out long ago by Ludwig Köhler, *Old Testament Theology*, trans. A. S. Todd (Philadelphia: Westminster, 1957) 44.

Abraham, Isaac, and Jacob.[8] In his study, Albrecht Alt (1883-1956) assumed that there was an actual cult connected with the God of Abraham (Gen 15:1), the Fear of Isaac (Gen 31:42), and the Mighty One of Jacob. The three patriarchs venerated three distinct numina, i.e., divine beings, of a similar type.

In the course of the occupation of Palestine, these numina were associated with different pre-Israelite sanctuaries, and finally merged into the God of the Fathers under the "leadership" of the God of Abraham.[9] Alt suggests that there certainly were other patriarchal gods, but only these three found their way into the Genesis narratives. According to Alt, some of their characteristic features, such as their ties to certain groups of people, their care for the welfare of their worshippers, and their inclination toward social and historical functions, also are characteristics that are to a higher degree constituent of Yahweh's character. Consequently he suggests that these gods of the Fathers were eventually absorbed into Yahweh, the God of all Israel. Thus the transition was made from tribal and local gods to a national god. Alt rightly calls the gods of the Fathers, "the *paidagogoi* leading to the greater God, who later replaced them completely."[10]

Alt's conclusions bear great merit, and many Old Testament scholars have accepted them, albeit with modifications. There seem to be two traditions, one specifying God through the addition of a proper name, such as the "God of Abraham" (Gen 31:53) or the other which used "God" and then later added "of your father" (Gen 26:24). The name of the deity reveals its true nature. While, for instance, the Canaanite deity Baal of Tyre bears the name of the place at which it had appeared, there is no relationship to a definite place discernible with this Old Testament God. Instead, the name emphasizes a relationship to definite persons. "Because the God of the fathers does not reveal himself in natural phenomena at a fixed place, he does not need to be 'sought' there either (cf. Amos 5:5). No pilgrimage needs to be undertaken to him, he does not 'dwell' anywhere; he is already present with man."[11]

---

8. Albrecht Alt, "The God of the Fathers," in *Essays on Old Testament History and Religion*, trans. by R. A. Wilson (Oxford: Blackwell, 1966) 3-77; cf. for the following 47.

9. Ibid., 55.

10. Ibid., 62.

11. So Werner H. Schmidt, *The Faith of the Old Testament: A History*, trans. John Sturdy (Philadelphia: Westminster, 1983) 14.

This God first appeared to one individual person after whom the God was named, such as the God of Abraham. But this person (Abraham) does not stand for itself. It represents a larger number, the person then being either the head of a clan or the first ancestor who had received this kind of revelation. We could talk here about a family or a clan religion in distinction to the later religion of the whole nation of Israel. This God was a nomadic deity, corresponding to those nomadic groups who did not yet have camels as did later nomadic groups, but donkeys for transport and sheep and goats on which to live. This "God of the Fathers" was deeply involved in the history of the group and guided it.[12] God led them, accompanied them, and guarded the group that was faithful to this God, deciding where they should go and keeping them safe on their journey. While "the gods of the ancient Near East were, to a large extent, associated with particular places and temples," the God of the Fathers whom we encounter in Genesis lacks all such territorial ties.[13] "The God of the fathers is not attached to places, but to persons!"

At the beginning of the patriarchal stories God said to Abraham: "Go from your country and your kindred and your father's house to the land that I will show you" (Gen 12:1). The God of the Fathers or of the ancestors also told Jacob to go back to Canaan (Gen 32:9), the God of Abraham went with Abraham and Sarah to Egypt (Gen 12:17), and the God of Jacob kept him safe wherever he went (Gen 28:15). This God who had disclosed himself to the ancestors of the people remained with the people and was committed to them especially through the promises given to them (Gen 12:2f). Eventually these nomadic groups which were associated with Abraham, Isaac, and Jacob gave up their migrating existence and settled in different regions of Palestine, where Abraham's group seems to have been associated with Mamre near Hebron (Gen 18:1), and that of Isaac with the area around Beersheba (Gen 26:23–33). The God of the ancestors seems to have merged with the local deities in such a way that the patriarchal tradition became associated with the deities venerated at these localities. "The first encounter of nomadic and

---

12. Roland de Vaux, *The Early History of Israel to the Exodus and Covenant of Sinai*, trans. David Smith (London: Darton Longman & Todd, 1978) 273.

13. Tryggve N. D. Mettinger, *In Search of God: The Meaning and Message of Everlasting Names*, trans. Frederick H. Cryer (Philadelphia: Fortress, 1988) 56 and 57 respectively for this and the following quote, in his insightful study.

settled religion in Israel's prehistory led to the gods of the clans and the gods of the land being equated with one another."[14]

Does this mean that these groups reverted again from worshipping just one God to some kind of polytheism? This was certainly not the case, because the deities connected with these different places were bestowed names with El, alone or as a prefix, such as El Olam in Beersheba (Gen 21:33), or El Bethel at Bethel (Gen 31:13). The divine name El is, however, common among Semitic tribes. If "El is not only the proper name for a particular deity but at the same time a general expression for 'god,'" an identification of the God of the ancestors with this polymorphic El would be understandable.[15] We should also not overlook that "the Hebrew Bible rarely distinguishes between El and Yahweh or offers polemics against El. West Semitic El lies behind the god of the patriarchs in Genesis 33:20 and 46:3 (and possibly elsewhere)."[16] The God of the ancestors, though initially the cult of the ancestor deity of a clan, was never a local god associated with one particular locality, nor was it a god of a polytheistic pantheon or a fertility god, such as Baal in Canaan. Through the association of the God of the ancestors with El, it is shown already at an early stage that the God of the ancestors was *the* God. Therefore it did not need a specific sanctuary and could be worshipped at different places.

The One Who Leads to a New Day: Exodus, Sinai, and the Promised Land

Up to this day the Exodus tradition and the entrance to the promised land are the foundational events from which the Jewish community derives it confidence in the Lord of history. "While the Exodus was the fundamental act of God for Israel, the Sinai event acquired the significance of the revelation of Yahweh without qualifications."[17] Yet we must notice that the "early biblical tradition preserves an association of the Exodus primarily with El and not Yahweh."[18] So even there the deity resembled

14. So Schmidt, *Faith of the Old Testament*, 17.
15. Ibid., 19.
16. So Mark S. Smith, *The Origins of Biblical Monotheism: Israel's Polytheistic Background and the Ugaritic Texts* (Oxford: University Press, 2001) 141.
17. Schmidt, *Faith of the Old Testament*, 39.
18. Smith, *Origin of Biblical Monotheism*, 147, for this and the following quote.

"the family god or 'god of the fathers' who accompanies the family on its journeys" as we remember it from the patriarchal narratives.

Moses has often been called the founder of the Israelite religion and the faith in Yahweh. In some ways Moses is that person. But it would be wrong to assume that he stands on the same level as Zoroaster, Buddha, or Confucius.[19] The Yahwistic tradition in the Pentateuch, for instance, does not designate Moses as the leader of Israel, but shows that the leadership of Israel is Yahweh's task alone. Moses is rather described as an inspired person through whom Yahweh makes himself known to Israel.[20] Similarly, the Elohist tradition depicts Moses as an instrument of God, his prophet who is actively involved in the events surrounding Yahweh's self-disclosure. Deuteronomy then portrays Moses as the example of a prophet through whose leadership Yahweh guarantees the continuous connection between Yahweh and his people. With its main interest in the Sinai events, the priestly tradition described Moses beyond the traditional concepts of miracle worker, prophet, or priest. Moses is seen as the mediator between God and the people, the only one through whom Yahweh speaks to his people and the one who alone can communicate with God. Though Moses' reflection of God's glory terrifies the people (Exod 34:29ff.), Moses is still totally human and not free from sin and rebellion against God.

All these traditions assume that Moses was a real person, who, as far as we know, was a Hebrew, born in Egypt and reared under strong Egyptian influence.[21] However, not Moses, but Yahweh is the center and starting point of the Exodus, the Sinai experience, and the conquest traditions. Moses can, however, be considered the connecting link between God and the people. The person of Moses also connects the tradition of the Exodus, the revelation at Mount Sinai, the wilderness experience, and the initial conquest of the promised land. He was buried at a place which was not precisely known to Israel (Deut 34:5f), a fact that most likely is historically reliable. He also married a Midianite woman. This

---

19. William Foxwell Albright, *From the Stone Age to Christianity. Monotheism and the Historical Process*, 2nd ed. (Garden City, NY: Doubleday, 1957) 258, claims, for instance, that "Moses was actually the founder of the Israelite commonwealth and the framer of Israel's religious system."

20. Cf. for the following the excellent analysis by Gerhard von Rad, *Old Testament Theology*, vol. 1: *The Theology of Israel's Historical Traditions*, trans. D. M. G. Stalker (Edinburgh: Oliver Boyd, 1962) 291–96.

21. Cf. Schmidt, *Faith of the Old Testament*, 65–68.

is interesting, because the Midianites were present "in the Arabah south of the Dead Sea" where one might locate Mount Sinai.[22] The Midianites, especially through Moses' father-in-law Jethro, who was a priest (Exod 18:12), could have come in contact with Yahweh, and brought that knowledge to the Israelites who were enslaved in Egypt.[23] If Gen 46:1–4 contains an historical core, then Israel's ancestors in Egypt could have known the God of the patriarchs and subsequently identified this God with Yahweh. Decisive for the Israelites was not this possible mediation of God, but first of all the Exodus experience through which they experienced God "first hand."

Why the ancestors of Israel came into Egypt we do not know exactly. Perhaps in times of famine, nomadic tribes moved into the Egyptian territory to keep themselves and their cattle alive (Gen 12:10; 43ff.). Those who stayed were then required to perform forced labor. Forced labor was also used later by Solomon when he built his cities (1 Kgs 9:15). The decisive point in the Exodus is "the miraculous deliverance of the Israelites from their pursuers at the sea."[24] What impact this event made on the Israelites can be gleaned from the Old Testament tradition which preserved it in at least in four versions, the prose version of Exodus 14 which includes the sources of the Yahwist, the priestly writer, and partially also the Elohist, and then the two hymns of Exodus 15. We do not know exactly where and how the Exodus occurred, we only hear in the oldest tradition, the victory song of Miriam: "Sing to the Lord [i.e., Yahweh], for he has triumphed gloriously; horse and rider he has thrown into the sea" (Exod 15:21). This event was not seen as a natural occurrence or as a victory of the Israelites. It was clearly interpreted as God's doing. Therefore the Egyptians realized: "Let us flee from the Israelites, for the Lord [i.e., Yahweh] is fighting for them against Egypt" (Exod 14:25). The Exodus was undertaken in God's name and the rescue from Egypt was totally God's doing.

Of course, the whole future Israelite nation had not been in Egypt. Nevertheless the Exodus experience had significance far beyond the individual group affected by it. The Psalmist attests to this when he says: "When Israel went out of Egypt, the house of Jacob from the people

---

22. Bright, *History of Israel*, 127.

23. Cf. Mettinger, *In Search of God*, 39, assumes the possibility of such a connection by referring to Nabatean inscriptions from Sinai.

24. Schmidt, *Faith of the Old Testament*, 30.

of strange language, Judah became God's sanctuary, Israel his dominion" (Ps 114:1–2). This means that through the events connected with the Exodus this God became the God of all of Israel. One rendering of the Exodus story refers to the natural cause, the "strong east wind" which blew all night so that the waters receded. But the Israelites were not interested in purely natural causality. For them it was clear that the natural causes had Yahweh as their originator (Exod 14:21). Attempts to explain how this miracle might have been possible are understandable in the light of critical reasoning. They contribute nothing, however, to its theological significance. The same is true of the next important event, Yahweh's self-disclosure at Mount Sinai.

While the Exodus event was the fundamental act of God through which Israel entered history, the Sinai event was the fundamental self-disclosure of God's will. It also established the relationship between God and Israel through a covenant. Since this self-disclosure was understood as decisive for recognizing God's will, legal instructions for daily life and extensive cultic ordinances were included later. One even surmises that the Decalogue was "subsequently included in the narrative of the revelation at Sinai."[25] Since the Sinai event was that important, again we have different versions from the various sources. In the Pentateuch it takes up the most space of all the events recorded there. In contrast to the Exodus event, God's self-disclosure at Mount Sinai is rarely mentioned outside the Pentateuch. Even the names Sinai or Horeb are scarcely found outside the Pentateuch. This might indicate that while God's self-disclosure was important, the place of the occurrence was not recognized as worthy of veneration. It was not understood as God's residence.

When we read that "there was thunder and lightening, as well as a thick cloud on the mountain" and "Mount Sinai was wrapped in smoke, because the Lord had descended upon it in fire; the smoke went up like the smoke of a kiln, while the whole mountain shook violently" (Exod 19:16, 18), we might think of a thunderstorm or of volcanic phenomena. On the southern tip of the Sinai peninsula, a mountain was identified with Sinai in the post-biblical period. But this is not a volcano. The nearest volcanoes are in north-western Arabia on the other side of the gulf of Aqaba. This again could point to the territory of the Midianites and give additional plausibility to Yahweh's self-disclosure there.[26]

25. So ibid., 38.
26. Bright, *History of Israel*, 124–25, even holds the traditional site as probable

The circumstances of God's appearance have sometimes led to the conclusion that Yahweh was originally a volcano or a storm deity. Yet we should note that "the natural phenomena do not show Yahweh himself, but are effects which accompany his coming. (Canaanite religion, too, did not by any means identify God and nature)."[27] Yahweh is not a God of nature and did not reside in nature, i.e., on Mount Sinai. The Yahwist clarified this when he mentioned: "The Lord [i.e., Yahweh] descended upon Mount Sinai, to the top of the mountain" (Exod 19:20). God is not identified with phenomena of the created order, but his activity is accompanied by them. The decisive event of Mt. Sinai was that "Israel received that law and covenant which made her a people."[28] The origins of Israel's faith were shaped by the Exodus and by the experience of Yahweh at Mt. Sinai, where the God who showed his power and might established a personal relationship with that emerging nation. This means that from the beginning of its history in the promised land, Israel worshipped Yahweh.

Yet how did that God disclose God's self? First of all, God disclosed his name. "Strictly Yahweh is not a personal name, but a statement about God in the third person. A proper name of this God is not found."[29] This is different from the Canaanite divine names, El and Baal, which are also general terms for god and personal names for a particular god. There seems to be a unity of name and being in Yahweh, because Yahweh can be translated as "the one who is." Yet "'to be' means in the Old Testament not an absolute 'being on one's own,' but specifically 'to be active in the present,' or even 'to appear as a helper.'" When Moses therefore asked Yahweh about his name, "God said to Moses, 'I am who I am.' He said further, thus you shall say to the Israelites, 'I am has sent me to you'" (Exod 3:14). God's name points to God's activity in the future. He is not just a divine presence, unchanging and eternal, but a God active in history. Yahweh not only discloses his name, but rather the goal of the self-disclosure is the covenant between God and this group of people who became the covenant community. After the theophany in Exodus 19, the commandments were introduced and then the covenant is concluded in

---

though he notes that the exact location is of no "crucial importance for the history of Israel."

27. Schmidt, *Faith of the Old Testament*, 51.

28. Bright, *History of Israel*, 125.

29. Schmidt, *Faith of the Old Testament*, 59, for this and the following quote.

Exodus 24 and 34. The people vow: "All that the Lord has spoken we will do, and we will be obedient" (Exod 24:7). The covenant is sealed with the blood of sacrificial animals.

The notion of making a covenant comes from Yahweh and he sets out his own agenda: "Before all your people I will perform marvels, such as have not been performed in all the earth or in any nation; and all the people among whom you live shall see the work of the Lord; for it is an awesome thing that I will do with you" (Exod 34:10). God vows to have a special relationship with the people of Israel and they are also to have a special relationship with Yahweh. Therefore he tells then: "I am the Lord your God, who brought you out of the land of Egypt, out of the house of slavery; you shall have no other gods before me" (Exod 20:2f). God does not pose certain demands on Israel. From what he has done for Israel in the past and what he is pledging to do for the people in the future, he is asking for a certain response. This response entails unconditional allegiance to Yahweh and abstinence from making any images of Yahweh.

The exclusive allegiance to Yahweh did not imply that Yahweh is the one and only God as creator, sustainer, and redeemer. If this were so, God would not have to be known by his specific name Yahweh. The general term God would have sufficed. Other gods may or may not still exist. For the Israelites, however, they are of little or no significance. Their well-being depends on Yahweh alone. This is evidenced by the iconographic findings of Othmar Keel (b. 1937) and Christoph Uehlinger who state: "There is no doubt that both Israel and Judah took for granted that other deities besides Yahweh existed. . . . Iconography, epigraphy, and biblical texts all point in the same direction: these powers and authorities, *asherahs*, Bes figures, *shaddayim*, cherubs, *uraei*, etc., were not of the same order as Yahweh, but rather subordinate to him, *mediating* the protection and blessing of Yahweh."[30] This means that ultimately it was Yahweh alone who counted. It is not coincidental then that "the prohibition upon acknowledging other gods (especially in association with the prohibition of images) is not found in the countries around Israel," but is a peculiarity of the Israelite faith.[31] Furthermore, this commandment is often repeated within the Old Testament (Hos 13:4; cf. Isa 43:11; Deut

---

30. Othmar Keel and Christoph Uehlinger, *Gods, Goddesses, and Images of God in Ancient Israel*, trans. Thomas H. Trapp (Minneapolis: Fortress, 1998) 280.

31. Schmidt, *Faith of the Old Testament*, 70.

32:12–39), which again indicates its importance for Israel. Nevertheless the historic reality was different.

The Israelites continued to be attracted in different ways to worship idols. This was not restricted to the common people. Often the kings, too, supported syncretism. Turning to other deities meant apostasy from Yahweh, straying away from the one, true God. The prohibition against worshipping other Gods and making images of Yahweh was not a theoretical, philosophical subject matter, but touched on Israel's relationship to Yahweh. Yahweh instructed the Israelites not to bow down to other gods and worship them, "for I the Lord your God am a jealous God" (Exod 20:5). "Jealous" does not imply that God was envious of other gods, but rather that God was protective of the Israelites lest they worship other gods. It is not that they are rivals against Yahweh, but that Yahweh feels betrayed if his chosen people worship other gods.

While there had been some attempts to foster the worship of one god only, as we noticed with the effort of Amenophis IV, the absence of any images in the Israelite faith was unique. At the end of the Bar Kochba revolt (135 CE), for instance, Roman soldiers entered the holy of holies in the temple in Jerusalem, and were surprised to find no portrayals or other images of Yahweh. It is also interesting that except for the golden calf (Exod 32) and the bronze serpent (Num 21:4ff.), there is no mention of images while the Israelites wandered through the wilderness. The prohibition against images may have been introduced for fear that with the representations of Yahweh, foreign images would also have crept in, thus leading to syncretism. Perhaps the second commandment was also meant to prevent the Israelites from getting control of the Godhead by making an image of Yahweh and using it in magic to make the Godhead do one's will. It could also mean that nothing of this world is able to represent God sufficiently.

When we finally consider the conquest of the promised land, the main account intimates a sudden, bloody, and complete victory of Israel over the inhabitants of Palestine.[32] Yet the other less visible picture of the occupation shows it as a long, drawn-out, and only partially successful process. This latter version is also attested more and more through the archaeological evidence. While much is still in flux, "if anything, a synthesis of Albrecht Alt's 'peaceful infiltration' model and an indigenous model is emerging, namely one that proposes the withdrawal of

---

32. Bright, *History of Israel*, 129.

a portion of the Canaanite population from established, urban settings without the violence of a social revolution or conquest."[33] This means that the Israelites were for the most part Canaanites who slowly evolved into Israelites.[34] This might explain why archaeology unearths so many idols in Israel, and it might also explain why the Deuteronomic reformers and the prophets accused the Israelites of polytheism. As Mark S. Smith (b. 1955) attests: "Early Israelite culture cannot be separated easily from the culture of 'Canaan.'"[35]

If the Israelites were really Canaanites who converted into Israelites, were then the Exodus, the wandering in the wilderness, and the Sinai event just literary devices by various writers or redactors, such as the Yahwist, the priestly writer, and the Elohist, not to mention the Deuteronomic reformers, designed to paint a more dramatic picture? If that were the case, the question is still to be answered how they gained their theological ideas. The formative influence could not have been all post-exilic, since at least the reform under King Josiah (639–609 BCE) was pre-exilic. Perhaps Robert Gnuse (b. 1947) is correct when he states "that every generation perceives the nature of the Israelite settlement process through its own eyes, through the values of its age, or according to the message which needs to be proclaimed in that age."[36] While this echoes what we have heard from Albert Schweitzer concerning the interpretation of Jesus that each generation constructs its own image of Jesus, we nevertheless must ask what actually did occur. If God is a God of history, certainly not just of literary history, how can we understand how Yahweh came to appear among the other gods?

Yahweh and the gods

"Yahweh was not part of a cosmogonic myth, he was not descended from a high god, nor was he associated with other gods in any clear way.... Furthermore, the early Yahweh cult either lacked good icons by which

---

33. So Brown, "An Update in the Search of Israel's History," 473.

34. Dever, *Did God Have a Wife?*, 269–70, claims that the Israelite religion "grew out of *Canaanite religion.*"

35. Mark S. Smith, *The Early History of God: Yahweh and the Other Deities in Ancient Israel*, 2nd ed., foreword Patrick D. Miller (Grand Rapids: Eerdmans, 2002) 19.

36. Robert Karl Gnuse, *No Other Gods: Emergent Monotheism in Israel* (Sheffield, UK: Academic, 1997) 58–59.

to represent Yahweh or used them sparingly, and this may have been reinforced by an aniconic tradition connected to Yahweh by those early immigrants who brought him into the land of Palestine."[37] While most near-Eastern gods were thought of as appearing in astral, zoomorphic, or composite forms, Yahweh was always experienced in anthropomorphic form. This is true for the whole Israelite history, starting with such crude anthropomorphisms as God "walking in the garden at the time of the evening breeze" (Gen 3:8) and continued in the New Testament with "Our father in heaven," which the Lord taught his disciples when he taught them how to call on God. Though his "mighty arm," his "loud voice," his love and hatred, his joy and sorrow, and his revenge and remorse intimate human form, Yahweh remains inaccessible and invisible because of his enveloping glory. The only exception in the Pentateuch is Exod 33:23 where Moses is allowed to see Yahweh's back, but not his face.[38]

It would be easy to claim that the anthropomorphic nature of Yahweh's appearance is patterned according to human needs and thus is a projection of the human mind. But we prefer rather to follow William Foxwell Albright's (1891–1971) suggestion that those anthropomorphisms were sheer necessities (and still are) if Yahweh were to remain a God for the individual Israelite as well as for the people as a whole. For the Israelite it was:

> very essential that his god be a divinity who can sympathize with his human feelings and emotions, a being whom he can love and fear alternately, and to whom he can transfer the holiest emotions connected with the memories of father and mother and friend. In other words, it was precisely the anthropomorphism of Yahweh which was essential to the initial success of Israel's religion.[39]

Even today when we advocate a much more spiritualized notion of God, it is still immensely difficult to have a meaningful relationship to "the ground of being" or to "the God who is love." Yet it was usually clear for Israel that these anthropomorphisms were not descriptions of Yahweh. Yahweh transcended all human characteristics that served as conceptualizations of his involvement with the individual and with

---

37. Gnuse, *No Other Gods*, 196.

38. Deut 34:10, which could also be cited, hardly fits here, because the writer emphasizes that Yahweh knew Moses face to face and not vice versa.

39. Albright, *From the Stone Age to Christianity*, 265.

Israel at large. It is noteworthy in this context that belief in Yahweh forbade any material representations. Whenever such representations are introduced, the Old Testament writers endeavor to show that these are trespasses against Yahweh's will which will not remain without consequences (Exodus 32).[40]

Another important feature of Yahweh is that, similar to the God of the ancestors, he was not conceived of as being restricted to a permanent residence or to a certain locale. He was not a territorial God, but a God who associated himself with a certain group of people and who came to their aid. Though he was the Lord of creation, controlling sun, moon, and the stars, Yahweh was not identified with any of them. Usually Yahweh was thought of as dwelling in heaven, coming down either to a lofty mountain such as Sinai or Horeb, or to a shrine such as the tent of meeting, or to any spot he chose. Occasionally Yahweh was also referred to as coming from Mount Seir or from Paran, or just from Edom. It almost appears as if the Israelites had no interest in localizing the exact place of Yahweh's habitation. This does not mean that there were no sacred places, such as Mount Sinai, but that, since there was no special cult associated with them, their precise name and location were unimportant. It was much more crucial for the Israelites that Yahweh came from those places to be with his faithful on their migrations, and to perform his mighty acts during the Exodus, in the wilderness, or in the cultivated land.

Yahweh's most important feature, however, was his relational character. Often this relational character was thought of in terms of a covenant which God makes with his people. Thus we speak of the old covenant or the Old Testament and the new covenant or the New Testament. But such terminology is easily misleading. The Hebrew term *berith*, which is used in the Yahwist (Exod 34:10, 27) and Elohist traditions (Exod 24:7f.) to denote the constitutive event which establishes the relationship between Yahweh and his people, does not mean covenant or treaty.[41] It means rather that either Yahweh is assuming an affirmative

---

40. Noth, *Exodus*, 247, in his exegesis of Exod 32:1–6, comments that the "calf" is explained as a representation of God, "indeed an image of the God who had brought Israel up out of Egypt." Cf. also Albright, *From the Stone Age to Christianity*, 266, for a slightly different interpretation of Exod 32:1–6.

41. The interpretation of the Old Testament meaning of the term "covenant," so central for the Sinai narratives, is highly controversial. We want to follow here with some modifications the argument of Georg Fohrer, *History of Israelite Religion*, trans.

obligation or that he confers an obligation upon Israel. Thus we are not surprised to find the cultic (Exod 34:10-26) and the ethical Decalogues (Exod 20:1-17) in the context of the "covenant." At Sinai a unique event had happened which was to establish a permanent relationship between Yahweh and those around Moses. Israel became Yahweh's people in the sense of being related to him as indicated in sharing the sacred meal (Exodus 24), and by conforming to the same standards. Decisive in this "covenant" concept is that this relationship was founded on Yahweh's unconditional will. God wanted to make himself known to Moses and he wanted to establish a lasting relationship with Israel. Thus this "covenant" was not a contractual relationship to secure certain services or to obtain certain privileges but it was Yahweh's offer to Israel mediated through their spokesperson Moses.

Israel was always aware that the "covenant" with Yahweh was not the result of the unconditional will of both partners, Yahweh and Israel. Also Israel was never so presumptuous as to think that it would make a "covenant" with Yahweh, since the covenant was clearly understood as the result of Yahweh's own doing.[42] Though the partners are infinitely unequal, the relationship does not result in mere domination of one partner over the other. On the contrary, Yahweh obliges himself to a certain way of looking out for Israel. Israel responds with its willingness to fulfill certain obligations. Thus Yahweh's relational character always implies a definite promise on his side. Israel also knows that the covenant entails Yahweh's dominion over those who are related to him through the covenant. This is, for instance, expressed in the conviction that Yahweh wants to be recognized as Israel's only God. As the German

---

David E. Green (Nashville: Abingdon, 1972) 80-81, who rejects the notion that the Sinai events can be compared with the model of an ancient vassal treaty. Of course, Dennis J. McCarthy, *Old Testament Covenant: A Survey of Current Opinions* (Oxford: Blackwell, 1972) 58, is right when he observes "that the apparent sequence of certain ceremonies reflects in large part the sequence of the elements in the treaty documents." Yet McCarthy also admits that many, if not most, recent writers are unwilling to assert that the treaty form is to be found in the Sinai narratives (72). Cf. also Ernst Kutsch, *Verheißung und Gesetz. Untersuchungen zum sogenannten "Bund" im Alten Testament* (Berlin: Walter de Gruyter, 1973) who strongly supports Fohrer at this point.

42. This is especially emphasized by Ludwig Köhler, *Old Testament Theology*, 61-62. One could, however, quote 2 Kgs 23:3 as an exception. But as Lothar Perlitt, *Bundestheologie im Alten Testament* (Neukirchen-Vluyn: Neukirchener, 1969) 262, has recognized, Josiah makes a covenant with his people before Yahweh in the sense of a pledge or oath of allegiance. Josiah would not dare to initiate a covenant with Yahweh.

Old Testament scholar Rolf Rendtorff (b. 1925) reminds us: "Yhwh is Israel's God—that is and remains the decisive content of the covenant."[43] As the Exodus events show, Yahweh's dominion also has a very comforting aspect, because it can even involve those nations who are linked with the well-being of his chosen people. This understanding of Yahweh's dominion was later expanded in two directions: that Yahweh is the Lord over all the world and that all of humanity is included in this covenant. Yet the realization of the promises implied in the covenant was always contingent upon the way the chosen people acted. Thus history seen in relationship to Yahweh became a decisional history, it was not simply a working out of Yahweh's promises, but was also seen as a consequence of Israel fulfilling or not fulfilling the obligations of its relationship to Yahweh.

One of the astounding phenomena of the Israelite faith was that the Israelites did not abandon their seemingly nomadic God once they settled in Palestine. This is even more surprising if we assume that these immigrants were a clear minority in the land. But the groups connected with the patriarchs did not leave behind their God of the Fathers once they moved into Canaanite territory. On the contrary, the Israelites kept allegiance to their God, though using pagan sanctuaries, and gradually they connected these with their own God. Some of the formerly Canaanite cult etiologies were reinterpreted and often used in such a way that the local gods were equated with the God of the ancestors. Especially the god El seems to have been identified with the God of the Fathers without even changing his name. Consequently, we still find narratives with El Olam (Gen 21:22–34) or El Bethel (Gen 28:10–22) or Peniel (Gen 32:25–32) in the Old Testament.[44] Of course, this was not mere equation. It meant that specific elements of the God of the ancestors were introduced into these narratives, while at the same time allowing for considerable influx of Canaanite ideas into the Israelite understanding of God. In the long run it proved to be an effective means for not only occupying Palestinian territory but for making any exclusive worship of Canaanite gods in the occupied territory impossible.

---

43. Rolf Rendtorff, *The Covenant Formula: An Exegetical and Theological Investigation*, trans. Margaret Kohl (Edinburgh: T. & T. Clark, 1998) 60.

44. Cf. Fohrer, *History of Israelite Religion*, 63–64, who cites many examples in which a local god El was identified with Israel's God.

When those whom Moses had gathered entered the promised land and merged with other tribes, the identification of Yahweh with the God of the ancestors, and with the god El, posed no problems. The story was different with Yahweh and the other gods present in Canaan. There was no doubt that those other gods were considered by the Israelites to be actual powers that were the masters over other nations (cf. 1 Kgs 11:7f.). Once the Israelites abandoned their nomadic existence and settled down in the cultivated land these gods were a great temptation for them. After all, the customs and language of the cultivated land deeply reflected the intrinsic connection between an agrarian way of life and the acceptance of those powers.[45] The statement in Deut 32:17, perhaps dating from the eleventh century BCE: "They sacrificed to demons, not God, to deities they had never known, to new ones recently arrived, whom your ancestors had not feared,"[46] portrays the magnitude of the spiritual struggle taking place during the first centuries after Israel had entered the promised land.

Gideon may serve as a prime example to document this inner strife within the emerging Israelite community (Judges 6–8).[47] Gideon was a strong supporter of Yahweh and one day destroyed an altar of Baal and cut down the sacred Asherah in his native town of Ophrah. For that reason he was renamed Jerubbaal, "that is to say, 'Let Baal contend against him'" (Judg 6:32). This name Jerubbaal betrays Canaanite influence, because it is a composite form of Baal, the name of a Canaanite deity. The name of Gideon's father, Joash, was still a composite form of Yahweh, the God of Israel. We also hear that Gideon's own Israelite people were enraged over his destructive acts against the Canaanite deities. But then

---

45. Cf. Fohrer, *History of Israelite Religion*, 102-3. We must agree here with James Barr, *Old and New in Interpretation: A Study of the Two Testaments* (London: SCM, 1966) 72, that gods outside of Israel were also conceived as acting in history. Barr is right too when he claims that revelation in history is not at the center of Hebrew thought. Yet the Old Testament emphasizes on almost every page that Israel enjoys a special relationship with a God who is actively involved in the history of Israel and who discloses himself through his involvement. Even wisdom literature follows this train of thinking though it emphasizes more the majesty and ultimate incomprehensibility of God (cf. Job 26:14).

46. Cf. also William Foxwell Albright, *Yahweh and the Gods of Canaan: A Historical Analysis of Two Contrasting Faiths* (Garden City, NY: Doubleday, 1969) 198, who refers to this passage.

47. Cf. Albright, *Yahweh and the Gods of Canaan*, 199-203, in his references to Gideon.

we are told that even Gideon himself set up a golden ephod in Ophrah. As far as we know, an ephod is a rich costume covered with gold or silver and studded with stars and other cosmic symbols. The Israelites who still adhered to the strict Mosaic tradition could easily interpret an ephod as an idol in analogy to Canaanite statues of gods. But in the official Yahwist cult of the day it could also be understood as the visible symbol of the invisible deity. The story of Gideon gives us some idea of the kind of absorption, adaptation, and rejection that took place in those first centuries after Israel settled down in the land of Canaan.

We have noticed that the Israelites sensed no difficulty identifying the Canaanite El first with the God of the Fathers and later also with Yahweh. But the story was different as far as the Canaanite fertility god Baal is concerned. Initially, some Israelites may have equated Baal with Yahweh or venerated him parallel to Yahweh. Even some of his characteristics may have been conferred upon Yahweh. For instance, we find names that are composites of the name Baal; such as Ishbaal, the son of Saul, and we see that, in analogy to Aliyan Baal, the god of thunder, Yahweh was praised as the one "who rides upon the clouds" (Ps 68:4).[48] However, the constant battle of the prophets against the worship under trees and in high places and sometimes even against the whole sacrificial cult (Amos 5:21–27) shows us in which direction prevailing thinking went.[49]

48. Cf. Hans-Joachim Kraus, *Psalms 60–150. A Commentary*, trans. Hilton C. Oswald (Minneapolis: Augsburg, 1989) 51, in his exegesis of Ps 68:4–6. Morton Smith in his provocative book, *Palestinian Parties and Politics that Shaped the Old Testament* (New York: Columbia University Press, 1971) 19, might be right when he claims: "Although the cult of Yahweh is the principle concern of the Old Testament, it may not have been the principal religious concern of the Israelites." While Smith recognizes that by the tenth century BCE the predominant cult in the hill country of Palestine was that of Yahweh, he asserts that this did not imply a neglect of the other gods of the common religion of the Near East (28–29). In other words, the popular piety was strongly syncretistic. However, Smith argues that a movement existed that wanted Yahweh alone to be worshiped. It gained stronger and stronger influence and finally culminated in the reconstruction and cult of the second temple in Jerusalem. From this movement and its influence stems not only the highly edited Old Testament, "but Christianity, rabbinic Judaism, and Islam" (30). Though Smith may have overstated his ease, it can hardly be doubted that popular pre-exilic piety was much more syncretistic than is commonly assumed.

49. Hans Walter Wolff, *Joel and Amos: A Commentary on the Books of the Prophets Joel and Amos*, trans. Waldemar Janzen et al., ed. S. Dean McBride, Jr. (Philadelphia: Fortress, 1977) 262, in his exegesis of Amos 5:21–27, sees in this passage a "fundamental statement which passionately rejects the cultic festivities." Gordon Kaufman,

In conclusion we can say that Yahweh merged quickly into the Palestinian religious melting-pot, but was not submerged. To the contrary, after assuming some of the attributes of those other deities, Yahweh became differentiated from these deities, assuming a position of primacy. This situation is reflected in Deuteronomy where we read:

> When you come into the land that the Lord your God is giving you, you must not learn to imitate the abhorrent practices of those nations. No one shall be found among you who makes a son or a daughter pass through fire, or who practices divination, or is a soothsayer, or an augur, or a sorcerer, or one who casts spells, or who consults ghosts or spirits, or who seeks oracles from the dead. For whoever does these things is abhorrent to the Lord; it is because of such abhorrent practices the Lord your God is driving them out before you. You must remain completely loyal to the Lord your God. Although these nations that you are about to dispossess do give heed to soothsayers and diviners, as for you, the Lord your God does not permit you to do so. (Deut 18:9–14)

This instruction still does not advance a monotheism in the modern sense of the word, namely the notion that there is only one god. The actuality of other powers besides Yahweh is still recognized. But there is no doubt in Israel's mind that guidance and help can come from Yahweh alone who offered his assistance to Israel and who demanded their allegiance. Monotheism could only emerge once the religion of Israel was no longer a tribal religion or reserved for one nation. Once it was understood that the whole of history is under God's guidance, then other gods lost their persuasive power. But for this to come we have to wait until the time of the exile, when the Israelites "being confronted with the universal claim of the gods of Mesopotamia . . . proclaimed in contrast their own God Yahweh as the universal ruler."[50] For instance, Yahweh announced through Deutero-Isaiah: "Then the glory of the Lord shall be revealed, and all people shall see it together" (Isa 40:5). This means that all people are confronted with the glory of Yahweh. And the word

---

God the Problem (Cambridge: Harvard University Press, 1972) 164, may have captured the truth well when he said: "The Old Testament is the principal extant record of the tumultuous and painful history of a growing consciousness, unparalleled elsewhere, of one God sovereign over the entire universe."

50. Hermann Vorländer, "Der Monotheismus Israels als Antwort auf die Krise des Exils," in Bernhard Lang, ed., *Der einzige Gott. Die Geburt des biblischen Monotheismus* (Munich: Kösel, 1981) 110.

of Yahweh came to Jeremiah telling him: "Before I formed you in the womb I knew you, and before you were born I consecrated you; I appointed you a prophet to all nations" (Jer 1:5). Jeremiah should serve as a prophet to the nations, not just to Israel. The salvational history of Israel was now expanded to include all nations and there was only one God left from whom help could be obtained, the God of Israel.

SEVEN

God's Ultimate Self-Disclosure

Over the centuries the understanding of God as it is reflected in the Bible has changed tremendously. There is a big difference between the picturesque anthropomorphism of the Yahwist who depicts "the Lord God walking in the garden at the time of the evening breeze" (Gen 3:8), Isaiah's experience in the temple when he encountered "the Lord sitting on a throne" (Isa 6:1), Ezekiel's "visions of God" by the river Chebar in Mesopotamia (Ezek 1:1), and Jesus' reference to God as his "Father in heaven" (Matt 18:10). Reflected here is a progressive and continuous reconceptualization of God, moving from a more objectified understanding of God to a more spiritualized one. Yet there is also a movement discernible with regard to the God and the gods. Beginning with Israel's ancestors and ending with Jesus, we encounter polytheism, a stage of henotheism (acceptance of just one god), or a monolatry, meaning the veneration of only one god, and finally arriving at monotheism, claiming that there is just one god, though this monotheism is often starkly dualistic, as in the apocalyptic writings. Apocalyptic provides both the conclusion of the Old Testament period and the background, if not the seedbed, for the New Testament message.

God as the Lord of History

The times of the apocalyptic writings are roughly the years between 250 BCE to 80–100 CE. Since this also includes the New Testament period, we can understand the dictum of the New Testament scholar Ernst Käsemann (1906–1998) that "apocalyptic was the mother of all Christian theology."[1] Preceding that period were the conquests of Alexander the

1. Ernst Käsemann, "The Beginnings of Christian Theology," in Ernst Käsemann,

Great (356-323 CE) and his successors through which the civilizations of the East and West were brought together on the basis of Greek culture. A *koine* or "common" Greek developed which facilitated the process of Hellenization. People of quite different backgrounds were made to feel that they belonged together within the *oikomene*, the inhabited world.

Beneath the surface of this syncretistic Hellenism which stretched from India all the way to Egypt and Spain, the religions of Babylonia and Persia continued to exercise a powerful influence.[2] This new "global" culture was perceived by many Jewish people as a major threat to their very existence. (This is similar to what many Muslims today feel about the pervasive Westernization and globalization of our world.) It introduced Hellenism, a common language, a new (Greek) philosophy which bore highly religious overtones, and it clashed with the promises of God enunciated through his prophets. The sense of apprehension of the Jewish people "was deepened still further by the fact that the promises made by God through his servants the prophets had not materialized. The Golden Age to which they had pointed with such assurance was slow in coming, and now the prophetic voices had long since fallen silent and prophecy itself was deemed to be dead." The situation came to a climax under the rule of the Seleucid king Antiochus Epiphanes IV (175-163 BCE), the period in which the Book of Daniel was written. He vigorously fostered the process of Hellenization to weld together his kingdom. Antiochus appointed a high priest of his own choosing and when the people rebelled, he desecrated the temple, took its treasures, and even issued a decree forbidding the people to live any longer according to their customary laws found in the Torah.

The intention of the apocalyptic writers was to tell the people that though prophecy may have become silent, then, the apocalyptists, were inspired by God to interpret the prophets' message to their own generation. They assured the faithful Jews that the realization of God's promises was not postponed. Now was the decisive and appointed hour. The divine acts of deliverance were going to start within history, a deliverance that was no longer restricted to history itself, but includes

---

New Testament Questions of Today, trans. W. J. Montague (Philadelphia: Fortress, 1969) 102; and the discussion of this thesis in Klaus Koch, *The Rediscovery of Apocalyptic*, trans. Margaret Kohl (Naperville, IL: Allenson, 1972) 78-85.

2. For the following, cf. the description of this new situation by D. S. Russell, *Divine Disclosure: An Introduction to Jewish Apocalyptic* (Minneapolis: Fortress, 1992) 14-17, quote on 15.

the whole cosmos. The sources on which these writers drew were not just the Old Testament prophets. Since they were children of their own time, their writings also betray Babylonian and Persian influences, even Canaanite traditions, and the Hellenistic religious mix of their time. In their visionary experiences the apocalyptists saw themselves standing so much at the edge of history that they could already foretell the unfolding of history and from their vantage point were able to perceive history as a unified whole.

The apocalyptists were utterly pessimistic with regard to what humans could do to change the course of history, since tyrants ruled and crushed everybody who stood in their way. However, "at heart they were men of faith who firmly believed, despite all signs to the contrary, that God was indeed in control."[3] They proclaimed that all earthly powers would be brought down at God's own preordained time and empires and rulers would fall due to God's judgment. Furthermore, rebellion against God was not just a human phenomenon. Satan was no longer conceived of as the accuser of humans before God's throne. He had split into many satanic forces, all devoted to wreaking havoc in God's creation and among people. These forces were even said to have seduced humanity into adoring the forces of darkness instead of the one and only God. But according to the apocalyptists, on judgment day "sinners will be punished and the evil cosmic powers will be destroyed."[4] This means that not just the earth but the whole cosmos will become the theater of God's glory and then God will finally triumph. The apocalyptists "looked beyond history for the fulfilment of the divine purpose; but for them history was still the arena of God's activity on behalf of his people. In this present age evil still prevailed and oppression was still commonplace; but the ultimate power lay in the hands of God and he would in the end prevail."[5]

"The Most High has made not one world but two" we read in 2 Esd 7:50. Of these two worlds, or aeons, we only know the present one, which is full of troubles and anxieties. "God who is himself a single person, made a clear separation by way of pairs of opposites, . . . in that he has set before their eyes first the small and then the great, first the world and then eternity, this world being transitory, but the one to come eter-

---

3. Ibid., 135.
4. Ibid., 136.
5. Ibid., 137.

nal" (*Pseudo-Clementines Hom.* II 15:1-2). The new world is an eternal one which is the opposite of this world and which will come when the time is fulfilled. "And when the whole of creation, visible and invisible, which the Lord has created, shall come to an end, then each person will go to the Lord's great judgment. And then all time will perish, and afterward there will be neither years nor months nor days nor hours. . . . And all the righteous, who escape from the Lord's great judgment, will be collected together in the great age" (2 *Enoch* 65:6ff.). This final judgment not only concerns Israel but has universal significance. Israel's own history is embedded in the totality of history. When this universal history is brought to consummation, Israel and its destiny will have been completed.

As the Old Testament scholar Gerhard von Rad (1901-1971) said long ago, the apocalyptic movement poses the danger of teaching "a great cosmological gnosis."[6] Indeed, the apocalyptists presented a great cosmological gnosis, if gnosis is literally understood as knowledge or understanding. They understood that the God in whom they believed was not indifferent to the cosmos. This cosmos provided the larger context for God's saving history. When later on von Rad changed his mind and thought that instead of understanding history as salvation history, as the prophets had done, history was understood by the apocalypticists in strictly deterministic terms, he was closer to the truth. The apocalyptists wanted to avoid the impression that God's dealing with history was anything but haphazard. God was in control and nothing could thwart his intention or undo God's power. While presently these powers and forces of darkness are still menacing and increasingly threaten us, they will be brought to nought. The British New Testament scholar Harold H. Rowley (1890-1969) captured this line of conviction in apocalyptic thinking very well when he wrote:

> They did not believe that God was indifferent to the world He had made; nor did they think He was impotent to take a hand in its course. They would have smiled at the idea so widespread in our day that God is of all beings the most helpless. . . . The apocalyptists believed in God, and believed that He had some purpose for the world He had made, and that His power was equal to its achievement. Their faith goes beyond the faith in the divine

---

6. Gerhard von Rad, *Old Testament Theology*, vol. 2: *The Theology of Israel's Prophetic Traditions*, trans. D. M. G. Stalker (New York: Harper & Row, 1965) 308.

control of history, indeed. It is a faith in the divine initiative in history for the attainment of its final goal. Such a belief is fundamental to the Christian view of God and the world.... Unless we believe in the eternity of human history in our world, we must expect that somehow, somewhere, the course of history will come to an end. We can look for it to peter out, or we can look for the world to be snuffed out ignominiously. But if we believe that it is God's world, and that He created it with some purpose, we must find some way of translating the faith of the apocalyptists that that purpose will be achieved.[7]

God is the sole agent of all historic and all comic processes. This understanding provides history with a basic unity. As Jürgen Moltmann (b. 1926) wrote: "This historifying of the world in the category of the universal eschatological future is of tremendous importance for theology, for indeed it makes eschatology the universal horizon of all theology as such. Without apocalyptic a theological eschatology remains bogged down in the ethnic history of men or the existential history of the individual."[8] This means that history presses on toward universal fulfillment. The one supra-nationalistic and supra-worldly God, the God of Israel, was now seen as the sole agent of this historic process shaping and destining the world to God's purpose, namely to the endtime-fulfillment. At the same time that God was perceived to stand for more than the ethnic history of Israel, God's name also underwent a significant change. While in the Hebrew Old Testament the prevailing name for God is the proper name Yahweh, the Greek translation of the Old Testament, the Septuagint, mostly uses Lord (*kyrios*) in place of Yahweh. The one who created the universe and with it humanity "is 'sovereign' in the absolute sense."[9]

Outside the Bible the term Lord or *kyrios* had been used for a long time to refer to deities or to the emperor. In the New Testament, however, the terminology employed in the Septuagint had changed again. Now *kyrios* or Lord is no longer the main term for God. It is usually su-

---

7. Harold H. Rowley, *The Relevance of Apocalyptic: A Study of Jewish and Christian Apocalypses from Daniel to the Revelation*, rev. ed. (New York: Association, 1963) 167-68 and 171.

8. Jürgen Moltmann, *Theology of Hope: On the Ground and the Implications of a Christian Eschatology*, trans. James W. Leitch (New York: Harper & Row, 1967) 137-38.

9. Werner Foerster, "*Kyrios*. The Choice of the Word *kyrios* in the LXX," in *ThDNT*, 3:1082.

perseded by the generic term *theos* or God. In other words, the growing awareness of God's universal domain goes hand in hand with changing his name from a proper name to the generic name for God. It is not surprising that Luke and Paul, both being in close touch with the Hellenistic world, even resort to stoic-pantheistic conceptuality to proclaim God (Acts 17:27f.; Rom 11:36). Since God is the only God, every (religious) person knows about God at least to some extent. Yet according to the Christian faith this knowledge is not sufficient, since without Christ, the full story of God's saving activity cannot be known.

The End of History Made Manifest: Christ's Resurrection

The New Testament writers took great pains to demonstrate the continuity of the Christian community with the people of Israel. Yet they also showed that something distinctively new had occurred. For instance, Paul, wrestling with the relationship between Israel and the Christian community, told the Christians in Rome to emphasize their continuity with Israel: "And you, a wild olive shoot, were grafted in their place to share the rich root of the olive tree" (Rom 11:17). In introducing Jesus Christ to that community he pointed to Christ's relationship with Israel, saying that Christ was he "who descended from David according to the flesh." But then he showed the difference by saying that Christ, "was declared to be Son of God with power according to the spirit of holiness by the resurrection from the dead" (Rom 1:3f.). The Gospel of John, too, emphasized continuity. In the prologue of the gospel the allusion to the creation narrative in Gen 1 is unmistakable. In contrast to Gen 1, however, creation is not just through God's creative and ordering word, but through the word that became flesh (John 1:14). In the synoptic gospels, too, the emphasis lies on continuity, yet with a difference.

According to the Gospel of Matthew the church founded by Jesus is the true Israel (Matt 16:18), since the historic nation of Israel has neglected its commission to be the light to the nations. The church is the new Israel and thereby stands in continuity with the Israel of promise. Jesus too is depicted as being in continuity with the Old Testament by referring to the promises and fulfilling them. He fulfilled the Immanuel promise (Isa 7:14; Matt 1:21f.), the Galilee promise (Isa 9:1f.; Matt 4:12–16), the Bethlehem promise (Micah 5:2; Matt 2:5f.), the servant of the Lord promise (Isa 53:4; Matt 8:17), and many others. Furthermore he did not come to abolish the law and the prophets, but to fulfill them (Matt 5:17f.). Moreover, he carries a multitude of Old Testament eschatological titles. He is the Messiah, the son of David, the king of Israel, the Son of God, and the Son of Man, to name just a few.

"The conviction that God fulfills his promises . . . underlies the Christian conviction that Jesus is the one promised as the fulfillment of the promises of a final redemption made to that chosen people."[10] Through Jesus not only a continuity with Israel is present, since he was born as a member of the Jewish community, and his God was the same that the Jewish community venerated, but in him the promissory history of Israel came to fulfillment. This did not just pertain to the particular history of the Jewish faith or the Jewish nation. In the apocalyptic frame of reference, that faith was now perceived as a faith in the God who governed the whole world. All history therefore came to fulfillment and conclusion in Jesus' destiny. Wolfhart Pannenberg (b. 1928) emphasized this especially when he claimed: "The universal revelation of the deity of God is not yet realized in the history of Israel, but first in the fate of Jesus of Nazareth, insofar as the end of all events is anticipated in his fate."[11]

While the apocalyptic writers envisioned the end of all things, in the destiny of Jesus Christ the end is not only envisioned, but experienced in a proleptic way. *Prolepsis* means that something in the future is anticipated to the point of being pre-actualized in the present. There is still something outstanding, something, however, that is not any different from that which has already occurred. Pannenberg reminds us that the apocalyptic expectation of the end of the world was linked with the general resurrection of the dead (ca. Dan 12:1–3, and other apocalyptic eschatologies). In and through the resurrection of Jesus "the resurrection of the dead had already taken place, though to all other men this is still something yet to be experienced."[12] One could not conclude, however, that Jesus was lucky while all others were not. The resurrection of Jesus must not be seen in isolation. The event of the resurrection gains its significance in the apocalyptic context in which it was experienced.

---

10. So Paul J. Achtemeier, *Romans* (Atlanta: John Knox, 1985) 31, in his comments on Rom 1:3–4.

11. Wolfhart Pannenberg, "Dogmatic Theses on the Doctrine of Revelation," in Wolfhart Pannenberg, ed., *Revelation as History*, trans. David Granskou (London: Macmillan, 1968) 139 (thesis 4).

12. Ibid., 141.

Jesus' resurrection meant that that which was envisioned for the end of time had already occurred in an individual so that all others could then know what was also in store for them.

The resurrection of Jesus must also be seen in the context of the life and destiny of a human being called Jesus. It refers back to the earthly Jesus who was more than just a human being. According to Mark, for instance, Jesus began his ministry with the words: "The time is fulfilled, and the kingdom has come near; repent, and believe in the good news" (Mark 1:15). Jesus understood himself as an end-time figure who was sent in that final period to confront his listeners with the eschatological message of the kingdom of God. In contrast to some present-day end-time evangelists, Jesus did not give his listeners a time-table and inform them in detail about things that were going to happen at some future point, but he addressed his audience in such a way that an immediate decision was called for. He confronted the people with a radical decision for or against God, which at the same time became a decision for or against Jesus and his actions. His proclamation, his own person, and his actions form a unity that provoked and called for a decision. "Follow me, and let the dead bury their own dead" (Matt 8:22); "no one who puts a hand to the plough and looks back is fit for the kingdom of God" (Luke 9:62); and "blessed is anyone who takes no offense at me" (Matt 11:6) are just a few passages that show the urgency of an immediate decision. In apocalyptic, in the message of John the Baptist, and in the promissory history of the Old Testament the emphasis was on the future. In the ministry of Jesus the now has become the decisive point of history.

When John the Baptist sent two of his disciples to ask Jesus whether he was the promised one or whether they should wait for someone else, Jesus referred them to his actions. He did not refer to any titles that were conferred upon him, but to his actions.[13] He said: "The blind receive their sight, the lame walk, the lepers are cleansed, the deaf hear, the dead

---

13. Many exegetes who are concerned about the historical Jesus also emphasize that only Jesus' actions can illuminate the significance of his person and his call for a decision. Ernst Fuchs, for instance, advocated this method in his programmatic essay "The Quest of the Historical Jesus," in *Studies of the Historical Jesus*, trans. Andrew Scobie (London: SCM, 1964) 11–31. This method seems to have been picked up by other students of Bultmann. But even Joachim Jeremias, coming from an entirely different direction, did extensive studies of the parables of Jesus in his quest for the *ipsissima vox Jesu* (original sayings of Jesus). Cf. Joachim Jeremias, *The Parables of Jesus*, trans. S. H. Hooke, 2nd rev. ed. (New York: Scribners, 1972).

are raised, the poor have good news brought to them" (Luke 7:22). With this remark Jesus applied Old Testament imagery which is connected with the time of salvation (Isa 35:5–6). At the wedding in Cana, Jesus reportedly turned water into wine. This "epiphany miracle" (John 2:11),[14] is a reference to the Old Testament understanding of wine as the symbol of the time of salvation. Jesus is portrayed as the one in whom this salvation had become manifest. Jesus also talked about the new wine that should not be poured into old wineskins (Matt 9:17). The old time is past; the time of salvation has been initiated. Jesus stated it even more clearly when he said: "But if it is by the finger of God that I cast out the demons, then the kingdom of God has come to you" (Luke 11:20). With Jesus of Nazareth the kingdom of God has already started. What had been expected for centuries, what had been projected into the future or into the present for so long, has now begun. The kingdom of God is in the midst of you, said Jesus. He did not call for an immediate decision because he was such an important preacher, or because he had such an important message. He called for an immediate decision because the kingdom of God had come with his appearance, and thus it was the time of decision. The today of Jesus is the goal of history.

Here we notice a decisive difference between Jesus' own proclamation and the apocalyptic environment in which he lived.[15] Apocalypticism had fostered a strong eschatological tension between the present conditions and the future expectations which partly resulted in an imminent expectation of the end. Jesus announced that which had been expected with fervent hope was already being fulfilled in the present. Yet both expectation and the tension connected with it made it possible that Jesus' proclamation of the coming of the kingdom of God was still related to the eschatological final disclosure. This means that Jesus pointed to the present in which the kingdom of God had been realized as well as also announcing the future dimension of the kingdom.[16] We could talk here

---

14. Rudolf Bultmann, *The Gospel of John: A Commentary*, trans. G. R. Beasley-Murray et al. (Philadelphia: Westminster, 1971) 118–19. Though Bultmann recognizes this miracle as an epiphanic miracle, he wants to connect it with a Hellenistic environment (Dionysus cult) instead of with the Old Testament.

15. Cf. for the following Eta Linnemann, "Zeitansage und Zeitvorstellung in der Verkündigung Jesu," in Georg Strecker, ed., *Jesus Christus in Historie und Theologie: Neutestamentliche Festschrift für Hans Conzelmann zum 60. Geburtstag* (Tübingen: J. C. B. Mohr, 1975) 262.

16. Cf. ibid., 254.

about a bipolar structure of this kingdom vision in which the one pole was realized in the present which in turn enabled the future realization of the second pole.

While Jesus' opponents could always claim that Jesus' proclamation was presumptuous and therefore unfounded, and that his actions only showed that he either was a trickster or performed his actions in alignment with other, anti-Godly powers, his resurrection vindicated him from charges like these. Through the resurrection "God confirmed the claim that was implicit in the work of Jesus, and that was also expressly made by him, namely, that the imminent rule of God that Jesus proclaimed was about to break in, and in fact was already doing so for those who trusted his message."[17] The resurrection also brought about the vindication from those charges that had brought him to the cross, namely that he had either political aspirations or had committed blasphemy. Yet, as we noted, within the apocalyptic context, Jesus' resurrection could not have been an isolated event. It was understood to be the beginning of the general resurrection of the dead. Paul therefore called Jesus "the first fruits of those who have died" (1 Cor 15:28).

While the hope of the early Christian community for an endtime resurrection of the dead corresponds by and large to the Jewish hope, there is one significant modification.[18] In Judaism the resurrection of the righteous was hoped for as a consequence of righteous activities. In Christianity the resurrection is expected as a consequence of the salvific efficacy of Christ's resurrection. Pertaining to anything beyond death the Christian faith focuses on Christ and his resurrection, not on some kind of common idea which was already present in Judaism. The resurrection of Jesus simply cannot be derived from some kind of Jewish expectation. While some Jewish concepts are present which correspond to the inauguration of Jesus as the endtime mediator of salvation and as judge, there is no notion of the resurrection of the Messiah. Occasionally we find the understanding of a revivification, such as with Lazarus or with the son of the widow who was brought back to life by Elijah (1

---

17. Wolfhart Pannenberg, *Systematic Theology*, trans. Geoffrey W. Bromiley (Grand Rapids: Eerdmans, 1994) 2:345.

18. So also Ulrich Wilckens, *Resurrection. Biblical Testimony to the Resurrection: An Historical Examination and Explanation*, trans. A. M. Stewart (Atlanta: John Knox, 1978) 109–10.

Kgs 17:22). But "there is nothing comparable to the resurrection of Jesus anywhere in Jewish literature."[19]

Nowhere, even in late Judaism, is there the expectation of a resurrection to glory as an event in history. Resurrection to glory means the beginning of God's new creation. Upon their encounter with the resurrected one the disciples interpreted the resurrection as this kind of endtime event, the beginning of the new eon, of the new world. The resurrection of Jesus as the Christ signifies the intersection between God's realm and our space-time continuum. The narratives of the encounter with the resurrected one amply demonstrate that the resurrected one was not a phantom, a vision, or the result of a hallucination. He was a being who was as concrete as any earthly human being. He could talk, eat, and be touched. He could be recognized as the crucified one and as the former Jesus of Nazareth. The resurrected one maintained historic continuity with the former Jesus. Yet the resurrected one is no longer confined to space and time, or to the necessities of this life, such as sleep, food, and even death. No bones of the resurrected one were ever found, in contrast to the claim that the bones of Peter had been discovered underneath St. Peter's Basilica in Rome. Jesus Christ is no longer a being confined to space and time. As the first-born of the new creation, he has new possibilities which stand in contrast to the possibilities of our space and time-bound existence. He was resurrected to a new and eternal life, to an imperishable existence in continuous community with God as the source of life. The resurrection is then only partially and in a limited sense an event in history. That which resulted in the resurrection transcends the boundaries of space and time and therewith of history.

It is significant that the resurrected one did not just seek union with God but visited his people, summoned them to a new task and a new mission, and thus showed that his destiny was both exemplary and proleptic. In Jesus of Nazareth the new creation reached down into the old. Through this divine intervention hope was inaugurated and strengthened in those living within this eon, a life that is both preliminary and transitory. The resurrection of Jesus as the Christ served both as a catalyst for hope and as a verification that such hope is not unfounded. The rapidly expanding movement which ensued in the Christian church owes its existence to the resurrection. Through Christ's resurrection the

---

19. So Joachim Jeremias, *New Testament Theology: The Proclamation of Jesus*, trans. John Bowden (New York: Scribners, 1971) 309.

true turning-point occurred from pre-Christian to Christian existence, from the wavering and questioning disciples prior to Easter to the dedicated and unwavering apostles of the Christian age. The resurrection is not a demonstration of the historical correctness of the Christian faith. It is rather the historic/transhistoric hinge which allows us already now to see the end of history, and thereby opens for us a new vision and a new reality. Since we get this glimpse of the end of history, it would be futile to expect anything radically new beyond that which is contained in the Christ-event except for its consummation and universalization. Therefore it is not presumptuous to claim that Jesus Christ is God's ultimate self-disclosure.

Jesus the Christ: God's Ultimate Self-Disclosure

If history had come to an end with the destiny of Jesus, then it is also to be expected that God's self-disclosure had come to an end. Indeed, Jesus was God's final self-disclosure. This has not only been the conviction of the Christian community, but it can also be traced to Jesus' own self-understanding. For instance, Jesus' call to a decision implied the notion that God's self-disclosure was taking place in this proclamation.[20] Those who rejected Jesus' proclamation also rejected God's self-disclosure. The uniqueness of Jesus' proclamation was not that he decreed propositional sentences about God and God's will as we find them in some of the sacred writings of the world's religions. As the New Testament scholar Ernst Fuchs (1903–1983) pointed out, Jesus "dares to affirm the will of God as though he himself stood in God's place."[21] For instance, in his parables Jesus did not simply tell us how God acts, but he told us that God acts the way Jesus acts. Luke wrote that the Pharisees and scribes remarked, "this fellow welcomes sinners and eats with them" (Luke 15:2). In response to these remarks Jesus told them parables of God's concern for the lost and sinful, implying once again that God acts like Jesus does. Moreover, Jesus claimed to forgive sins, he reinterpreted the law authoritatively (Mark 2:10, 28), and he drew the outcasts of society to himself

---

20. Cf. Rudolf Bultmann, *Theology of the New Testament*, trans. Kendrick Grobel (New York: Scribners, 1951) 1:43, who states that "Jesus' call to decision implies a christology."

21. For the following, see Fuchs, "Quest for the Historical Jesus," 21.

and condemned those who were self-righteous (Matt 11:16ff.). No sane person before him had dared to assume such a position.

Furthermore, Jesus also allowed *proskynesis*, meaning the oriental custom of casting oneself to the ground before a deity. In the Septuagint, this term is also used in relation "to veneration and worship of the true God and Lord or to that of false gods. The angels, God's messengers, are also greeted in this way by the righteous."[22] In the New Testament *proskynesis* is always reserved for a divine object.[23] For instance, the Gospel of Matthew relates the incident of the *proskynesis* of the wise men before Jesus (Matt 2:2, 11) to show that he is the ruler of the world. Then we have it again in the temptation story (Matt 4:9) where the tempter asks Jesus to perform before him the *proskynesis*, which belongs to God alone. When Cornelius wants to conduct the *proskynesis* before Peter, Peter rejects this with the words: "Stand up; I am only a mortal" (Acts 10:26). The story is different with Jesus. For instance, the leper performs the *proskynesis* before Jesus who in turn heals him (Mark 1:40). Or there was the case of the Syro-Phoenician woman who performed the *proskynesis* before Jesus begging him to heal her daughter, which he did (Mark 7:25ff.). We have also the story of the blind man who was healed. When Jesus related to him who he was this formerly blind man performed the *proskynesis* before Jesus (John 9:38). Some of these examples of *proskynesis* may reflect the interpretation of the Evangelists. But the usage is too widespread in the gospels that it would only reflect later theological considerations.

In his survey of the biblical records, the New Testament scholar Heinrich Greeven (1906–1990) stated: "Proskynesis demands visible majesty before which the worshipper bows. The Son of God was visible to all on earth (the Gospels) and the exalted Lord will again be visible to His own when faith gives way to sight (Revelation)."[24] It is interesting that the term *proskynesis* is still used today in the Orthodox community with regard to the veneration of icons. While *proskynesis* may be offered to icons, *latreia* as worship or adoration is reserved for the divine *physis* only, meaning for the one true God. Yet the notion of the icon is that it allows us a vision for what it represents. This would then be exactly what

---

22. Heinrich Greeven, "*Proskyneo, Proskynesis,*" in *ThDNT*, 6:761.
23. So ibid., 6:763.
24. Ibid., 6:765.

Jesus was, the gate through which we can perceive the one for whom he represents, God's own self.

This sentiment was also shared by the Christian community, as we can see with the title *kyrios* when it is used in an absolute sense, as *ho kyrios*. We remember that in the Septuagint, God was addressed as *kyrios*, a title which then was conferred on Jesus in the New Testament. The absolute use of the term *ho kyrios* for Jesus can be explained "as taken over from the use of *kyrios* as a title for gods or human rulers in the eastern Mediterranean Hellenistic world."[25] Yet this title could also have a Palestinian Semitic background and be derived from a title "that Palestinian Jews already used for Yahweh." This term *ho kyrios* was then applied to Jesus by the early Christian community, as can be seen in the Jewish-Christian liturgical hymn in Phil 2:11 where it says that "every tongue should confess that Jesus Christ is Lord, to the glory of God the father." Similarly the *maranatha* of 1 Cor 16:22, "Our Lord, come!" would point us in the Jewish-Christian direction.

We can gather from these and other uses of the *kyrios* title in the New Testament that "early Christians regarded Jesus as sharing in some sense in the transcendence of Yahweh, that he was somehow on a par with him. This, however, is meant in an egalitarian sense, not in an identifiying sense."[26] Since Jesus shared in Yahweh's transcendence, he could mediate Yahweh to us though he was not the same as Yahweh. Therefore only in the later writings of the New Testament (Heb 1:8, John 1:1, etc.) is Jesus called God (*theos*). Gradually, the Christian community conceded to address Jesus also as God, on a par with Yahweh, but not Yahweh himself. Because of his closeness with God, he could mediate God to us as God's human face. This also shows the unique way in which Jesus talked about himself.

In the Gospel of John, for instance, we read that Jesus speaks of himself figuratively saying: "I am the bread of life" (John 6:35), or "I am the light of the world" (John 8:12). Yet there is also the use of the "I am" (in Greek: *ego eimi*), with no predicate following. For instance, Jesus says: "I told you that you would die in your sins, for you will die in your sins unless you believe that I am" (John 8:24), or "I tell you this now, before it

---

25. Joseph A. Fitzmeyer, "The Semitic Background of the New Testament *Kyrios*-Title," in Joseph A. Fitzmeyer, *The Semitic Background of the New Testament* (Grand Rapids: Eerdmans, 1997) 2:116, for this and the following quote.

26. Ibid., 2:130.

occurs, so that when it does occur, you may believe that I am he" (John 13:19). It is interesting that the English translation always changed the Greek "I am" to "I am he," because there is a natural tendency to assume that the statements as they stand in the Greek are incomplete. The use of the "I am" with no predicate following, however, is not restricted to John. For instance, according to Mark 13:5, Jesus cautions his disciples: "Many will come in my name and say, 'I am he!' and they will lead many astray" (Mark 13:6). Again in the English translation the original Greek "I am" is changed to "I am he." This addition was left off at the trial before the council, where Jesus confessed: "I am; and 'you will see the Son of Man seated at the right hand of the Power,' and 'coming with the clouds of heaven'" (Mark 14:62).

While it is difficult to find parallels in Gnosticism or Hellenism for the "I am" formula, the Old Testament "offers excellent examples of the use of 'I am,' including the only good examples of the absolute use."[27] The "I am" formulas are a means of divine self-presentation, as we see for instance in Gen 28:13 and Isa 43:25, where we hear Yahweh say: "I, I am he who plots out your transgressions for my own sake." Similarly we read in Isa 51:12: "I, I am he who comforts you." The Hebrew form is *ani hu*, the equivalent of the Greek *ego eimi*. Against this background the absolute use of the *ego eimi* becomes understandable. Jesus is presented as speaking in the same manner in which Yahweh speaks in the Old Testament, especially in Deutero-Isaiah. Therefore we can understand the adverse reaction by the Jewish religious establishment. For instance, in the Gospel of John, after Jesus used the *ego eimi* (John 8:58), the Jews try to stone him. After the use of "I am" in John 18:5, those who hear it fall to the ground. Here we are confronted with a divine majesty which in the first instance the Jews rejected as presumptuous and therefore reacted accordingly, whereas in the second instance they are taken aback. The same is true in the Synoptics.

As mentioned, when Jesus is asked by the high priest during the court trial whether he is the Messiah, the son of the Blessed One, he answers with "I am." One might understand this simply as an affirmative reply in the sense of "yes, you are right." But if this were the case the immediate charge of blasphemy would hardly be understandable, since

---

27. So Raymond E. Brown, *The Gospel According to John (I-XII)* (Garden City, NY: Doubleday, 1966) 535. For the whole discussion, cf. the "Appendix IV: Ego Eimi—'I am,'" 533–38.

being a messianic pretender was nothing unusual at that time. If Jesus, however, had claimed here that he is indeed the embodiment of Yahweh, the disbelieving reaction of the high priest and the charge of blasphemy would have been warranted.[28] Similarly, in Matt 14:26 the reaction to "I am, do not be afraid" after Jesus walked across the water and had entered the boat of the disciples is understandable. The reaction is the *proskynesis* and the confession by the disciples: "Truly, you are the Son of God" (Matt 14:33). We can therefore conclude that at least "some of the *ego eimi* passages without predicates do indeed reflect Hebrew-Jewish usage, and that in these passages the evangelist understands the statements to imply a self-revelation of deity on the part of Jesus."[29] Jesus is God's self-disclosure and he is on a par with Yahweh. This was the conviction of both Jesus and the early Christian community.

Finally, we should also mention that Jesus often referred to himself as son and to God as his father. With this terminology, Jesus picked up on the father-son relationship between God and David, and God and God and David, and God and Israel. According to the Old Testament, "Israel has a particular relationship to God. Israel is God's first-born, chosen out of all peoples" (Deut 14:1f.; Exod 4:22; Jer 31:9).[30] Though this election had been made historically manifest in the Exodus from Egypt, the Old Testament prophets constantly reminded Israel that this Father-Son or Father-Child relationship was threatened by Israel's sinfulness (cf. Deut 32:5f.; Jer 3:19f.; Mal 1:6; Isa 64:7f, and many others). As the New Testament scholar Joachim Jeremias (1900–1979) has pointed out, Jesus took up this Father-Son imagery in a unique way. Jesus referred to God as *abba* (Father) indicating "his certainty that he is in possession of the revelation because the Father has granted him complete divine knowledge."[31] Small wonder that this usage of the Father-

---

28. Catrin H. Williams, *I am He. The Interpretation of 'Ani Hu' in Jewish and Early Christian Literature* (Tübingen: Mohr Siebeck, 2000) 308, claims rightly in her dissertation: "The primary significance of *ego eimi* for Mark lies in its role as the expression used by Jesus to disclose his true identity."

29. So Harvey K. McArthur, "Christology in the Predicates of the Johannine *Ego Eimi* Sayings," in Robert F. Berkey and Sarah A. Edwards, eds., *Christology in Dialogue* (Cleveland, OH: Pilgrim, 1993) 123.

30. Joachim Jeremias, *The Prayers of Jesus*, trans. John Bowden and Christoph Burchard (London: SCM, 1976) 13.

31. Jeremias, *The Prayers of Jesus*, 63. Jeremias emphasizes the connection of the address *abba* with the way children address their father (58–61) indicating the intimacy

Son imagery, though foreshadowed in the Old Testament, does not find any correspondence in rabbinic literature. It is patterned according to the exclusive promise given to David to whom Yahweh spoke through his prophet Nathan: "I will be a father to him, and he shall be a son to me" (2 Sam 7:14), and according to the royal announcements in Ps 2:7 and 89:19f. Only later was this promise expanded to include all Israel. By using the Father-Son imagery in analogy to the relationship between Yahweh and David, the indication is made that in Jesus we face the true continuance of the promise to David.

Moreover, Jesus often connects the reference to the Father with the immediate disclosure of God's will (Matt 11:25; 27). He does not act as a prophet who announces the establishment of the Father-Son relationship, but he acts as the Son who asserts his unique relationship with his Father. Bearing this in mind we are not surprised that Jesus always distinguishes between "my Father" and "your Father." In other words, the relationship between God and Jesus is exclusive and finds only its analogy and not its sameness in the relationship between God and Jesus' disciples. Even the opening words of the Lord's Prayer were originally "Father" or "Dear Father" and not "Our Father" (cf. Luke 11:2).[32] Nevertheless Jesus encouraged his disciples to trust God as their Father. Due to Jesus' own influence the first Christian community dared to call God their Father (Gal 4:6; Rom 8:15f), and at the same time they called Jesus their Lord.[33] Both moves seem to be inextricably interrelated, if we consider the concept of a new covenant as the connecting link. Since Jesus is God's self-disclosure and therefore on a par with God, he can extend to his followers a new covenant in analogy to the old one. This new covenant opens for his followers as the new Israel the possibility to understand themselves as sons and daughters of God their Father. This

---

implied in using this word.

32. Cf. Joachim Jeremias, *The Lord's Prayer*, trans. J. Reumann (Philadelphia: Fortress, 1964) 17.

33. Jeremias, *New Testament Theology*, 197, rightly mentions: "As members of the family of God, they may say 'Father' to God, and ask him for his good gifts. The earliest church right from the beginning regarded it as a great privilege that Jesus in this way gave the disciples a share in his authority as Son." Cf. also Donald Guthrie, *Galatians* (Grand Rapids: Eerdmans, 1981) 115, who mentions in his exegesis of Gal 4:6f. that "the apostle assumes that adoption into the status of sons carries with it the full privileges of sonship." He also states that the apostle is strangely attracted to the idea of the connection between sonship and heritage. Yet, we might be safe to assume that Paul only brings to its appropriate conclusion the implications of the newly gained sonship.

new familial relationship looks back to its historical manifestation, this time not in the Exodus, but in the life, death, (and resurrection) of Jesus the Christ. Since the former ethnic preference is no longer valid, Jesus the Christ now becomes decisive for every cognizant relationship with God.

Jesus the Christ: Decisive but not Exclusive

Since Jesus is God's ultimate self-disclosure, the question needs to be addressed whether anyone can circumvent this ultimate self-disclosure. The Gospel of John sets the record straight when we hear Jesus say to his disciples: "I am the way, and the truth, and the life. No one comes to the Father except through me" (John 14:6). Here the conviction is expressed that Jesus provides the only access to God. Contrary to our innermost yearning, there is no immediate access to God. God is only approachable in and through the historic Jesus of Nazareth who is the Christ. The encounter with Jesus, not the assent to certain esoteric rules or words of wisdom, is decisive for our knowledge of God or, to use Johannine terminology, for our "being in truth." If one rejects Jesus, one rejects God and the opportunity for being in communion with God (John 3:18). In a similar way we hear Peter confess: "There is salvation in no one else, for there is no other name under heaven given among mortals by which we must be saved" (Acts 4:12). The name which provides salvation of course is the name of Jesus. Considering the Jewish background of Peter's statement, only the name of Yahweh could have been referred to in this way. This means that here again the exclusiveness of God's self-disclosure is emphasized by identifying Jesus the Christ with Yahweh.

Since the New Testament writers were convinced that God had identified God's self with Jesus of Nazareth and consequently Jesus identified himself with God, they concluded that this divine self-disclosure could not be surpassed. It had final character. We are confronted here with an actual self-mediation of God in a human being. God became human so that we could become divine, giving us a chance to understand God and to attain communion with God. Of course, God is not tied to this one self-disclosure, and could therefore also use other avenues in the history of humanity for an analogous self-disclosure. Moreover, there could be new covenants similar to the new covenant, namely the New Testament, that the Christian community experienced. Since God remains God, we cannot determine God's ways, and, in principle, the possibility of a plurality of ultimate self-disclosures would not be unwarranted. But God's own intentions run contrary to such an assumption.

The writer of the Letter to the Hebrews reminds us in the opening sentence: "Long ago God spoke to our ancestors in many and various ways by the prophets, but in these last days he has spoken to us by a Son, whom he appointed heir of all things, through whom he also created the worlds" (Heb 1:1f). The writer of this letter seems to remind the readers of the various ways through which God disclosed himself in Old Testament times, such as through dreams, visions, and auditions, through angels, and through animals. But now things are different, because God has spoken in an eschatological time. And Jesus is the decisive factor, because, as we remember, Jesus spoke in an eschatological time as an eschatological figure and preached an eschatological message. This means that in Jesus the end-time has broken in and in Jesus God's ultimate disclosure has been made.

In the apocalyptic environment in which Jesus lived there were many others with whom eschatological expectations were connected, such as John the Baptist, the Zealots, Judas the Galilean, Simon, son of Giora, and, above all, Bar Kochba.[34] However, only in the life and destiny of Jesus can we recognize that the still outstanding eschaton has already commenced. Moreover the movements inaugurated by these other "eschatological" figures soon ended. Only the emerging Christian community multiplied and spread to the very ends of the earth. The reason for this is that the Christian community did not simply preserve Jesus' message and the record of his actions. Under the impact of the Easter events, the proclaimer became the proclaimed and therewith the focal point of the Christian gospel. What they had previously surmised and assumed but not ever really known, the followers of Jesus could now recognize from the Easter experience: Jesus actually was that which he said he was, the initiator of the eschaton which had been brought about through his own resurrection by proleptic anticipation. The idea of an ongoing revelation, apart from Jesus Christ and his destiny, or even beyond it, would

---

34. For more information on the numerous figures and movements with whom eschatological and messianic expectations were connected cf. the informative study by Craig A. Evans, *Jesus and his Contemporaries: Comparative Studies* (Leiden: Brill, 2001) 58–81, especially in the chapter on "Messianic Claimants of the First and Second Centuries" the section on "Messiahs, Prophets, and Deliverers."

contradict this anticipatory character. There is no need for any separate or ongoing revelations, only for clarification of what it means that God disclosed God's own self in a final way in and through Jesus Christ. If this self-disclosure is so decisive and so final, what does this mean for other religions? Are they simply products of the human mind?

As soon as one reflects on human history beyond the confines of the Judeo-Christian tradition, it becomes clear that outside this covenant community there was not a godless vacuum. Even the covenant community asserted God's presence, since eventually God had been understood as the creator, sustainer, and redeemer, not only of the covenant community, but of the whole inhabited world and of the whole universe. It is not accidental that in the prologue of the Gospel of John the divine logos is given a universal status. This divine logos entered human existence in and as Jesus of Nazareth. In a similar way as God's presence is asserted throughout the world, Christ's presence must be universally asserted. Therefore Karl Rahner's term "anonymous Christians," though misleading, contains a kernel of truth. As we have seen, the revelatory history of God, starting with the ancestors of Israel and culminating in the life and destiny of Jesus the Christ, is basically a history of God's initiative, or in other words, the history of a great invitation.

The religious history of humanity outside this great invitation is neither just an expression of humanity's sinfulness nor a history leading up to Christ. It is the history of humans as God's creatures who are moved by the existential separation from their creator. Humans cannot gain insight of this separation just by themselves, as modern day secularists testify when they ignore this separation. While some religious manifestations express the misconception that finite humanity can heal on its own its existential separation from God, the vast majority of religions convey the notion that God alone can reconcile the world and humanity to God's self. Virtually all great religious traditions admit the necessity of grace. Even in Buddhism, which seems to contradict this notion, there developed a strand called Amida Buddhism, the Buddhism of the loving Buddha. The understanding prevails almost everywhere in religions that only God can redeem us. If redemption does take place in these other religions, something Christians hope and pray for, but do not know, it would only be because God is the kind of God that has shown itself in Jesus Christ. Just as we cannot pronounce the inclusion of everybody and every movement into God's kingdom, we also cannot exclude anybody or any religion. Such a decision is God's alone.

The emphasis on the exclusiveness of God's self-disclosure in Jesus Christ is not directed against other religions. The decisiveness with which Jesus encountered people was not theoretical, but an existential address. Those who are encountered by the gospel and its call for a decision, cannot but respond, and, as far as we know, their response will have eternal significance. With regard to other religions, however, our conclusions must be of a much more modest character. Since God disclosed himself in an unsurpassable way in Jesus Christ, we emphasize that this kind of self-disclosure is the preferred option. Moreover, since God is perceived in the Judeo-Christian tradition as a God who beckons our response, this also allows for freedom to develop our innate potential so that we can be good stewards of creation. Therefore the charge of the great commission once addressed to the disciples is still valid for us: "Go therefore and make disciples of all nations, baptizing them in the name of the Father and of the Son and of the Holy Spirit, and teaching them to obey everything that I have commanded you" (Matt 28:19f.). Those who were never properly confronted with the Christian gospel are not without hope, because through Jesus Christ we know that God is not just a God of holiness, but also of compassion. This means that the God-disclosive history of the Judeo-Christian tradition becomes a source of clarity and hope in understanding all of religious history. If the question is still raised as to why this self-disclosure must be exclusive and unsurpassable, then such objection can only be adequately dealt with by referring to God's own primacy in the whole God-disclosive process. The recognition of "it pleased God" is the deepest reason for this process, since we cannot adduce any external criteria why Israel or the Christian community should have had such privileged status.

We must, however, voice a further caution. At first, the emerging Christian community asserted, as we have seen, that in Jesus of Nazareth we really encounter God's self-disclosure. If this means that this human person Jesus of Nazareth is on a par with God, how are the two related beyond the figurative speech that Jesus is the son of God? Intensive theological reflection led to the conclusion that Jesus could be not a demi-God, because, as Christians knew from their environment, such demi-Gods at most could only provide temporary relief from human finitude. At the Council of Nicea (325 CE), a city close to present-day

Istanbul, Turkey, the church decided that since Jesus the Christ mediated salvation, he must be of the same being as God the Father, he must be *homoousios* (i.e., of the same being). Yet almost immediately came the realization that Jesus was also a human being, not just a divine entity. This observation made it difficult for many faithful Christians to agree to the decision of Nicea. Again after several generations of intensive spiritual and political struggle, it became more and more evident that the issue of how the human being Jesus of Nazareth was related to his God-disclosive or divine nature could not be settled that easily. The church understood Jesus to be on a par with God (the decision of Nicea) and still a truly human being: in other words that he was true God and true human. When the church assembled for its ecumenical council at Chalcedon (451 CE), a city not far from Nicea, it finally recognized the limits of human reason and instead of defining the relationship between the divine and the human nature in Jesus Christ it restricted itself to only a negative solution. Both natures, it said, were present in Jesus in such a way that they were neither mixed together nor changed to a "higher" entity, neither torn apart nor separated. This restraint from defining how both natures are related to each other in Jesus the Christ while at the same time insisting on their actual presence in an inextricable togetherness saved God's ultimate self-disclosure from being distorted into a timeless philosophical truth.

The church stated first of all that what happened to Jesus occurred within space and time. At the same time it affirmed that that which happened is not something available or accessible within the space-time continuum. If the opposite were true, there would be no reason why the church could not rationally define how God's self-disclosure in Jesus is related to another phenomenon of space and time, namely Jesus' human nature. Consequently, empirical research can never come up with a statement like, "Jesus was God's self-disclosure." Even exegesis can only unearth bits about a truly human being called Jesus of Nazareth. If it arrived at assertions about Jesus' divine nature, it would leave its empirical ground and enter either the realm of faith or of speculation. Naturally, such conclusions must affect our understanding of Jesus Christ as the God-disclosive event.

We observed earlier that the significance of Jesus can only be appropriately understood in the context of Israel's history of promise and expectation. Only in the contextual history of Israel and not as an isolated event does the Christ event reveal the Godhead of Yahweh. But the history of Israel is not a special case of history whose course, culminating in the Christ event, would make God's self-disclosure unmistakably evident. On the other hand through these historical events both Israel and the Christian community gained an insight which transcends empirical verification. In other words, the history of Israel and the Christ event seem to have God-disclosive power. How can God then be disclosed in such events if, as the Chalcedonian confession recognized, he is neither an additional component of the historic process nor separable from it? The only solution is to consider this process as an obvious paradox.

Though every cause and component of the Judeo-Christian salvation history *(Heilsgeschichte)* can be explained within a strictly empirical reference system, it must at the same time be understood as a totally God-wrought process. Observing this paradox, Jesus' proclamation, action, and destiny are not the result of a religious fanatic, but a disclosure of God's demand and promise. This paradox will not allow us to forget that it is the human being Jesus of Nazareth through whom God becomes transparent. Since we always perceive God's ultimate pronouncement and action through an anthropomorphic veil, we do not perceive God's self, but God's approximative anthropomorphic form. The ultimate self-disclosure of God is still disclosure in approximation, namely God becoming communicable in human form.

The necessary approximation through which God descends to our phenomenal level together with the paradox of Jesus being true God and true human results in the decision-demanding character of God's self-disclosure in Jesus Christ. Since the Judeo-Christian *Heilsgeschichte* confronts listeners with the claim that it is *the* God-disclosive history, they cannot escape from making a choice. Yet a positive decision does not simply result from an option between two possibilities. Since the Judeo-Christian history of salvation has the power to convince the skeptic as well as to withhold its God-wrought nature from the seeker, the believers recognize that God's own self is involved in the decision making process. Once the decision of accepting the basic paradox has been reached, the approximation character of this self-disclosure allows for increasingly deeper investigation of this disclosive process. The result will be an ever deeper understanding of God's self-disclosure contained in the human form of Jesus of Nazareth. But what is God like in this self-disclosure?

EIGHT

Theomorphous Humanity—Curse or Blessing?

We have extensively discussed God's ultimate self-disclosure, yet only implicitly the content of this self-disclosure. If God makes a difference to our world and to us human beings then this cannot be derived just from God's "thatness," but from the peculiarity of God. Yet how can we as humans even talk about God? Søren Kierkegaard emphasized the otherness of God, stating that "between God and a human being . . . there is an absolute difference."[1] Pursuing a similar line, Karl Barth stated the resulting problem very precisely: "As ministers we ought to speak of God. We are human, however, and so cannot speak of God. We ought therefore to recognize both, our obligation and our inability and by that very recognition give God the glory. This is our perplexity. The rest of our task fades into insignificance in comparison."[2] Indeed, how can we bridge that gap between God and us? If we are confronted with God's self-disclosure, how can we with our human conceptuality express that which is not directly expressible in human conceptuality? Given this task the temptation and also the reality of human projection in our God talk looms high on the horizon. Instead of actually talking about God, we talk in a magnified way about ourselves.

---

1. Kierkegaard, *Concluding Unscientific Postscript*, 1:412.
2. Karl Barth, "The Word of God and the Task of the Ministry," in Karl Barth, *The Word of God and the Word of Man*, trans. Douglas Horton (New York: Harper, 1957) 186. The German original reads "theologians" instead of "ministers." Cf. *Anfänge der dialektischen Theologie*, ed. Jürgen Moltmann (Munich: Christian Kaiser, 1966) 1:199.

After God's Likeness: Projection or Experience?

An interesting and influential way to talk about the divine attributes was advanced by the anonymous writer who, writing ca. 500 CE, used the pseudonym Dionysius the Areopagite, the name of a convert of St. Paul in Athens. This writer was influenced by late neo-Platonism as it was represented especially in the neo-Platonic school of Athens, and also by Christian Platonism, especially that of Gregory of Nyssa.[3] His treatise *The Divine Names* "has played a central role in a long conceptual tradition, neo-Platonic and scholastic, that has influenced Western thought" including that of Thomas Aquinas.[4]

Pseudo-Dionysius wondered how we can talk about God, because human words do not capture the transcendent God. He concluded: "He [God] is all things in all things and he is no thing among things. He is known to all from all things and he is known to no one from anything."[5] This means, God is present and elusive at the same time. Pseudo-Dionysius therefore suggested:

> It might be more accurate to say that we cannot know God in his nature, since this is unknowable and is beyond the reach of mind or of reason. But we know him from the arrangement of everything, because everything is, in a sense, projected out from him, and this order possesses certain images and semblances of his divine paradigms. We therefore approach that which is beyond all as far as our capacities allow us and we pass by way of the denial and the transcendence of all things and by way of the cause of all things.[6]

Pseudo-Dionysius advocated a threefold way to arrive at assertions about God, starting from the created order (1) by way of denial, meaning the *via negativa* or the negative way, (2) the *via eminentia* or the way in which God excels all else, and (3) the way of the cause of all things, meaning the *via causalitatis*. We attribute to God adjectives such as infinite, immortal, and incomprehensible according to the negative way by trying to negate attributes that are usually consigned to human be-

---

3. For details, cf. Gerard O'Daly, "Dionysius Areopagita," in *TRE* 8:772.

4. So Paul Rorem, *Pseudo-Dionysius: A Commentary on the Texts and an Introduction to Their Influence* (New York: Oxford University, 1993) 174.

5. *The Divine Names* (7.872A) in Pseudo-Dionysius, *The Complete Works*, trans. Colm Luibheid (New York: Paulist, 1987) 109.

6. Ibid. (7.869C–872A) 109.

ings, such as finite, mortal and comprehensible. Or we confer upon God adjectives such as omnipotent, omniscient, or omnipresent according to the superlative way by attempting to surpass attributes that are usually associated with human beings, such as potency, knowledge, or presence. Finally God is referred to as the first uncaused cause or the creator of all things according to the way of causal inference. Even statements defining God as the moral order of the world (Kant) or holy (Otto) or pure act (scholasticism) are ultimately related to one of the three ways that Pseudo-Dionysius outlined.

Of course, hardly any of these descriptions of God were ever taken literally. They were usually immediately qualified "by the admission that they are not intended literally."[7] Paul Tillich, for instance, has pointed out in volume 1 of his *Systematic Theology* that all statements about God are of a symbolic nature. Only "the statement that God is being-itself is a non-symbolic statement. It does not point beyond itself. It means what it says directly and properly."[8] In volume 2 he is still more cautious, saying: "Thus it follows that everything religion has to say about God, including his qualities, actions, and manifestations, has a symbolic character and that the meaning of 'God' is completely missed if one takes the symbolic language literally." Asking himself whether a non-symbolic statement about God is possible he concludes: ". . . There is a point at which a non-symbolic assertion about God must be made . . . , namely, the statement that everything we say about God is symbolic."[9] With this concession Tillich has recognized that regardless of what we say about God all our assertions have at best a symbolic character. However, for Tillich this does not mean they are of no value.

Tillich distinguishes between sign and symbol saying "while the sign bears no necessary relation to that to which it points, the symbol

---

7. This has been pointed out especially well by Gordon D. Kaufman, *Systematic Theology: A Historicist Perspective* (New York: Scribners, 1968) 121; cf. also his book *God the Problem* (Cambridge: Harvard University Press, 1972) 113, where he says: "*All conceptions of God . . . including that of scripture and faith, must be understood as creations of the human imagination: the 'real God' is never available to us or directly knowable by us.*"

8. Paul Tillich, *Systematic Theology*, vol. 1: *Reason and Revelation. Being and God* (Chicago: University of Chicago Press, 1951) 238.

9. Paul Tillich, *Systematic Theology*, vol. 2: *Existence and the Christ* (Chicago: University of Chicago Press, 1957) 9.

participates in the reality of that for which it stands."[10] Characteristics we attribute to God can be regarded as symbols that not only point to the divine, but if they are true symbols, even participate in the power of the divine. When we remember, however, that we often want to win God for our side and try to rationalize that God is actually in agreement with our own self-centered preferences, we must question whether any of the characteristics attributed to God do indeed disclose something about God.

Already Friedrich Schleiermacher sensed this subjective and speculative tendency in our God-talk when he mentioned that after the age of scholasticism metaphysics was treated separately and apart from Christian doctrine in the philosophical discipline called natural theology. Therefore he reminds us that the representations of the divine attributes are of religious and not of philosophical origin. "All attributes which we ascribe to God are to be taken as denoting not something special in God, but only something special in the manner in which the feeling of absolute dependence is to be related to Him."[11] In other words, the adjectives we attribute to God are neither descriptive of him nor do they originate from human fantasy. They are an attempt to express how we experience God's relationship to us. Thus to talk about God and God's likeness is different from speaking in a raised voice about humanity.[12] If these concepts truly express how we experience God's relationship to us, they do disclose some modality of God to us. Or to use Tillich's terminology, they are true symbols and participate in the power of the divine to which they point.

But it should also become clear that these concepts do not disclose how God is in his divine "essence," namely apart from God's self-disclosure. Martin Luther cautioned about this restriction when he said in his drastic and picturesque manner:

> It is therefore insane to argue about God and the divine nature without the word or any covering. . . . Whoever desires to be

---

10. Tillich, *Systematic Theology*, 1:239.

11. Friedrich Schleiermacher, *The Christian Faith* (par. 50) trans. H. R. Mackintosh and J. S. Stewart, intro. Richard R. Niebuhr (New York: Harper Torchbook 1963) 1:194–96.

12. Cf. Barth, "Word of God and the Task of the Ministry," 196. However, it is difficult to side with Barth and blame Schleiermacher for speaking about God "simply by speaking of man in a loud voice." It seems that especially Schleiermacher attempted to escape from an anthropocentric God language.

saved or to be safe when he deals with such great matters, let him simply hold to the forms, the signs, and the coverings of the Godhead, such as His Word and His works. For in His Word and in His works He shows Himself to us.[13]

At another occasion he also warned:

Through their speculations some ascend into heaven and speculate about God the creator, etc. Do not get mixed up with this God. Whoever wishes to be saved should move away from God in his majesty, for He and the human creature are enemies. Rather grasp that God whom David also grasps. He is the God who is clothed in his promises. . . . Such a God one must have. . . . We know no other God than the one who is clothed in his promises. If he would talk to me in his majesty I would run away like the Jews did. But when he is clothed in the voice of man and accommodates himself to our capacity to understand, I can approach him.[14]

It would certainly be interesting to speculate about the omnipotence or the aseity of God. Yet the only directive we can get in our desire to talk theologically about God is to use as our sole criterion the God-disclosive history which culminated in Jesus Christ. This does not mean that philosophic concepts concerning God's likeness are without any validity. The reflection on God's self-disclosure as recorded in the Bible is not written in original "Bible language." It shows on almost every page that its conceptuality is borrowed from many different sources. But all conceptual tools must be judged, transformed, or verified by the degree to which they support the coming into language of the one disclosed in this history. Since the whole disclosive history culminated in God's final self-disclosure in Jesus Christ, we might also say that the meaning and truth attributed to all such (philosophic and religious) experiences and concepts must be determined with reference to Jesus the Christ.

The New Testament scholar Rudolf Bultmann (1884–1976) made a very important point in his essay "What Does It Mean to Speak of God?" (1925) when he said: "If 'speaking of God' is understood as '*speaking*

---

13. Martin Luther, *Lectures on Genesis*, in *LW* 1:13, in his exegesis of Gen. 1:2; cf. also Paul Althaus, *The Theology of Martin Luther*, trans. Robert C. Schultz (Philadelphia: Fortress, 1966) 20–24, in his section on "God in Himself and God as He Reveals Himself."

14. Martin Luther, *Ennaratio Psalmi LI*, in *WA* 40/2:329, 8–12 and 330, 1–7, in his exegesis of Ps 51:3.

about God," then such speaking has no meaning whatever, for its subject, God, is lost in the very moment it takes place. Whenever the idea, God, comes to mind, it connotes that God is the Almighty; in other words, God is the reality determining all else. But this idea is not recognized at all when I speak *about* God."[15] In speaking about God I take a standpoint external to that which is being talked about. But how is this possible if God determines all reality? Bultmann therefore claimed: "To speak of God in this sense is not only error and without meaning—it is *sin*."[16] Therefore Bultmann argued, we should not speak *about* God but *from* God. But "speaking of God as *from* God can evidently be only the gift of God himself."[17] Only when God gives his own self to us, as God discloses Godself, can we speak from God.

Even then we are forced again to speak about God, since we must assess the divine self-disclosure. Therefore all our action and speech has meaning only under the aspect of the forgiveness of sins, as Bultmann assured us. It must be kept in mind that we can only talk *from* God if such talk is preceded by God's self-disclosure and focuses on God's self-disclosure. By focusing on it, we must necessarily set ourselves over against it and are consequently in danger of misappropriating God's self-disclosure. Unless we want to resign ourselves to silence, we must proceed on this path, trying to avoid the danger of substituting our own projection for the self-disclosure we attempt to interpret.

The Personification of God

In the Judeo-Christian tradition, God is represented with attributes which imply that God acts like a person. God is an addressable Thou and in analogy to other religions, God can be invoked in the cult and approached through prayer. In many religions the first things we hear of God are stories about God. In the Judeo-Christian tradition, however, the initial focus is on God's relationship to certain persons, to the patriarchs, to Moses, to David, to the prophets in the Old Testament, and in the New Testament, of course, God's relationship to Jesus of Nazareth.

---

15. Rudolf Bultmann, "What Does It Mean to Speak of God?," in Rudolf Bultmann, *Faith and Understanding*, ed. with intro. Robert W. Funk, trans. Louise Pettibone Smith (New York: Harper & Row, 1969) 53.

16. Ibid., 54.

17. Ibid., 55.

Then this relationship is extended to a select group of people, the Israelites, and finally to all of humanity. In the Judeo-Christian tradition God is experienced as an active God who relates to humans. Therefore God is described with characteristics usually applied to a person. The Jewish philosopher and theologian Martin Buber (1878–1965) justified God's personification saying:

> The designation of God as a person is indispensable for all who, like myself, do not mean a principle when they say "God" although mystics like Eckhart occasionally equate him with "Being," and who, like myself, do not mean an idea when they say "God" although philosophers like Plato could at times take him for one—all who like myself mean by "God" him that, whatever else he may be in addition, enters into a direct relationship to us human beings through creative, revelatory, and redemptive acts, and thus makes it possible for us to enter into a direct relationship to him.[18]

Buber did not want to imply that we describe God by attributing features to God which imply a personal being, since God is beyond description, nor do we determine who God is in his essence. The only thing we can know about God is what is disclosed to us through God's own activity. Since God encounters people as a Thou, as an addressing and addressable being, they are enabled and encouraged to respond to him as an I, which means as persons. The German theologian Helmut Thielicke (1908–1986) observed:

> When we speak of the God of revelation, we can also speak of his attributes only in terms of revelation. When revelation tells me that God speaks to me and acts on and with me, the word 'attribute' can denote, not a constituent of God in himself, but only the nature of God as it is declared in his speech and action. Hence attributes such as his omnicausality, eternity, immutability, om-

---

18. Martin Buber in his classic *I and Thou*, with a prologue 'I and You,' trans. and notes Walter Kaufmann (New York: Scribners, 1970) 180–81. Karl Barth very rightly reminds us that the concept of the "'personality' of God . . . is a product of the struggle against modern naturalism and pantheism" (Karl Barth, *Church Dogmatics*, vol. 1/I: *The Doctrine of the Word of God*, trans. G. T. Thomson [Edinburgh: T. & T. Clark, 1969] 403). Cf. also Harminus Martinus Kuitert, *Gott in Menschengestalt. Eine dogmatisch-hermeneutische Studie über der Anthropomorphismen der Bibel* (Munich: Chr. Kaiser, 1967) 27, who attempts to show that the anthropomorphisms in the Bible are not human and therefore are not inadequate concepts projected into God.

nipotence, omniscience, etc., are to be expounded as modes of his historical revelation to the cosmos and man.[19]

Since God relates to us, we can become God-responsive and are in this responsiveness distinguished from all other living beings on earth. We are persons in the true sense.

Thielicke therefore wrote: "When we speak of God as person we do not mean this anthropomorphously. On the contrary, we mean it theomorphously when we speak of man as person."[20] This means a reversal of the usual question "How can God be conceived of in personal terms?" to "How can we speak of a human being as a person unless we consider that person's relationship with God?"—Parenthetically it must be noted here that a different understanding of God also implies a different understanding of humanity and its role on earth. This must be taken into consideration when we view other religions.—This new question reflects the experience of the Judeo-Christian tradition according to which God first addresses us before we can address God. This new question is further consonant with the creation accounts where the priestly writer stated: "So God created human kind in his image, in the image of God he created them; male and female he created them" (Gen 1:27). This text was shaped by the experience of the Babylonian exile. According to Babylonian mythology, "people were created to minister to the gods."[21] But of this we hear nothing in Genesis. Humans are not created as domestic servants of the gods. They have their own task here on earth. Being created in God's image separates humanity from all other creatures made by God. We could speculate which parts or functions of humanity correspond especially well to being created in God's image. Yet such differentiating speculations are foreign to this text. We are simply reminded that a whole human person as a person is created in God's image.

A view of the cultural historical context can be enlightening.[22] In Mesopotamia and in Egypt images of the gods were often used in reli-

---

19. Helmut Thielicke, *The Evangelical Faith*, vol. 2: *The Doctrine of God and of Christ*, trans. and ed. Geoffrey W. Bromiley (Grand Rapids: Eerdmans, 1977) 122–23.

20. Ibid., 2:114.

21. Claus Westermann, *Genesis 1–11. A Commentary*, trans. John J. Scullion (Minneapolis: Augsburg, 1984) 157, in his explanation of Gen 1:26f.

22. To the following, cf. Edward M. Curtis, "Image of God (OT)," in *The Anchor Bible Dictionary*, 3:390–91.

gious cultic life. The significance of an image did not lie in the fact that it would describe or actually depict the godhead, though this may not have been completely off the mark. What was decisive was that the image was the place at which the godhead was present and made manifest. The presence of the god and the blessing of his or her presence was mediated through the image. In Egypt the pharaoh was even regarded as the earthly manifestation of the godhead and he functioned analogously to the image of the god which was kept in the temple. For a short period in Mesopotamia the king was considered the representation of the godhead. In post-exilic Israel, according to Genesis 1, the image of God was extended to humans in general. Therefore, being created in the image of God means: "that the human being rules over the rest of creation as king, governor, and God's representative on earth."[23]

According to Genesis 1:26ff., being created in the image of God does not imply a special ontological quality, but it is an assertion about the function of humanity. That is to say that humanity has been created and is called forth to rule over the rest of creation. This is also expressed in Psalm 8, where the psalmist writes:

> What are human beings that you are mindful of them, mortals
> that you care for them?
>
> You have made them a little lower than God, and crowned them
> with glory and honor.
>
> You have given them dominion over the works of your hands;
> you have put all things under their feet. (Ps 8:4ff.).

Being created in the image of God is not intended to deify or idolize humanity. It is also no license to exploit creation and to subjugate it to one's desires. Being created in God's image means rather to act in God's place, as God's administrator and representative. This understanding is reinforced in the New Testament. The Pauline corpus is the main—almost exclusive—source of this understanding. In the New Testament, to be created in God's image means to be ethically shaped in conformity with God and to act in a manner for which God serves as the prototype. Such conduct can be derived from God's ways as they become transparent in Jesus of Nazareth (cf. Phil 2:5; Rom 15:5).

As humans we are supposed to represent God and to model our conduct according to God. Yet in our attempt to assert our own au-

---

23. Jacob Jervell, "Bild Gottes I," in *TRE*, 6:492.

tonomy, we abandon God as the guiding influence for our lives. Instead of caring about God's dominion over the earth, we seek to establish our own dominion. Since we have lost sight of God as the integrating power by caring only about our own selves, humanity is no longer striving for a common goal; everybody is striving for his or her own goal. This can result either in the domination of one or a few at the expense of everyone else (dictatorship or oligarchy), or as Thomas Hobbes (1588–1679) spelled it out in his *Leviathan,* everyone pursues his or her own goal at the expense of everyone else's.

Both of these positions and variations of the two have been repeated in human history in many different ways, showing that the loss of our awareness of being created in the image of God results in a loss of personhood. This is especially true for our emerging global village. In the secular pursuit of progress we have abandoned any guidance beyond our own self. In all of human history we have never been so independent, presumably being able to do whatever we want. But at the same time we have never been so enslaved to hidden and overt pressures, be it by institutions, society, or business enterprises. Pure science reduces us to biological or psychological entities, and the economic establishment regards us as consumers who can fuel the various economies. The implicit or explicit treatment we receive is to be expected, since we are items manipulated by transpersonal forces.

We notice that the understanding of humans as persons who are of infinite value and have inalienable rights is by no means self-evident. These rights and the value accorded to humans are denied especially in economic and political arrangements where either the reference to God is ignored or deliberately omitted. It is not by accident that violation of human rights goes hand in hand with suppression of religious freedom. Therefore Wolfhart Pannenberg asks: "Should we not perhaps look for the origin of the idea of person precisely in the phenomenology of religious experience . . . ? Was not the personality of man originally thought of as a participation in the inviolable majesty of God, just as the ancient commandment against murder in Israel was motivated by man's being in the image of God (Gen 9:6)? Do we not have in the idea of the image of God in man the Old Testament expression for what we call personality?"[24] And then he answers: "The fact that the modern concept

---

24. Wolfhart Pannenberg, "The Question of God," in Wolfhart Pannenberg, *Basic Questions in Theology: Collected Essays,* trans. George H. Kehm (Philadelphia: Fortress, 1971) 2:228–29, for this and the following quote.

of the personal has arisen out of Christian theology . . . points in the same direction."

It would be utterly wrong to assume that we infringe upon our personhood and upon our relationship with other persons once we acknowledge a personal God. The opposite is true. Only through our awareness of God as deeply personal and through the mutual relationship between God and ourselves do we become persons in the truest sense, able to respect other individuals as persons. Once we have attained this awareness, the dangers associated with secularisation do not suddenly subside, but they no longer determine our personal existence and cannot enslave us. As Christians we still live in this world and our life continues to be a historical existence governed by the powers of this world. But our vision is no longer confined to the power play of these worldly forces. Recognizing Christ as the Lord at whose name "every knee should bend, in heaven and on earth and under the earth, and every tongue should confess that Jesus Christ is Lord" (Phil 2:10f), our ultimate destiny is taken up into the God-provided destiny of history. Through God's self-disclosure in Jesus Christ we are able to recognize that the God whom we acknowledge as Lord has not only provided the beginning of our history, but will also provide its fulfilment as foreshadowed in the Christ event.

It is becoming increasingly evident that the spirit of materialistic and pragmatic secularity ultimately turns against humanity itself. The Christian faith, however, without abandoning the dynamic drive shown in this movement, leads to true humanity. Therefore, we must pursue a reintegration of the Judeo-Christian vision of God and God's history into this dynamic drive. In the pursuit of this reintegration lies the great task and promise of the Christian faith for the whole of humanity.

With regard to the personification of God, we must also consider God's gender and locality. Though these issues are interesting, they are clearly secondary and their expositions depend on the available conceptual tools. While for the patriarchal society of Israel masculine features for Yahweh were dominant, female-like features were not forgotten. The Jewish scholar Howard Eilberg-Schwartz (b. 1956), who deals extensively with the sexual imagery in the Old Testament, especially as it pertains to the image of marriage in the relationship between God and Israel, comes to the conclusion: "While the anatomical maleness of God is never fully conceptualized, God is sometimes imagined not only in feminine imagery but as anatomically female."²⁵ A sexual differentiation for Yahweh, however, was of no interest, since in contradistinction to the gods of the surrounding nations, Yahweh was not considered a fertility god. This is fundamentally different, for instance, from Zeus whose sexual imagery points to real acts and does not stand for something beyond that which is imaged. Similarly, for the community of the first temple it was evident that Yahweh was present in his temple. Yet, we are also told that King Solomon conceded: "But will God indeed dwell on the earth? Even heaven and the highest heaven cannot contain you, much less this house that I have built!" (1 Kgs 8:27). While there is a preferential presence for God, i.e., God's temple, God is not limited to a physical habitation or a geographical region.

The decisive point concerning God being a personal God is not where God is or what God looks like, but that a human being can only be a true person in being related to a personal God. This is substantiated by our earlier observation that a human being is basically a religious being. While a human being can to some extent attain personhood in being related to the God who comes into language in the multitude of religions, a human being can only be a person in the full sense if related to God as God comes to us through the ultimate and final self-disclosure in Jesus Christ. Only there a human being's primordially intended wholeness becomes an actual proleptic possibility, because only there, in the redemptive Christ event, do we encounter God's ultimate compassion and holiness.

The whole invitational history is an illustration of God's compassion with us.²⁶ There is no indication in the Bible that God needed humans as

---

25. Howard Eilberg-Schwartz, *God's Phallus and Other Problems with Men and Monotheism* (Boston: Beacon, 1994) 114.

26. Yehezkel Kaufmann, *The Religion of Israel: From Its Beginnings to the Babylonian Exile*, trans. and abridged by Moshe Greenberg (Chicago: University of Chicago Press, 1960) 212–13, very interestingly ties this invitational history with the status of the prophet in Israel. The prophet acts on behalf of God, not of the people. He is sent to the people to bring the word of God and God's command to the people. But he is not the only one since there is a succession of emissaries of God that come to the people through the centuries. Kaufmann sees here a distinctive difference from the pagan religions. In pagan religions prophets are exceptional figures endowed with a charisma that was theirs alone. Therefore, Buddha, Zoroaster, or Mohammad were exceptional figures whose "mission" ended with them as founders or reorganizers of religions. In Israel, however, there was a continuous commissioning of people of God throughout the ages. In other words, Kaufmann's reference to the succession of prophets as spokespeople of

companions. God created man and woman out of God's free will. Even hereditary research implicitly attests to this when it states that humans are not a necessary but an accidental product of evolution. There is also no indication that God needed another chosen people after the first had turned away from God. The frequently used imagery that we are like clay in the potter's hand (Jer 18:6; Isa 64:8, etc.) reinforces this point.

While there is absolutely no necessity for God's compassion we nevertheless read: "Although heaven and the heaven of heavens belong to the Lord your God, the earth with all that is in it, yet the Lord set his heart in love on your ancestors alone and chose you, their descendants after them, all peoples, as it is today" (Deut 10:14f.). God has once shown unconditional compassion to Israel's ancestors and now God shows it to Israel itself. This compassion is expressed in the unconditional love to the people despite their shortcomings. Since love in the Old Testament's understanding is the attitude of a superior toward an inferior it does not describe the relationship between humanity and God, but between God and humanity. Yet only in a few cases are we told that God loves individuals (cf. 2 Sam 12:24 and Neh 13:26), and in those instances the individuals are of royal blood. In the vast majority of cases love denotes God's relationship to the chosen people. Due to God's love for them, they are then in turn enabled and encouraged to love God.

Often God's relationship to his people is expressed in the image of love, of a filial relationship, or one of husband and wife. God states through the prophet Hosea: "When Israel was a child, I loved him, and out of Egypt I called my son" (Hos 11:1). This divine love, though not bare of emotions, indicates God's faithfulness. The foundation for God's faithfulness is the covenant God has made with Israel (1 Kgs 8:23).[27] Herewith we have encountered three constitutive terms for God's compassion: love (*'ahabah*), faithfulness (*chesed*) and covenant (*berith*).[28]

God illustrates what we have called God's invitational history.

27. Cf. Hans-Jürgen Zobel, "*chesed*," in *ThDOT*, 5:60. Yet there *chesed* is always translated as "kindness" in contrast to *NRSV* which uses "faithfulness" (cf. Jer 31:3).

28. Norman H. Snaith, in his helpful book, *The Distinctive Ideas of the Old Testament* (London: Epworth, 1960) 95, mentions that *chesed* ("love" or, as we rather say, "faithfulness") is conditional upon there being a covenant, while *'ahabah* (love) is unconditional love and the very basis and cause of the existence of the covenant between God and Israel. "Without the prior existence of a covenant, there could never be any *chesed* at all." Thus Snaith calls *'ahabah* (love) God's election love, while he terms *chesed* (faithfulness) God's covenant love.

Each of them is different, yet all are interrelated. In the book of Jeremiah, for instance, the relation between love and faithfulness is expressed in God saying: "I have loved you with an everlasting love; therefore I have continued my faithfulness to you" (Jer 31:3). In other words, God's compassion implies that God does not revoke his initial choice. God continues his faithfulness towards Israel. This faithfulness is the power which guarantees God's covenant with Israel and which makes it strong and durable. "Know therefore that the Lord your God is God, the faithful God who maintains covenant loyalty with those who love him and keep his commandments, to a thousand generations," we read in Deut 7:9. Again the triad of love, faithfulness, and covenant, is mentioned with its components intimately related.

By making a covenant with Israel God has shown his faithfulness. The likeness of God is described here not in terms of God's being, but in the way God relates to his people. From passages such as Micah 6:8 "He [Yahweh] has told you, O mortal, what is good; and what does the Lord require of you but to do justice, and to love kindness [*chesed*], and to walk humbly with your God?" we gather that faithfulness and love are not conceived of as having originated in humanity's own sphere.[29] They are derived from the way God relates to humanity. Only then do they become human possibilities. Yet love, faithfulness, and covenant not only characterize God's present relation to Israel. Israel can recognize from its history of broken covenants, broken by Israel yet renewed by God, that God's compassion emerged out of the past and extends itself into the future. God will even make "an everlasting covenant" with Israel (Isa 55:3) whose fulfillment the people await. God's steadfast love is also expanded beyond the confines of Israel. History as well as the whole creative and

---

29. The term "good" that Micah uses here is not a "perfectly general term" (*Allerweltsbegriff* in the German original) as Gerhard von Rad assumes, *Old Testament Theology*, vol. 2: *The Theology of Israel's Prophetic Traditions*, trans. by D. M. G. Stalker (New York: Harper, 1965) 186. Theodor Lescow, *Micha 6, 6–8. Studien zur Sprache, Form und Auslegung* (Stuttgart: Calwer, 1966) 45, rightly objected to von Rad and claimed that doing good and knowing God is intimately correlated in the Old Testament, since without knowing God one cannot do good and without doing good one does not really express that one knows God. Cf. also Artur Weiser, *Das Buch der Zwölf kleinen Propheten* (Göttingen: Vandenhoeck & Ruprecht, 1985) 1:281, in his exegesis of Mic. 6:8, who emphasizes that "demanding the good is presupposed as a foundation on which alone a relationship of humanity to God is possible."

life-sustaining activity of God is interpreted as an expression of God's steadfast love (Ps 136).[30]

Since the Christian community understood itself in succession to God's chosen people, God's compassion assumes a prominent place in the New Testament. The compassion of God finds its central expression in a new covenant. Already in the book of Jeremiah we hear the promise of a new covenant which will be radically different from the old one.

> The days are surely coming, says the Lord, when I will make a new covenant with the house of Israel and the house of Judah. It will not be like the covenant that I made with their ancestors when I took them by the hand to bring them out of the land of Egypt—a covenant that they broke, though I was their husband, says the Lord. But this is the covenant that I will make with the house of Israel after those days, says the Lord: I will put my law within them, and I will write it on their hearts; and I will be their God, and they shall be my people. (Jer 31:31ff.)

But not until Jesus the Christ did this new covenant become a reality. Through the power of Jesus' sacrificial death a new covenant was instituted (1 Cor 11:25). While the Old Testament understanding of the covenant concept is continued it is no longer the same covenant. There is now an old covenant (2 Cor 3:14) and a new one. But "there is no contradiction between the old and new covenants. The one is preparatory; it leads to Christ . . . it is fulfilled in and therefore superseded by the other."[31] But it is still the sameness of God's compassionate will that finally prevails over human sinfulness. The term covenant denotes "from first to last the 'disposition' of God, the mighty declaration of the sovereign will of God in history, by which He orders the relation between Himself and men according to His own saving purpose, and which carries with it the authoritative divine ordering, the one order of things which is in accordance with it."[32] Thus compassion cannot be equated with senile stubbornness. It is the sovereign will of God that comes to

---

30. Cf. Walther Eichrodt, *Theology of the Old Testament*, trans. J. A. Baker (Philadelphia: Westminster, 1961) 1:239, who shows that creation itself is a work of the divine *chesed*. However, in making the covenant relationship the overriding concept of Old Testament theology Eichrodt has to shortchange other equally important concepts in the relationship between God and God's people.

31. So Philip Edgcumbe Hughes, *Paul's Second Epistle to the Corinthians* (Grand Rapids: Eerdmans, 1962) in his exegesis of 2 Cor 3:14.

32. Johannes Behm, "*diatheke*," in *ThDNT*, 2:134.

expression here in his concern for humanity, a concern so radical that God does not hesitate to dissolve one covenant to further the advance of God's salvational interest in humanity.

In analogy to Old Testament thinking, in the New Testament God's compassion for humanity is again expressed through the term love. For instance, in the Gospel of John we read the conviction that "God so loved the world that he gave his only Son, so that everyone who believes in him may not perish but may have eternal life" (John 3:16). Through his love God calls his people into communion with God and with each other (Rom 1:7). While love is also the sign of those whom God loves, God and humanity do not gather around the common concern to love, but because God loved those whom he called they in turn love each other and their neighbors (1 John 4:19). Though God is also the "object" of human love, love toward God is only tangentially mentioned in the New Testament.[33] God's love is primarily intended to enable human love to extend itself to others. The ethical demands of the New Testament concerning our neighbors are understood to be fulfillable only because of the primacy of God's love.

We can see from the life and destiny of Jesus Christ, the prime example of God's love, that love is neither sentimental nor sexual. As the extension of God's love Jesus Christ shows compassion and solidarity even to the point of suffering and self-annihilation. Therefore the faithfulness of Jesus Christ and the love of God are at times mentioned in one breath (2 Cor 13:14). The love of God expresses itself in the faithfulness of Jesus Christ, in his sacrificial death, and in his continued presence with the Christian community. God's faithfulness in the New Testament is enunciated with terms such as mercy (*eleos*) and grace (*charis*). In the New Testament *eleos* is often used for "the divinely required attitude" of one person to another.[34] But Titus 3:5 ("he [God] saved us, not because of any works of righteousness that we had done, but according to his mercy") makes it clear that such a "requirement" is not determinative for God's *eleos*, for his eschatological act of salvation in Jesus Christ. A human being's "required" *eleos* to another human being is rather seen as in response to God's grace.

---

33. Cf. Ethelbert Stauffer, "*agapao*," *ThDNT*, 1:50, esp. n. 140.

34. Rudolf Bultmann, "*eleos*," *ThDNT*, 2:482–84. We find Bultmann's expression of "the divinely required attitude of man" somewhat misleading. "Response" would have been more appropriate than the legalistically sounding term "requirement."

Charis is used in a way very similar to *eleos*.[35] For instance, Paul uses *charis* as the central term to express God's saving event in Jesus Christ. The whole structure of the saving event is seen under the aspect of God's faithfulness or God's grace. It is an undeserved gift of God (Rom 3:24f) which culminates in Jesus' sacrificial death. Its undeserved character excludes any cooperative disposition of humanity. Grace as God's compassion for humanity is not only the presupposition for making humanity acceptable to God, but it constitutes itself in the gifts of grace (1 Corinthians 13) and it institutes the apostolate to communicate grace to others (cf. Rom 1:5). In other words, a human being's Christian existence is an existence through grace and in grace. To avoid the impression that the compassion of God would be misunderstood as God's indulgence of human alienation from God, we now must turn to the other basic trait in God's self-disclosure, God's holiness.

We remember that holiness is a basic concept of religion, closely related to mana and taboo. The understanding of holiness as a supernatural and mysterious force which confers a special quality upon particular persons and things is not foreign to the Old Testament.[36] For instance, when Uzzah touched the ark, the place of God's presence, he had to die, because he had come in contact with the holy (2 Sam 6:6f). Holiness is always a manifestation of power. According to the Old Testament all power is concentrated in the person of Yahweh, apart from whom no life is possible in nature or humanity. Therefore, it is only after "the revelation to Moses in Exod 3" that we hear of God's holiness.[37] Holiness is not a divine quality beside other qualities, it is the characteristic of Yahweh. Israelites and non-Israelites alike experienced that God is a holy God before whom no one can stand (1 Sam 6:20). God is a holy God who makes humanity realize the infinite qualitative difference between God and humanity and who causes fear and dread (Isa 8:13).[38] The places of God's presence are also holy and, because of him, are treated with special respect (Ps 93:5; Exod 3:5).

---

35. Cf. for the following Hans Conzelmann, "*charis*," in *ThDNT*, 9:394–398.

36. For a good introduction to the Old Testament understanding of this aspect of God's holiness, cf. Snaith, *Distinctive Ideas of the Old Testament*, 40–41.

37. Walter Kornfeld, "*kadosh*," in *ThDOT*, 12:529.

38. Th. C. Vriezen, *An Outline of Old Testament Theology*, 2nd ed. (Newton, MA: Charles T. Bradford, 1970) 149, rightly observes that Yahweh's holiness "first of all involves *unapproachableness*, even for the angels around His throne."

While the essential aspect of holiness is that of power, it is "power in the service of a God who uses all things to make his kingdom triumph."[39] The prohibitive aspect of holiness is no longer decisive, as in many other religions, but the aspect of communion which bestows life. Holiness is always and particularly connected with the God of the covenant. The prophet Isaiah expresses this with the thought that Yahweh is the holy one of Israel (Isa 5:24). "Yahweh is the holy one of Israel not because he is consecrated to Israel but because he has consecrated Israel to himself, and Israel itself is holy only because of this consecration to Yahweh."[40] "Sanctify yourselves therefore, and be holy, for I am holy" says the Lord (Lev 11:44). Since the holy one of Israel is experienced as a God who is always near to help (Isa 31:1), God's mighty acts in history through which Israel was delivered from its enemies are seen as manifestations of his holiness. Even the gathering of Israel after the exile and the reestablishment of its own nation is understood as a demonstration of God's holiness (Ezek 20:41). Hosea already interprets God's presence among the people as a sign of God's holiness (Hos 11:9). Through God's holiness Israel is gathered and preserved in the face of all other nations and inspired to become a holy or God-dedicated nation.

Closely connected with God's holiness is God's righteousness. Righteousness is understood as conformity to a norm and not primarily punitive, distributive, or justificatory. It expresses itself in a certain way of acting and manifests itself in God's relation to humanity which is experienced in God's action in history. God is a righteous God and delights in righteousness (Ps 11:7). Neither wickedness is left unpunished nor the good unrecognized. Therefore the righteous and upright shall dwell in the presence of the Lord (Ps 140:13). Righteousness can sometimes become almost identical with God's faithfulness, since God recognizes the pleading of the people (Ps 143:1). This means that though righteousness implies justice and judgment, it is exercised in conformity with God's covenantal compassion with the people. This is summed up best in the book of Jeremiah where we read: "Let those who boast boast in this, that they understand and know me, that I am the Lord; I act

---

39. Edmond Jacob, *Theology of the Old Testament*, trans. Arthur W. Heathcote and Philip J. Allcock (London: Hoder & Stoughton, 1958) 87. Cf. also Horst Dietrich Preuss, *Old Testament Theology*, trans. Leo G. Perdue (Louisville: Westminster John Knox, 1995) 1:240–41.

40. Jacob, *Theology of the Old Testament*, 89.

with steadfast love, justice, and righteousness in the earth, for in these things I delight, says the Lord" (Jer 9:24). God is not the primordial tyrant who uncompassionately distributes good and evil to those who deserve it. Norman Snaith (1898–1982) appropriately reminds us that in the Israelite understanding there is "no *Ananke* (Necessity) and no *Dike* (Justice) to which both gods and men must conform. God is His own necessity,"[41] and God's will shows a persistent tendency to ensue in benevolent action. God's salvational activity, though shy of any sentimental leniency, always looks out for the benefit of humanity and for the ultimate victory of God's kingship. This is also true when we now consider another facet of God's holiness, his wrath.

Naturally, the thought emerges that wrath reflects a human characteristic that in turn was projected into God. Yet the overwhelming number of passages that talk about wrath in the Old Testament do not talk about a human disposition, but about God. "Wrath is so much part of the figure of God in the Old Testament that the ancient Israelites saw no problem in it, but they accepted this reality as being a normal part of the irrational and mysterious in God."[42] It is the prerogative of God to show his power and wrath even if nothing has provoked it (cf. the classic example of Job, or 2 Sam 24:1).[43] Israel, however, realized that the wrath of God is not just a demonstration of God's power and sovereignty. The Pentateuch, especially in its exhortations in Deuteronomy, as well as the prophets, relates the outburst of God's wrath to Israel's transgression of the covenant (Deut 6:15; Ezek 5:13). God is a jealous God, we hear, and his anger will be kindled against the people if they neglect God's laws. Other nations too are under God's wrath for their pride and their contempt of the elementary rules of humanity. We also hear of a day of wrath when definite sins are judged (cf. Am 1 and 2).

Israel's whole history can be understood as a history of God's wrath, since it is a history of Israel's aversion to God. Though the day of the Lord as a day of wrath looms high over Israel, we hear from God: "I

---

41. Snaith, *Distinctive Ideas of the Old Testament*, 77.

42. Cf. Jacob, *Theology of the Old Testament*, 114, who also quotes statistics according to which the most frequently used Hebrew terms for "wrath" are used roughly four times more often for describing a disposition of God than of humanity.

43. It must be mentioned, however, that the later Chronicles no longer attributed the incitement to number Israel to Yahweh but to Satan (1 Chr 21:1). Should this indicate an emerging doubt whether the dreadful feature in God was compatible with his moral integrity?

will not execute my fierce anger; I will not again destroy Ephraim; for I am God and no mortal, the Holy One in your midst, and I will not come in wrath" (Hos 11:9).[44] Was the Psalmist right, when he said of God: "For his anger is but for a moment; his favor is for a lifetime" (Ps 30:5)? God's self-disclosive history, we have noticed, is the history of a great invitation. It seems that even God's wrath has as its ultimate goal the accomplishment of this invitation. This is at least the conviction as far as the New Testament is concerned.

The trends present in the Old Testament concerning the understanding of God's holiness are in part continued and in part modified in the New. In analogy to the Old Testament, God is still regarded as the Holy One (Rev 4:8; 1 Pet 1:15f.), but this attribute is now also conferred upon Jesus the Christ (cf. Mark 1:24) and upon the Spirit. Similarly to Noah's dove indicating a new age after the flood (Gen 8:8ff.), so the Spirit of God descending upon Jesus in the form of a dove signifies the dawn of a new age initiated through Jesus' baptism (1 Pet 3:19ff.). The Holy Spirit of God, first exclusively connected with the figure of Jesus, is set free through Christ's resurrection (John 20:22) and communicated to his disciples. Especially Luke emphasizes the activity of the Holy Spirit who since Pentecost works creatively and giving directions to the Christian community. The Holy Spirit of God who at the time of Moses and even in the post-exilic period had lived in Israel (Isa 63:10f.; Hag 2:5), dwells now in the Christian community (1 Thess 4:8).[45] The signs of this new community are baptism by the Holy Spirit of God, made possible through the death of Jesus the Christ, and the Lord's Supper (1 Cor 12:13). Therefore Christians can be called the holy ones (Col 3:12) who are sanctified through the sacrificial death of Christ. The intention of God's holiness to create a community of those who are again one with God has been accomplished by God's coming to us in Jesus the Christ and by the creative and guiding function of God's Spirit. The aspect of God's holiness in fulfilling salvation is even more emphasized in the understanding of his righteousness.

---

44. Artur Weiser, *Das Buch der zwölf kleinen Propheten*, 1:86, comments about this passage that, in contrast to our reasoning, the seriousness of God's judgment and his seeking, pedagogical love do not exclude each other. "God's wrath does not suffocate his love; it is only the other side of his same fundamental divine disposition that Yahweh never abandoned with his people."

45. Cf. for the following Otto Procksch, *"hagios,"* in *ThDNT*, 1:103-5.

Already in the Septuagint, the Greek translation of the Hebrew Old Testament, we notice that *dikaiosyne* (righteousness) *is* not only used to translate the Hebrew word *tsedaka* (righteousness), but also to render the Hebrew *chesed* (faithfulness, compassion, or steadfast love) into Greek (cf. Gen 19:19).[46] This gives us some indication that already in the Septuagint God's righteousness is being interpreted with greater emphasis on his dispensing of salvation. In a few New Testament instances righteousness is still understood as God's righteous judgment at the parousia of Christ (Acts 17:31) or as God's righteousness which guides the activity of the Christian community (2 Pet 1:1). Yet outside the Pauline writings the term righteousness describes in most cases a human condition. It is the term "for the right conduct of man which follows the will of God and is pleasing to Him, for rectitude of life before God, for uprightness before His judgment."[47]

The clue to the change of the term righteousness from describing primarily an attitude of God to denoting almost exclusively a human condition may be found in Paul's view of the term righteousness of God. Paul understands the righteousness of God as God's alone. This reflects the second part of Isaiah, where righteousness and salvation are conjoined (Isa 45:9, 21). This means that righteousness is God's saving activity. Righteousness is a conjunction of judgment and grace which God enjoys and demonstrates. Ultimately, it is a pardoning sentence by which God draws humanity into a new life in the kingdom and which will be fully manifested in the last judgment (cf. Rom 1:16f.). Paul's interpretation of God's righteousness must be seen against the background of the Old Testament. There God was conceived of as the judge who demands obedience and who rewards and punishes. Through the encounter with Christ, however, Paul deeply realized—far more than the Judaism out of which he came—that to accomplish obedience to God through exact fulfilment of the Law is an optimistic utopian idea. While Paul maintained that only the righteous can enjoy fellowship with a holy and righteous God, he was convinced that righteousness that enables fellowship with God can no longer be—if it ever has been—established by us; it is solely God's doing. This righteousness has been brought about

---

46. Cf. Gottlob Schrenk, "*dikaiosyne*," in *ThDNT*, 2:195–97, for an extensive treatment of this topic.

47. Schrenk, "*dikaiosyne*," 2:198.

through God's sovereign, gracious, and decisive intervention in Jesus the Christ (Rom 3:25f).

The righteousness of God is now considered a power that leads to new life. Since God's activity is always tending toward fulfilment of his kingship, God's righteousness concerns itself not just with the present, but equally important with the eschatological fulfilment in life eternal (Rom 5:21). Now we understand why in the New Testament the righteousness of God is so frequently used to denote an anthropological phenomenon. The righteousness of God, demonstrated in the Christ event, enables humanity to be righteous again and to attain communion with the one who is righteous (cf. Matt 6:33 and Luke 1:75). This also implies a shift in the understanding of God's wrath.

It would be a gross misunderstanding to assume that the New Testament gospel suddenly enlightens us "as to God's hitherto misunderstood nature as if till now He had been wrongly conceived as wrathful and ought henceforth to be regarded as gracious."[48] God is and remains a God of wrath even for Christians. Both Jesus and John the Baptist are portrayed in the New Testament as proclaiming a gospel that includes the pronouncement of God's wrath (cf. Matt 3:7; Luke 21:23). The wrath of God is intrinsic to understanding God even in the New Testament, since "it is a fearful thing to fall into the hands of the living God" (Heb 10:31). Biblical thought can hardly substantiate Schleiermacher's claim that apart from Christ humanity need not be "the object of divine displeasure and wrath, for there is no such object."[49] We must rather agree with the Lutheran theologian Paul Althaus (1888–1966) that one cannot disclaim the reality of God's wrath by referring to God's unconditional love.[50] Both the magnitude of God's wrath and of God's compassion must be taken with utmost seriousness. Passages such as Rom 1:17f and 3:23f, however, might intimate that the disclosure of God's wrath is rather the necessary background over against which the disclosure of God's grace gains its brightness. This would mean that human sinfulness and God's resulting wrath in the last analysis only magnify the triumph of God's compassionate righteousness.

---

48. Bultmann, *Theology of the New Testament*, 1:288.

49. Schleiermacher, *Christian Faith* (par. 109/4) 2:503.

50. Cf. Paul Althaus, *Die christliche Wahrheit*, 5th ed. (Gütersloh: Carl Bertelsmann, 1959) 398.

Yet we are confronted here with a paradoxical mystery: On the one hand everything is founded in and contributes to the salvational plan of God. On the other hand the guilt of all anti-Godly moves cannot be undone and deserve the unlimited wrath of God. This wrath, indicated in the wrath of Jesus over all anti-Godly resistance (cf. Matt 12:34; Mark 1:25, etc.), will find its culmination in his wrath as the eschatological judge (cf. Matt 22:13). Since Christ is both the judge and was also judged for our sake, those who claim Christ on their side, need no longer be afraid of the still outstanding finalization of God's wrath.[51] For such people the time of the wrath has passed away and something new has come, because through Christ God reconciled the world to himself (2 Cor 5:17f).

In attempting to outline the biblical understanding of God's compassion and holiness we have seen that the main terms which describe these characteristics, such as love, faithfulness, covenant, righteousness, and wrath, are not conceived of as originating from the observation of human conditions which then are projected unto God. They are regarded as originating from the experience of God relating Godself to humanity, an experience which in turn enables humanity to display characteristics such as love, faithfulness, covenant, and righteousness.[52] Furthermore, compassion and holiness were not understood as telling us something about God's essence, but about the way God encounters us. George Ernest Wright (1909–1974) pointed this out very well when he said: "The so-called 'attributes' of God are inferences drawn from the way he has acted. His righteousness, justice, love, grace, jealousy, and wrath are not abstractions with which we are free to deal abstractly—that is, apart from history. They are descriptive of the way God has directed history; and hence it is inferred that they all find their unity in him."[53] These "attributes" of God tell the story of how the Judeo-Christian community was encountered by God and they invite us to be encountered likewise so that our existence is also characterized by such actions as love, faithfulness, righteousness, and holiness. Since these terms describe a history

---

51. Cf. Gustav Stählin, "*orge*," in *ThDNT*, 5:427, who claims that there is only one refuge from the unqualified wrath of God, "namely, Christ and faith in Him."

52. In the New Testament wrath is seen as something bad, if it is just a human attitude. It is justified only as holy wrath "which hates what God hates and which is seen above all in Jesus Himself" (cf. Stählin, "*orge*," in *ThDNT*, 5:419).

53. G. Ernest Wright, *God Who Acts. Biblical Theology as Recital* (Chicago: Henry Regnery, 1952) 84.

they also tell us about a movement of this history, a movement that culminates in the full realization of God's compassion and holiness for all humanity. In being confronted with Christ as the focal point and goal of this history we are invited to anticipate this full realization now proleptically in the Christian community.

History—Human and Divine

Throughout our investigation we have noted that the God experienced in the Judeo-Christian tradition is a God of history who discloses himself in historical events, which means in the categories of space and time. As a God of history God is intimately involved not only in the present process, but also in the ultimate outcome of history. Dietrich Bonhoeffer (1906–1945) captured well God's involvement in the historical process when he said: "God does not give us everything we want, but he does fulfill all his promises."[54] Not every historical event can be interpreted as the result of God's activity, and even the technical term "an act of God" does not imply that God was indeed active in a particular event, but that we are at a loss to explain why it actually happened.

It is not without significance that in both the Old and the New Testaments God is introduced as the one for whom nothing is impossible and who determines the cause of history. This confession of God's almighty power and God's predetermination of history, however, only serves to emphasize the conviction that God will bring his plan of salvation to completion (Gen 18:14 and Luke 1:37). This confession does not imply that all of history runs according to God's preconceived plan so that humans became reduced to puppets with God and his mighty arm as puppeteer. When Jesus was asked for theological interpretation of the death of the Galileans that Pilate had slain, or of the eighteen men who were killed when the tower collapsed at Siloam (Luke 13:1–5), he did not equate the course of history with God's judgment. Jesus also reacted similarly when his disciples asked him why a specific person was born blind (John 9:3). At the same time, Jesus did not simply shrug his shoulders in ignorance and declare that history is without meaning. In the first two instances Jesus answered in an existential fashion that events like these remind us of our own mortality and sinfulness. In the latter

---

54. Dietrich Bonhoeffer, *Letters and Papers from Prison*, Eberhard Bethge, ed., rev. and enlarged ed. (New York: Macmillan, 1968) 206.

case he commented, according to the Evangelist, that this case serves to make manifest God's works.

Historical events are not ends in themselves. They also are not simply a piece of a larger puzzle called world history. Ultimately, but only ultimately, historical events have eschatological significance. They are "a living reminder of the End, speaking sometimes with certainty and more often with utter ambiguity."[55] While Jesus alerted his audience to watch for the signs of the end, he did not provide us with a time-table for events leading to the eschatological fulfilment of history and creation (Matt 24:32f and 36f).

Can we, however, so easily penetrate through the scriptural texts to the underlying events, if there are any, and then relate them to God's doing? Archaeology and Old Testament research have shown that at least with regard to the Old Testament the factual history covering Israelite and Jewish history is not identical with the history recorded in the Old Testament documents. In his monumental *Theology of the Old Testament* Gerhard von Rad demonstrated that the Old Testament reflections on Israel's history basically are of a confessional nature. They were handed down to us by a variety of witnesses and ways of understanding. While von Rad's own endeavor to delineate the origin and transformation of such traditions presupposes a fairly solid reconstruction of Israel's history, he came close to advancing the idea that in the Old Testament we have only a kerygmatic history, i.e., a history of proclamation.[56] Yet he

---

55. Evigenii Lampert, *The Apocalypse of History: Problems of Providence and Human Destiny* (London: Faber and Faber, 1948) 176, who convincingly asserts an apocalyptic and eschatological interpretation of history.

56. This impression is reinforced by Gerhard von Rad's comment, *Old Testament Theology*, trans. D. M. G. Stalker (London: SCM, 1975) 1:121: "Thus, re-telling remains the most legitimate form of theological discourse on the Old Testament." Cf. also Friedrich Baumgärtel, "Gerhard von Rad's 'Theologie des Alten Testaments,'" *Theologische Literaturzeitung*, LXXXVI (November, 1961) col. 803, where he vehemently objects to this comment. However, in his preface to the fourth edition of his *Old Testament Theology* von Rad mentioned to his critics that he never thought of "separating between the historical and the less or not at all historical" (*Theologie des Alten Testaments*, 4th ed. [Munich: Chr. Kaiser, 1962] 1:11–12). Evidently this is exactly the point that Baumgärtel attacked. Faith and history seem inextricably interwoven in von Rad's *Old Testament Theology*.

For an excellent introduction to the issue of history and salvation history, cf. Carl E. Braaten, *History and Hermeneutics*, vol. 2 of *New Directions in Theology Today*, ed. William Hordern (Philadelphia: Westminster, 1966). Braaten himself comes close to Pannenberg in emphasizing the progressive, eschatological character of history of

admitted that "even the earliest avowals to Jahweh were historically determined, that is, they connect the name of this God with some statement about an action in history."[57] One of these confessions is that Yahweh brought Israel out of Egypt, while others designate Yahweh as the one who called the patriarchs and who promised them the land, etc.

Yet Walter Brueggemann (b. 1933) and others assert that the time of Gerhard von Rad is over and that we cannot that easily penetrate to history as an earlier generation of scholars thought.[58] Since Brueggemann realizes that the Old Testament text as it now stands is a result of post-exilic Judaism, meaning that older texts were reappropriated, we need therefore "to turn away from history to the actual rhetoric of text" to become aware "of the *intertextuality* of the text," because "texts are primarily related to other texts."[59] We are primarily confronted just with texts which we have to interpret. Brueggemann now advances a post-liberal approach to the biblical texts similar to what the Yale School of the systematician George Lindbeck (b. 1923) has propagated. Brueggemann proposes as his task: "to pay attention to the internal logic of the texts, and to attend, as best I can, to the peculiar grammar and dialect of this textual tradition."[60] With this linguistic or textual approach, Brueggemann wants to circumvent the complex issue of historicity because he is no longer asking what happened but what is said. Therefore, according to him, the historical referent does not belong "to the work of Old Testament theology."[61] This does not mean for Brueggemann that he finds no historicity pertaining to Israel's faith, but rather that this is not the point of his inquiry.

---

which the Christ event is its proleptically anticipated goal. Cf. his book *The Future of God. The Revolutionary Dynamics of Hope.* (New York: Harper, 1969) 109 in which he characterizes "the church as the prolepsis of a new world."

57. von Rad, *Old Testament Theology*, 1:121.

58. Cf. Walter Brueggemann, *Theology of the Old Testament. Testimony, Dispute, Advocacy* (Minneapolis: Fortress, 1997) 42, who claims: "It is now conventional to recognize that the great period of Old Testament theology dominated by Eichrodt, and even more by von Rad, came to an end around 1970."

59. Ibid., 78.

60. Ibid., 86; cf. the criticism of Lindbeck by Alister McGrath, *A Scientific Theology*, vol. 2: *Reality* (London: T. & T. Clark, 2002) 38–54, where he rightly accuses Lindbeck of "fideism."

61. Brueggemann, *Theology of the Old Testament*, 118.

The reason Brueggeman brackets the issue of the historicity is that he wants to circumvent the issue of historicity of the so-called "acts of God." He is aware that "the notion of 'God's action in history' has been a privileged reference point in Old Testament theology, especially under the influence of von Rad and Wright."[62] But now "it is evident that a naïve biblical notion of God's action is not plausible in the categories of modernism. Thus one is faced with either abandoning the notion of God's action or trimming it down to irrelevance (which Old Testament theology can scarcely do), or refusing the categories of modernity that make one susceptible to the charge of fideism." Indeed, modernism in the gown of modern materialistic secularity has eliminated any transcendent referent and thereby also the notion of God's action. Brueggemann is correct in not wanting to trim down the notion of God's action to irrelevance or to adopt some kind of fideism, which might mean simply believing everything that the biblical authors relate. Therefore he, like an interpreter of other literary texts, attempts "to explicate the rhetoric of ancient Israel in terms of its own claims."

Such allegiance to these texts is certainly to be lauded. Yet the question must be asked whether "the categories of modernism," as Brueggemann calls them, are indeed binding and beyond criticism. As we have noted they are highly reductive and therefore felt wanting. The resultant void is noticed by the vast majority of people everywhere. Whether learned or not, rich or poor, denominationally affiliated or unattached, people all yearn for and seek transcendent guidance. Many fill this void by following modern-day gurus or come up with a self-created, often highly syncretistic religion. Many are very much convinced of divine interference with human activities and the natural processes in this world, though their everyday lives may witness to the opposite. Observing all this there is no need to give in to some kind of reductive modernism that would call the biblical notion of God's action implausible.

Even Brueggemann himself cannot refrain from at least implicitly acknowledging God's action in history as the starting-point of his theological enterprise when he writes: "The reader will note well that I have proposed that *the beginning point for articulating Old Testament theol-*

---

62. Ibid., 124–25 n. 18, for this and the other two quotes.

ogy is the liturgical, public acknowledgement of a new reality wrought by Yahweh in the life of the speaker and in the community of the speaker."[63]

If the beginning point of Old Testament theology—and I would even venture to say of the Judeo-Christian tradition—is the public acknowledgment of a new reality brought about by Yahweh, then this new reality certainly has a historical reference point. It must have occurred in space and time. And this is exactly what the Israelite community affirms. For example in the creed in Deuteronomy 26:5–9 the main events in the salvation history of Israel are recapitulated from the time of the Patriarchs to the entrance into the promised land:

> A wandering Aramean was my ancestor; he went down into Egypt and lived there as an alien, few in number, and there he became a great nation, mighty and populous. When the Egyptians treated us harshly and afflicted us, by imposing hard labor on us, we cried to the Lord, the God of our ancestors; the Lord heard our voice and saw our affliction, our toil, and our oppression. The Lord brought us out of Egypt with a mighty hand and an outstretched arm, with a terrifying display of power, and with signs and wonders; and he brought us into this place and gave us this land, a land flowing with milk and honey.

We will easily notice that the passage cited does not just contain objective facts, though we nevertheless observe a close concentration on objective facts. The general outline of Israel's history which is reported here is seen in the light of God's activity. Archaeology has unearthed a plethora of external data which serve "as a tool for isolating a very reliable 'historical core' of events in the narrative of the Hebrew Bible."[64] This is true for early Israel, for the so-called United Monarchy, i.e., the period when Israel was united under the first two kings of Israel, and for the divided monarchy, when from the tenth [ca. 922] through the eighth [722, fall of Samaria] centuries BC, Israel was divided into a Northern and Southern kingdom, and for the last years of Judah until the Exile. Since, as we have seen, God and God's activity cannot be proven by external means, these archaeological findings are silent about God's activity. The same is true for epigraphic, historical, social scientific and other data. Yet, as the

---

63. Brueggemann, *Theology of the Old Testament*, 128.

64. William G. Dever, *What Did the Biblical Writers Know and When Did They Know It? What Archaeology Can Tell Us about the Reality of Ancient Israel* (Grand Rapids, MI: Eerdmans, 2001) 267, who discredits the approach of the biblical minimalists who disclaim that the biblical witness is historically reliable.

Theomorphous Humanity—Curse or Blessing?

Old Testament scholar Paul Hanson (b. 1939) stated in his criticism of Brueggemann's rhetorical approach, they "add clarity, depth, and precision to our understanding of that testimony" of the biblical witness "and remind us of the earth-groundedness of our own theologizing."[65] Together with the biblical witness, however, these external data are significant pointers in the direction of God's involvement in history.

Therefore it is unwarranted to stay with *"the practice of rhetoric"* and affirm that "utterance is an act of imagination that produces worlds and/or counterworlds."[66] With such a claim Brueggemann plays into the hands of those who suggest with Feuerbach that religion is predominantly imagination and fabricates its own reality. We should rather side with Brueggemann's earlier insight that the biblical texts "are in their main reference anticipatory, either in the Old Testament or in the New Testament, as the coming Kingdom or the coming Messiah."[67] While in other reports of ancient history attention is focused on the past, retelling the deeds of God or humans, biblical history is largely a promissory history. It retells the promises of God and shows how through his mighty acts history has been propelled forward.

The factual course of history, however, necessitated a continual and progressive re-interpretation of the traditions of Israel by incorporating the older promises in a fulfilled, modified, or expanded way. There is no linear progression of history, but a tension between promise and fulfillment which was strongly creative of Israel's own historic progress. History thereby is understood as a kind of salvation history which eventually was expanded not only towards the future, but also into transnational and transhuman terms. As we have seen, the prophets understood that other nations too were included in God's plan for Israel and vice versa (cf. Isa 2:2–4; Amos 1:6–8). In the period of apocalyptic God's salvation history was understood to extend to all of humanity and to the whole cosmos. Beginning with the patriarchs, God's salvation history eventually included all of Israel, all nations, and the whole world. This

---

65. Paul. D. Hanson, "A New Challenge to Biblical Theology," *Journal of the American Academy of Religion* (June 1999) 67:452, in his review essay on Brueggemann's *Theology of the Old Testament*.

66. So Walter Brueggemann, "Theology of the Old Testament: A Prompt Retrospect," in *God in the Fray. A Tribute to Walter Brueggemann*, Tod Linafelt and Timothy K. Beal, eds. (Minneapolis: Fortress, 1998) 309.

67. Walter Brueggemann, *Old Testament Theology: Essays on Structure, Theme, and Text*, Patrick D. Miller, ed. (Minneapolis: Fortress, 1992) 116.

means that at the beginning of the New Testament, history was understood as the working out of God's purposes or as salvation history.

How universal salvation history has become in the New Testament is evident from the prologue of the Gospel of John. There, in obvious analogy to the creation story of Genesis 1, the incarnation of the world creating *logos* or word is narrated. In Stoicism "*logos* is a term for the ordered and teleologically orientated nature of the world. . . . It is thus equated with the concept of God."[68] As John tells us, this *logos*, i.e., "the Word became flesh and lived among us, and we have seen his glory" (John 1:14). It is not simply an apparition of the divine, such as in a theophany, but an indwelling of the divine in a human being. The goal or intention of God coming in human form is to provide salvation, even if "the world did not know him" (John 1:10). Therefore salvation history can no longer be tucked away in a corner of the then known world, meaning Palestine, but salvation history has now become actual history.

Wolfhart Pannenberg consequently wanted to do away with the usual distinction between a special salvation history and the rest of history. He asserts: "It belongs to the full meaning of the Incarnation that God's redemptive deed took place within the universal correlative connections of human history and not in a ghetto of redemptive history, or in a primal history belonging to a dimension which is 'oblique' to ordinary history."[69] If God has anything to do with the world, God cannot only be its creator and preserver. In some way or other, God must also see to it that the world eventuates into its promised destiny, the new world of God. As we are confronted with the daily news, be it politics, economics, or social affairs, we can discern in these events nothing of God's salvational activity. As the longing for the good old days indicates, many people are even convinced that things are getting worse instead of better. Salvation or a new world is seen nowhere around the corner.

Even the church father Augustine (354–430) asserted on the one hand: "If all these things are so, then, let us not attribute the power to grant kingdoms and empires to any save the true God."[70] But then he

---

68. Hermann Kleinknecht, "The *Logos* in Hellenism," in *ThDNT*, 4:84.

69. Wolfhart Pannenberg, "Redemptive Event and History," in Wolfhart Pannenberg, *Basic Questions in Theology. Collected Essays*, trans. George H. Kehm (Philadelphia: Fortress, 1970) 1:41–42.

70. Augustine, *The City of God against the Pagans* (5.21) trans. and ed. R.W. Dyson (Cambridge: Cambridge University Press, 1998) 227, for this and the following quote.

also conceded: "It is a task too great and too far surpassing my powers to search out the secrets of human affairs and by clear inspection give judgment as to the merits of kingdoms." In other words, Augustine claimed that the constellations in this world are due to God's activity. At the same time he admitted, however, that he could not make sense of these earthly proceedings. In the same way as we cannot prove God's activity by adducing external data, we also cannot discern how God is involved either in our personal affairs or in the world at large. We can only make sense out of history by returning to the Judeo-Christian tradition as recorded in the biblical witness. There we encounter a promissory history that eventually impacts world history. This salvation history as recorded in the Bible is like a red thread which can help us to discern God's way even in present-day history.

Yet why would this promissory history still have any relevance for us today? The reason for this is not because it is sacred history. "Sacred" histories are also recorded in other ancient texts. The reason for its relevancy lies in the New Testament witness. There the claim is made that God has acted decisively by identifying with us in Jesus of Nazareth and most importantly by raising Jesus from the dead. In and through the resurrection event the goal of this world and its history has not only been decided upon, it has already been proleptically anticipated. That which had been expected as the goal of history, the new creation, has been anticipated in a proleptic way in Christ's resurrection. We are not stuck with a promissory history, as one might surmise, but we are given a definite clue that through Christ's destiny the fate of the world had been decided upon. Looking in the biblical witness for guidance in today's world is no futile endeavor, since it is the source of inspiration for a new world to come.

If history's ultimate goal is already predetermined, what then is the significance of our involvement in that history? First of all we are freed from playing God. Salvation or the future of the world does not depend on us. God provides the future already now and God will provide a new world in God's own time. So where do we come into the picture? The significance of our activities lies in understanding ourselves as being created in God's image and being entrusted with dominion over the world. As our eternal parent God has entrusted to us this world as our inheritance and as God's sons and daughters we should prove ourselves as trustworthy heirs of God's creation.[71] As foreshadowed in the Christ event the overall outcome of this world has already been decided. In response to this salvific action we are God's free and acceptable partners who are invited to work out the details of history within the larger framework of God's salvation.

While we need not worry whether things will come out alright, our position is still of utmost significance. As heirs of this world we must continuously ask ourselves what kind of message we spread in word and deed. This is all the more important, since Jesus Christ, the human face of God "was in the world . . . yet the world did not know him" (John 1:10). Faithfulness to our calling as heirs also entails spreading the good news of God's salvational activity and intent to those who do not know him through his incarnation in Jesus Christ. This does not mean winning missionary victories for Christ, but enabling others to live a God-responsible life in freedom and yet in faithfulness, in thankfulness, and in all seriousness.

We have come to the conclusion of our investigation on the God who is. As has been noticeable throughout, we have done this from a Christian standpoint. No one can address existential issues from a vacuum. At the same time we have wanted to be fair to other positions and hope that we have succeeded within the limits that a particular starting-point entails. But what has been the outcome? In contrast to the heavy criticism of the God notion in the nineteenth century, we can confidently say that the God issue is alive and well today. There has been a rejuvenation of religion in general and also of trust in God.

We have also seen that it makes a big difference as to what kind of God it is that we trust. Not only is the "object matter" of this trust quite different, as we noticed in a survey of the world's religions, but conversely the way we relate to this God also makes a huge difference in our self-understanding, both in religious devotion (such as worship life) and in everyday living. We have concluded that the Christian understanding of God, disclosed throughout the Judeo-Christian tradition, and culminating in the Christ event, opens up the most positive possibilities for humanity.

---

71. Friedrich Gogarten, *The Reality of Faith. The Problem of Subjectivism in Theology*, trans. Carl Michalson et al. (Philadelphia: Westminster, 1959) 55, who has convincingly shown our position as heirs of this world.

Since this God is not perceived as overpowering, but as a compassionately faithful and nevertheless sovereign God, we have the possibility of cultivating the talents given to us and responding to this God as caretakers of this beautiful planet. God does not abandon us, but we are encouraged to relate to God as to a personal other. Moreover, we are given the assurance that our lives will conclude in eternal communion with this God. Other perceptions of God are not worthless nor do they necessarily lead humanity astray. We can only trust that the one compassionate God disclosed in Jesus Christ will ensure that others may also find an appropriate response to the revelation from this God which they perceive.

Index of Names

Abbott, Walther M., 162n
Abu Hanifa, 124
Achtemeier, Paul J., 222
Ackerman, Robert, 84n
Aeschylus, 78, 96
Akhnaton, 114–15, 117
Albright, William Foxwell, 201n, 208, 209n, 212n
Allegro, John, 80–82
Allen, John L., 169
Alt, Albrecht, 197–98
Althaus, Paul, 175n, 186n, 243n, 260
Ambrose, 144, 145n
Anaxagoras, 29, 49
Anselm of Canterbury, 38–42, 44, 60–61
Aristotle, 24–25, 30–51, 33–37, 45, 60–61, 117
Ashoka, 132
Atatürk, Mustafa Kemal, 128
Atkins, Peter W., 22
Augustine, 35, 66, 268–69

Bachofen, Johann Jacob, 78, 79n
Bandaranaike, Sirimaro, 136
Bar Kochba, 206, 234
Barrow, John D., 55
Barth, Karl, 41, 65, 143, 149–52, 239, 242n, 245n
Baumgärtel, Friedrich, 263n
Behe, Michael, 54
Behm, Johannes, 253n
Bhattacharji, Sukumari, 78n
Birk, Kasimir, 100n
Bonhoeffer, Dietrich, 63, 262
Botiveau, Bernard, 122n

Bright, John, 196n, 202n, 203n, 204n, 206n, 207n
Brown, Raymond E., 230n
Brown, William P., 196, 207n
Brueggeman, Walter, 264–65, 266n, 267
Buber, Martin, 186n, 245
Bultmann, Rudolf, 223n, 224n, 227n, 243–44, 254n, 260
Burleigh, J. H. S., 66n

Calvin, John, 148–49, 156, 186
Carruthers, Gregory H., 173n
Carter, Brandon, 54
Carter, John Ross, 132n, 133n
Charlesworth M. J., 39n
Cicero, Marcus Tullius, 49, 65–66, 149
Clayton, John, 38n, 45n, 59n
Clayton, John, 59
Cobb, John, 178, 180–81
Comstock, W. Richard, 92n
Comte, August, 82–83, 85, 154
Conze, Edward, 133n, 135n, 138n, 139
Conzelmann, Hans, 224n, 255n
Cook, James, 102
Cousins, L. S., 131n, 132n
Curtis, Edward M., 246n

Danby, Herbert, 104n
Darwin, Charles, 23, 25, 49, 50n, 53
Dawkins, Richard, 22–28, 52
de Vaux, Roland, 199n
Denzinger, Heinrich, 60
Descartes, René, 42–44
Dever, William G., 79n, 207, 266n
Dharmasiri, Gunapala, 136n
Dilthey, Wilhelm, 100

Diocletian, 152
Dobbelaere, Karel, 137n
Driesch, Hans, 49
Dupuis, Jacques, 163n, 164n

Edgerton, Franklin, 117n
Eichrodt, Walther, 253n, 264n
Eilberg-Schwartz, Howard, 249, 250n
Einstein, Albert, 22
Eliade, Mircea, 67n, 84n, 90n, 93n, 108, 111n
Ende, W., 127n
Engels, Friedrich, 10, 11n
Engnell, Ivan, 103
Epicurus, 145n
Euler, Walter Andreas, 56n
Euripides, 78
Evans, Craig A., 234n
Evans-Pritchard, E. E., 110n

Feuerbach, Ludwig, 1–2, 4–14, 20, 22, 44, 62, 69, 100, 148, 150–51, 170, 267
Feynman, Richard P., 26
Fichte, Johann Gottlieb, 58
Finegan, Jack, 78n
Fitzmyer, Joseph A., 229n
Foerster, Werner, 220n
Fohrer, Georg, 104, 209n, 210n, 211n, 212n
Frankl, Victor, 136n
Frazer, James G., 74, 83, 84n, 85, 88
Freeman, Kathleen, 113n, 116n
Frend H. C., 29n
Freud Sigmund, 1, 14–22, 27, 59, 62, 98–101
Fritz, Volkmar, 111n
Fuchs, Ernst, 223n, 227

Gardet, L., 124n
Gaunilo, 39n, 40
Gerlitz, Peter, 77n, 78n, 79n
Ghorbal, Shafik, 125n, 126n
Gideon, 212–13
Glassé, Cyril, 123n
Gnuse, Robert, 207, 208n
Gogarten, Friedrich, 270n

Gray, Asa, 50n
Greaves, Ron, 125n, 126n
Greenberg, Moshe, 250n
Greeven, Heinrich, 228
Guirdham, Arthur, 100n
Guthrie, Donald, 232n

Hallisey, Charles, 131n, 132n
Hamann, Johann Georg, 60
Hans-Georg Gadamer, 70n
Vogler, Paul, 70n
Hanson Paul D., 267n
Hartshorne Charles, 39n, 40n, 41n
Hawking, Stephen, 23
Hegel, Georg Wilhelm Friedrich, 1–3, 6, 13, 60, 154
Heiler Friedrich, 105n, 122n, 183n, 186
Heisenberg, Werner, 44n
Henry, Francis, Eighth Earl of Bridgewater, 53
Hesiod, 30, 96, 112–13, 115
Hick, John, 70n, 170–75, 178
Hobbes, Thomas, 248
Hodge, Charles, 53
Hoefler, Herbert E., 152n
Homerin, Emil, 128n, 129n
Houtman, Cornelius, 197n
Hughes, Philip Edacumbe, 253n
Hume, David, 3, 53, 56

Humphreys, Christmas, 134n

Ibn-Rushd (see also Averroes), 126
Ikbal, Muhammad, 127

Jacob, Edmond, 256n, 257
Jagadish Kashyab, 133n
James, William, 85, 86n, 87–88, 98
Jaspers, Karl, 111, 172
Jeremias, Joachim, 223n, 226n, 231, 232n
Jervell, Jacob, 247n
John of Damascus, 45, 91
John the Baptist, 223, 234, 260
Josephus, Flavius, 118, 144
Josiah (King), 207
Judas the Galilean, 234

Index of Names

Jung, Carl Gustav, 98
Justin Martyr, 144n

Kamali, Mohammad Hashim, 123n
Kant, Immanuel, 3, 40, 47–48, 50–51, 56–58, 60, 62, 68, 147, 154, 241
Käsemann, Ernst, 216
Kaufman, Gordon D., 213, 241
Kaufmann, Jehezkel, 250n
Kaufman, Walter, 245n
Keel, Othmar, 205
Kenny, Anthony, 25n
Kierkegaard, Søren, 61, 239

King, John C., 81n
King, Winston L., 67
Kitagawa, Joseph M., 88n, 93n, 189n
Kleinknecht, Hermann, 268n
Knitter, Paul F., 174–78, 179n
Köhler, Ludwig, 197n, 210n
Kornfeld, Walter, 255n
Kraemer, Hendrik, 65n, 152
Kraus, Hans-Joachim, 213
Kuitert, Harminus Martinus, 245n
Küng, Hans, 166–68, 178

Lactantius, 66
Lampert, Evgenii, 263n
Lang, Andrew, 75, 92n
Lawrence, Chellaian, 130n
Leeuw, Gerhardus van der, 76n
Leibniz, Gottfried Wilhelm, 51
Leibrecht, Walter, 60n
Lescow, Theodor, 252n
Linnemann, Eta, 224n
Locke, John, 3
Löwith, Karl, 157n
Ludwig, Theodore M., 117n
Luther, Martin, 21, 91, 145–49, 156, 168, 186, 188, 242, 243n

Maier, Paul L., 118n
Maimonides, Moses, 31, 35–38
Makiguchi, Tunesaburo, 137
Malinowski Bronislaw, 91, 92n, 102n, 109
Marett, Robert R., 73–75, 101

Martin, Marie-Louise, 111n
Marx, Karl, 1–2, 10–14, 20–22, 62, 149
McArthur, Harvey K., 231n
McCarter, P. Kyle, Jr., 79n

McCalla, Arthur, 27, 54n
McCarthy, Dennis J., 210n
McGrath, Alister, 23, 25n, 26n, 264
Meister Eckart, 140
Mensching, Gustav, 75n, 102n, 186
Metraux, Daniel A., 137n
Mettinger, Tryggve N. D., 199n, 202n
Miller, Patrick D., 80n, 207n
Mohammed, 115, 120n, 121–12, 124
Mohammad Ali Jinnah, 127
Moltmann, Jürgen, 220
Moore, Edward C., 86n, 87n, 88n
Morenz, Siegfried, 77, 114n
Moses, 97, 101, 114, 118, 184, 196–97, 201–2, 204, 208, 210, 212, 244, 255, 258
Mowinckel Sigmund, 103
Muhammad Ibn Abd al-Wahhab 126
Murata, Kiyoaki, 137n
Myers, Gerald E., 88n

Narr, Karl J. 70
Nasr Hamed Abu Zeid 129
Nelson, Benjamin, 99n
Nelson, J. Robert, 185n, 190
Nero (Emperor), 152
Newton, Isaac, 44, 52–53
Noth, Martin, 197n, 209n

O'Brien, John A., 58n
O'Daly, Gerard, 240n
Oedipus, 15, 100
Ohlig, Karl-Heinz, 120n
Origen, 35, 112
Otto, Rudolf, 73 n., 76n, 96–98, 140, 186, 241
Owen, Thomas C., 190n
Ozols, Jakob 70–71

Pahlavi, Mohammed Reza (Shah), 128
Paley, William, 23–24, 51, 52n, 53
Panikkar, Raimundo, 175, 178, 189

Index of Names

Pannenberg, Wolfhart, 181, 182n, 222n, 225n, 248, 263, 268
Pascal, Blaise, 61
Paul (Apostle), 16, 30, 62, 141, 143–44, 151, 164, 181, 184, 188–89, 221, 225
Pelikan, Jaroslav, 144n
Perlitt, Lothar, 210n
Petry, Michael John, 44n
Pettazzoni, Raffaele, 93–94
Philipp, Wolfgang, 138n, 140n
Philo of Alexandria, 118, 119n
Pindar, 113
Pinnock, Clark H., 179n
Plato, 29–35, 45, 60–61, 111, 117, 147
Pope Benedict XVI, 169
Pope John Paul II, 163–64, 168
Pope Paul VI, 162
Preuss, Horst Dietrich, 256n
Procksch, Ott, 258n

Rad, Gerhard von, 197n, 201n, 219, 252n, 263–65
Radin, Paul, 109n, 110n
Ragip Robert Frager al Jerrahi, 125n
Rahman, Fazlur, 120n, 121n, 127, 129–30
Raimund of Sabund, 56
Ratschow, Carl-Heinz, 102n, 188n
Ratzinger, Joseph (Cardinal), 169
Ray, John, 52
Rendtorff, Rolf, 211
Nicholson, Reynold Alleyne, 125n
Reynolds, Frank E, 131n, 132n, 136n
Richards, Jay Wesley, 54
Ricoeur, Paul, 100n
Boyle, Robert, 52
Rorem, Paul, 240n
Rössler, Dietrich, 100n
Rowley, Harold H., 219, 220n
Ruether, Rosemary Radford, 77, 79n, 175
Russell, Bertrand, 47
Russell, D. S., 217n
Saddhatissa, H., 136n
Samartha, Stanley J., 175
Sanders, John P., 179–80

Saunders, E. Dale, 137n
Schaer, Hans, 98n
Schall, Anton, 120n
Scherer, James E., 179n
Schiller, Friedrich, 58
Schimmel, Annemarie, 122n, 126n, 127n
Schmidt, Wilhelm, 75–76, 92–93, 100
Schmidt, Werner H., 198n, 200n, 201n, 202n, 203n, 204, 205n
Schoeps, Hans-Joachim, 74
Schrenk, Gottlob, 259n
Schwarz, Hans, 23n, 103n, 130n, 187n
Schweitzer, Albert, 195, 207
Shaltout, Mahmud, 123n, 124n
Simon, son of Giora, 234
Seneca, 149
Smith, Huston, 120n, 123n, 182n, 184n
Smith, Mark S., 80n, 200n, 207
Smith, Morton, 213n
Smith, Norman Kemp, 43n
Smith, Ronald Gregor, 60n
Smith, Wilfred Cantwell, 175, 187n
Snaith, Norman H., 251n, 255n, 257
Socrates, 29, 114, 144
Söderblom, Nathan, 92n, 93, 98n, 186n, 187n
Suzuki, Beatrice Lane, 134n, 135n, 136, 139n
Suzuki, Daisetz Taitaro, 139n, 140
Stählin, Gustav, 261n
Starobinski-Safran, Esther, 118n
Stauffer, Ethelbert, 254n
Stietencron, Heinrich von, 78n
Swanson, Ted, viii

Teilhard de Chardin, Pierre, 51
Thielicke, Helmut, 245–46
Thomas Aquinas, 38, 45, 46n, 47n, 49n, 50, 59n, 60, 240
Thomas, Terance, 160n
Tillich, Paul, 42, 61, 67, 143, 149–62, 241–42
Tipler, Frank, 22, 55
Troeltsch, Ernst, 153–56, 162, 185
Towers, Bernard, 185n
Toynbee, Arnold, 156, 157n
Tylor, Sir Edward Burnett, 71–75

Uehlinger, Christoph, 79n, 205

Visser't Hooft, V. A., 175, 176n
Vogler, Paul, 70n
Voll, John Obert, 126n
Vorländer, Hermann, 214n
Vriezen, Theodor C., 255n

Wagner, Falk, 63
Waley, Arthur, 133n
Wallace, Howard N., 184n
Wayman, Alex, 134n
Weber, Max, 110n
Weber, Otto, 151n
Weinberg, Steven, 22
Weiser, Artur, 251n, 258n
Werblowsky, Zwi, 112
Westermann, Claus, 247
Whitehead, Alfred N., 180
Whitelam, Keith W., 104n
Widengren, Geo, 92n, 94
Wilckens, Ulrich, 225n
Wilcox, David, 56n
William, Catrin H., 231n
Williams, John Alden, 122n
Wolf, Hans Walter, 213n
Wright, G. Ernest, 261
Wundt, Wilhelm, 99

Xenophanes of Colophon, 113n

Zobel, Hans-Jürgen, 251n

Index of Subjects

absoluteness of Christian faith, 174
acts of God, 265
adoration, 30, 66, 90–91, 95, 228
African religions, 94
agnosticism, 25
Allah, 21, 80, 122–25, 130, 143
ancestor, 16, 107–8, 197, 199, 200, 202, 209, 211–12, 216, 234–35, 251, 253, 266
    worship, 73
Amida, 117, 139
animism, 16, 70–73, 76, 92, 111
anonymous Christian, 165–66, 171, 188, 235
anthropic principle, 54–55
anthropocentric, 5, 7, 242
anthropology (-ical), 4, 20, 110, 150, 189, 260
anthropomorphism, 60, 82, 208, 216
anthropomorphous, 242
apocalyptic (-ist, -ism), 177, 217–20, 222–25, 234, 263, 267
apologetic (-s), 39, 54, 61, 76
apostasy, 121, 129, 206,
Arab religion, 107
archaeology (-ical), 77, 79, 108–9, 196, 206–7, 263, 266
atheism (-ist, -istic), 8, 12, 20, 22–23, 25, 29, 44, 112, 145, 151, 177
attributes of God, 5, 261
autonomy (-ous), 44, 147
axial period, 172
avatar, 113, 117, 170

Babylonian, 77, 218, 246
biblical minimalists, 266

Black Muslims, 128
bodhisattva, 115, 134, 138, 170
Buddha, 69, 89, 111, 115, 117, 131–35, 137–40, 170–71, 184, 201, 235, 250
Buddhism (-ist), x, 115, 121, 131–33, 135–40, 181, 187, 189
    Amida, 117, 139, 235
    Hinayana, 117, 134
    Mahayana, 115, 134, 139, 170–1
    Nichiren, 135, 137
    Shin, 135
    Shingon, 134
    Soka Gakkai, 137
    Tantric, 134
    Theravada, 132, 134
    Zen, 135

Canaan(ite), 79, 81, 118, 198–200, 204, 207, 211–13, 218
cargo cult, 111
causality, 45, 48–49, 57, 203
cause and effect sequence, 25, 32, 38
Christianity, x, 8, 12, 16, 29, 65–68, 80, 84–85, 117, 119–20, 128, 137–39, 141, 144, 151–52, 154–55, 157–61, 164–66, 171–74, 181–83, 213, 225
Christology, 170, 173, 176–78, 227
    theocentric, 176–77
Christocentricity, 169
Communism (-ist) ix, 1–2, 12
compassion, 138, 171, 188, 236, 251, 253–54, 259, 261
complementarity, 17, 169
Confucianism, 73

Index of Subjects

consciousness, x, 4, 6, 13, 16, 72, 84, 102, 165, 175, 214
Copernican Revolution, 169–71, 173
cosmos, 55, 56, 218–19, 246, 267
convenant, 104, 186–87, 203–5, 209–11, 232–33, 235, 251–57, 261
creation, 19–20, 22–23, 26, 51, 57–58, 60, 62, 76–77, 89, 94, 99, 104, 127, 141, 144, 149, 164, 193, 209, 218–19, 221, 226, 236, 241, 246–47, 253, 263, 268–70
    account, 191, 193, 246
creative transformation, 180
Crusades, 21
culture, 67, 78, 92–93, 96, 100, 195, 110–12, 115, 139, 141, 155–56, 159–60, 163–64, 166, 170, 175–76, 181, 185, 187, 190, 207, 217
cyclical, 119, 157

demiurge, 32
desacralization, 119, 190, 193
design, 24–25, 50, 53–54
divine kingship, 103–4
    watchmaker, 51–52
drugs, 80–82
dualism (-istic), 117, 216

Early Christian Apologists, 144
El, 196–97, 200, 204, 211–13
Elohim, 196
Egypt, 77, 81, 112, 118, 122, 128, 141, 199, 201–2, 205, 209, 217, 231, 246–47, 251, 253, 264, 266
Enlightenment, 51, 67, 88, 147, 175
enthronement festival, 103
entelechy, 49
eschatology (-ical), 139, 157, 177, 179, 195, 220, 222–24, 234, 254, 260–61, 263
eternal life, 179, 226, 254
ethnology, 79, 100
European civilization, 155
evangelism, 179
evolution (-ary), 1, 11, 19, 24–25, 53–56, 75, 79, 84–85, 92, 114, 182, 251
    theory of, 24

exclusiveness (-ity, -ism), 114, 121, 171, 173, 233, 236
exile, 118, 214, 246, 256, 266
existence of God, 22, 25, 28, 30–31, 38–41, 43, 45–48, 50–52, 56–57, 59, 62, 86, 186
    cosmological argument, 32, 35, 45, 47–48, 50
    historical, 58–59
    moral, 56, 62
    ontological, 38, 40–42, 44, 47–48, 50
    teleological, 35, 48, 50–52, 56
Exodus, 81, 196, 200–205, 207, 209, 211, 231, 233

faithfulness, 251–52, 254, 259, 261, 270
fatalistic, 130
feeling, 6, 9, 68, 73–74, 83, 96, 98, 102, 133, 135, 152, 148, 183, 208, 242,
fertility, 77–82, 91, 94–95, 109
    god, 94, 118, 200, 213, 250
    goddess, 79, 114, 118
finite, 6–7, 9, 47, 68, 156, 191–92, 235, 241
    substance, 42
first cause, 25, 35, 37, 46–48
first unmoved mover, 24–25, 34, 61
French Revolution, 3, 83, 183
fulfillment, 81, 122, 193, 220, 222, 252, 267

global village, 248
globalization, 190–92, 217
Gnosis, Gnosticism, 219, 230
God-is-dead theologians, 87
God of the Fathers, 198–99, 201, 211, 213
God (knowledge of –), 4, 59–60, 62, 140, 145–47, 149, 174, 233
God's
    action, 142, 256, 265
    compassion, 25056, 260–62
    dominion, 248
    faithfulness, 251, 254–56
    image, 18, 186, 209, 248, 246–49, 269
    likeness, x, 242–43, 252
    righteousness, 256, 258–61
    wrath, 257–58, 260–61

Greek religion, 73, 76, 95–96, 112
   antiquity, 49, 112

Hadith, 122, 124
Hellenistic (-ism), 20, 30, 35, 217–18, 221, 224, 229–30
Hellenization, 67, 217
henotheism, 216
high god(s), 76, 92–93, 95, 104, 110–11, 114, 116, 182, 188, 207
Hinduism, 107, 117, 158, 163, 183
historicism, 153
history
   of religion, 73, 75–76, 79, 100, 153, 162, 186, 196
   of salvation, 175, 215, 219, 238, 263, 266–69
   end of, 227
   goal of, 224, 269
   human, 11, 13, 30, 106, 160, 186, 220, 235, 248, 268
   promissory, 222–3, 267, 269
   sacred, 269
   universal, 219
   world, 13, 58, 263, 269
holiness, 96–97, 101–2, 105–6, 221, 236, 250, 255–58, 261–62
Holy War, 21, 127–28

illusion, 9, 13, 17, 19, 25, 81
image, 72, 77, 91, 99, 167, 181, 205–7, 240, 246–47, 249, 251
immortality, 7, 17, 57, 62, 99
indigenization of religion, 157
infinite, 6–8, 34, 42, 47–48, 57, 68, 88, 114, 120, 130, 139, 184, 192, 240, 248, 255
   substance, 42
inquisition, 21, 143
intelligent design movement, 28, 54
Islam (-ic), x, 1, 35, 67, 90, 107, 116–17, 119–20, 122–30, 136, 141, 158, 163, 182–84, 213
Islamic law, 122
Israel (-ite), 16, 30, 79–81, 94, 104, 107, 110, 115–20, 141, 184, 187, 196– 216, 219–22, 231–32, 235–36, 238, 245, 247–58, 264–67
   history, 116, 144, 196–97, 200, 204, 208, 212, 219–20, 222, 237–38, 257, 263, 266
   religion, 16, 89, 101, 103–4, 112, 115, 117, 119, 141, 201, 208, 214

Jesus Christ, 60, 66, 75, 143–45, 148–49, 151, 159, 167–69, 176–77, 179–80, 185, 187–89, 221–22, 227, 229, 235–38, 243, 249–50, 254–55, 270–71
Jewish, 16, 35, 104, 110, 116, 118, 120, 143–45, 155, 163, 176–77, 200, 217, 222, 225–26, 229–31, 233, 245, 249, 263
Jihad, 127–28
Judaism, 16, 29, 117–19, 141, 145, 158, 213, 225–26, 259, 264
Judeo-Christian, 20, 58, 93, 102, 120, 125, 138, 140–42, 156–57, 175, 183–84, 192–93, 249, 261
   history, x, 10, 154, 238
   tradition, 20, 44, 136, 141, 149, 175, 181–82, 185, 187, 190–92, 235–36, 244–46, 262, 266, 269–70

Ka'bah, 90–91
karma, 134, 136
kingdom of God, 182, 223–24
kingship (divine or sacred), 103–5, 257, 260
koine, 217
kyrios, 220, 229

Latin, 61, 97, 174
   America, 1, 111, 181
logos, 144, 170, 173, 180, 235, 268
   incarnate, 144, 161, 180
   seminal, 144
   universal, 160–61
Lord of history, 200

magic (-al), 16, 22, 69, 74–75, 83–85, 101–2, 108–11, 206
Maitreya, 139

mana, 74, 101–2, 109, 111, 255
martyr(s), ix, 152
Marxism (-ist), 2, 12, 27
materialism (-istic), 2, 5, 10, 13, 44, 87, 191–92, 249, 265
matriarchy, 78–79
meme, 27
Mesopotamia, 112, 128, 214, 216, 246–47
messianic, 110, 120, 195, 231, 234
metaphysics (-cal), 13, 27–28, 59, 68, 82, 242
Middle Ages, 50, 138
middle path, 141
missionary, 65, 75–76, 92, 135, 152, 157, 160–61, 165–66, 169
Mithras cult, 89
monasticism, 125, 135, 140–41
monistic, 115, 117, 119–20
monolatry, 216
monotheism (-istic), x, 16, 18, 59, 73, 82–83, 92, 109–12, 114–20, 182, 186, 188, 193, 214, 216
   original, 75–76, 93
moral law, 57
mother goddess, 16, 77–79, 99
Muslim (Moslem), 21, 107, 110, 116, 120–29
mysticism, 91, 127, 140, 151
myth (-ical), 77, 79, 89, 92, 99, 207
mythology (-ical), 15–17, 30, 75, 81, 92, 99, 114, 167, 246

natural selection, 22–25, 27, 53
naturalism, 27–28, 245
Neolithic, 27, 108
Neo-Platonism (-istic), 45, 240
nirvana, x, 115, 117, 120, 133, 135, 139–40
noumena, 3
numinous, 96–98
numina, 198

ontology (-ical), 38, 40–42, 44, 47–48, 50, 61, 173, 178, 247
optimism, 7, 19, 98, 115
Ottoman Empire, 128

Paleolithic, 70, 77, 108–9
pantheism (-istic), 33, 58, 76, 95, 127, 221
patriarch (-al, -y), 79, 81, 143, 191, 196–202, 249, 266–67
Peking Man, 70
personal God, 44, 109, 249–50
personification of God, 249
physicist, 22, 26, 54
physico-theology (-ical), 50, 52
Platonic (-ism, -ist), 35, 90, 147, 240
pluralism, 169–70, 175, 177, 179, 186
prime mover (see also first cause), 34, 36
polydemonism, 92, 111
polytheism, 16, 73, 76, 82–83, 92, 111–12, 114–18, 182, 200, 207, 216
positivism, 20, 82–83
pre-established harmony, 51
pre-historic, 109–10
profane, 66–67, 90, 102, 125, 189
progress (-ive), 2, 7, 17–20, 26, 53, 57, 82–83, 115–16, 119, 126, 136–38, 155, 157, 184–85, 192, 216, 248, 263, 267
   western, 157
projection, 5, 14, 16–19, 21, 44, 69, 98–100, 130, 148, 151, 170, 208, 239, 244
proletariat, 12
proleptic, 184, 186, 222, 226, 234, 250, 262, 264, 269
promised land, 200–201, 204, 206, 212, 266
proskynesis, 228, 231
Protestant (-ism), 60, 153, 159, 161, 174–75
psychological, ix, 19–20, 86, 99, 248
psychoanalysis, 1, 14, 98, 100

Qur'an, 120–27, 129–30

reason, 3–5, 7–9, 19–20, 22, 28, 30, 35, 45, 47–48, 50, 57, 60–62, 83, 87, 98, 145–48, 237, 240
   divine, 35
reincarnation, 134, 136

282 Index of Subjects

religion (s) (see also under particular religion)
  ethnic, 119
  lawful, 165
  monotheistic, x, 16, 109, 111, 115, 120, 188
  natural, 72, 85–86
  polytheistic, x, 111–12, 114, 119
  pre-historic, x, 109–12
  pre-literate, 66, 73–75, 89, 92, 94, 107, 188
  tribal, x, 66, 94, 107–11, 214
  true, 8, 66, 121, 137, 150
  world, 68, 115, 119, 128, 141, 151–52, 155, 160, 162, 166–69, 171–73, 178, 181–83, 186
  definition of, 67, 73, 84
  origin of, 5, 11, 17, 20, 27, 69, 71–73, 75–77, 80, 82
resurrection, 3, 26, 77, 85, 103, 124, 176, 181, 221–23, 225–27, 233–34, 258, 269
revelation, 3, 52, 144, 150, 158, 161, 169, 173, 182–83, 186–87, 197, 199–201, 203, 212, 222, 228, 231, 235, 245–46, 255, 271
revolution (-ary), 3, 10–12, 128, 151, 169–70, 207
Roman, 49, 65, 78, 83, 89, 113–15, 139, 144, 152, 157, 206
  Catholic (-ism), 16, 59, 75, 113, 115, 146, 153, 159, 161–62, 164, 166–70, 175
  Empire, 1, 29, 89, 141, 170, 174, 177
  religion, 73, 113

saints, 113, 115–16, 125–26, 133–34, 138
salvation (-al), x, 16, 88, 90, 96, 121, 135, 140–41, 149, 152, 156, 165–69, 171–73, 175–76, 178–80, 183–84, 187–89, 193, 215, 224–25, 233, 237, 254, 257–59, 261–62, 268–70
samsara, 134–35
Sangha, 131–32

science, 20–21, 27, 33, 43–44, 52, 59, 83–84, 86, 96, 111, 155, 185, 190, 248
  modern, 20, 44, 59
scientific, 18–20, 25–26, 28, 54, 74, 82, 84–85, 87, 266
secular(-ity, -ization), ix, 11–12, 20, 66–67, 102, 106, 128–29, 157–58, 190–91, 235, 248–49, 265
self-consciousness, 4, 6, 10
self-disclosure, 144–45, 148–50, 181, 183–85, 189, 201, 203–4, 227, 231–39, 243–44, 249
self-estrangement, 11
sexual (-ity), 17, 21, 80–81, 249–50, 254
shamanism, 70
Shari'a, 122, 124, 126, 130
Shema Israel, 118
Sinai (tradition), 184, 200–204, 207, 209–10
Son of Man, 81, 222, 230
soul, 16–7, 31–33, 66, 70–73, 118, 143
space-time continuum, 25, 48, 226
spirit, 4, 7, 15, 18, 20, 71, 73, 86, 98, 101, 115, 117, 135–38, 147, 153, 155, 157–58, 164, 170, 173, 185, 191, 221, 249
(Holy) Spirit, 13, 148, 156, 164–65, 185, 188, 236, 258
  absolute, 4–5
Spiritual Community, 159–60
Stoic (-ism), 116, 141, 144, 221, 268
Sufism, 125–26
Sunnah, 123–24
supreme being (- deity), 23, 50, 75–77, 90, 92–94, 109, 145
symbol (-ic), 89, 90, 92, 100–102, 106, 108, 139, 213, 224, 241–42
syncretism (-istic), 137, 158–60, 183, 206, 213, 217, 265

taboo, 74, 101–3, 109, 111, 255
teleological, 35, 48–52, 55–56, 58, 268
theist (-ic), 5, 40, 167
theomorphous, 246
theophany, 204, 268
totem (-ism), 15–17, 100, 109

transcendent (-ce), 9, 63, 66–67, 83, 102, 112, 121, 125, 133, 135, 170, 181, 186, 229, 240, 265
trickster , 96, 225
Trinity, 5, 114
triune God, 69, 164, 168, 173, 185

uniqueness, 158, 167, 175–57, 178, 227
universalism, 167
veneration, ix, 63, 66, 73, 79, 91, 126, 203, 228
voodoo, 111

Wahhabism, 126–27
world architect, 50–51, 61

Yahweh, 69, 76, 79, 80–81, 94, 97, 101–4, 107, 117, 182, 184, 196–98, 200–215, 220, 229–33, 238, 249–50, 252, 255–58, 264, 266

Zoroastianism, 117, 158

Index of Scripture References

Old Testament

Genesis

1	121, 199, 221
1–11	76
1:11	247n
1:27	246
1:28	193
2:15	193
2:7	191
3:8	208, 216
8:8ff.	258
9:6	248
12	142
12:1	199
12:10	42ff., 202
12:17	199
12:2f.	199
15:1	198
17:1	197
17:7	145n
18:1	199
18:14	262
19:19	259
21:13	200
21:22–34	211
21:33	200
26:23–33	199
26:24	198
28:10–22	211
28:13	230
28:15	199
28:17	97
31:42	198
31:53	198
32:25–32	211
32:9	199
33:20	200
46:1–4	202
46:3	200

Exodus

2:2	118
3:5	97, 255
3:13	197
3:14	204
4:22	231
5	202
5:1	196
6:2–3	197
14:21	203
18:12	202
19:16	203
19:18	203
19:20	204
20:1–17	210
20:2f.	205
20:5	206
24:7	205, 209
24	204, 210
32	206, 209
32:1–6	209n
33:23	208
34	204
34:10	205
34:10–26	210
34:10	209

Index of Scripture References

34:27	209
34:29ff.	201

Leviticus

5:2ff.	103
11:44	256

Numbers

19:9	101
21:4ff.	206

Joshua

24:15	107

Judges

3:7	118
6:32	212

Deuteronomy

6:4	118
6:4ff.	118
6:15	257
10:14f.	251
14:1f.	231
18:9–14	214
26:5–9	264
32:12–39	205f.
32:5f.	231
32:17	212
34:5f.	201
34:10	208n

1 Samuel

6:20	255
8:4–9	104
15:10	104

2 Samuel

6:6f.	255
7	104
7:14	232
12:24	251
23:5	104
24:1	257
24:21	110

1 Kings

9:15	202
11:7ff.	212
17:22	225f.
8:27	250

1 Chronicles

21:1	257n

2 Chronicles

33:6	101

Nehemiah

13:26	251

Psalms

2:7	232
3:5	258
8:4ff.	247
11:7	256
14:1	29
68:4–6	213
89:19f.	232
93:5	255
114:–2	203
136	253
140:13	256
143:1	256

Isaiah

2:2–4	267
5:24	256
6:1	216
6:5	69, 97
7:14	221
8:13	255
8:1f.	221
35:5–6	224
40:5	214
43:11	205
43:25	230
45:9	259
45:21	259
51:12	230
53:4	221
63:10f.	258
64:7	231
64:8	251

Jeremiah

1:5	215
3:19f.	231
9:24	257
18:6	251
31:3	251
31:9	231
31:13ff.	253

Ezekiel

1:1	216
5:13	257
10:20	118
20:41	256

Daniel

2:1–3	222

Hosea

11:1	251
11:9	256, 258
13:4	205

Amos

1 and 2	257
1:6–8	267
5:5	198

Micah

1:5–7	117f.
5:2	221
6:8	252

Haggai

2:5	258

Malachi

1:8	231

New Testament

Matthew

1:21f.	221
2:2	228
2:5f.	221
3:7	260
4:12–16	221
4:4	191
4:9	228
5:17f.	222
6:33	260
8:17	221
8:22	223
9:17	224
11	228
11:6	223
11:16ff.	228
11:25	232
12:34	261
14:26	231

Index of Scripture References

14:33	231
16:18	221
18:10	216
22:13	261
24:32f., and 36f.	263
27	232
28:19	188
28:19f.	236

Mark

1:15	223
1:18	185
1:25	261
1:24	258
1:40	228
2:10	226
7:25ff.	228
13:5	230
13:6	230
14:62	230
28	226

John

1:1	229
1:10	270
1:14	221, 268
2:1	224
3:16	254
3:18	233
8:24	230
8:58	230
9:3	262
9:38	228
13:19	230
14:6	188, 233
20:22	258

Luke

1:75	260
7:22	224
9:62	223
11:2	232
11:20	224
11:31	262
13:1–5	262
15:2	227
19:38	104
21:23	260
24:11	26

Acts

2:13	82
4:12	233
10:26	228
14:17	163
17:13	259
17:23	144, 164
17:26	163
18	

Romans

1:3	104
1:3f.	221
1:5	255
1:16f.	259
1:17	254
1:19	145n
1:19f.	61
1:19ff.	145
1:20	60, 146
1:21	61
11:17	221
15:5	247
2:6–7	163
3:24f.	255
3:25f.	260
4:12	143
5:21	260
8:15f.	232
9–11	144

1 Corinthians

11:25	253
12:13	258
13	255
15:28	225
16:22	229

2 Corinthians

3:14	253
5:17f.	261
13:14	254

Galatians

4:6	232

Philipppians

2:11	229
2:5	247
3:12	190

Colossians

3:12	248

1 Thessalonians

4:8	258

1 Timothy

2:4	163
2:4–6	167

Titus

3:5	254

Hebrews

1:1f.	234
1:8	229
10:31	260

1 Peter

1:15f.	258
3:19ff.	258

2 Peter

1:1	259

1 John

4:19	254

Revelation

1:13–16	81
4:8	258
21:3f.	193
21:23f.	163

Deutero-Canonical Books

2 Esdras

7:50	218

Extracanonical Writings

2 Enoch

65:6ff.	219

Wisdom of Solomon

8:1	163

Pseudo-Clementines

Hom. II 15:1–2	219

www.ingramcontent.com/pod-product-compliance
Lightning Source LLC
Chambersburg PA
CBHW021653230426
43668CB00008B/607